The Development of Postsecondary Education Systems in Canada

A Comparison between British Columbia, Ontario, and Quebec, 1980–2010

EDITED BY
Donald Fisher, Kjell Rubenson,
Theresa Shanahan, and Claude Trottier

McGill-Queen's University Press
Montreal & Kingston • London • Ithaca

© McGill-Queen's University Press 2014
ISBN 978-0-7735-4307-2 (cloth)
ISBN 978-0-7735-4308-9 (paper)
ISBN 978-0-7735-9042-7 (ePDF)
ISBN 978-0-7735-9043-4 (ePUB)

Legal deposit third quarter 2014
Bibliothèque nationale du Québec

Printed in Canada on acid-free paper that is 100% ancient forest free (100% post-consumer recycled), processed chlorine free

McGill-Queen's University Press acknowledges the support of the Canada Council for the Arts for our publishing program. We also acknowledge the financial support of the Government of Canada through the Canada Book Fund for our publishing activities.

Library and Archives Canada Cataloguing in Publication

The development of postsecondary education systems in Canada: a comparison between British Columbia, Ontario, and Quebec, 1980–2010 / edited by Donald Fisher, Kjell Rubenson, Theresa Shanahan, and Claude Trottier.

Includes bibliographical references and index.
Issued in print and electronic formats.
ISBN 978-0-7735-4307-2 (bound). – ISBN 978-0-7735-4308-9 (pbk.).
ISBN 978-0-7735-9042-7 (ePDF). – ISBN 978-0-7735-9043-4 (ePUB)

1. Postsecondary education – Government policy – British Columbia – History – 20th century – Case studies. 2. Postsecondary education – Government policy – British Columbia – History – 21st century – Case studies. 3. Postsecondary education – Government policy – Ontario – History – 20th century – Case studies. 4. Postsecondary education – Government policy – Ontario – History – 21st century – Case studies. 5. Postsecondary education – Government policy – Québec (Province) – History – 20th century – Case studies. 6. Postsecondary education – Government policy – Québec (Province) – History – 21st century – Case studies. I. Fisher, Donald, author, editor of compilation II. Rubenson, Kjell, 1944–, author, editor of compilation III. Trottier, Claude R. (Claude René), 1941–, author, editor of compilation IV. Shanahan, Theresa, 1963–, author, editor of compilation

LA417.D49 2014   378.7109'045   C2014-901466-X
                                       C2014-901467-8

This book was typeset by Interscript in 10.5/13 Sabon.

THE DEVELOPMENT OF POSTSECONDARY
EDUCATION SYSTEMS IN CANADA

Contents

Figures and Tables   vii
Acronyms and Abbreviations   xiii
Acknowledgments   xix
Preface   xxi

1 Introduction and Overview: PSE in Three Canadian Provinces   3
   DONALD FISHER AND KJELL RUBENSON

2 The Transformation of the PSE System in British Columbia   35
   DONALD FISHER, KJELL RUBENSON, JACY LEE, ROBERT CLIFT, MADELEINE MACIVOR, AND JOHN MEREDITH

3 Contradictory Trends in PSE Policy in Ontario   122
   THERESA SHANAHAN, GLEN JONES, DONALD FISHER, AND KJELL RUBENSON

4 PSE Policy in Quebec: A Case Study   200
   CLAUDE TROTTIER, JEAN BERNATCHEZ, DONALD FISHER, AND KJELL RUBENSON

5 Trends across the Three Provinces: Similarities and Differences   291
   DONALD FISHER AND KJELL RUBENSON

Conclusion   334
   DONALD FISHER AND KJELL RUBENSON

Appendices   353
Notes   371
References   395
Index   423

Figures and Tables

FIGURES

1.1 Linking state and federal policies to higher education performance 6
2.1 Changes in provincial operating grants for BC colleges and institutes, university/college and university sectors, and total postsecondary education, 1986–87 to 2009–10 in constant 2002 dollars, 1986–87 = 100 92
2.2 Changes in provincial operating grants for BC college and institute, university college, and university sectors, 1986–87 to 2006–07 in constant 1992 dollars, 1986–87 = 100 93
2.3 Changes in provincial grants per funded FTE for BC college and institute and university sectors, 1986–87 to 2009–10 in constant 2002 dollars, 1986–87 = 100 95
2.4 Proportion of revenue from own-source revenue and government funding, British Columbia, 1988–89 to 2008–09 99
2.5 Average university tuition by program in BC, 1985–86 to 2009–10 (2002 dollars) 102
2.6 Average undergraduate university tuition fees as a proportion of selected after-tax average income quintiles, British Columbia, 1985–86 to 2008–09 (constant 2002 dollars) 104
2.7 Postsecondary education and participation rate, 18–24 and 18–29 age groups in British Columbia, 1986–87 to 2009–10 106
2.8 Postsecondary education participation rate (18–24 age group) by sector in British Columbia, 1986–87 to 2009–10 107
2.9 Postsecondary education participation rate (18–24 age group) in adult basic education, career/vocational, academic/bachelor and

graduate (master and doctoral) programs in British Columbia, 1985–86 to 2004–05   109

2.10 Changes in postsecondary education participation rate (18–24 age group) in adult basic education, career/vocational, academic/bachelor and graduate programs in British Columbia, 1985–86 to 2004–05   110

2.11 Gross expenditures on research and development for British Columbia as a proportion of gross domestic product, 1985–2008   112

2.12 Proportion of gross expenditure on research funded by business, government, higher education, and foreign and private non-profit funders for British Columbia, 1985–2008   113

2.13 Provincial operating grant for BC college and institute, university college, and university sectors (in 1992 dollars) and postsecondary education policies, 1986–87 to 2009–10   118

2.14 Percent change in gross domestic product and postsecondary education operating grants, 1987–88 to 2009–10   120

3.1 Changes in provincial operating grants for Ontario college and university sectors and total postsecondary education, 1986–87 to 2009–10 in constant 2002 dollars, 1986–87 = 100   173

3.2 Changes in provincial grants per funded FTE for Ontario college and university sectors, 1986–87 to 2009–10 in constant 2002 dollars, 1986–87 = 100   176

3.3 Proportion of revenue from own-source revenue and government funding, 1988–89 to 2008–09   179

3.4 Average university tuition by program in Ontario, 1985–86 to 2009–10 (constant 2002 dollars)   182

3.5 Average undergraduate university tuition fees as proportion of selected after-tax average income quintiles, Ontario, 1985–86 to 2008–09 (constant 2002 dollars)   183

3.6 Change in headcount enrolment for Ontario universities undergraduate, 1992–93 to 2008–09   186

3.7 Change in university participation rate, Ontario and Canada, 1992–93 to 2008–09   189

3.8 Gross expenditures on research and development for Ontario as a proportion of gross domestic product, 1985–2008   192

3.9 Proportion of gross expenditure on research funded by business, government, higher education, and foreign and private non-profit funders for Ontario, 1985–2008   193

3.10 Provincial operating grants for Ontario college and university sectors (in 2002 dollars) and postsecondary education policies, 1986–87 to 2009–10   197
4.1 Changes in provincial operating grants for Quebec college and university sectors and total postsecondary education, 1986–87 to 2006–07 in constant 2002 dollars, 1986–87 = 100   267
4.2 Changes in global provincial expenses per funded FTE for college and university sectors in constant 2002 dollars, 1986–87 to 2009–10   269
4.3 Proportion of revenue from own-source revenue and government funding in Quebec, 1988–89 to 2008–09   272
4.4 Average undergraduate tuition by program in Quebec, 1985–86 to 2009–10   276
4.5 Average undergraduate university tuition fees as proportion of selected after-tax income quintiles, Quebec, 1985–86 to 2008–09   277
4.6 Gross expenditures on research and development for Quebec as a proportion of gross domestic product, 1985–2008   280
4.7 Proportion of gross expenditure on research funded by business, government, higher education, and foreign and private non-profit funders for Quebec, 1985–2008   281
5.1 Change in provincial grants for postsecondary education in BC, Ontario, and Quebec, 1988–89 to 2008–09 in constant 2002 dollars, 1988–89 = 100   294
5.2 Average undergraduate full-time fees in constant 2002 dollars   309
5.3 Gross domestic expenditures on research and development (GERD) as a proportion of GDP, 1985 to 2008   331

TABLES

2.1 Expenditure: Budget plan 1986–87 to 2011–12 in percentage of total expenditure   97
2.2 Funding sources as a percent of total funding: BC postsecondary education, 1988–89 to 2008–09   100
2.3 FTEs by grouped major programs 1985–86 to 2004–05 in BC, percentage distribution   111
3.1 Applications submitted to PEQAB 2001 to 2010   129
3.2 Expenditure – Budget plan 1986–87 to 2010–11 in percentage of total Ontario government expenditure   177

3.3 Funding sources percent of total funding: Ontario postsecondary education, 1988–89 to 2008–09   180
3.4 Postsecondary participation rates of young adults aged 24 to 26 by December 2005, by province and type of institution attended   184
3.5 University headcount enrolment undergraduate–level instructional programs, 1992–93, 1998–99, 2004–05, 2008–09   185
3.6 University headcount enrolment graduate-level instructional programs, 1992–93, 1998–99, 2004–05, 2008–09   187
3.7 Ontario total university enrolment and university participation rates (18–24 years and 18–29 years). Selected years: 1992–93, 1995–96, 1998–99, 2001–02, 2004–05, and 2008–09   188
3.8 Highest degree, certificate, or diploma attained for population 15 years and over, Ontario, 1986–2006   190
3.9 Degree production, Ontario, 1992–2008–09   191
4.1 Expenditure, budget plan 1986–87 to 2011–12 in percentage of total Quebec government expenditure (in million dollars)   270
4.2 Funding sources as a percent of total funding: Quebec postsecondary education, 1988–89 to 2008–09   273
4.3 Proportion of financial aid to Quebec university students in the form of loan and bursary (%)   278
4.4 Participation rates (1) in college education (2) and university programs   279
5.1 Provincial government transfers to colleges and universities per FTE student enrolments, 1993–94 to 2008–09 (2008 dollars)   296
5.2 Expenditure, budget plan 1988–89 to 2008–09 in percentage of total government expenditure in BC, Ontario, and Quebec   297
5.3 Proportion of revenue from own-source revenue and government funding as a percentage, selected years, 1988–89, 2003–04, and 2008–09 in BC, Ontario, and Quebec   298
5.4 Average undergraduate tuition fees, selected years, 1993–94, 1997–98, 2001–02, 2005–06, and 2009–10   304
5.5 Weighted average tuition fees for full-time Canadian students by province and program, 1993–94, 1997–98, 2001–02, 2006–07, and 2009–10   304
5.6 Maximum provincial student loan (full-time, with no dependent, single, based on 34 weeks of study) and total maximum assistance for selected years: 2011 and 2011–12   307

5.7 PSE participation rates by age (18–24 and 25–29) using full-time equivalent enrolment figures by province, BC, Ontario, and Quebec 309
5.8 Canadian population 15 years and over by highest degree, certificate or diploma, 2006 312
5.9 Literacy and numeracy scores 313
5.10 Proportion of GERD by source of funding and by province, 1990–2008 332
6.1 Total government spending and tuition fees as a percentage of university operating revenue, 1994 to 2008 346

Acronyms and Abbreviations

ABE	adult basic education
ACAATO	Association of Colleges of Applied Arts and Technology of Ontario
ACCC	Association of Canadian Community Colleges
ACS	Attestation of College Studies
ADQ	Party l'Action démocratique du Québec
AECBC	Advanced Education Council of British Columbia
AEF	Apprenticeship Enhancement Fund Program
AIHEPS	Alliance for International Higher Education Policy Studies
ATOP	Access to Opportunities Fund
AUCC	Association of Universities and Colleges of Canada
BCCP	British Columbia College Presidents
BCCAT	British Columbia Council on Admissions and Transfer
BCIT	British Columbia Institute of Technology
BCKDF	British Columbia Knowledge Development Fund
BCLFDB	British Columbia Labour Force Development Board
BCUCC	British Columbia University Colleges Consortium
BERD	Business Expenditure on Research and Development
C2T2	Centre for Curriculum, Transfer and Technology
CAAT	Colleges of Applied Arts and Technology
CANSIM	Canadian Socio-Economic Information Management System
CAUBO	Canadian Association of University Business Officers
CAUT	Canadian Association of University Teachers
CBIE	Canadian Bureau for International Education
CC	Canada Council

CCAC	Colleges Compensation and Appointments Council
CCAFE	Comité consultatif sur l'accessibilité financière aux études
CCF	Co-operative Commonwealth Federation
CEC	Commission de l'enseignement collégial
CEEC	Commission d'évaluation de l'enseignement collégial
CEGEP	Collèges d'enseignement général et professionnel
CEISS	Centre for Education Information Standards and Services
CEN	Canadian Education Network
CERU	Commission de l'enseignement et de la recherche universitaires
CFHSS	Canadian Federation for the Humanities and Social Sciences
CFI	Canada Foundation for Innovation
CFS	Canadian Federation of Students
CGPSS	Canadian Graduate and Professional Student Survey
CHET	Centre for Policy Studies in Higher Education and Training
CHST	Canada Health and Social Transfer
CIHR	Canadian Institutes of Health Research
CJS	Canadian Jobs Strategy
CLFDB	Canadian Labour Force Development Board
CMEC	Council of Ministers of Education Canada
CMSF	Canada Millennium Scholarship Foundation
COU	Council of Ontario Universities
CQRS	Conseil québécois de la recherche sociale
CRC	Canada Research Chairs Program
CRCS	Canada Research Chairs
CRÉPUQ	Conference of Rectors and Principals of the Universities of Québec
CSAC	College Standards and Accreditation Council
CSE	Conseil supérieur de l'éducation
CSLP	Canada Student Loans Program
CSR	Common-Sense Revolution
CSSRC	Canadian Social Science Research Council
CST	Conseil de la science et de la technologie
CTMS	Contract Training Marketing Society
CTTCS	College Technology Transfer Centres
CUCC	College University Consortium Council

CUP	Commission des universités sur les programmes
CVS	Credentials Validation Service
DCS	Diploma of College Studies
DFAIT	Department of Foreign Affairs and International Trade
DVS	diploma of vocational studies
EPF	Established Programs Financing Act
EQAO	Education Quality and Accountability Office
FCAC	Formation des chercheurs et action concertée
FCAR	Formation de chercheurs et d'aide a la recherche
FCSQ	Fédération des commissions scolaires du Québec
FLQ	Front de libération du Québec
FQRNT	Fonds du recherche du Québec
FQRSC	Fonds québécois de la recherche sur la société et la culture
FRSQ	Fonds de la recherche en santé du Québec
FTE	full-time equivalent
GDP	gross domestic product
GERD	gross domestic expenditure on R&D
GNP	gross national product
GPOG	general purpose operating grants
HEB	Higher Education Board
HEPC	Higher Education Presidents' Council
HEQCO	HigherEducation Quality Council of Ontario
HERD	Higher Education Expenditure on R&D
HRDC	Human Resources and Development Canada
HRSDC	Human Resources and Skills Development Canada
IMF	International Monetary Fund
INAC	Indian and Northern Affairs Canada
INRS	Institut national de la recherche scientifique
ISSP	Indian Studies Support Program
ITA	Industry Training Authority
ITAC	Industry Training and Apprenticeship Commission
ITAL	Institute of Technology and Advanced Learning
KPI	key performance indicators
LMDA	Labour Market Development Agreement
LMPA	Labour Market Partnership Agreements
MDEIE	Ministère du Développement Économique, de l'Innovation et de l'Exportation
MDERR	Ministère du Développement économique et régional et de la Recherche

MELS	Ministère de l'Éducation du Loisir et du Sport
MESS	Ministère de l'Enseignement Supérieur et de la Science
MEQ	Ministère de l'Éducation
MRC	Medical Research Council
MTCU	Minister of Training Colleges and Universities
MYAA	multi-year accountability agreement
NAFTA	North American Free Trade Agreement
NCE	Networks of Centres of Excellence Program
NDP	New Democratic Party
NSERC	Natural Sciences and Engineering Council of Canada
NSSE	National Survey on Student Engagement
OCAD	Ontario College of Art and Design
OCE	Ontario Centres of Excellence
OCQAS	Ontario Colleges Quality Assurance Service
OCUA	Ontario Council on University Affairs
OCUFA	Ontario Council of University Faculty Associations
OECD	Organization for Economic Cooperation and Development
OISE	Ontario Institute for Studies in Education
OLA	Open Learning Agency
OPSEU	Ontario Public Service Employees Union
ORF	Ontario Research Fund
OSAP	Ontario Student Assistance Program
OSOTF	Ontario Student Opportunity Trust Fund
OTSS	Ontario Trust for Student Support
OYAP	Ontario Youth Apprenticeship Program
PAC	Provincial Access Committee
PC	Progressive Conservative
PCC	Private Career Colleges
PCTIA	Private Career Training Institutions Agency
PEQAB	Postsecondary Education Quality Assessment Board
PLA	prior learning assessment
PPSEC	Private PSE Commission
PQAPA	Program Quality Assurance Process Audit
PSE	Postsecondary Education
QIF	Quality Improvement Fund
RLC	Regional Learning Council
RRU	Royal Roads University
RRU Act	Royal Roads University Act
SFU	Simon Fraser University

SPOG	Special Purpose Operating Grants
SSD	Secondary School diploma
SSHRC	Social Sciences and Humanities Research Council of Canada
TCAF	Training Completion Assurance Fund
TechBC	Technical University of British Columbia
TRU	Thompson Rivers University
TUPC	The University Presidents' Council of British Columbia
UBC	University of British Columbia
UNBC	University of Northern British Columbia
UNESCO	United Nations Educational, Scientific and Cultural Organization
UOIT	University of Ontario Institute of Technology
URIF	University Research Incentive Fund
UVic	University of Victoria
WTO	World Trade Organization

Acknowledgments

The editors and contributors wish to express their gratitude to the people and institutions that made this book possible. The work would not have been possible without the generous funding from the Ford Foundation for the Alliance for International Higher Education Policy Studies (AIHEPS) project. We are especially grateful to Richard Richardson Jr. of New York University and Roland Kent of the Autonomous University of Peubla and the respective teams of researchers they lead in the United States and Mexico for their insights, patience, good humour, and thoughtful comments throughout this study. The books *Las Politicas de Educación Superior en México duante la Modernización: Un Análisis Regional* (Kent 2009) and *Policy and Performance in American Higher Education* (Richardson and Martinez 2009) report the results of the Mexican and American studies. We have also benefitted from the advice and input from other colleagues who have attended some of the meetings held by the Canadian team. Included here are Adrienne Chan, Karen Evans, Garnet Grosjean, and Amy Metcalfe. The four editors wish to acknowledge the support of their respective institutions as well as to recognize specific financial support for the publication of this book from the Université du Québec à Rimouski and the Faculty of Education, Minor Research Grant Program, at York University.

We acknowledge the encouragement received from Philip Cercone during the early stages of this project. More recently we have received invaluable support from editor in chief Jonathan Crago and Joanne Richardson our trusted copy editor. Thanks must also go to Christine Dudgeon, who did such a fine job of compiling the index. Finally, we are grateful to two anonymous readers who peer-reviewed the manuscript and offered valuable suggestions to streamline and strengthen our message.

Preface

A note about the way we have assigned authorship of this volume. The collaborative nature of the research project and the writing that followed made it difficult for us to opt for either an edited volume or one with multiple authors. To avoid confusion we have opted for the following compromise. The four main authors (Fisher, Rubenson, Trottier, and Shanahan) are the overall editors. Among the four editors, Fisher and Rubenson took responsibility for writing and editing the case study chapter on British Columbia, Trottier took primary responsibility for Quebec, and Shanahan for Ontario. The contributing authors co-wrote the initial versions of each chapter in which they are listed and participated in the updating of the text. With consultation from the other two editors, Fisher and Rubenson wrote chapters 1, 5, and 6. Fisher and Rubenson have taken overall responsibility for the final rewriting and revision of the entire text. Finally, while Jacy Lee and Robert Clift are only listed as authors of the BC chapter, they were, between them, responsible for producing all the figures and tables.

THE DEVELOPMENT OF POSTSECONDARY
EDUCATION SYSTEMS IN CANADA

1

Introduction and Overview: PSE in Three Canadian Provinces

DONALD FISHER AND KJELL RUBENSON

This book emerges from work that a Canadian team of researchers is conducting on the impact of educational policy on the performance of postsecondary education (PSE) systems in Canada, the United States, and Mexico. This research was funded by the Ford Foundation through the Alliance for International Higher Education Policy Studies (AIHEPS). The purpose of the larger study is to illuminate the relationship between policy environments, the process of decision making ("rules of the game"), and performance of PSE systems in selected jurisdictions in the United States, Mexico, and Canada. The first part of the study began in September 1999 and was conducted by researchers at New York University and the Centro de Investigacion y Estudios Avanzados in Mexico City. The second part of the study began in September 2002 and marked the addition of Canada to the project. The Canadian team included researchers from Quebec, Ontario, and British Columbia, and the Centre for Policy Studies in Higher Education and Training (CHET) at the University of British Columbia (UBC) took on the task of coordination.

The purpose of this book is to present three case studies of the evolution of PSE systems in British Columbia, Ontario, and Quebec over the last thirty years. The impact of PSE policies is analyzed and compared between the three provinces. This analysis comes at a time when both senior levels of government have come to recognize that PSE is a key institution in liberal democratic knowledge societies, a time when governments across the political and ideological spectrum have subscribed to the belief that investments in PSE will translate into economic security and economic development at the individual, provincial, and national levels. For some state theorists, PSE systems play a central role in the state's legitimation function and an increasingly important role in its accumulation function. Universities in particular have been strongly implicated in the market language of production, distribution, and utilization of knowledge. The role of research in the production of knowledge is increasingly influenced by ideologies that support the commodification of knowledge. It follows that this book draws from recent research that examines changes within PSE systems in the context of human capital and human resource theory, the marketplace, and international competitiveness.

This work is located within the sociological tradition, and our approach is set within the field of policy sociology.[1] This field has its origins in the 1970s and began to take off in the 1980s. These researchers were part of what was called the "new" sociology of education. Following the lead of sociologists in Britain and Europe a "new" form of policy studies took on the task of conducting "critical" policy research that went beyond description and understanding to include explanation. Just as the new sociology has two broad foundations housed in interpretive and structuralist traditions, so the new policy research divides into two strands: one focusing on discourse analysis and using Foucault as a major starting point, the other focusing more on explanation and using classical theorists like Marx, Weber, and Durkheim as well as the current theorizing of Bourdieu.

Our work is located specifically in the latter strand of the distinction drawn above. This means that we, as a group of researchers, start from the position that, in order to understand and explain the role of PSE in Canadian society, we must locate systemic change in the broader structural context. By definition, policies are part of and help construct the socio-political-economic context. For these reasons, current theorizing on the liberal-democratic state, academic capitalism, and marketization became our key sensitizing concepts. We aim to contribute to theory in these areas as we expose the gap between policy and outcomes. The focus here is upon the contradictions and unintended consequences of public policy. We use the classic Weberian device of trying to understand the relation between policy and outcomes by focusing on the factors that both enable and constrain implementation.

While beyond the time period of our study, we contend that recent events in Quebec illustrate the relevance of our work. The student strike, the subsequent defeat of the Liberal government, and the current difficulties faced by the Parti Québecois (February 2013) all speak to the importance of accessibility and accountability and, further, the need to explicate the complex relations between states, governments, and PSE systems.

DESIGN AND PURPOSE OF OUR STUDY

The AIHEPS framework as it appeared at the point when Canada joined the study (see figure 1.1) envisioned examining links between state/province and federal policies and PSE performance across the following dimensions:

- The general context, or "policy environments," which includes population demographics, history, geography (regionalism), political culture, economics, political philosophies/ideologies, and constitutional issues;
  - The priorities of the government at both the federal and provincial (or state) levels concerning PSE policy;
  - The organization of the PSE system (system design), including the types of institutions, coordinating agencies, information systems, technology, and the private sector;
- The financial strategies (fiscal policies) concerning the functioning of institutions, operating support, capital funding, incentive funding, student assistance, and tax policy;
- The behaviour of the system contextualized by jurisdiction, including communication, collaboration, accountability, and priorities; and
- The performance of the system based on indicators developed by the participants.

The focus is on how policy priorities get translated into the PSE system as reflected in "system" behaviours, performance, funding arrangements, design, and structural components. The framework presents the relationship as a multidimensional, dynamic exchange between policy makers, the PSE community, and the behaviour and performance of PSE systems. This framework has been revisited and refined upon discussion between the three national academic teams.

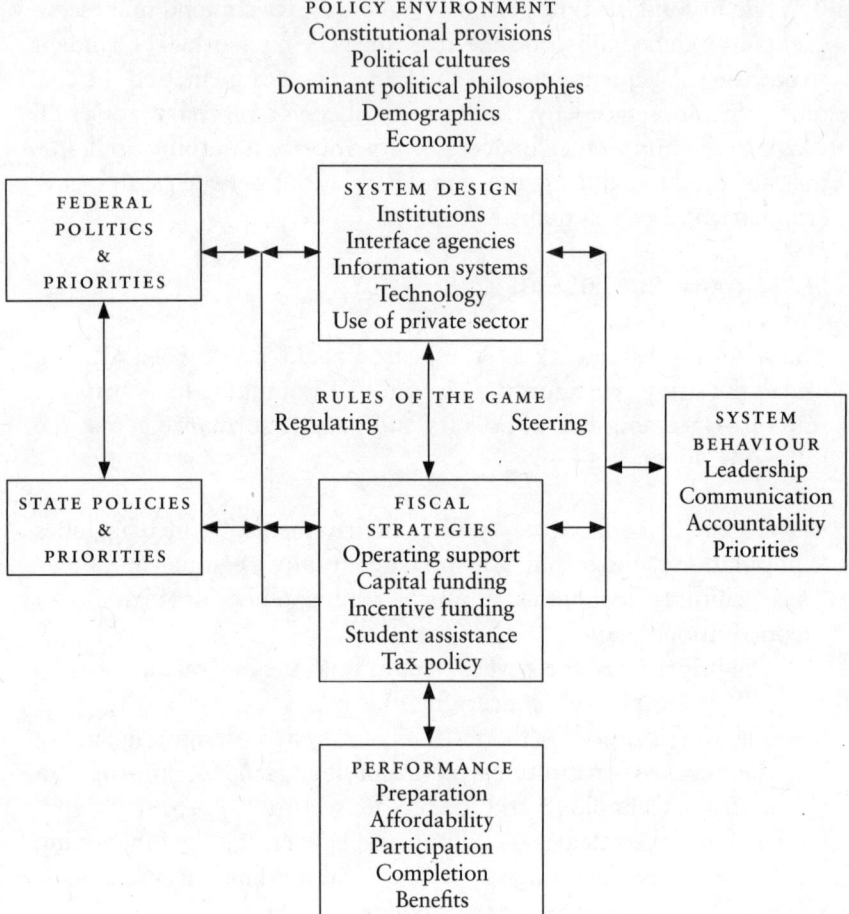

Figure 1.1
Linking state and federal policies to higher education performance

To document the policy environment we decided to use a set of policy priorities as sensitizing concepts. These priorities also cut across the AIHEPS model (see figure 1.1). We grouped these priorities under three overlapping headings: Political, Economic, and Academic (see below).

Political priorities (ideology of governments)
- Accountability (fiscal reporting, use of funds, responsibility to citizens, contribution to democratic process)
- Marketization/globalization (deregulation of fees, competition, promotion of market behaviour)
- Academic-industry partnerships

- Public-private relationships
- Expansion of private sector
- Access and equity (particular focus on Aboriginal/Indigenous populations)
- Quality
  - Participation
  - Levels of completion
  - Total quality management
  - Relevance of Education: Employment of students/starting salaries, access/participation/outcome "benefits";
  - Question: Do performance indicator policies actually measure quality?

Economic priorities
- Economic development
- Funding
- Transfer payments
- R & D
- Internationalization
- Vocationalism (accountability, academic-industry partnerships)

Academic priorities
- Life-long learning
- Distance education
- Information and communication technologies
- Academic-industry partnerships, R & D, Internationalization

So while not losing sight of the original intention, the Canadian team has focused on a series of questions that emerge from the framework. The underlying questions are as follows: What are the conditions that make the emergence of a particular policy agenda possible? How do these rules and regularities shape policy choices? How have provinces attempted to alter their policy environments? What particular combinations within policy environments have either enabled or constrained the capacity of a province to adapt to changes in the external environment? What aspects of the policy environment are associated with particular performance patterns?

The policy priorities were drawn from three relevant literatures – namely, policy sociology, sociology of higher education, and theories of the state. These priorities became sensitizing concepts that we used as a screen throughout the research process. From the interplay between these concepts and our sources of evidence we were able to identify and document emergent policy themes. Our aim was both accurate description and reasonable explanation.

The most important substantive policy themes to emerge from our analysis are accessibility, accountability, marketization, labour force development, and research and development. The way we defined these themes also emerged from our analysis. We define accessibility as participation in, and graduation from, the PSE system by all willing and capable persons regardless of age, gender, socio-economic status, race, culture, religion, and geographic region. This is based on the principle that everyone with the intellectual ability and the desire has the right to PSE. The objective is to enable the greatest number of these people not only to attend postsecondary institutions but also to obtain the diploma or degree in question within a reasonable time frame.

Accountability refers to the possibility of making organizations responsible for their actions. It is defined at the institutional level as an institution's ability to demonstrate meeting its mandate, or competency, and the achievement of its mission. Concomitant with academic autonomy and a measure of self-governance comes the responsibility to demonstrate accountability to the public and the government that has determined its mandate. Accountability is actualized through reporting. Efficiency is closely linked to accountability, and it emerged as a priority within the same context. It refers to the achievement of objectives at the least possible cost to (not necessarily defined in monetary terms), and the least possible effort from, an organization. Similarly, accountability is associated with the "quality" of both management and outcomes.

For both levels of government, labour force development refers to the wish to bring training programs closer to socio-economic realities and to meet the demand for highly skilled human resources. Vocational and skills training is articulated within the context of work organization changes, new technologies, and increased productivity as well as economic development and competitiveness requirements related to globalization. Provincial policies are designed to adapt the structure of the economy, modernize companies, and develop value-added light industry in technology sectors. The emphasis has been placed on training quality human resources in the belief that PSE systems must ensure both initial training and upgrading to help people adapt to these changes. This goal entails collaboration with business and the forging of partnerships so that market requirements can be properly met.

Marketization in PSE is reflected in a shift of the education system from state-centred towards market–driven approaches through the introduction of notions of market primacy, free trade, deregulation, and privatization, with a corresponding reduction in the role of the public sphere (Shanahan 2002). This trend has been particularly strong in Ontario and British Columbia, which have introduced legislation that creates the conditions for the establishment of quasi-markets in PSE (Marginson 1997; Marginson and Considine 2000; Chan and Fisher 2008).

The research and development policy theme is an integral part of PSE policy in Ontario and Quebec and is based on the principle that research must contribute more closely than it did before to the state's economic and social goals, and it most often links provincial research policy to competitiveness in a global economy.

The rest of this introduction is divided into the following sections: research design, federal-provincial relationship, literature in the field, and a chapter outline.

RESEARCH DESIGN

The research design aims to construct provincial and federal profiles of the relationship between policy environments, the decision-making process, and the performance of PSE systems. To this end, the Canadian team employs a comparative, multiple, nested case study research design (Feagin et al. 1991; Stake 1995; Merriam 1998; Yin 2003; Gerring 2007). The case study method of inquiry covers the overall design, data collection techniques, and data analysis. The application of a case study is to explain, to describe, to illustrate, to explore, and to evaluate (Stake 1995, 14). According to Stake, comparative case studies can be understood in terms of their disciplinary framework, which, in our case, means sociology, history, education, and policy studies.

For Feagin, et. al., (1991), case studies can offer an understanding of the critical importance of contextual, global, and environmental circumstances. Comparative social science typically draws attention to "convergent causal conditions, causes that fit together or combine in a certain manner" (Ragin 1987, 13). Our intent is to "illuminate features of a broader set of cases" (Gerring 2007, 29). The use of a multiple comparative case study design makes our analytic conclusions more powerful than those obtained from a single case and expands the external validity of our general conclusions (Yin 2003).

The case studies were conducted at the provincial and national levels. Each of the three provincial teams (Quebec, Ontario, and British Columbia) of Canadian researchers is responsible for one provincial case study.[2] The team and the choice of cases was somewhat determined by the availability of funds and people. Initially, the Canadian part of the study was limited to British Columbia, but, with the encouragement of the principal investigators of the larger study, we decided to extend the study to include Ontario and Quebec. These choices were made, in part, because of an existing network of scholars in higher education who were located in the universities of Toronto, York, and Laval, but they were also made because, in our judgment, these three provinces taken together provide significant insight into the Canadian setting and increase the potential generalizability of our conclusions. They provided an excellent opportunity to examine the specific elements that connect social forces to policy environments.

In choosing our comparative, multiple, nested case study research design we were conscious of the fact that Canada, because of the constitutional division of powers between the federal and provincial governments, provides a unique, laboratory-type setting for comparative work on PSE systems. With regard to the particular cases, we contend that both the size and mainstream position of the three provincial PSE systems, along with their diversity, makes them at least somewhat representative of the other provinces in Canada. In 2007, Quebec, Ontario, and British Columbia accounted for 75 percent of university full-time equivalent (FTE) enrolment, 79 percent of the graduates (undergraduate and postgraduate), and 79 percent of postgraduate degrees awarded in Canada. Similarly, in the area of R&D, the three provinces in 2007–08 accounted for 79 percent of federal granting councils funding, 77 percent of Canada Foundation for Innovation (CFI) funding, and 78 percent of Canada Research Chairs (CRCS) (cumulative 2000–08) in Canada. On the crucial variable of tuition fees, the three provinces are representative of the range of increases across Canada as a whole. The range of increases of "average undergraduate tuition fees" between 1991–92 and 2009–10 went from 70 percent in Newfoundland and Labrador to

258 percent in Alberta. Over the same period, the increases for Quebec, British Columbia, and Ontario were 73 percent, 146 percent, and 227 percent, respectively.[3] Finally, we argue that the array of political administrations that have been elected in these three provinces over the last three decades is representative of the Canadian political spectrum. For all of the above reasons, this comparison provides an excellent opportunity to examine the specific elements that connect state policies to PSE system outcomes.

Beyond the use of indicators and other secondary statistical data, we rely upon documentary and policy analysis and qualitative interviews. We have created a relevant documentary database for each province (including policy statements, committee reports, laws, regulations, by-laws, briefs, periodicals, pamphlets, association newsletters, government reports and commissions, and PSE-related websites) that explicate the policies that have guided PSE over the last three decades (1980 to 2010). This documentary analysis was complemented by semi-structured interviews with key policy makers in each province.[4]

The aim is to reconstruct and render sociologically intelligible the divergence in political, ideological, and socio-educational positions among the major social actors in Canadian PSE (e.g., governments, government departments, unions, institutional leaders, professional associations). In the analysis, policies are treated as operational statements of values, "statements of prescriptive intent" (Kogan 1975). Defining policy and policies in this way draws our attention to the importance of power, control, and conflict in the policy-making process. Logically, we cannot divorce policies from interests, from domination, and from justice (Ball 1994). We are also concerned with theorizing the nature of policy and its production.

Over the period of this study each province has elected a wide array of political administrations. In each case, the political ideology of these administrations has moved to the right. The trend begins in Ontario in 1995 with the election of the Progressive Conservatives under Premier Michael Harris. The Harris government and subsequent Progressive Conservative administrations until 2003 set out to change the society through what they called the "Common Sense Revolution." In classic neoliberal manner, Ontario was moved dramatically closer to the market. British Columbia followed suit in 2001 when the Liberals under Premier Gordon Campbell were elected on a clear neoliberal platform. In both cases, the new right took over from the old left New Democratic Party (NDP). Finally, in Quebec, a neoliberal version of the Liberal Party under Premier Jean Charest took power from the left-wing Parti Québecois.

We define the PSE system as the sum of component institutions, agencies and government departments which provide, regulate and coordinate PSE (Skolnik 1992 and 1997). As PSE is under the jurisdiction of provincial governments, so it is the combined influences of the history, demographics, politics, and economics of the province in question that produces the policies shaping its PSE system and the priorities assigned to it. At the same time, we were conscious of the importance of federal PSE policy and the similarities and differences between the provinces in the federal-provincial relationship. Our definition of the PSE system includes all public and private institutions operating in each province. Following Skolnik, Jones, and Soren (1998) we posit three major approaches to the coordination of PSE systems: institutional-level, sector-level, and system-level. No province is yet at the system level of coordination, whereby agencies transcend institutional and sector boundaries.

In trying to arrive at a broader explanation of the transition from elite to mass to universal systems (Trow 1973),[5] and as a means of bringing some uniformity to our analysis, we utilized a typology of four broad types of PSE system that was first developed by Clark (1987a) and discussed by Scott (1995, 37). The types are as follows: dual systems (Holland, Germany), binary systems (most Canadian provinces), unified systems (Britain, Australia), and stratified systems (California). Absent is the original type in which universities dominate the system. Arguably, systems evolve through this typology. Therefore, a system might begin as a university-dominated system in which universities are the postsecondary sector and all other institutional types are secondary sectors. The movement to a dual system (such as Holland's, beginning in 1992) involves the inclusion of other institutions in the postsecondary sector, along with universities, as a properly acknowledged system develops. Coordination of the system emerges as a priority even though universities remain dominant. In the binary stage there are two parallel sectors. Usually one sector is created as an alternative to universities to serve a complementary function, but this function often becomes blurred, which creates competition between the sectors. A unified system (i.e., Australia 1988 and the United Kingdom 1992) is comprehensive. All institutions are recognized as part of one system, with regulatory and co-coordinating institutions. The stratified system is the final type (e.g., as in California, 1960). A stratified system has differential missions attached to its different sectors (strata).[6]

Given the importance of the federal role in PSE, in the next section we focus directly on the federal-provincial relationship and the development of federal PSE policy.

FEDERAL-PROVINCIAL RELATIONSHIP[7]

Canadian federalism is characterized by a major paradox. On the one hand we have the provinces' constitutionally derived responsibility for social welfare, health, and education; on the other hand, we have the federal government's responsibility for concerns of national interest, equality of treatment and opportunity, economic development, and Aboriginal peoples and lands reserved for them. This paradox has led to a major line of tension in federal-provincial relations as each jurisdiction attempts to fulfil its respective responsibilities. The provinces have, to varying degrees, attempted to protect the constitutional division of powers by either blocking or accommodating federal interference. Quebec has played the most significant role in both protecting its own autonomy and, by extension, pushing the federal government to observe at least the relative autonomy of the other provinces. Federal governments have used the powerful instrument of "federal spending power" to intervene with the enormous weight of federal taxes in precisely the same areas that come under provincial jurisdiction.[8] Over time, the major line of tension is influenced by structural factors that are simultaneously national and global. The key factors that affect PSE are war, demography, and the economy. The most recent phase in federal PSE policy, with its emphasis on research leading to the creation of applied knowledge, is clearly set within, and has contributed to, the emergence of the knowledge society (Drucker 2002).

Federal PSE policy has gone through some significant and at times dramatic shifts. Because there is an overlap of responsibilities between the federal and provincial levels of government, we can observe a continuous struggle for recognition and credit as well as an increased emphasis on accountability. Federal governments have used their spending powers both as a means of channelling funds directly to federal priorities and as a lever for realigning the behaviour of provincial legislatures. What has emerged from the basic line of tension and the ensuing struggle is a patchwork of indirect and direct federal spending, and an assortment of conditional and unconditional federal-provincial agreements governing grants and transfers. Commentators have variously labelled the federal-provincial PSE relationship as "soft federalism" (Jones 1996), "chequerboard federalism" (Bakvis 2002), and "collaborative federalism" (Robinson and Simeon 1999; Noël 2002; Cameron 2004). We should note that, while federal ministerial portfolios cover health and social welfare,[9] this is not the case for PSE (Young and Levin 2002),[10] except indirectly in the case of First Nations and Inuit education through Indian and Northern Affairs Canada (INAC).

Federal governments have always viewed PSE in relation to their own responsibilities for national well-being. These include supra-provincial issues such as defence, foreign affairs, and the national economy as well as the imperative to ensure that all citizens enjoy similar rights and living standards regardless of their province or territory of residence. The federal case for involvement in PSE has repeatedly invoked the senior government's responsibility for national economic policy, including human resource development, and for the educational and occupational standards that ensure citizens' inter-provincial mobility and equity. To these has often been added a paternalistic (but occasionally justified) doubt concerning the will and/or capacity of provincial governments to make the long-term investment that their individual and collective interests entail.

Even before the Canadian state was officially born, PSE was an area of contention. The 1864 Charlottetown draft of what would become the Constitution placed universities under federal responsibility. However, when the final version of the British North America Act was signed in 1867, the entire educational sphere had been relegated to provincial jurisdiction, primarily at the urging of Lower Canada (Standing Senate Committee on National Finance and Leblanc 1987, 1–2).[11] The provinces therefore have a central role in providing direct operating support to educational institutions as well as in developing legislation for them and ensuring their regulation and coordination. The federal government does not have a direct role in coordinating PSE institutions in Canada. Thus, different arrangements exist in each province with regard to education.

Major areas of federal involvement in education evolve out of areas of federal responsibility,[12] such as national defence, Indian affairs, the territories, prisons, external affairs, and the economy. A central responsibility involves the education of Aboriginal peoples, which has been and continues to be a controversial and critical issue in Canada. Section 91(24) of the Canadian Constitution Act, 1982, designates "Indians and Lands reserved for the Indians" as a federal responsibility. This means registered (status) Indians (living on reserve or on Crown land) are under the legal jurisdiction of the Indian Act, kept on register by INAC, and their schooling is a federal responsibility.[13] INAC is also responsible for Indian education in the three territories. However, despite the recognition of Métis as Aboriginal people in section 35(2) of the Constitution, the federal government does not accept responsibility for Métis education.

The federal government is involved in educational areas that contribute to the national interest. In the 1970s and 1980s, this resulted in federal resources being allocated to the Canada Studies Program for educational programs and curricula that focus on elevating student awareness of Canada at home and abroad. This work is currently handled by the academic relations unit within the Department of Foreign Affairs and International Trade (DFAIT) and is mostly directed towards Canadian studies programs in other countries. Similarly, the Official Languages in Education Program focuses on educating official minority language students in their mother tongue and promoting bilingualism.[14]

The federal government has a history of involvement in vocational and technical training. Its role in this area is seen as an extension of its responsibility for national economic development. The federal government's concern with producing a well-trained work force that would allow Canada to compete in the global economy heightened in the 1980s and 1990s. The responsibility for these programs has moved between different ministries; however, beginning in 1994, it was housed in the renamed Ministry of Human Resources and Development Canada (HRDC) and is currently housed in Human Resources and Skills Development Canada (HRSDC). Federal involvement is most obviously seen in the federal government's support of community college skills training programs. Federal support for these programs reached a high point in the late 1980s. More recent agreements with the provinces have largely placed this activity in the hands of the provinces.

The federal government's responsibility for economic development has led it to support university-based research. Through national research councils and institutes, as well as various intermediary bodies such as the Canadian Foundation for Innovation (CFI), the federal government has become the largest source of support for university-based research. Consequently, it wields considerable influence over this aspect of PSE.

Similarly, the federal government has a role in financing student PSE, in the past through the Canada Student Loans Program (CSLP) and currently through the Canada Millennium Scholarship Foundation (CMSF). The CSLP was the responsibility of the Secretary of State until 1994,[15] when this function was taken over by the HRDC and then, in 2003, by the HRSDC. The federal government also funds PSE for Aboriginal and Inuit students, initially through the Postsecondary Assistance Program (1977) and now through the University and College Entrance Preparation Program (1983) and the Postsecondary Student Assistance Program (1989).

Finally, there are national organizations involved in PSE that have connections with the federal government. The Council of Ministers of Education Canada (CMEC) is made up of all the provincial ministers of education and PSE, and it represents and protects the interests of the provinces. While historically it has had limited impact on education in Canada because it only acts when all the ministers are in agreement, there are examples of its having initiated pan-Canadian activities. Some examples of national bodies representing constituent interest groups include the Association of Universities and Colleges of Canada (AUCC), the Canadian Association of University Teachers (CAUT), the Canadian Federation for the Humanities and Social Sciences (CFHSS), the Canadian Federation of Students (CFS), the Association of Canadian Community Colleges (ACCC), the Canadian Bureau of International Education (CBIE), and the Canadian Education Network (CEN).

The financial relationships between the provinces and the federal government are complex and controversial. In the Canadian federal system the federal government enjoys the largest share of revenues from economic growth (e.g., through income tax). However, constitutionally the provinces have responsibility for providing essential and expensive services such as health and education. Transfer payments from the federal government to the provinces were formerly known as established programs financing (EPF). The transfer program was revised, renamed the Canada Health and Social Transfer (CHST), and reduced. During the 1990s, as part of an overall spending reduction effort, the federal government limited or reduced its financial support to the provinces. In turn, the provinces have had to make up the shortfall in various ways, by reducing provincial grants to PSE institutions, thus setting the stage for the search for alternative sources of revenue for the PSE system. Currently, provincial governments provide almost all the funding for education (exceptions have been noted above, particularly in the federal government's support of university research). Provincial funds for PSE are drawn from the general revenue of the province (which includes any federal government transfers and provincial tax revenue). While part of the annual provincial government's budget is set aside for education, other provincial ministries outside of education have been involved in initiatives that have benefited education.

The struggle over who controls the boundary territory between the federal and provincial governments has become more prominent since the 1970s as the federal government shifted the emphasis from indirect and unconditional funding to more direct and, at times, conditional funding for researchers, students, and universities. Over the last three decades, the federal government has used its spending power to reduce indirect transfers to PSE and to channel that money into direct funding to universities for research, research chairs, research infrastructure, and the "indirect costs" of research. In this way, since the mid-1990s, federal governments have become stronger and more dominant in the federal-provincial relationship. National well-being housed in a free-market economic ideology has become the watchword for successive federal governments. Yet Quebec has been firm about protecting its constitutional powers while, at the same time, benefiting just as much as the other provinces from federal policies. Quebec "exceptionalism" has been a key feature of the federal-provincial relationship in PSE and, by extension, has pushed the federal government to take into account the relative autonomy of the other provinces.

The main sources of academic research funding are grounded in a dual support system. Until recently, infrastructure has been covered primarily through block grants from the provinces, which, in turn, have been heavily dependent on transfers from the federal government. Project and program research grants have come primarily from three national funding bodies; and, in some provinces – notably Quebec and Ontario – additional funds have been provided through a parallel set of granting structures. Since 1996, the federal government has created a series of R&D programs that cuts directly across the infrastructure/project divide. Funds are disbursed primarily through three mechanisms: (1) direct grants to faculty members for research projects, (2) capital funding on a shared-cost basis for research infrastructure projects, and (3) direct grants to universities for indirect costs of research. The funding is disbursed by federal agencies on a competitive basis and is awarded in accordance with federal criteria, which include merit and national interests.

As noted earlier, while the federal government's commitment to providing unconditional transfers to the province for PSE has decreased over the last twenty years (1988–89 to 2010–11), those transfers have risen since reaching a low point in 2003–04. At the same time, the federal government has substantially increased the funds allocated for R&D (Doern and Sharaput 2000; Fisher et al. 2006; Fisher and Rubenson 2010). The underlying policy decisions are set within a science and technology policy that emerged from competing definitions of science, utility, and the "public good." By promoting industry access to publicly funded research, the science and technology policy recognizes that scientific research is both fundamental and useful; however, it also shifts the balance in favour of private interests and commercial science.

The Canadian academic research enterprise has three main components: (1) government and quasi-government funding agencies, (2) universities, and (3) faculty and doctoral students. Currently, the federal government provides research funding for academic disciplines and fields through three national funding bodies: Canadian Institutes of Health Research (CIHR), the Natural Sciences and Engineering Research Council (NSERC), and the Social Sciences and Humanities Research Council (SSHRC) (for details, see Fisher et al. 2006, chart 1, app. 2).[16] In addition, the government has created a series of policy instruments to provide additional research and capital funding. This list includes the Networks of Centres of Excellence program (NCE), the CFI, the Canadian Research Chairs program (CRC), and the indirect costs of research funding.[17]

Given the combined impact of the major federal research policy instruments (the NCE, the CFI, the CRC, and the research councils and "indirect costs") as well as the provincial R&D policies in Ontario, Quebec, and British Columbia, the trend has favoured the natural, applied, and health sciences. Furthermore, given the links between R&D policy and commercialization and economic development, we can conclude that the research-intensive universities have been pushed closer to the boundary separating the academy from industry and the market.

Federal R&D policy has been successful on two fronts. The increase in public funding has guaranteed that a high proportion of the research continues to be conducted in the PSE sector. At the same time, the emphasis on commercialization and academic-industry partnerships has resulted in business enterprise increasing the proportion of the gross domestic expenditure on R&D (GERD) that it funds. Alongside these intended consequences are the unintended consequences of increased stratification between regions and institutions. The emphasis on competition and knowledge production has created quasi-markets within Canada as provinces and universities compete for resources and status.

When we turn to federal transfers, we find that the differential emphasis between health, on the one hand, and education and social assistance, on the other, is profound. Between 1988–89 and 2010–11, the federal transfers to the provinces for health and for social programs (PSE and social assistance) combined, in 1988 dollars, increased 84.7 percent and 14.1 percent, respectively. The difference is even more pronounced if we only report the cash transfers. Over the same period, again using constant 1988 dollars, we find that, while health increased by an enormous 132.7 percent, PSE and social assistance actually declined by -9.8 percent. The gap between the transfers for health, and for PSE and social assistance combined, becomes more pronounced if we just focus on the last fifteen years. Between 1995–96 and 2010–11, the federal transfers to the provinces for health and for PSE and social assistance combined, in 1988 dollars, increased 94.6 percent and 2.4 percent, respectively. The difference is even more pronounced if one only reports the cash transfers. Over the same period, again using constant 1988 dollars, we find that, while health increased by an enormous 168 percent, PSE and social assistance actually declined by -22.2 percent.

In many ways the differential emphasis and the invisibility of PSE is predictable, given the way decisions are made in a parliamentary democracy. Both health and social welfare have ministers at the cabinet table, whereas PSE does not. The best estimate we have of the decline in federal transfers to PSE provides startling confirmation of how this area has moved to the bottom of the policy agenda. Between 1988–89 and 2010–11, the total transfer (both cash and tax points) for PSE in 1988 dollars decreased from $5.084 billion in 1988–89, to $2.527 billion in 2003–04 and, finally, to $3.571 billion in 2010–11, for a total of $1.513 billion, or -29.8 percent. From the late 1980s, the federal government turned its attention to funding research and infrastructure through the granting councils and special programs. So, for example, between 1988–89 and 2010–11, the federal government spending on granting councils in 1988 dollars had risen from $721 million to $1.462 billion.

THREE FIELDS OF LITERATURE

This book is set within three overlapping scholarly fields: policy sociology, sociology of PSE, and theories of the state. The cross-disciplinary nature of research in the field of PSE means that, by definition, our work draws on other social science disciplines and fields (such as political science and historical sociology).

Policy sociology emerged as a response, and in opposition, to the traditional technocratic and managerialist orientation present in policy studies. In the mainstream disciplines of political science and sociology we can observe the creation of the subfield known as political sociology. More recently, in a series of publications, sociologist Michael Burrawoy (2005) distinguishes between four types of sociology: professional, policy, critical, and public. In professional sociology, other academics are the intended audience and the focus is on providing "instrumental" knowledge and information. In policy sociology, the knowledge is "instrumental" but the audience consists of non-academic clients who engage sociologists in the service of a pre-defined goal. In critical sociology, other sociologists are the intended audience but, rather than "instrumental," the knowledge is "reflexive" because the focus is on appropriate outcomes. In public sociology the audience is the "communities" with whom sociologists work reflexively to produce knowledge that will serve the public good.

In the field of education it was the subfield known as the sociology of education that provided the intellectual foundation for change and the emergence of a different policy sociology. Yet, just as the elements of the Burrawoy taxonomy are not mutually exclusive, so in education we find that the labels "critical" and "sociology" have been used in overlapping and confusing ways. This means that we can observe a blurring of the boundary between the two strands of work identified earlier. Even so, the "new" policy researchers in education agreed that to present a linear representation of the policy process, without also acknowledging that decisions are influenced by the material and social circumstances within which they are made, was to miss the basic premise of policy as process. Further, with a nod to the complexity of the policy process, these researchers observed that policy texts, policy production, and policy producers change within and across contexts – so much so that sometimes there is little that is shared from one context to another and that it is actually difficult to identify what a policy is and what it is intended to achieve. These reactions highlighted the need for new conceptual tools to provide a more adequate account of the discontinuities, compromises, omissions, and exceptions in policy production.

By the late 1980s and early 1990s, a group of sociologists was attempting to draw a clear boundary around a field it labelled as "policy sociology" (Ozga 1987; Ball 1990; Lingard 1993; Gale 2001). At this stage, the intent was to take account of context and complexity but to house the analysis historically and politically. For Bowe, Ball, and Gold (1992), one way to account for the variation in context was to look at a cycle of policy production and reproduction. They highlighted three contexts of policy making: context of influence, policy text production, and context of practice (i.e., the localities within which policy is initiated, articulated, and rearticulated). Yet, even in these early stages, we can see the emergence of one major strand of work that was inspired by Foucault and that focuses on text and discourse (Ball 1993, 1997, 1999; Scheurich 1997; Taylor 1997; Olssen et al., 2004). The intent is to display the relation between power and politics by using the methodology of discourse analysis. For Ball (1994, 23), policy discourse as a process "articulate(s) and control(s) the possibilities and probabilities of interpretation and enactment." Further, the analysis can uncover "dominant discourses" in social policy, such as neoliberalism.

Taylor (1997, 2004) builds on Ball's work and draws on Foucault and Fairclough (1989, 1995) to enhance the scope of what she calls "critical policy studies." For Taylor, discourse theory allows one to simultaneously examine the historic, economic, social, political, and cultural contexts of policy production. In turn, this analysis helps to determine how policy problems are constructed and positioned on the policy and political agenda, which then shapes both the content and the language of the policy text. Critical policy analysis can then show how implicit and explicit meanings in the language and the historical and political contexts come together to shape the policy environment. Goldberg (2005) develops what he calls "critical policy discourse analysis," which he utilizes to identify and locate "predominant discourses," which are the equivalent of major policy themes.

Everett (2003) refers to this Foucauldian turn as the "postmodern" approach to policy analysis. He makes the interplay between power and politics the centre of his approach. Policies and policy directions are the result of the struggle between groups that use their capital to arrive at a solution. The results of these struggles, Everett contends, are unlikely to be based on fair and objective analysis, and he concludes that "policies and their resultant outcomes are more likely to be determined on the bases of political clout and expedients" (70).

The other major strand takes a structural approach and has drawn inspiration from the work of Bourdieu (Rothstein 1999; Thompson 2005; Lingard, Rawolle, and Taylor 2005). As noted earlier, the two strands are not mutually exclusive as they share ideas and authors. The boundary-defining difference is the move away from a reliance on Foucault and on discourse analysis. This strand of policy sociology is an amalgam of two approaches – namely, the "social science project" (Ozga 2000) and "critical policy analysis" (Taylor et al. 1997; Rizvi and Lingard 2010). More emphasis is placed on political economy in this approach than in earlier approaches. The state is assumed to be crucially involved in all phases of the policy-making cycle (Rizvi and Lingard 2010). Further, this strand of policy sociology takes more fully into account the structural context and the social forces impinging on the system.

As noted earlier, our work is located within this second strand of policy sociology. We utilize and build upon the work of researchers like Gale (1999, 2001); Bourdieu (1988); Bowe, Ball, and Gold (1992); Rothstein (1999); Schugurensky 2003; Dale (1999, 2005); Robertson et al. (2007); and Rizvi and Lingard (2010). Because policy texts, policy production, and policy producers change within and across contexts, analysts like Gale highlight the need for new conceptual tools to provide a more adequate account of the discontinuities, compromises, omissions, and exceptions of policy production.

In doing policy sociology we are aware that we must try to explicate the intellectual climate and the wider debates that characterize the policy context. Policy sociology makes use of historical methods in drawing attention to the historical context of the policy process and how the combined influences of the history, demographics, politics, and economics that produce the policies have shaped the education system and the priorities assigned to it. In this sense, one needs to take into account the unique properties of systems. The aim must be to link these unique properties to broader structural trends (Rothstein 1999).

Bourdieu (1988) draws attention to the concept of a "critical moment" in the development of an academic field. In *Homo Academicus*, Bourdieu describes May 1968 as a "historical event," a point at which the equilibrium of the academic field in France was broken and the existing lines of fracture were made more visible (30). Similarly, in the development of educational policy we are able to determine key moments when governments change direction. At these moments the structural forces present before and after the event are more visible and, hence, more amenable to analysis. Finally, Dale (1999, 2005) and Robertson et al. (2007) draw attention to the importance of the influence of the knowledge-based economy and globalization when trying to understand the relation between state policy and the development of PSE systems.

When we turn to the sociology of PSE, we focus on the general PSE literature and the accumulating literature on academic capitalism, marketization, and commercialization. Within the general literature on Canadian PSE, Glen Jones (1997a, 2006) provides an overview of provincial PSE systems. Yet our emphasis is different from that of Jones as we draw attention to the relation between state PSE policy and performance outcomes. Our work fits into the efforts found in the United States (Clark 1978, 1983, 1988, 1998; Altbach, Berdhal, and Gumport 1999), Europe (Thurow 1977; Teichler and Sadlak 2000; Neave and van Vught 1991; Brennan, Kogan, and Teichler 1998; Scott 2000), and internationally (Altbach 1998, 2007; Altbach, Arnove, and Kelly 1982; Currie and Newson 1998; Arnove and Torres 2003; Amaral, Jones, and Karseth 2002; Dill and Van Vught 2010) to make sense of the role of PSE systems in society at large. More concretely, in the Canadian setting, our work contributes to the literature on access and equality of opportunity (Anisef, Okihiro, and James 1982; Axelrod 1982, 2002; Lee 2005).

If privatization was the symbol of the tension between the public and the private sectors during the 1980s, then marketization and the corollary of commodification took over that role in the 1990s. In particular, the university has been described as the centre of the drive towards the "commodification" of PSE (Rooney and Hearn 2000), while Etzkowitz, Webster, and Healey (1998) invoke the image of the "triple helix" to describe the revolution that has occurred with the intertwining of the interests of the state, the market, and PSE. Bok (2003) draws attention to the "commercialization" of PSE, while Noble (1976, 2001), looking at an extended period of time, pushes us to think about education as a mode of production. For Clark (1998), the new model for our universities is characterized by "entrepreneurship," while Marginson and Considine (2000) speak of the "enterprise university." At the heart of the changes is the "marketization" of liberal democratic societies and, necessarily, of PSE (Slaughter and Leslie, 1997; Fisher and Rubenson 1998; Bourdieu 1999; Currie 2004). We have begun to look at this change as what has produced the "exchange university" (Chan and Fisher 2008).

Simon Marginson and Sheila Slaughter are two authors who have led the way in helping us to understand and explain the impact of capital and market ideology on our PSE systems. For Marginson, all markets in education are "quasi-markets," involving a mix of use and exchange values and a mix of both public and private interests. Slaughter and Leslie (1997) build on the earlier work of Slaughter and Rhoades (1996) to map the rise of what they call "academic capitalism." This concept is useful because it captures how commercialization and marketization overlap to change the power relations within universities. It provides a basis for understanding how academic culture is changing as academic entrepreneurs move their institutions closer to the market. Slaughter and Rhoades (2004, 2008) take us yet further by describing the "academic capitalist knowledge learning regime." In documenting the dominance of this regime, they provide us with a way to understand changes in the territory that connects the public and the private sectors in PSE, between the state, PSE, and the market. For Slaughter and Rhoades, academic capitalism is not privatization but, rather, a redefinition of public space and of the activity appropriate to that space. As the configuration of state resources changes and public universities and colleges are pushed to seek alternative sources of funding, our conception of "public" becomes blurred and altered. In Canada, the analysis focuses on policies that have encouraged the creation of quasi-markets as institutions compete with each other over both public funding and students.

A dominant policy paradigm in industrialized countries over our period of study is accountability. This paradigm rejects the idea that the state is primarily responsible for the public good function of education. Its advocates calls for less taxation, less government interference, more public choice, more deregulation and privatization, and more accountability to taxpayers on the part of the government and its subsidiaries (Dale 1997). In a neoliberal framework, public choice, marketization, and the privatization of education are prevalent themes, emphasizing stronger links between industry training needs and the postsecondary sector. These changes manifest themselves in education and other public services in two major ways. First, there is a reluctance to use public funds to fund public services; second, public institutions are expected to engage in market behaviour in order to fund more of their services. This shift creates changes to organizational forms, managerial practices, and institutional cultures (Deem 2001). Policy changes are accompanied by downloading more financial responsibility onto postsecondary institutions and are characterized by less state funding and an increased emphasis on business practices (Currie 1998). Clark (1998) contends that themes of efficiency, effectiveness, excellence, and continuous quality improvement are examples of the type of thinking that prevail within the entrepreneurial university. Governments strategically promote increased efficiency and innovation using education markets (Dill 1997a, 1997b; Slaughter and Leslie 1997; Mok 2002).

The work on academic capitalism, marketization, and accountability leads to a discussion of the restructuring of the state. If we accept the general proposition that we are living in a globalized knowledge society (Castells 2000) and that PSE has, as a result, become an important legitimating institution in capitalist states, then it follows that an examination of the relation between state PSE policy and the development of PSE systems should provide insight into the restructuring process (Dale 2005).

There is general agreement on the proposition that the rise of the modern interventionist state and the expansion and development of social scientific knowledge are interdependent (Poggi 1990). Social empiricism goes hand in hand with the growth of government. Further, most authors accept to some degree the idea that states perform a legitimation function under conditions of relative autonomy. What is contested is the relation between capital, power, and the state. On one side is the "bringing-the-state-back-in" school, which posits a diffuse relation between state officials and elites, with the state at times acting in an independent manner (Skocpol 1980). On the other side is the more traditional perspective (Domhoff 1998; Milliband and Panitch 1994), which posits a close relation between state officials and capital, with the state acting in the interests of the ruling class. Somewhere between these two positions we find the "public sphere" (Habermas 1989) theorists, who posit that the state and the public sphere are synonymous. This sphere is open, democratic, and egalitarian. Social policy is formulated through a rational communication process, through which the power of elites is held in check.

The change in the Canadian political economy has been achieved over the last two decades through two processes: "neoliberal constitutionalism" and "disciplinary neoliberalism" (Gill 2003). The former term refers to the legal institutionalizing of neoliberalism through supranational organizations such as the World Trade Organization (WTO) or the International Monetary Fund (IMF) or through free trade agreements such as the North American Free Trade Agreement (NAFTA). The latter term refers to the internalization of neoliberal ideology that occurs within governments and individuals. Through self-governance and self-regulation, individuals come to pursue a neoliberal agenda, even though there may be no legal requirement or policy that dictates such action. Consider, for example, the message that global economic forces leave us no choice, which is stressed time after time by politicians and the business community. David O'Brian, former CEO of one of the most influential lobby groups in Canada, the Canadian Council of Chief Executives, states: "The Global economy is at our doors. It is not a question of deciding what we want to do: it is deciding for us" (Watkins 2003, 4).

A central concern over the last two decades has been the relation between globalization theory and state theory. A major debate concerns whether globalization leads to convergence or divergence when it comes to the formulation of internal policies. Contained within this general debate is the view that the ideology of neoliberalism is dominant and that social policy is, in general, subjugated to economic policy (Dale and Robertson 2003a, 9). Further, it is argued that states have for the most part accepted the idea that we are living in a global knowledge economy so that, increasingly, economic development at the collective level and economic security at the individual level (Spitzer 1987; Sears 2003; Frauley 2012) depend on the work being done in PSE systems. Thus, increasing R&D funding of and access to PSE become the main tools for legitimation. Security and competitiveness are served at both the individual and the national levels.

At the same time, it is argued that global neoliberalism has contributed to the decline, retreat, or disappearance of the state (Ohmae 1990; Giddens 2000b). So, on the convergence side of the debate, globalization leads states to a form of isomorphism as they adopt neoliberal principles and become more homogenous. On the divergence side of the debate, researchers accept the global assumptions stated above but posit differential outcomes at the level of internal policy making. Connected to this view, although not synonymous with it, is the idea that the state is alive and well and that what we are experiencing is a restructuring of, rather than a retreat from, the state formation. At its extreme, this body of literature suggests that the new "evaluative" state is even stronger than the Keynesian welfare state because of its emphasis on accountability and its reliance upon what has become known as governmentality (Rose 1999).

PSE has undergone a massive transformation across the globe. In many countries, access to postsecondary institutions has increased to meet the demand of citizens who realize that they need credentials in order to secure jobs in a competitive, global marketplace. Globalization, characterized by economic and cultural convergence towards a model that valorizes free-market ideology and cultural homogenization, is helping to determine policy decisions in postsecondary instruction in countries from Australia to Argentina (Wagner 2004). Those critical of globalization tend to look at how certain tenets of neoliberalism have come to underpin policies formed in entirely different countries with different political systems: policies that de-emphasize the role of the state in certain areas (e.g., financial support) but over-emphasize it in other areas (e.g., institutional accountability). According to critics, this combination results in greater responsibility, but less freedom, for the institutions affected (Van Damme 2002). The interconnectedness between states, some argue, is not so much based on symbiotic relationships but, rather, on a convergence in culture, economies, and, consequently, national policies that favours a free-market, neoliberal, and, arguably, American model (see Dale and Robertson 2003a; Schugurensky and Davidson-Harden 2003; Mundy and Iga 2003; Vidovich and Slee

2001). Helping to proliferate neoliberal ideology, some argue, are supranational institutions, such as the IMF, the World Bank, and the WTO (Schugurensky Davidson-Harden 2003; Dale and Robertson 2003a, 2003b; Ginzburg et al. 2003). Under globalization, state power is significantly reduced.

Another body of work that is critical of the application of neoliberal economics to PSE also focuses attention on how countries differ in their approaches to PSE and how governments react to and help construct globalization (e.g., Green 2000; Amaral, Jones, and Karseth 2002; Mundy and Iga 2003; Mok 2003). These academics are not naive to the ways in which the nation-state is changing; yet, at the same time, they do not espouse the "globalization-is-nothing-new" mantra championed by some political scientists and sociologists, such as Hirst and Thomson (1996). Nor do they welcome all the changes that have occurred within PSE over the past twenty years. Different countries enact policies for different reasons. According to this body of literature, due to a variety of factors there is both convergence and divergence in national policy.

Critics of these trends believe certain disciplines within universities suffer as a consequence of them. In particular, disciplines not deemed integral to the economy are given short shrift while institutional autonomy, academic freedom, culture, and environment are eroded (Gould 2003). Amaral et al. (2000) claim that, due to globalization, the university is losing its hegemony and power while, paradoxically, fulfilling an even more important role. However, as universities and PSE systems are increasingly linked to economic activity and interests their role has changed (Enders 2005). Additionally, they are deemed important actors in the areas of technological advancement and the bolstering of the knowledge economy (Dale 1999). Institutions equip students with the skills needed to survive in the information age, enabling them to become Reich's (1992) "symbolic analysts," flexible enough to adapt to any situation.

A number of studies illustrate the divergence in national policies on PSE, suggesting that there are different levels of autonomy and agency in different states. Furthermore, policies are often particular to the individual country's circumstance and political situation. These studies indicate that the "golden straitjacket" is not a one-size fits all and that perhaps there is space to move within it. Indeed, states are not always victims of globalization. McBride (2001) claims that globalization has been the result of domestic neoliberalism, not the reverse. Sometimes the state cooperates with the market not because of coercion but, rather, because of the agendas and desires of the government involved. Brodie (1995, 386) argues that, rather than hapless recipients of neoliberalism, "governments act as the midwives of globalization." As Hallak (2000) argues, states can use globalization to justify their own needs. In other words, states use the rhetoric and supposed pressure of globalization for different purposes: they may "buy into" certain elements of neoliberalism but not others.

Carnoy (2000, 58) claims that states decide how globalization will affect their national policy and that sometimes the reason governments do not fund or support public education is at least partially a result of "ideological preference rather than helplessness." In addition, there are reasons other than globalization behind policy formation. Christopher Hood offers four: (1) policy change, which is influenced by new ideas; (2) pressure from interest groups; (3) change in environment (often due to socio-economic/political changes); and (4) the legacies of previous policies (cited in Mok 2002). Every state's situation is different. Often there is a hybrid, or mix, of divergence and convergence, sometimes through choice and sometimes through imposition.

Some states are stronger than others. Immanuel Wallerstein assigns countries to core, semi-peripheral, or peripheral status, while Susan Strange defines state strength in terms of both structural and relational strength (Volgy and Bailin 2003). Structural strength refers to a state's capacity to create rules and norms for engaging with other states, while relational strength refers to its capacity to deter or minimize challenges from others. According to Volgy and Bailin, a strong nation-state is able to write and rewrite the rules of the game. Using these definitions and concepts, it appears obvious that the United States remains a strong, indeed the strongest, nation-state in the world, while other Western Organization for Economic Cooperation and Development (OECD) countries retain some strength, although they are not always able to "write the rules of the game." As Canadian political scientist Stephen McBride (2005) contends, strong states facilitate globalization while weak states receive the outcomes.

Many have argued that the United States is the force behind globalization and that the values espoused and transported around the globe are essentially "American values" (see Mundy and Iga 2003). While Canada may be "an enthusiastic echo of US policy" (McBride

2001, 105), PSE policy has not been the same here as in the United States. As this text demonstrates, there have been marked differences in PSE policy across and between the provinces (e.g., with respect to student fees, marketization, and privatization). In part, the differences might be explained by the fact that Canada is part of what Hall and Soskice (2001) refer to as the Anglo-Saxon model of welfare provision. These two authors separate the economies of OECD countries into two distinct categories: the *liberal market*, which comprises Anglo-Saxon countries, and the *coordinated market system*, which includes the Nordic countries, Germany, Belgium, and Switzerland. Anglo-Saxon countries, they argue, have been more affected by the rhetoric and reality of neoliberalism than have those within the coordinated market system. In the end, according to McBride (2001), the close relationship Canada shares with its neighbour impinges on its capacity to be autonomous.

In the last two decades much attention has been given to the idea of a Third Way (Giddens 1999, 2003) that sits somewhere between "welfare liberalism" (see Keynes 2007; Esping-Andersen 1985) and "neoliberalism" (see Friedman 1991; von Hayek 1976). Since the turn of the century, however, some have claimed that a new form of liberalism has emerged (see Saul 2005; Giddens 2003; Craig and Porter 2003, 2004; Roelvink and Craig 2004) – what Craig and Porter call "inclusive liberalism." As the term suggests, the notion of "inclusion" is at the heart of this "new" form of liberalism, which seeks to carve out a path between Keynesian welfarism and Friedmanesque neoliberalism. Taking up Anthony Giddens's suggestions for centre-left governments regarding how to cope with globalization, inclusively liberal states bridge the market/state, economy/society, public/private, company/non-profit divides and seek to bring in, or include, those who may have been left behind by the changes in the economy and society in general. In Canada, Prime Minister Jean Chrétien labelled his version of the Third Way as the "Canadian Way" (Coyne 2000). Chretien describes the Canadian Way as "*a balance that promotes individual freedom and economic prosperity while at the same time sharing risks and benefits*" (Coyne 2001, 1, emphasis added). As former minister of finance and former prime minister Paul Martin declared in the 2000 budget speech: "The success we have achieved as a nation has come not only from strong growth but from an abiding commitment to strong values – caring and compassion, an insistence that there be an equitable sharing of the benefits of economic growth" (Department of Finance, Canada, 2000, 5).

In *Canada's Performance 2002* the president of the Treasury Board (2002, 8) describes the Canadian Way as "an approach marked by an accommodation of cultures, a recognition of diversity, a partnership between citizens and the state, a sharing of risks and benefits, and a positioning of government as an instrument of collective action. It is an approach centred on a goal that is common to all Canadians – improving the quality of life for all."

Like the Third Way, the Canadian Way strongly embraces the "no-rights-without-responsibilities" philosophy (Giddens 2000, 165). However, we would argue that the Canadian Way goes beyond the Third Way, injecting a distinct Canadian flavour in an effort to revive a sense of national allegiance. Yet the "New Canadian Nationalism" promoted by the Chrétien Liberal government differs from other interpretations of Canadian nationalism. Critics argue that the particular understanding of "nation," "nation building," and "national identity" that was integral to post-Second World War citizenship efforts is missing from the new version of Canadian nationalism (Brodie 2002). Although in the two quotations above Chrétien (as cited in Coyne 2000) mentions or alludes to diversity and multiculturalism (two factors deemed important to Canadians in defining their identity) (see Kunz 2001), values associated with state services are absent. Brodie laments Canada's abandonment of "the social covenant upon which the postwar social citizenship regime was built" (378). Now, Canadian values are alleged to be most suited to a competitive marketplace (Carroll and Ratner 2005). Indeed, at a summit for the Business Council on National Issues, the speaker opened with a tribute to Canadian values, asserting that these are what will triumph in a competitive world (Carroll 2010).

Critics of the Third Way and inclusive liberalism charge either that it is not particularly different from neoliberalism or that it is a return to classical liberalism. A variety of authors accuse Third Way policies of being neoliberalism as presented by a revamped marketing campaign (see Bastow and Martin 2003; Newman and De Zoysa 2001; Kelsey 2002; Callinicos 2001). A variety of authors believe that, by appearing to focus on civil society, Third Way policies are a cynical ploy to make individuals take more responsibility for their own well-being while continuing to privilege one part of the original public/private binary over the other. In other words, a public-private partnership is rarely made up of equal partners, with the private almost invariably being favoured over the public. For Craig and Porter (2004) "inclusive liberalism" can look much like classical liberalism as governments appear to be on the side of the disadvantaged while in reality maintaining an unequal distribution of property and power.

Barrow (2005) and others (Wood 2003) argue that, rather than the decline of the nation-state, we are witnessing a transition to a new form of capitalist state. Through an examination of the changing relation between globalization theory and state theory, Barrow (2005, 125) concludes that, "within the new global political economy, state elites must still manage the contradictory pressures of (global) accumulation and (national) legitimation. This enduring contradiction is being managed by a restructuring of the capitalist state form and a realignment of internal power relations within the national state apparatuses." This means that the form of state intervention in the economy has changed to mediating between externally established policy and the internal social forces to which the state is accountable (Panitch 1994). Barrow (2005) incorporates in this restructuring of the nation-state the processes of destatization, internationalization, and denationalization described by Offe (1984, 1996) and Jessop (1990, 2002). According to Claus Offe (1984, 1996), the state has relative autonomy and is not directly controlled by the capitalist classes. The democratic capitalist state is an institutionalized form of political power that operates to achieve and guarantee the collective interests of all members of a class society dominated by capital. For Offe, three conditions guide the institutional operation of the state. First, the state does not directly organize production (in a liberal democracy this is outside its direct control). Second, as the state is dependent for its taxation revenue on successful capital accumulation, it is in the interest of state officials to ensure a healthy capital accumulation. Third, in order to legitimate its role, including its role in the capitalist mode of production, the state needs democratic legitimization. The state must try to avoid legitimation crises that can threaten long-term capital accumulation. According to Poulantzas (1978), the autonomy of the state allows it to adopt measures that serve the subordinate classes if such measures are found to be politically unavoidable and/or necessary for promoting the long-term interests of capital. Offe's point is that state institutions, although not directly controlled by the interests of the capitalist class, will, through their dependence on capital accumulation, generate policies that tend to guarantee and enhance these very interests. The promotion of Third Way policies can, in this perspective, be seen as a way of protecting capitalism from itself.

Part of the current debate focuses attention on the way states use PSE policy to promote economic security. The idea is that states restructure PSE systems primarily as a means of increasing access in order to foster active, entrepreneurial, independent, and employable citizens who organize their activities around commercial norms. These policies define university campuses as sites of capital accumulation (Chan and Fisher 2008). They identify "the campus as a site creating or enhancing the profit-making capacity of individuals, business or the country itself" (Carroll and Beaton 2000, 72). We argue that state PSE policies are a central component in the process of redefining the public space in Canadian society.

CHAPTER OUTLINE

This book is divided into five chapters and a conclusion. Following chapter 1, the next three chapters present the provincial case studies: British Columbia, Ontario, and Quebec, respectively. While each case study has unique qualities, in order to allow for an effective comparison, we attempt to make them commensurate and compatible. Each of chapters 2, 3, and 4 contains sections that, in this order, deal with: current system design and funding mechanisms, political economy and the changing shape of the policy environment, policy themes and the policy-making process, funding, and outcomes. While the emphasis on the policy themes differs for each province, each chapter does have sections on accessibility, participation, and choice as well as on useful and relevant research development. Finally, at the end of the book, three appendices (one per province) chart the political parties, the ministers responsible for PSE, the names of the ministries, and the relevant legislation from the mid-1980s to the present.

Chapter 5 focuses on cross-provincial analysis through time. We begin with a section on political economy and funding, wherein we document changes in the funding relationship between the federal and provincial levels of government as federal transfers decreased and R&D spending increased. Further, we document the different reactions of the three provinces to these changes and to the shifting policy environment at the provincial level. We focus on a series of indicators: provincial operating grants for PSE (total and by sector), total government spending as a share of university operating revenue, provincial transfers to colleges and universities per FTE student enrolment, the share of public expenditure allocated to PSE, and, finally, a comparison of the proportion of revenue from own sources as compared to government sources. The rest of the chapter is divided into five sections devoted to the themes that dominated the PSE policy-making process. In order of presentation, these are: accessibility, accountability, marketization, labour force development, and R&D. In discussing these themes, we illustrate their impact on and within the three provincial PSE systems of British Columbia, Ontario and Quebec.

We begin the conclusion by revisiting the questions that we asked at the start of our journey. The next section documents and compares the policy-making process in each of our three case-study provinces. We then draw the material together and interpret our findings within the three literature fields that inform our study. Our sociological lens brings together the political economy of PSE with the five major policy themes and places the analysis within the current debates concerning the role of PSE in the process of restructuring the state. We explore how central PSE has become to the legitimation and accumulation functions served by the state, focusing on the relationships between PSE policy and economic and social development.

2

The Transformation of the PSE System in British Columbia

DONALD FISHER, KJELL RUBENSON, JACY LEE,
ROBERT CLIFT, MADELEINE MacIVOR,
AND JOHN MEREDITH

INTRODUCTION

The story of PSE policy in British Columbia provides a rich opportunity not only to chart the parallel unfolding of events within and outside government but also to examine questions of causation and judgment in PSE policy. The period since the early 1980s has certainly been one of dramatic, perhaps even revolutionary, change. The pressure for access has led to the emergence of new institutional types and new lines of stratification, raising new questions about differentiation, mandate, and identity. A trend towards vocationalism in the university sector has coincided with "academic drift" in the community college sector, leading to convergences in programming and institutional functions across the system as well as competition for resources, students, and external partners. Unprecedented demand has made education a viable industry, sustaining both a proliferation of private providers and a range of new entrepreneurial activities within public institutions. Levels and objectives of public funding have swung dramatically over the period. Public investments in PSE, in the form of capital grants and tuition subsidies, have alternately expanded and contracted, being sometimes applied across the board and sometimes targeted to specific social groups or economic sectors. Likewise, sometimes policy makers have treated PSE as a mechanism for social inclusion and equality, sometimes as an instrument for labour force development, and sometimes as a market sector in its own right.

This chapter is divided into seven sections. First, we provide some demographic information about the province before describing the current design and organization of its PSE system and funding arrangements. Second, we trace the development of British Columbia's postsecondary system with a particular focus on how the general policy environment has been driven by the changing political economy. After a brief historical section we organize the narrative according to changes in political administration. Three political parties have held power in British Columbia since the mid-1980s: the Social Credit Party, the New Democratic Party, and the Liberal Party. Third, we relate the dominant policy themes and then describe and analyze the policy-making process using the concepts of policy communities, policy institutions, and policy capacity. The major policy themes are accessibility, vocationalism and skills, accountability, science and technology, and marketization. Fourth, we trace fiscal policy and the financing of the postsecondary system. This leads into two sections that provide a summary of the impact of the policy themes and the aligned fiscal policies on system design and organization as well as on a range of outcomes. Here we pay special attention to accessibility, participation and choice, and research and development. Finally, we draw some conclusions about the relationship between the policy environment, system design, and outcomes in British Columbia.

CURRENT SYSTEM DESIGN AND FUNDING MECHANISMS

British Columbia is Canada's most western province. The population in 2010 stood at 4.5 million, which represented 13.2 percent of the total population of Canada.[1] Between 1986 and 2010, the total population of the province grew from just over 3 million, or by approximately 50 percent. The most rapid growth occurred in the first decade (22 percent) as opposed to the last decade (11 percent). Over the same twenty-four-year period, the province's 18 to 24-year-old population increased by a somewhat smaller amount, from 341,000 to 444,000, or 30 percent. All this growth has occurred since 1990. For the first four years the province recorded negative growth in this age cohort. The most rapid growth in this population occurred since 2000 and, particularly, since 2005. The rise over the last decade accounts for approximately 70 percent of the total change since 1986. In 2010, the 18- to 24-year-old population of British Columbia as a proportion of the total Canadian 18- to 24-year-old population was 13.5 percent and, therefore, slightly higher than the overall population ratio. The pattern for the 18- to 29-year-old population is quite similar to that for the 18- to 24-year-olds. Over the same period, the province's 18- to 29-year-old population increased from 614,000 to 786,000, or 28 percent. In 2010, the 18- to 29-year-old population of British Columbia as a proportion of the total Canadian 18- to 29-year-old population was 13.5 percent and, therefore, somewhat over the overall population ratio.

Public Sector

In 2010, the PSE system contained a total of twenty-five public institutions serving the needs of the people of the province: eleven universities, eleven colleges, and three institutes. As in the rest of Canada (Skolnik and Jones 1992; Smith 2011), in British Columbia the structure of the public PSE system had remained basically unchanged from the mid-1960s to the mid-1990s. During this period existing legislation divided the public PSE system into two distinct segments: (1) the university sector and (2) the college and institute sector, whereby only the former could offer degrees. The NDP government, elected in 1991, introduced several new structures to the public system in an attempt to respond to low university participation rates, particularly outside the Lower Mainland, and economic demands for the expansion of technical education. In 1995, two Aboriginal institutions – the Nicola Valley Institute of Technology in Merritt and the Institute of Indigenous Government in Vancouver – were designated as public institutions under the College and Institute Act. Royal Roads University was established in 1995 under its own legislation, the Royal Roads University Act (RRU Act). This university differs from the other BC universities in various aspects. It offers undergraduate and graduate degrees as well as certificates and diplomas in selected applied and professional fields. Similarly, in 1997 a special act for the creation of a new technical university of British Columbia (TechBC) was passed, and the institution opened in 1999. However, it only operated for three years before it was closed down by the incoming Liberal government and was incorporated into Simon Fraser University (SFU). In another major initiative to open up more spaces for a university education, the Social Credit government in 1988 transformed three former colleges into a new hybrid institution: university colleges that could offer bachelor degrees. This number was subsequently increased to five by the NDP government.

With these university colleges continuing to be governed under the College and Institute Act, the defining binary characteristic of the BC PSE system began to break up. The new hybrid institutions created considerable tension in the system, and it soon became clear that the new structure was less than optimal to respond to British Columbians' increasing demand for a university education. The disappearance of university colleges began under the Liberal regime in 2004, when the University of British Columbia expanded to incorporate part of the Okanagan University College in Kelowna as a campus of UBC. In the same year, the Open University component of the Open Learning Agency (OLA) was combined with the University College of the Cariboo,[2] and the resulting institution was renamed the Thompson Rivers University (TRU) governed by the Thompson Rivers University Act. TRU has a mandate both as a regional university and as a provincial distance education provider and offers undergraduate programs as well as master's degrees in applied and professional fields. In perhaps the most dramatic change to the BC university system since the Macdonald Report (1962), the Liberal government, acting on recommendations from the Campus 2020 review (Plant 2007), introduced a new category of universities under the University Act, the so-called special purpose, teaching universities (Bill 34, 2008 [the University Amendment Act, 2008]). Bill 34 designated the three remaining university colleges, one community college (Capilano), and one institute (Emily Carr Institute of Art and Design) as special purpose, teaching universities: Capilano University, the Emily Carr University of Art and Design, Kwantlen Polytechnic University, Vancouver Island University, and University of the Fraser Valley. In 2007, the Institute of Indigenous Government closed and became the Vancouver campus of the Nicola Valley Institute of Technology.

The many changes in the system since the mid-1990s have substantially altered the structure of British Columbia's public PSE system, particularly the university sector, which has become highly diversified and increasingly stratified (see, e.g., Metcalfe 2009). The diversity of the university system is upheld through a set of legislative acts regulating the governance, functions, and duties of the institutions.

Universities operate as independent corporations with a significant degree of autonomy. Like most traditional Canadian universities, the nine BC universities that are guided by the University Act adopt a bicameral governance model. Each board of governors has responsibility for management, administration, control of property, and revenue; it also has other general powers associated with managing the affairs of the university, including the power to set and collect fees and enter into agreements on behalf of the university. As with bicameralism, the senate has powers related to academic and program issues. Under the University Act, the Board of Governors must consider recommendations from the senate when making decisions concerning the establishment of faculties and departments. The only powers of the minister of advanced education referenced in the legislation concern the approval of new degree programs and the right to request reports and information from the universities. The amended University Act notes the different functions of the four traditional universities (UBC, SFU, the University of Victoria [UVic], and UNBC) and the five new special purpose, teaching universities. The respective functions of the traditional research universities and the new special purpose, teaching universities are set out in the University Act (paragraph 47) as follows:

(2) A university must, so far as and to the full extent that its resources from time to time permit, do all of the following:
(a) establish and maintain colleges, schools, institutes, faculties, departments, chairs and courses of instruction;
(b) provide instruction in all branches of knowledge;
(c) establish facilities for the pursuit of original research in all branches of knowledge;
(d) establish fellowships, scholarships, exhibitions, bursaries, prizes, rewards and pecuniary and other aids to facilitate or encourage proficiency in the subjects taught in the university and original research in all branches of knowledge;
(e) provide a program of continuing education in all academic and cultural fields throughout British Columbia;
(f) generally, promote and carry on the work of a university in all its branches, through the cooperative effort of the board, senate and other constituent parts of the university.
The functions of the five special purpose, teaching universities:
47.1 A special purpose, teaching university must do all of the following:
(a) in the case of a special purpose, teaching university that serves a geographic area or region of the province, provide adult

basic education, career, technical, trade and academic programs leading to certificates, diplomas and baccalaureate and master degrees, subject to and in accordance with regulations under section 71 (3) (c) (i);

(b) in the case of a special purpose, teaching university that serves the whole province, provide applied and professional programs leading to baccalaureate and master degrees, subject to and in accordance with regulations under section 71 (3) (c) (ii);

(c) provide, in addition to post-secondary programs referred to in paragraph (a) or (b), post-secondary programs specified in regulations under section 71 (3) (c) (iii);

(d) so far as and to the extent that its resources from time to time permit, undertake and maintain applied research and scholarly activities to support the programs of the special purpose, teaching university.

The University Act makes it unequivocally clear that research is not a core function of the new special purpose, teaching universities. The mandate for the senate of the special purpose, teaching universities reflects the differences in functions between the traditional and the new universities. The changes to the University Act partly address one of the key recommendations of *The Campus 2020 Plan for British Columbia's PSE System* (Plant 2007) released in April 2007. In July 2006, Geoff Plant, QC, had been asked by the premier and the minister of advanced education to undertake a comprehensive review of the BC postsecondary system with the aim of helping to shape the future of PSE in the province. The report recognized that "BC cannot have a system of higher learning in which all institutions aspire equally to undertake all responsibilities with an equal amount of success" (4). The report made it clear that, while regional universities could offer master's degree programs and undertake and maintain research and scholarly activities, the latter were for the "purposes of supporting teaching" (67).

As noted above, Royal Roads University does not fall under the University Act but, rather, the RRU Act. Unlike the nine universities under the University Act, RRU does not follow a bicameral governance model but, rather, has adopted a corporate governance model whereby the president, who is also the chief executive officer, holds the powers traditionally vested in a senate. The RRU Act stipulates the establishment of a program and research council to advise the

Board of Governors on instructional programs, research priorities, program objectives, and learning outcomes. The council is comprised of a majority of board-appointed external representatives to ensure relevance of the mandate of the university. An academic council also exists to advise the president on such matters as qualifications for admission; curriculum content; academic standards; criteria for awarding certificates, diplomas, and degrees; and other academic matters typically vested in a senate. The Academic Council is composed of elected internal representatives.

The colleges and provincial institutes are established and regulated under the College and Institute Act. The objects of a college (section 6) are to provide comprehensive (a) courses of study at the first-and second-year levels of a baccalaureate degree program, (a.1) courses of study for an applied baccalaureate degree program, (b) postsecondary education or training, (b.1) adult basic education, and (c) continuing education. The purposes of a provincial institute (section 8) are to provide (a) technical, vocational, artistic and other postsecondary education or training or (b) other functions designated by the minister. The College and Institute Act (section 8.1) states that the objects of BCIT are to act as a polytechnic institution for British Columbia by (a) providing courses of instruction in technological and vocational matters and subjects, (b) providing courses of instruction at the baccalaureate and applied master's degree levels, and (c) performing other functions designated by the minister.

Each of the institutions under the College and Institute Act has a board of governors, which has the responsibility to manage, administer, and direct the affairs of the institution. As "agents of the Crown," colleges, university colleges, and institutions are more closely tied to government than are the universities. The College and Institute Act lists a number of ministerial powers and duties that relate to institutions' programs, budgets, and credentials. Another dissimilarity with universities is that, instead of a senate, the colleges and institutes, with the exception of the Justice Institute of British Columbia, each has an education council. Each Education Council is comprised of twenty voting members. The role of an education council is primarily to advise the Board of Governors on the development of educational policy, including the implementation, cancellation, and evaluation of programs; policies on faculty qualifications; admission policies; and matters of student discipline. In addition, the Education Council has the power to set policies concerning a variety of areas, including student performance, academic standards and grading, awards, and curriculum content.

Degree granting and use of the name "university" were formerly limited to those institutions named in the University Act. These functions are now regulated under the Degree Authorization Act, passed by the Legislature in May 2002. The necessary policies and procedures to make the legislation fully operational were established in November 2003. Sections 3(1) and (2) of the act are as follows:

> 3(1) A person must not directly or indirectly do the following things unless the person is authorized to do so by the minister under section 4:
> (a) grant or confer a degree;
> (b) provide a program leading to a degree to be conferred by a person inside or outside British Columbia;
> (c) advertise a program offered in British Columbia leading to a degree to be conferred by a person inside or outside British Columbia;
> (d) sell, offer for sale, or advertise for sale or provide by agreement for a fee, reward or other remuneration, a diploma, certificate, document or other material that indicates or implies the granting or conferring of a degree.
> 3(2) A person must not directly or indirectly make use of the word "university" or any derivation or abbreviation of the word "university" to indicate that an educational program is available, from or through the person, unless the person is authorized to do so by the minister under section 4 or by an Act.

Private Sector

The PSE system has seen a massive expansion in the number and variety of private institutions offering a range of postsecondary credentials to British Columbians. To grant a degree, an institution must be established either under an individual act or be authorized under the Degree Authorization Act. This act provides a mechanism for private institutions to offer degree programs in British Columbia and thus sets the stage for the addition of a number of private universities and other institutions offering degree-level education. The minister responsible for PSE has the authority to give consent to an applicant to grant a degree if the applicant satisfactorily passes a quality assessment process administered by the government-appointed Degree Quality Assessment Board.

In 2011, there were four BC-based private universities: three established by private legislation and one authorized under the Degree Authorization Act.[3] Trinity Western University was founded in 1962 as a liberal arts Christian college. In 1979, it was granted university status by means of a private member's bill. Beyond the recognition of a private institution, Trinity Western also expanded the boundary of what counted as a university in British Columbia. Fundamental Christian beliefs not only defined the culture of the campus but also infused much of the learning. In addition to bachelor's degrees, Trinity Western also offers master's degrees in leadership, biblical studies, counselling psychology, TESOL, linguistics, and interdisciplinary humanities.

In 2002, Quest University Canada (originally Sea to Sky University) was established with its own legislation. Quest is a non-profit, non-sectarian institution founded by former UBC president David Strangway and located in Squamish. Quest began offering a non-discipline-based bachelor of arts and sciences as its only degree in the fall of 2007.

In May 2007, Pacific Coast University for Workplace Health Sciences (PCU-WHS) was established by private legislation as a private, not-for-profit university. The institution was founded by Wolfgang Zimmerman as an outgrowth of his National Institute of Disability Management and Research (NIDMAR), a non-profit agency jointly governed by representatives of employers and employees whose primary focus is the implementation of workplace-based reintegration programs for injured and disabled workers. The Port Alberni campus opened in September 2011, and the university intends to offer its first degree program in 2013.

The one university established through the process provided for by the Degree Authorization Act is University Canada West. University Canada West was founded as a for-profit institution by former UVic president David Strong and a group of investors. Originally located in Victoria, the institution received approval to offer undergraduate degrees in commerce, communications, geography, tourism and economics, and a master's degree in business administration. Subsequently, the geography, tourism, and economics programs were discontinued. First approved in 2004, the institution had intended to cater to those students turned away from BC public universities due to a lack of spaces as well as to the Asia Pacific market. Like Quest University, University Canada West has failed to attract the expected number of students and has had financial problems. In 2009, it was sold to a large educational conglomerate, the Eminata Group, which also owns a small college in Vancouver. In 2011, Eminata shut down the Victoria campus of University Canada West for "business reasons."

So far the experience of the last decade of establishing new, BC-based private universities has been less than successful. Not only are two universities struggling to recruit students, but two other approved institutions (one for-profit and one not-for-profit) were forced to shut down.

Lansbridge University was the BC incarnation of the for-profit institution first established in Fredericton, New Brunswick, in 1999 as Unexus University. In 2001, Lansbridge University was bought by Vancouver-based entrepreneur Michael Lo, who, through his Kingston Education Group, also owned Kingston College and other education businesses in Canada and China. In 2005, Lo received government permission through the Degree Authorization Act to operate Lansbridge University in British Columbia as a distinct legal entity separate from the New Brunswick campus but sharing the brand name and the focus on business education. Student complaints led to revelations in fall 2006 that Michael Lo had been illegally offering degree programs at his other BC postsecondary institution, Kingston College. As a consequence, Kingston College was ordered shut down and an investigation was launched into Lansbridge University and the process by which it had received permission to operate in British Columbia. Following the two-month investigation, the minister of advanced education ordered Lansbridge University to close because the institution had not lived up to the requirements of its consent to operate and because Michael Lo and his officials had deceived government officials about the illegal degree programs at Kingston College in the course of applying for permission to operate it.

Another failed attempt, the not-for-profit World Trade University (WTU), was established in 2005 via a private member's bill to offer degree and non-degree programs in international trade, economics, business, and related subjects. Founded by Sujit Chowdhury, a specialist in youth entrepreneurship, the non-profit institution was criticized for bypassing the quality-control process contained in the

Degree Authorization Act. Rather than subjecting the proposed institution to external academic review, its founder sought and obtained private legislation from the Liberal government that enabled it to call itself a university and to grant degrees. Eventually it was revealed that Chowdhury did not possess a doctorate, despite allowing himself to be called "Dr Chowdury," and that his implied connections to the United Nations did not exist. In February 2008, WTU quietly withdrew its application to offer a degree program in British Columbia. By the summer of 2008, the campus in Chilliwack had been abandoned.

The Degree Authorization Act also provides for the approval of individual degrees, including associate degrees in private institutions that have undergone the assessment process of the Degree Quality Assessment Board (DQAB) and have been authorized by the minister of advanced education for delivery. These degrees are eligible for articulation within the BC transfer system. By 2011, only two BC-based private, non-university institutions had been granted permission to offer baccalaureate degree programs: Sprott Shaw Community College (also known as Sprott Shaw Degree College), which received approval in November 2004; and the Art Institute of Vancouver, which received approval in 2010. So far, five additional private institutions have received approval to offer two-year associate degrees: Alexander College, Columbia College, Coquitlam College, Corpus Christi College, and Fraser International College. The BC transfer system also includes two publicly funded, out-of-province institutions (Athabasca University [Alberta] and Yukon College [Yukon]) and one private US university with a campus in Vancouver (Fairleigh Dickinson University [New Jersey]).

Prior to the adoption of the Degree Authorization Act, a number of US-based institutions had offered degree programs in British Columbia either through branch campuses or in partnership with BC-based private colleges. Although such activity was prohibited by the University Act, successive provincial governments of all political stripes had turned a blind eye to the activity, arguing that these institutions were not violating the act because they were not offering "BC degrees." The government's position changed in January 2002, when it suffered an embarrassing defeat in trying to shut down an illegal BC-based institution called Vancouver University. The judge in the case refused the government's application for an injunction, which would have effectively killed the institution. The application was refused in part because the government had known about Vancouver University's activities for almost twenty years and did not take action against it and because the government had applied different standards to the US-based institutions than it had to this BC-based institution.

With the adoption of the Degree Authorization Act in May 2002, both out-of-province and in-province institutions wishing to offer degree programs were brought under the same regulatory framework. At the time the act was introduced, eleven US-based institutions had tacit government approval to offer their degree programs in British Columbia. These institutions were given five years to become compliant with the new regulatory framework. By 2011, five of these institutions had received approval under the new process. The other six either failed to apply to operate in British Columbia or received approval and subsequently ceased operations in the province. British Columbia remains a popular destination for out-of-province providers of degree programs. Since 2007, in addition to the grand-parented US institutions, two Canadian institutions, two US institutions, and one Australian company have received permission to operate in the province

As of 2011, about 350 registered private postsecondary institutions offer non-degree programs in British Columbia. The most popular fields of study are: computer technology, business studies, occupations in health care administration and support, preparatory programs for teaching English as a second language, and traditional Chinese medicine. Governments of all political stripes have consistently attempted to include the private postsecondary sector as part of the overall provincial postsecondary system. In 2000, the NDP government extended eligibility for student financial assistance grants to students at private institutions that had been "accredited" by the Private PSE Commission (PPSEC).

In November 2004, the Liberal government brought into force the Private Career Training Institutes Act, which replaced the Private Post Secondary Education Act. Under the new act, PPSEC was replaced by the Private Career Training Institutions Agency (PCTIA), which assumed responsibility for registering private postsecondary institutions, running the voluntary "accreditation" program, and managing the Student Training Completion Fund to reimburse students at institutions that close without notice. PCTIA is significantly different from the PPSEC in that the former is largely an industry-controlled agency, whereas the latter was a largely government-controlled agency. English as a second language schools were exempted from registration, dropping the number of registered institutions by about one-third overnight. Finally, the Student Training Completion Fund had much narrower grounds for granting students refunds than had been the case under PPSEC. These changes were hailed by the private PSE industry as long-awaited relief from government oversight but were criticized by public-sector students and educators as ceding too much control to industry. The naysayers were proven right when the serious weaknesses in the regulatory system were revealed in light of the Kingston College scandal (mentioned earlier). In the summer of 2007, the Liberal government launched a review of the PCTIA legislation led by John Watson, former president of the British Columbia Institute of Technology (BCIT). The Watson Report was released in January 2008 and included recommendations on improving governance and accountability, on improving quality of institutions and programs, on increasing protections for students, and on providing more independence for the registrar, giving her or him more leeway to take action against delinquent institutions. Many of Watson's recommendations were subsequently incorporated into the PCTIA legislation and its governing bylaws. A similar review of the Degree Quality Assessment Board was carried out in 2010–11, but it is not yet clear if government will act on its recommendations, which are aimed primarily at improving the quality of degree programs and the "BC Brand."

Intermediary Bodies

Intermediary governing bodies play a lesser role in British Columbia than they do in Ontario. The most significant has been the University Presidents' Council of British Columbia (TUPC) and its replacement the Research Universities Council of British Columbia (RUBC). The TUPC was an offshoot of the former Universities Council of British Columbia, established under the University Act in 1974. In the spring of 1987, the Universities Council was abolished and provincial funding was withdrawn. Consequently, the presidents of UBC, SFU, and UVic established the Tri-University Presidents' Council in 1987 by informal agreement. The name was subsequently changed to the TUPC when it was expanded from three to six institutions in order to include new public universities. The mandate was to identify issues facing the universities, provide system-wide leadership in the development of relevant public policy, and communicate on behalf of the university system. It also provided a coordinating forum for its members and acted as a focal point for dealing with the Government of British Columbia and provincial or national bodies associated with universities. Rather than the universities submitting individual budget requests, this was done for the whole sector through the TUPC. In a response to the recent restructuring and expansion of the public university system, the four research-intensive universities reached the conclusion that the TUPC could not properly serve their interests, and, in 2008, they announced the founding of the Research Universities' Council of British Columbia (RUCBC). Similar in function to the TUPC, the RUCBC's distinguishing feature is that its focus is on the interests of the four research-intensive universities rather than on the public university system as a whole. Similar organizations in the college and institute and former university college sectors – the British Columbia College Presidents (BCCP), the now-defunct British Columbia University Colleges Consortium (BCUCC), and the Advanced Education Council of British Columbia (AECBC) – have not developed the necessary cohesion to successfully fulfill the coordination functions exhibited by the RUCBC. The establishment of the British Columbia Association of Institutes and Universities (BCAIU) in 2009 to represent the teaching-intensive universities, BCIT, the Justice Institute, and the Nicola Valley Institute of Technology suggests that this may be changing and that the RUCBC may have competition in Victoria.

Within the college and institute sector, the British Columbia Council on Admissions and Transfer (BCCAT) has been instrumental in ensuring articulation and transferability of credits within the postsecondary system. British Columbia has one of the most sophisticated sets of transfer arrangements in Canada (Andres and Dawson 1998). The BCCAT was established in 1989 by the minister of advanced education and job training to provide a formal forum and mechanism to deal with the transfer of academic credit between colleges and universities. This function has expanded as the number and diversity of public postsecondary institutions has grown, and the private sector has pressed for inclusion in the system. The council's key role is to encourage collaborative leadership throughout the BC PSE system in order to develop and maintain a system of articulation and to improve the transferability of academic credits for the benefit of students (British Columbia Council of Admission and Transfer 2003). Other core agencies for system integration in the college sector, the provincial curriculum, and professional development agency – the Centre for Curriculum, Transfer and Technology (C2T2) and the technical information agency known as the Centre for Education Information Standards and Services (CEISS) – were dissolved in March 2004.

While, to a considerable extent, the Liberal government has implemented *Campus 2020's* (Plant 2007) recommendation regarding the structure of the BC postsecondary system, it has so far not acted on its call for the implementation of system-wide coordinating and planning. The report recommended the creation of a higher education presidents' council and a higher education board. The former would have the role of implementing the policies while the latter would assess the implementation from the point of view of the public interest. The HEPC would be made up of all the presidents in the system: public and private degree-granting institutions and others. The council was charged with facilitating "collaborative, coordinated planning among all postsecondary institutions in the province" (3). The council would formulate the "common purpose" referred to above. The council would also oversee and manage data collection and analysis for the whole system. The board was charged with measuring the "progress of the entire sector in achieving government's PSE from an integrated life-long learning perspective" (3). It would include representatives of the PSE sector but should be controlled by representatives of the larger community.

The work of these two provincial bodies would be conducted in concert with five regional learning councils (RLCs) that cover the same physical territory covered by the current fifteen college regions and the five provincial health authorities. The RLCs (Northern, Interior, Fraser, Vancouver, and Vancouver Island) were charged with bringing the K-12 and PSE sectors together to ensure that each individual would have the maximum opportunity to enrol, participate, and learn close to where she or he lives. Membership in each RLC would consist of all presidents of public colleges and universities and private degree-granting agencies, school superintendents, representatives of the institutes, and community representatives appointed by government to ensure broad representation of community interests. These suggestions were strongly opposed by the research universities, and there was no political will to challenge this opposition, with the result that British Columbia still suffers from a lack of system-wide coordination.

Funding Mechanisms

The British Columbia Ministry of Advanced Education provided block operating grants totalling $1.6 billion in 2009–10 (using 2002 dollars) to public postsecondary institutions to deliver a comprehensive mix of educational programming that best suits their mandates and meets the needs of their communities or constituencies. Although block grants have been commonplace in the universities for decades, it was not until the 2002–03 fiscal year that university colleges, colleges, and institutes were released from formula-based funding. Block operating grants provide institutions with the flexibility and autonomy to manage their institutions within available financial resources. The ministry does not specify how the funds are to be spent but does set overall student full-time equivalent (FTE) enrolment targets. Despite this, the ministry has also targeted some of the funded enrolment growth to specific provincial government priorities such as information technology, nursing, critical health care professions, doctors, social work, on-line learning, and Aboriginal education. In the initial development of the ministry's Strategic Investment Plan (twenty-five thousand new FTE student spaces expansion over the 2004–05 to 2009–10 period), the planning assumptions were based on 55 percent targeted FTE growth and 45 percent general FTE growth. These proportions were based on the FTE allocations for 2002–03 and 2003–04 and projections out for 2004–05 and beyond. The 2009–10 to 2011–12 Service Plan that projects student spaces does not indicate any further expansion.

Operating grants provided through block funding are used for instruction, support services, student services, administration, and, in the case of the universities, non-sponsored research. About $300 million annually is allocated for debt servicing costs to fund capital projects. This funding is provided under a separate process and is not included in the operating grants. The Ministry of Advanced Education develops a budget proposal covering all public postsecondary institutions, which is subsequently submitted to the Treasury Board. The Treasury Board reviews the overall budget proposal in light of the proposals from other ministries and the government's fiscal and policy objectives, and it determines, often through negotiation with the ministry, the amount of money the ministry will receive. Typically, institutions are informed of their individual allocations in March each year.

The overall level of funding for an institution is based on a review of regional demographics, historical performance (i.e., student FTE utilization), anticipated demand, and fiscal, economic, and social priorities. The ministry strives to provide equitable funding to similar institutions within each subsector (i.e., research-intensive universities, teaching-intensive university colleges, rural colleges, and urban colleges).

The Ministry of Advanced Education and institutions communicate on a regular basis regarding funding issues and funding levels. Although the ministry sets the overall budget and funding levels for institutions, this is done within the context of an assessment of the available funding, government priorities, and the requirements of the PSE system.

As indicated earlier, the six public universities had formerly submitted their budgets as a group. Since the RUBC replaced the TUPC, this is now true only of the four research universities, while the special purpose, teaching universities, institutes, and colleges bring forward budget issues through annual face-to-face budget and accountability meetings. These generally occur in the late fall (late October to early January). These meetings provide the Ministry of Advanced Education with an opportunity to communicate ministry and government priorities to institutions. In turn, institutions have the opportunity to provide an update on themselves and the issues they are facing, which range from budgets to programs and other assorted issues. The colleges have not generally submitted individual budget requests through their collective organizations (i.e., BCCP and the now defunct BCUCC and AECBC). Nothing prevents the colleges from doing this, and on rare occasions they have provided subsector budget requests to the ministry.

POLITICAL ECONOMY AND THE CHANGING SHAPE OF
THE POLICY ENVIRONMENT

Political Context

Geography and resources have shaped the province's social and political landscape, renowned for dramatic valleys and divides of their own. Postwar electoral politics in British Columbia have been dominated by two parties whose persistent antagonism reflects ideological and practical rifts that extend far beyond the electoral arena. On one side is the Social Credit Party, which, along with its recent successor, the BC Liberal Party, held power for about thirty-five of the last fifty years. The party's electoral base has historically been among the independent farmers, ranchers, and merchants of rural British Columbia, along with the small-business sector of the urban areas, and underwritten by the financial backing of the corporate sector. Regarding its ideological appeal, Social Credit has consistently presented a socially and fiscally conservative brand of populism, stressing virtues of self-help and entrepreneurialism, and warning against welfare-state dependency and intrusive government, particularly as manifested in business taxes and regulations.

Standing opposite the Socreds throughout this period has been the BC New Democratic Party (NDP). The party was formed as a wing of the federal NDP in October 1961 from an alliance between two quite distinct working-class movements. One of these was the Commonwealth Co-operative Federation (CCF), a social democratic party formed in Saskatchewan during the "dustbowl" years of the Great Depression and the pioneer of public health insurance in Canada. The other party to the marriage was organized labour, an entity with its own internal divisions. The abundance of British Columbia's natural resources had supported high profits in the extraction industries and led to the growth of a well-paid, unionized, blue-collar workforce in forestry, mining, and fishing (Marchak 1983). The formation of the NDP in 1961 was an attempt to meld a pair of political tendencies that, while occasionally and superficially congruent, harboured quite divergent interests and values.

Since 1983, three political parties have been in power in British Columbia: the Social Credit under Bill Bennett (1975–86); William Vander Zalm (1986–91); and Rita Johnson (1991); the NDP under Michael Harcourt (1991–96); Glen Clark (1996–99); Daniel Miller (1999–2000); and Ujjal Dosanjh (2000–01); and the Liberal Party under Gordon Campbell (2001–11) and Christy Clark (2011–). The current iteration of the Liberal party has adopted a neoliberal ideology emphasizing individualism and market ideology, although during its second term in power it moved somewhat to the centre of the political spectrum.[4]

Social Credit Era (1983-91)

The 1960s and 1970s were the halcyon period for PSE in British Columbia. The beginning of the period that is the main focus of our work was marked by the most tumultuous episode in British Columbia's modern political history. The Socreds were narrowly returned to power in 1979 under Bill Bennett. The economic boom that had sustained public-sector expansion through the 1970s was by now faltering and moving into what would become the deepest worldwide recession since the 1930s. With its dependency on commodities, British Columbia was hit harder than any other region of the country, and the unemployment rate doubled from 6.8 percent to 13.8 percent (Schworm and Rosenbluth 1984). Campaigning on a platform of fiscal restraint, the Social Credit Party was re-elected in May 1983. In July the government introduced a notorious restraint budget along with thirty-four pieces of proposed legislation that were passed mostly intact in the Legislature. The legislation package included the Public Service Restraint Act, which gave public-sector employers authority to dismiss employees without cause. The government aimed to reduce the public sector by 25 percent through dismissals, privatization, and reorganization. Amendments to the College and Institute Act removed local representation from governing boards, leaving only government appointees (Dennison and Gallagher 1986, 93). Legislation to control salary increases was also introduced to control college budgets (Dennison 1987). The swift and comprehensive restraint program was partially made possible by the government's sizeable majority. The aggressiveness of the restraint program was due partially to the desire of Premier Bennett to make the resource industries more competitive and to have them adopt a neoconservative outlook consistent with the worldwide trend (Prince 1996, 254).

In the social area, the government proceeded with a series of initiatives to deregulate business activities and to privatize public services, including the transfer of government-operated child care facilities to non-profit societies. Agencies like the Office of the Rentalsman, human rights commissions, and the Employment Standards Board were eliminated. The Ministry of the Attorney General shrank by 20 percent, and the reduction was perceived to be a de-emphasis on the goals of equality, fairness, and civil liberties

(Prince 1996, 255–6). The government presented its actions as a prudent response to declining revenues and rising social welfare costs and as a necessary corrective to public "mismanagement" under the NDP. Its many critics, however, saw far more sinister intent. At one level, Socred policies were regarded as a local experiment with the emergent neoconservative model associated with Thatcher and Reagan (Magnusson et al. 1984).

The Socred's restraint policies forced the PSE sector into survival mode. Legislated changes to educational governance gave the province centralized control over school and college budgets. Deep cuts were made with little warning. David Thompson University Centre was closed in 1984.[5] The universities responded by imposing enrolment quotas, increasing tuition, eliminating programs, and laying off staff and faculty (Dennison 1987; Fisher and Gilgoff 1987). Students paid more for less service, and, effective in 1984, provincial grants were replaced with student loans, putting British Columbia in tenth place among the provinces in terms of expenditure per fulltime enrolment (Orum 1992, 8).

University and college budgets were clawed back midway through 1982–83 by $12 million and $8.5 million, respectively (Cameron 1991, 252; Moran 1991, 120). By 1984–85, the university budgets were reduced by 5 percent and universities were under great financial pressure. Inflation was at 12 percent and enrolments had increased by 11.4 percent. During the same period, college budgets were cut by 3.5 percent and colleges were similarly faced with attempting to enrol more students while reducing staff and faculty. Other restraint measures included the elimination of the three intermediary councils, including the University Council, which had long been unpopular with at least two of the universities. Consolidation measures included the melding of the Knowledge Network with the Open Learning Institute (OLI) to become the Open Learning Agency and the amalgamation of the Pacific Vocational Institute with BCIT (Dennison 1987).

The economy began to improve in 1985. By 1986, it had recovered from the recession and was growing. Unemployment in British Columbia dropped from 12.5 percent in 1986 to 8.3 percent in 1990. Despite the glittering success of Expo '86 and the Coquihalla Highway, SkyTrain, and the Tumbler Ridge coal development project, barely three years into his third term Premier Bennett resigned.

As Rayner (2000, 210) puts it: "He knew his government, after almost eleven years in office had become stagnant."

On 6 August 1986, William Vander Zalm led the Social Credit Party to an election victory. Vander Zalm was a proponent of neoconservatism, and, during his premiership, privatization continued as a policy direction, albeit in conjunction with the easing of some aspects of restraint. By 1986, with the Mulroney government, a neoconservative agenda was also apparent in Ottawa. Due to prior cuts, strong revenue growth, and new accounting practices,[6] the province's budget was balanced by 1987-88 and ran surpluses in the next two years; however, deficit budgets followed and reached a record $2.4 billion in 1991-92 (Prince 1996, 257). In February 1987, Stanley Hagen was appointed minister of the new portfolio of advanced education and job training. A political newcomer and owner of a rural road construction firm, Hagen had no background in education issues, yet he proved to be a collaborative minister with a genuine interest in PSE.

As the economy began to improve in 1985, the BC PSE system entered a period of sustained expansion and transformation. The first phase of recovery involved ministerial restructuring. The ministry responsible for PSE was renamed and expanded twice in 1986, first acquiring the postsecondary department of the Ministry of Education and, later, the job training department of the Ministry of Labour. This change reflected the government's acknowledgment of the role to be played by education and educational institutions in its economic renewal strategy: "One of the aims of this government is to enable all students who would profit from a PSE to pursue that goal if they so choose, and to encourage the best students to make that choice" (Ministry of Advanced Education 1988, 13). This encouragement to potential students came in the form of providing loans to finance their education, granting partial remissions of loans upon graduation, and scholarships for the top 30 percent of high school students.

Over the next four years, the overriding policy goal for Minister Hagen and his successor Bruce Strachan was to increase access to degree-granting programs for rural interior populations. In March 1988, Hagen announced the "Access for All" initiative, thus setting the stage for a massive expansion in degree-granting programs over the next decade. Appointed by Stanley Hagen, the Social Credit minister of advanced education and job training in 1987, the Provincial Access Committee (PAC) was charged with studying financial need and regional access in the PSE system. PAC concluded that, relative to its population, British Columbia ranked ninth among provinces with respect to first degrees awarded, and seventh in terms of full-time postsecondary enrolment of 18- to 24-year olds (Ministry of Advanced Education 1988), 4; Dennison 1995c, 15). The report highlighted two overarching policy goals: (1) improving equitable access for all citizens of the province and (2) improving "the overall rate of transition of students from high school into advanced education and job training institutions of all kinds" (Dennison 1995c, 5). Its specific recommendations were comprehensive and, in some cases, quite novel.[7]

PAC's recommendations had a clear impact on the structure of the PSE system. PAC suggested not only adding a "University of the North" but also introducing a completely new institutional species previously unseen in Canada (Dennison 1995c, 16). University colleges would expand access to degree programs in densely populated areas not adequately served by universities. Access to academic qualifications was also to be expanded by means of a "credit bank," in which learners would be able to accumulate credits from open learning courses through OLA and even to receive recognition for prior learning (ibid., 17). Anticipating the need to align programs and academic standards in an increasingly diverse system, PAC also recommended the creation of a council on admissions, transfer and articulation to resolve issues of program equivalency, degree requirements, and credit transfer. In recognition of the unmet education and training needs of Aboriginal people, the Ministry of Advanced Education (1988, 20) recommended that the government develop a strategy in consultation with Aboriginal people and postsecondary institutions.

The report was enthusiastically received across the PSE system. In March 1988, Hagen, in what was described by one commentator as a "brilliant policy move,"[8] announced the government's Access for All policy initiative, which embodied the report's main recommendations and ushered in British Columbia's second major period of PSE expansion and transformation. Hagen faced the need to expand access to degree-granting programs but recognized that he did not have the resource capacity to create four new true universities. In 1989, the government designated three community colleges as university colleges,[9] enabling them to offer baccalaureate studies in partnership with an existing university, which would grant the degree. The changes in legislation also authorized BCIT and the Emily Carr Institute of Art and Design to offer baccalaureate degrees. The BCCAT was also created to organize and facilitate student transfer from community colleges to degree-granting programs, in line with PAC's recommendation. Funds were committed to further develop the concept of a "University in the North."

The Provincial Advisory Committee on Post-Secondary Education for Native Learners was established in 1989. The committee was co-chaired by Chief Gordon Antoine from the Coldwater Band and Dr Peter Jones, then president of Fraser Valley College, and committee membership was primarily Aboriginal. After extensive consultation with Aboriginal people and organizations, postsecondary institutions, and others, the 1990 *Report of the Provincial Advisory Committee on Post-Secondary Education for Native Learners* (also known as the Green Report) was released. This document initiated policy discourse about Aboriginal PSE in British Columbia.

Key to the Green Report are four principles that not only provided a guide for writing the report but also the foundation for implementing recommendations. These principles include: (1) that First Nations have a right to self-determination in education and, therefore, must be part of the decision-making process; (2) that, because education is an inherent Aboriginal right, it is a federal responsibility that can only be devolved to the province with First Nations approval; (3) that contemporary PSE reflect a holistic approach, consistent with traditional education, that enhances First Nations languages and values; and (4) that Aboriginal access and this holistic approach to PSE would require cooperative planning by First Nations and postsecondary authorities (Provincial Advisory Committee on PSE for Native Learners 1990, 11). The report's twenty-one recommendations were framed as "Challenges to the Post-Secondary System" and include governance, jurisdictional, cultural, program, financial, and geographic challenges. A number of the recommendations were quickly implemented, and the Green Report became the basis for developments in Aboriginal postsecondary education implemented by subsequent governments (MacIvor 2012, 96–7).

In April 1990, the government unveiled a renamed Ministry of Advanced Education, Training and Technology, under Bruce Strachan. Perhaps Strachan's most visible achievement, and the

Socreds' last major step in fulfilment of the Access for All initiative, was to introduce the University of Northern British Columbia Act on 1 June 1990. Located in Prince George, the most northerly major town in the interior of British Columbia, UNBC honoured a long-standing commitment to make university education locally accessible to the people of the North.

Before leaving office the Social Credit government introduced legislation in 1990 establishing the independent Private PSE Commission to take over the functions previously performed by the Independent Schools Branch in the Ministry of Education. As an independent agency, with industry representation, the PPSEC gave the private training industry greater control over its own governance and introduced stronger consumer protection measures in the wake of several high-profile bankruptcies and complaints over educational quality in the sector. According to numerous observers, the public furor that followed the collapse of Alpha College in 1987 was the catalyst for change. Alpha College had offered ESL and high school education to an international clientele (Culos 2005). The commission would continue to operate through the NDP years, only to be transformed again under the subsequent Liberal government from a quasi-independent oversight agency into a largely self-regulating, industry-controlled body.

The NDP Mandate (1991–2001)

The 1991 provincial elections marked the end of the Social Credit era in BC politics as the New Democrats under Mike Harcourt claimed fifty-one of seventy-five seats. With its strong legislative majority, the NDP was free to pursue an ambitious reform agenda, in which PSE policy would play an integral part.

More than any previous government, the NDP was determined to link PSE and work in the most transparent manner. Accessibility continued to be a major policy priority, but the major goal would be the expansion of the vocational and skill-building capacity of the system as a whole. In adopting its skills agenda, the government was clearly influenced by the broader environment. Since the middle of the 1980s, economic policy across the OECD had emphasized the growing importance of education as a determinant of economic prosperity. National differences in economic performance were increasingly attributed to measures of educational effectiveness and countries' learning capabilities. In particular, educational success was seen as a crucial factor in a nation's capacity to participate in and benefit from technological change. Since new technologies were expected to increase productivity and efficiency, an educated workforce would be a critical asset in global economic competition (OECD 1989).

This general sense of urgency was heightened by economic conditions nearer to home. A deep economic recession engulfed Canada in the early 1990s. Even though British Columbia was somewhat shielded by its resource sector, the unemployment rate rose to 10.4 percent within a year of the NDP's electoral victory (Prince 1996, 259). Between 1989 and 1993, the portion of the BC population living in low-income poverty rose from 13.8 to 17.3 percent. While poverty among senior citizens had been dropping for over a decade, poverty among families with children had been rising (263). The government's major policy themes were to reduce provincial debt, eliminate the deficit, protect the social safety net, maintain stability in the health care system, and invest in people through education and skills training. Other government priorities included equality 1996 for women, pay equity, child care, personal safety, assistance to victims of violence, and forging relationships with Aboriginal peoples. The Harcourt government also invested heavily in social infrastructure such as public schools, colleges, universities, hospitals, courthouses, non-profit housing, and recreational facilities. To finance the infrastructure projects, the NDP borrowed and thus increased the provincial deficit, arguing that today's taxpayers should not have to shoulder the entire cost of services and facilities that would benefit future British Columbians for decades to come (260–3). By the same token, with the aim of eliminating the provincial deficit by the start of the 1996–97 fiscal year, the NDP also committed itself to reducing the growth of program spending and raising taxes in its budgets.

In a period when skills and learning took the centre of the policy agenda, the ten-year NDP reign would be marked by its activism in policy research and stakeholder engagement, and its robustness (if not always its coherence) in policy experimentation. On the research side, an influential report (in fact commissioned in 1989 under the previous administration) was put together by the BC Task Force on Employment and Training. It is entitled *Learning and Work: The Way Ahead for British Columbians* and is also known as the Strand

Report, for its chairman Kenneth Strand as well as by part of its subtitle (i.e., *The Way Ahead*). The task force's objectives had been: to examine training and employment issues, to recommend long-term responses to structural unemployment, and to recommend how to build greater consensus among labour market stakeholders. Not surprisingly, it traced structural unemployment in British Columbia to three basic drivers found in many other jurisdictions: globalization, technological change, and demographic trends, including an aging workforce and a relatively large cohort of young job-seekers. But it also found that the problem in British Columbia was more widespread and longer-lasting than it was in other parts of the country due to relatively low skills and education and to a weak labour market information system.

The Strand Report made twenty-eight recommendations, many of which would be enacted in the course of the NDP's skills agenda over the next decade. Regarding structural unemployment, the task force gave priority to reducing long-term unemployment by addressing the needs of low-skilled or low-educated workers. It recommended better alignment of federal and provincial labour market policies, with a general preference for "active" remedies, and better coordination among training providers. It called for improved management of labour force development issues – for instance, through better integration of government functions and through enhanced labour market research, data management, and decision-making capabilities. It also touched on the long-troubled area of trades training and apprenticeship, noting the imperative to raise employers' participation in training and suggesting that the key to this would be to reform the Provincial Apprenticeship Board, giving employers and labour greater influence over the system's governance.

In 1992 a further study, *Forces of Change*, reinforced the main recommendations of the Strand Report (Ministry of Advanced Education Training and Technology 1992). In addition to reinforcing the question of educational "relevance" (to work and employment), it identified three other challenges for British Columbia's education and training system: the challenge of quantity, as public demand for access continued to rise; the challenge of quality, cast as an imperative to find alternate delivery methods in the face of rising demand; and the challenge of resources in an environment of fiscal restraint.

The participatory approach to policy formation/promulgation continued with a major summit in 1992 on trade and economic opportunities, followed in 1993 by another on skill development and training. In his opening remarks for the latter, Premier Harcourt announced his government's intention to treat education "as intimately interwoven with social, economic and workplace concerns."[10] The announcement was followed in the fall of 1993 by the creation of a new ministry of skills, training and labour. Apart from symbolically highlighting the government's emphasis on non-university learning, the new super ministry gathered responsibility for PSE, labour force development, and industrial relations under a single portfolio. In the next legislative session cabinet approved a package of initiatives under the name *Skills Now*.

Skills Now defined a central thrust of the government's integrated agenda over the next two years, and it marks the high point of the emphasis on vocationalism under the NDP. But, like much of the NDP's policy approach during this period, the initiative would also incorporate an eclectic and sometimes uneasy mix of philosophical objectives and strategies, in part reflecting the diversity of the NDP's political base. Certainly, one priority was to enhance access and participation, largely through the expansion of public provision. During the first year of the initiative, the number of new spaces in the college, institute, and university sector tripled from 2,700 in 1993 to 8,100 in 1994, bringing enrolments to over 180,000. The government established a "challenge" fund of $12 million for colleges and universities "to find innovative and cost-effective ways to teach skills to more students" (Ministry of Skills, Training and Labour 1995, 4). At the same time, it created six new programs in advanced technology areas. Six million dollars was pledged for new equipment purchases, subject to matching by the private sector. In line with the Strand Report recommendations, the government pilot tested a number of "Training and Enterprise Centres" to provide comprehensive employment, training, and labour market information services, eventually opening sixteen community skills centres throughout the province.

In July 1994, the government followed through on another key Strand Report recommendation by creating the British Columbia Labour Force Development Board (BCLFDB). The story of the board illustrates a variety of influences on policy and the complexity of the NDP's agenda. According to Hommen (1997), an important factor behind the BCLFDB's creation was a perception of growing federal encroachment onto provincial labour force policy, specifically through the Canadian Labour Forces Development Board (CLFDB). In creating the board, the province sought partly to head off this interference while addressing a range of well-known labour market management challenges. With a rather loose mandate to facilitate multipartite cooperation and dialogue on labour market policy, the board's most notable achievement was its controversial 1995 report entitled *Training for What?*, which noted an under-supply of skilled graduates in technological and scientific fields as well as a pronounced "imbalance in the public post-secondary system toward degree and university transfer programs" (British Columbia Labour Force Development Board [BCLFDB] 1995, 5). The clearly vocationalist slant of the report's recommendations on educational "balance" drew a vociferous critique from academics, who saw it not only as anti-elitist university-bashing but also as a misguided assessment of academic education's benefits for the labour market. As it turned out, both the controversy and the board itself were short-lived. Minister Miller announced its dissolution in the fall of 1996, only two years after it was formed.

As British Columbia's PSE system continued to expand and diversify through the 1990s, as new institutions and types of academic credit emerged, and as educational planning became more entwined with other policy objectives, the need for system-wide coordination became ever more apparent. In 1996, the Ministry of Skills, Training and Labour articulated this imperative in a major policy paper on non-university PSE: *Charting a New Course: A Strategic Plan for the Future of British Columbia's College, Institute and Agency System* (Ministry of Education, Skills and Training 1996b). This "milestone policy" document highlighted the need for greater integration and coherence across the provincial college and institute system.[11] It set out four principal goals for reform in the non-university sector:

1 Relevance and quality in college programming would be achieved by establishing "outcomes-based" standards for all general education and liberal arts programs. Students and programs would be expected to meet objective standards, defined not only in terms of job performance but also in terms of learners' ability to interact and participate successfully in the community.
2 Access to educational opportunity would be expanded by continued expansion of institutions, but also by means of new learning

technologies (PLA and expanded use of educational technology) and by smoother mechanisms for credit recognition and transfer.

3 Affordability would be achieved through greater efficiency in instructional delivery, including distance education and the reduction of program duplication. Provincial funding for colleges and institutes would be restructured. Apart from the Basic Operating Grant there would be three separate "envelopes" contingent on colleges' progress towards partnerships (with the private sector and other levels of government); the development of on-line courses; and capital expansion.

4 Accountability would be enhanced by requiring colleges and institutes to develop "key performance indicators" (KPIS) and to report on the definition and achievement of learning outcomes in all program areas.

Charting a New Course had multiple effects on the system. On the one hand, the new funding formula and accountability measures imposed managerialist constraints on colleges; on the other hand, the plan brought a more conciliatory and inclusive tone to skills policy discourse.

The plan also set out roles for three provincial educational agencies in order to help achieve the goals of system integration. OLA would continue to play a role in educational broadcasting and distance learning as well as in administering a credit bank for open learning. The Centre for Curriculum, Transfer and Technology (C2T2) would provide a range of services in relation to the government's goals of "quality and relevance." It promoted professional development for college instructors and administrators, particularly in relation to outcomes-based curriculum development and instruction, and the use of new learning technologies, including on-line delivery. It would receive about half its funding as a core operating grant, and it would generate funds by contracting with the ministry and other clients. A third key agency, in this case oriented to the government's "accountability" goal, was the Centre for Education Information Standards and Services (CEISS). The CEISS was responsible for gathering and disseminating data on labour market demand and PSE supply. It compiled an annual report on employment outcomes for graduates of the college and institute system, and it provided consulting and technical services on management information systems for the colleges. The CEISS also provided an internet portal to provincial and federal labour market information and career planning services.

Another interesting example of system-wide integration during the NDP tenure involved the creation of a central marketing agency for the public college system. The Contract Training Marketing Society (CTMS) was established to support the efforts of community colleges to win contracts for customized training services, particularly with the provincial government. While the initiative was consistent with the government's general goals for the college system it also illustrates the complexity of the policy environment. The impetus for a centralized contract training body came from several directions at once. It aligned well with the themes of *Charting a New Course*, in particular the focus on system-wide efficiencies and synergies, and on building colleges' capacity for "flexible" and innovative delivery. It also fit with the recommendations of a 1993 inquiry into public sector efficiency (British Columbia 1993), which had urged the government to harmonize its procurement and collective bargaining practices across ministries. But other, more direct pressures and interests were also involved. Faced with this combination of increased competition and vanishing contracts, colleges and their employee groups were highly motivated to find new sources of revenue,[12] and the most immediate was the province. However, there was a perception that provincial government procurement rules were stacked against public providers. "Using a very broad definition of training, the BC Government and its Crowns and agencies were spending an estimated $250 million, annually, on training purchases. Very little of this went to the public colleges" (Calvert 2000). Meanwhile, the provincial government had its own motivations. On the one hand, it wished to see the public colleges become more responsive to government training needs and more flexible in their delivery schedules and formats. In pursuit of these goals, the government, as noted earlier, established the CTMS as a "one-stop shop" where provincial public servants could gain access to the training services of all colleges in the province. The real victory for the public colleges, however, was in securing a change to the government's purportedly biased procurement practices. The "Training Accord" of 1998 was not a part of the formal bargaining process but, rather, a side agreement, understood to be contingent on a contract settlement. In effect, it gave the public colleges a "right to first consideration" for government training contracts ("all else being equal") in return for their unions' accepting wage increases of only zero, zero, and 2 percent over the next three years.

General accessibility continued as a major policy objective throughout the 1990s. In parallel with its skills agenda, the NDP government pursued a range of integrated reforms in academic PSE. The main policy thrusts can be placed under three headings: institutional expansion and diversification, low tuition fees, and system-wide integration.

The government addressed the explosive demand for academic qualifications through two strategies: (1) by conferring degree-granting powers on a wider range of institutions and (2) by building more (and more specialized) universities. In 1992, Tom Perry, the minister of advanced education, training and technology, launched an initiative in the former direction by introducing an amendment to the University Act that would authorize public colleges and institutes to develop two-year associate degree programs in arts or science (*Hansard*, 27 April 1992, 1126). In May 1994, Dan Miller introduced the College and Institute Amendment Act, further extending the powers of two technical institutes and the newly created university colleges to grant designated four-year baccalaureate degrees. The effect was to expand by six the number of degree-granting postsecondary institutions in the province.[13] Reflecting the labour market orientation of *Skills Now*, and particularly the emphasis on educational "relevance," the new degrees would be offered in applied areas of the arts, sciences, and technology. In 1995, the government changed the status of Kwantlen College to a university college with a mandate to offer applied degrees. In addition, three new universities were established between 1990 and 1997. Each was oriented to a specialized educational purpose and constituency, and all were enthusiastically supported by the public and the legislative opposition.

The first, UNBC in Prince George, was not so much an NDP initiative as the culmination of long-standing efforts by local community activists. The second new university established under the NDP mandate was Royal Roads University. RRU's creation emerges from the key themes of the NDP's PSE policy, including an emphasis on vocational relevance, and the need to balance student demand against fiscal limitations. The precipitating factor, however, was the federal government's decision in 1994 to close Royal Roads Military

College and to dispose of its historic, park-like campus outside the provincial capital, Victoria. The university offers a range of short, modularized programs, primarily at the master's level. Access is facilitated by the extensive use of prior learning assessment (PLA) strategies. Academic organization is not by traditional disciplines and permanent departments but, rather, by "themes" such as entrepreneurship, organizational leadership, environmental sustainability, and conflict resolution.

The Technical University of British Columbia was the third and last new degree-granting institution created by the NDP. As with UNBC, the original plan emerged from the Social Credit's Access for All initiative and the urgent need to address PSE access in the Fraser Valley. The objective was explicitly vocational: the new institution would help fuel a regional high-tech economy both by producing "market-ready" technical graduates and by incubating R&D innovations through strategic partnerships with private industry. Despite fierce opposition from the university community the new institution had, from its inception, a corporate model of governance, justified by the purported need for "flexibility" and "responsiveness" to industry requirements. In this sense, the government moved the institution much closer to the market.

This experiment with TechBC was only one instance in which the NDP's PSE reforms encountered questions of governance and labour relations. In 1992, the University Amendment Act that empowered colleges to grant two-year associate degrees had also granted university professors the right to form faculty associations or trade unions, bringing BC law into line with international labour standards. In the college and institute sector, the rights and roles of faculty members continued to evolve as well. The College and Institute Amendment Act, 1994, which opened the way to college degrees, also amended provincial college boards to include elected representatives from faculty, students, and support staff in addition to government appointees. At the same time, it created a new governance body in the college sector – the "education council" – which, in the absence of a university-style senate, would be the college sector's mechanism for democratic oversight in academic matters and an important symbolic acknowledgment of college instructors' status as professional educators rather than classroom technicians.

The NDP government was concerned about issues of minority groups, including First Nations. While Aboriginal youth (0–18 years) accounted for 7 percent of the total youth population in 1995–96, they represented less than 3 percent of the college population and less than 2 percent of the university population (British Columbia Labour Force Development Board 1996). During the Harcourt regime, in 1995, the cabinet approved the *Aboriginal Post-Secondary Education and Training Policy Framework* (Ministry of Education, Skills and Training 1996a; MacIvor 2012).

The policy framework set out the following three fundamental strategies:

- Strengthen public postsecondary institutions in meeting the needs of aboriginal people;
- Stabilize partnership agreements between public and private deliverers of PSE for Aboriginal people; and
- Provide for designation of public Aboriginally controlled institutions.

In the same year, the NDP government designated two Aboriginally controlled institutions as provincial institutes under the College and Institute Act: the Institute of Indigenous Government in Vancouver Downtown and the Nicola Valley Institute of Technology (NVIT) located in Merritt.

A second major thrust of NDP policy in the academic sector was to promote access to PSE through a series of college and university tuition freezes. The first of these was part of the broadly targeted Tax and Consumer Rate Freeze Act, 1996, which imposed a three-year freeze on postsecondary tuition. In April 1998, Premier Glen Clark introduced a further Tuition Freeze Act,[14] which extended the freeze on public postsecondary tuition rates to 31 March 1999 and was also apply to mandatory ancillary fees as well as to new programs. Over the next few years, what amounted to an extra subsidy seemed to acquire the status of a fundamental right. In all, the freeze would be sustained from 1996–97 through 2001–02, renewed by five separate legislative acts. In every case the freezes were overwhelmingly supported in the Legislature by the opposition Liberals. In defence of the 1999 extension, Advanced Education Minister Andrew Petter drew a parallel between the contemporary process of globalization and the Industrial Revolution of the eighteenth century, observing that current transformations in work and skill requirements implied the risk of replicating "the huge disparities that arose in wealth and power between those who had access to capital and those who didn't" (*Hansard*, 18 May 1999, 12570). He argued the imperative "that education becomes more of a universal right and entitlement and less of a market commodity" (ibid.). Petter's successor, Graeme Bowbrick, invoked the same vision of social solidarity a year later as he announced the next extension of the freeze:

> We believe that PSE is an inherent public good and should therefore be funded out of public resources to the greatest extent possible. That's what the tuition fee freeze is all about. What we're saying to students with this legislation is this: "You're not alone. We collectively, as a society and as your government, will support you if you seek higher education." (*Hansard*, 5 April 2000, 14812)

In March 2001, the government introduced legislation that not only extended the freeze but also mandated a 5 percent cut in tuition.

The tuition fees policy initiative was an attempt to increase equity in the system. This initiative, along with the vocational policy thrust, resulted in the largest increase in student spaces in British Columbia's history. More than forty thousand seats (38 percent) were added to the system between 1990–91 and 2003–04. Yet the NDP government did not provide sufficient core funding to cover either inflation or the cost of the extra spaces. The real per-student funding declined significantly since the early 1990s – by 21 percent for universities and 10 percent for colleges. Most of this decline occurred prior to the tuition freeze during the years of the most rapid expansion (CCPA/BC 2004).

From 1996 to 2001, the tuition freeze policy was seen by the NDP as an important instrument of public policy. But, as one commentator put it, this was a good example of "a triumph of great politics over good public policy."[15] Members of the university sector were critical of the policy because, as they saw it, they were caught in a double bind. On the one hand, government was telling them to expand capacity but refused to provide more funds; on the other, government was tying their hands by not allowing them to increase student fees. This policy conflict was set against the background of a rapid increase in demand due to an expanding cohort of academically qualified 18- to 24-year-olds. Opposition to the freeze became particularly intense in the last part of the NDP mandate as a restructured TUPC became a far more effective advocate on both the provincial and federal policy stages.

For the TUPC and its newly appointed president Don Avison, the freeze policy led to a series of adverse and unintended consequences. Faced with frozen tuition revenues, the universities found it necessary to raise their academic admission requirements, making it much more difficult for students to transfer into degree programs after their second year in college. Thus, rather than benefit working-class students, the freeze arguably had the indirect effect of securing university access for members of the middle and upper-middle classes, who could afford to take their first year at university.

On the other hand, events at the institutional level in British Columbia would occasionally align with others elsewhere in the system to produce new opportunities. In an interesting example of this, as a result of developments at the federal level, the TUPC came to play a key role in research advocacy. Historically, the province has placed a very low premium on funding research capacity. However, two federal programs (Canadian Research Chairs and the Canadian Foundation for Innovation) that either encouraged or required matching funding from the provinces were introduced. Now speaking through the TUPC with a single voice rather than six, the university presidents were able to leverage these federal opportunities into stronger research commitments from the province. The provincial government set up the BC Knowledge Development Fund (BCKDF) with an initial installment of $100 million to engage the federal opportunities, and Premier Dosanjh added a further $117 million in the budget prior to the 2001 election.

The third policy thrust involved the integration of the non-university sector. Here, the NDP's vision was in many ways consistent with positions taken during the Socred years. If anything, the exigencies of globalization and structural adjustment had only heightened the urgency for a vocational training system that could, on the one hand, accommodate a highly diverse learner population (including traditionally under-served groups) and, on the other, offer relevant instruction and efficient pathways to employment and/or further education. Though terms like "laddering," "seamlessness," and "curricular flexibility" may have sounded fresh, the underlying questions of structure within the growing PSE system had been the subject of reform initiatives – and of growing stakeholder conflict – since at least the mid-1970s. A central issue here was the distinction between *vocational training* as a field of public policy, oriented to economic and social-welfare objectives, and *apprenticeship* as an institution essentially oriented to "craft" practice and the preservation of defined occupational groups.

British Columbia's first apprenticeship legislation, introduced in 1935, had explicitly aimed to promote private skill development within self-regulating craft groups (employers and labour) by setting minimum standards for the employment of apprentice labour. Over the subsequent decades, the simultaneous erosion of those regulations and expansion of in-class vocational training for the same trades would seriously undermine the economic incentives to apprentice training, while also threatening the skills advantage formerly enjoyed by exclusive producer groups (and, in particular, craft unions). In the mid-1990s, the NDP found itself uncomfortably astride this policy dilemma: committed, on the one hand, to a more accessible and flexible training system consistent with its principles of equity and, on the other, to defending the interests of a vital constituency – organized labour. Regarding the latter, a key component of *Skills Now* was the Skill Development and Fair Wage Act, 1994, which stipulated that workers on government-funded construction projects either be certified journeypersons or registered apprentices and that they be paid at specified rates. However, while the Fair Wage Act played directly to the interests of craft construction unions in their bitter struggle with the open-shop movement, other elements of the NDP's training agenda were surprisingly cool towards traditional labour interests. In 1996, skills minister Moe Sihota launched two commissions of enquiry: (1) the Inter-Ministry Committee on Equity in Apprenticeship and (2) the Minister's Committee on Entry-Level Trades Training and Apprenticeship. The former called for action to remedy the long-standing underrepresentation of women and equity groups in the skilled trades, and the latter aimed to settle once and for all the chronic question of whether entry-level trades training should be offered on principles of open access and flexibility or on principles of craft solidarity. Both commissions ultimately tilted in the latter direction, clearly envisioning the training system more as a public resource than as a forum of self-regulating private actors.

The NDP's ambivalence regarding the basic purpose of trades training became evident again when, after narrowly winning re-election in

1996, it introduced its major overhaul of the apprenticeship system. In June 1997, the government passed Bill 43, creating the Industry Training and Apprenticeship Commission (ITAC). Judged by its mandate, ITAC clearly reflected a vision of access, flexibility, efficiency, and equity in the skills system. The new body was to: (1) facilitate school-to-work transition and life-long learning, (2) raise the number of skilled persons in designated trades, (3) increase participation in skilled trades by underrepresented groups, (4) promote labour mobility by creating a provincial system of recognized and articulated vocational credentials, and (5) make the best use of available resources. Yet, in its operations and governance, the ITAC was a strange amalgam. Operationally, it retained regulations and workplace enforcement powers of earlier apprenticeship law, now bolstered by the Fair Wage Act. Meanwhile, its governance structure included elements of European-style "social partnership" – such as a twenty-five-member board representing capital, labour, and equity groups – but also neoliberal borrowings from Australia and New Zealand, including an argument for "devolving" the management of the skills system to industry. In the end, only four years later, ITAC's very incoherence would make it a convenient platform from which the NDP's successors could pick and choose the elements that served them.

The NDP also made inroads into the university sector. The New Programs Committee (later called the Degree Program Review Committee), while ostensibly a response to the rapid expansion of degree programs in the university colleges and the institutes, became the gatekeeper for all new degree programs. Although the minister responsible for advanced education had long possessed legislative authority to approve or deny new degree programs, until the establishment of the Degree Program Review Committee, such approval had largely been pro forma. While the monitoring process was closely tied to the emergence and spread of applied degrees across the PSE sector, it was also used to evaluate non-applied programs in the established universities. Finally, the creation of university colleges, TechBC, and RRU increased the permeability of the boundary that had separated the university and the non-university sectors. As the vocational orientation of the system increased, the NDP was achieving its underlying goal of making the system accountable.

In summary, the period of NDP government from 1991 to 2001 saw the energetic and sustained expansion of the PSE system. While it was broadly consistent with provincial policies dating from the 1960s and had much in common with policy trends in other industrialized countries, this expansion included some distinctive developments. Access to PSE was dramatically expanded by building new institutions and, more controversially, by creating new kinds and sources of academic credit. The creation of the university colleges and the specialized universities and institutes not only added numerical capacity but also hastened qualitative stratification of the system. By the turn of the century the former, binary system of universities and applied institutions had fragmented into a range of institutional types no longer distinguished by their exclusive focus on liberal education, vocational training, or research but, rather, performing any or all of these to varying degrees. Meanwhile, system-wide planning frameworks and support structures were used to align this diverse activity with a finite budget and a set of fundamental principles. One of these was a view of skills and knowledge and, hence, of the education system as critical resources for economic prosperity. Another concerned the role of the state, particularly in assuring equitable access to the opportunities that education promised. Given the province's history, both before and after this period, it is highly doubtful that the political opposition or the majority of the public overtly embraced the NDP's social democratic vision. Arguably, though, the party has succeeded in harnessing a spectrum of disparate constituencies and motivations to its concrete policy agenda.

The Liberal Government (2001–present)

After a crushing defeat leaving only two members of the former NDP government in the Legislative Assembly, a Liberal administration assumed office on 5 June 2001 under Premier Gordon Campbell. The Liberal campaign was vague, promising to build a "new era of hope and prosperity" by cutting taxes and red tape, revitalizing investment, and job creation. In the often tumultuous postwar history of PSE policy in British Columbia, the Liberals' initial agenda marked the most radical shift in both substance and philosophical orientation in forty years.

The fiscal policy during the first Liberal mandate was based upon the government's commitment to New Right philosophy. When taking office in June 2001, the government made market ideology the cornerstone of its fiscal policy. The first policy intervention was the announcement that personal income taxes would be cut by 25 percent. In its July Economic and Fiscal Update in 2001, Minister of Finance Gary Collins indicated:

> The Fiscal Review Panel made it clear that BC has a structural fiscal imbalance and if we did nothing we could face a deficit of more than $5 billion within three years. The Panel also said that our fiscal problems can be solved with fundamental changes in the way government operates. I'm announcing action on both fronts today to get our economy growing again: 1) we need to make our tax system competitive as a first step to revitalizing economic growth; 2) we need to bring some discipline to spending, with strong, accountable fiscal management. (British Columbia Ministry of Finance 2001)

The Liberal government provided health authorities, school boards, and postsecondary institutions with three-year funding commitments. Consequently, starting in 2002–03, budgeting has been conducted on a three-year plan basis. The government committed to reducing government red tape and eliminating business subsidies so as to foster suitable conditions for market forces. In its first year in government, a core review task force was established to review every government program and service. Any program and service that was deemed inappropriate or not within the scope of government was eliminated or phased out. Only programs and services considered "core services" received government funding. The government's first budget, released 18 February 2002, reported a deficit of $3.4 billion and $4.4 billion in fiscal 2003 but promised to balance the budget by 2004–05. Its means of doing this involved privatization and deregulation.

As a preliminary step, the government announced the establishment of a cabinet core review and deregulation task force to undertake a thorough overhaul of public-sector priorities and functions. The worst fears of educators were allayed somewhat by the announcement of a three-year spending freeze on education and health. This amounted to preferential treatment. On "Black Thursday," 17 January 2002, the government announced a 25 percent average reduction in the budgets of all ministries apart from health and education over the next three years. The government also announced an end to the six-year tuition fee freeze and the total deregulation of fees for public postsecondary institutions. The announcement was soon followed by tuition fee hikes of 30 to 40 percent in many institutions and almost 100 percent in some. Public institutions soon discovered that the pledge to protect postsecondary funding only applied to overall government spending. In March 2002, the Ministry of Advanced Education sent budget letters to all PSE institutions, outlining institutional budget reductions of between 1.6 and 8 percent for the 2002–03 and 2004–05 fiscal years. The effects of these cuts were compounded by government expectations that the public PSE system would increase enrolment by 8,500 seats over the period 2002–05.

Targeted and matching funding schemes were emphasized, giving preference to programs in computer science, computer engineering, electrical engineering, medicine, and health-related fields. For example, the Leading Edge Endowment Fund, a cost-sharing arrangement with the private sector, was launched in April 2002. The intention was to add $45 million to postsecondary research and skills training in high-tech fields and to establish twenty permanent research chairs in medical, social, environment, and technology fields (the first chair was in spinal cord research). Furthermore, the budgets for several programs government previously supported were eliminated entirely, pushing postsecondary institutions to become more self-sustaining. For example, government funding for cooperative education, work-study, and graduate assistantship programs was cut, and these programs had to draw on institutional funds or partnering arrangements or be discontinued.

With a rising economy over the course of their four-year term, the Liberals came to present balanced budgets and began to increase funding for PSE. After winning a second mandate in the May 2005 provincial election, the Liberal government made a series of shifts that are somewhat divergent from the neoliberal philosophy that defined their first period in power. Henceforth, student fees were not allowed to increase at a rate beyond the annual rate of inflation (projected at about 2 percent over the next three years). The government promised $600 million over a four-year period to fund the extra twenty-five thousand student spaces in universities and colleges that they announced in 2004. The government thus recognized a system capacity problem and, on the surface, responded through the creation of fully funded student spaces. During the first two years, only 7,417 of these spaces were created, which, according to the government's Annual Service Plan Report (Ministry of Advanced Education 2006, 23), was 2,526 spaces short of the target for 2005–06. Moreover, per student funding continued to drop.

During the second administration, the government turned its attention to funding graduate study. Two programs were introduced in 2007: (1) ACCELERATE BC Graduate Research Internships and (2) the Pacific Century Graduate Scholarships. The former program set aside $10 million to fund 650 industry-based internships between 2007 and 2011; the latter program set aside $40 million to fund one thousand scholarships at $10,000 each year over the same four-year period. The scholarships have been awarded to magistral, doctoral, and postdoctoral students at the four research-intensive universities.

Beyond the fiscal orientation, the changes can be grouped under two headings: (1) institutional changes and (2) legislation. In its first few months in office in 2001, the Liberal government eliminated or radically transformed most of the system-wide agencies and support structures for PSE that had been built up over the previous decade and a half. But it also disbanded all of the core agencies deployed by the NDP for system integration under *Charting a New Course*. The provincial curriculum and professional development agency, C2T2, had its budget sharply reduced in the first fiscal year, and in 2003 it was announced that both it and the technical information agency, CEISS, would be dissolved by the end of March 2004. The PPSEC was dissolved and replaced with the Private Career Training Institutions Agency (PCTIA), a self-regulating, industry-dominated body with minimal government oversight.[16] OLA was dissolved, and a process initiated to sell off the educational television broadcaster, the Knowledge Network. The government contended that rapid diffusion of distance-education technology and on-line learning capabilities throughout the PSE system had rendered OLA redundant. Partly as a replacement for OLA, in 2002 the Ministry announced the creation of "BC Campus," a distance education network involving the province's public colleges, university colleges, universities, and institutes. In January 2003, BC Campus reported that sixteen institutions were involved in providing on-line training to approximately twenty-eight hundred learners (390 FTES) in six programs (C2T2 News, January 2003). The Open University division of OLA was subsequently merged with University College of the Cariboo to become Thompson Rivers University, and the Knowledge Network division was established as a separate publicly supported broadcaster.

Many of the institutional changes described above involved the government's use of its law-making powers. But the Liberals also used legislation to change the "rules of the game" more broadly in the PSE sector.

In trades training policy, for instance, the government acted quickly to realign the influence of specific interest groups over the institutional machinery of the skills system. Shortly after taking office in 2001 it repealed the Skill Development and Fair Wage Act as well as other laws and regulations requiring trades workers to hold formal certification. In 2002, it dismantled ITAC, eliminating 115 staff positions, many formerly responsible for monitoring regulatory compliance. Meanwhile, it announced plans to restructure the governance of the trades training system on a blueprint drawn up by open-shop employers (Coalition of BC Businesses 2001). Retaining core elements of ITAC, the "New Model" would strengthen the central body's budgetary and administrative autonomy from government, but it would also trim its membership from twenty-five members to nine and redefine "industry representation" to denote employers only. A new governance body, the Industry Training Authority (ITA) was established in 2003 through legislation that, for the first time in BC history, was entirely silent on employers' responsibilities in workforce training and, instead, limited the governing body's powers to defining the performance standards to be met by trainees and training providers and distributing the public trades training budget.

In another example of rule changing, the Public Education Flexibility and Choice Act, or Bill 28, authorized the boards of public institutions to over-ride collective agreement provisions regarding class size, length of academic year, and use of distance education methods in schools, colleges, institutes, and university colleges. Predictably, it brought outrage from teachers' organizations and a charge from the NDP opposition that the government's objective was not educational reform but union-busting (*Hansard*, 26 January 2002, 897).[17] A third piece of legislation that would have major implications for the shape and structure of the PSE system was tabled by the minister of advanced education in April 2002. Bill 15, the Degree Authorization Act, set out criteria under which new institutions, including private and public institutions from outside the province, would be authorized to offer degree programs and grant degrees in British Columbia. In addition, the bill allowed public colleges and institutes to offer "applied baccalaureate degrees" and university colleges to offer "applied master's degrees" (*Hansard*, 11 April 2002).

In a move reflecting the spirit of Bill 15 but not directly related to it, during their first year in office the Liberals also authorized the creation of a new, private degree-granting institution in Squamish. While Squamish is a working-class, resource-based town, it is also close to the upscale ski resort of Whistler. A private member's bill was introduced in May 2002 to establish Sea to Sky University, and it passed without debate in the Legislature, although, when the bill was before the Private Bills Committee, there were interventions on the part of the Confederation of University Faculty Associations of BC to ensure that the new institution would be subject to the degree program approval process established under the newly approved Degree Authorization Act. In 2007, the university began offering intense, three-week liberal arts courses for $3,000 per course ($24,000 per year), plus room and board for $11,000 for the eight-month academic year. University Canada West and Sprott Shaw Community College were the first new private institutions to be approved to grant degrees under Bill 15.

Although the result of policy, not legislation, the rules of the game were changing in other ways. In 2002, the Ministry of Advanced Education's Aboriginal Program Unit, which was established under the NDP, was dissolved, and targeted funding for Aboriginal coordinators (which was initially instituted by the Socreds) was rolled into institutional base funding, giving institutions discretion over how this money was spent. In 2002, the ministry tuned its attention to revising the *Aboriginal Post-Secondary Education and Training Policy Framework*. In 2003, a highly contentious draft policy (Ministry of Advanced Education 2003) was completed. Following a consultation forum attended by some 150 people in February 2004, a final draft was completed (Ministry of Advanced Education 2004) but was shelved.

By this time the Liberals were developing a "New Relationship" with British Columbia's Aboriginal people, "based on respect, recognition and accommodation of aboriginal title and rights" (Ministry of Advanced Education 2004, 1) in order to resolve title and jurisdiction issues and to address socio-economic concerns, including education, children and families, health, and the environment. This New Relationship had a profound influence on Aboriginal post-secondary education.

In November 2005, Campbell hosted and emerged as a leader in the First Ministers' and Aboriginal leaders' meeting in Kelowna, British Columbia, which culminated in the Kelowna Accord.[18] The accord proposed to eliminate broad-ranging socio-economic disparities between Aboriginal and non-Aboriginal people in ten years (Patterson 2006).

The same day the Kelowna Accord was signed (25 November 2005), Canada, British Columbia, and the First Nations Leadership Council signed the Transformative Change Accord. Like the New Relationship, this accord aimed to establish new relationships between First Nations, Canada, and the province based on respect and recognition; to reconcile Aboriginal rights with the rights of the Crown; and to address socio-economic disparities within ten years (British Columbia First Nations, the Province of British Columbia, and the Government of Canada 2005, 25 November, 362; Patterson 2006, 361). While Canada's commitment to the Kelowna and Transformative Change accords ended with Paul Martin's defeat, BC continues to pursue the objectives through the Transformative Change Accord (McKee 2009).

An Aboriginal postsecondary education unit was re-established. In 2007, after significant consultation with Aboriginal political leaders, postsecondary institutions, and others, the ministry released the Aboriginal Post-Secondary Education Strategy and Action Plan (Ministry of Advanced Education 2007b, 1), which was intended to "fulfill the post-secondary component of the Transformative Change Accord." The strategy proposes two goals. The first is to "close the educational gap for Aboriginal learners" by increasing "access, retention, completion and transitions opportunities"; increasing institutional "receptivity and relevance"; and "strengthening partnerships and collaborations." The second is to ensure that "effective and accountable programs and services implementation and delivery" is to be achieved through measurement and monitoring (2). Between 2006–07 and 2009–10 the ministry disbursed $58 million of the $65 million budget to BC postsecondary institutions to support a wide range of initiatives to meet the goals of the strategy (Jothen et al. 2011).

On the matter of student costs, rather than letting student organizations control the debate on the future of the tuition fee freeze after the 2001 election, the government launched a province-wide consultation through which it shaped the public dialogue about fees. It did so by, at every opportunity, advancing the proposition that student concerns about the availability of classes, quality of education, and general accessibility could only be solved by removing the fee freeze. This position conveniently ignored government's responsibility for funding its share of increasing institutional operating costs connected to larger student numbers. The government's message was reinforced at the consultation meetings by hand-picked student presenters, who were either sympathetic to the government's message or who were members of the youth wing of the governing Liberal Party. Thus, it was no great surprise when the government announced the complete deregulation of tuition fees in early 2002.

The Liberal government also took steps to introduce market concepts into student financial assistance programs. The system of student loans, grants, and loan remission is generally considered to be an entitlement program to the extent that all applicants with demonstrated financial need, and who meet other eligibility criteria, receive funding. Although the government increased funding for the program to offset the effects of the ending of the tuition fee freeze, new student financial assistance initiatives were not aimed specifically at needy students but, rather, were designed to keep students in high-demand fields from leaving the province. In August 2001, the Liberal government announced that medical school graduates would be eligible for a 20 percent remission of their BC student loans for each year that they practised in a rural area. The program was expanded to include nurses and then midwives. Eventually, nine health professions became eligible for the program, and the rate of loan remission increased to 33.5 percent for each year the graduates practised their profession in an underserved area of the province. Subsequent changes to the student financial assistance program were aimed at replacing upfront grants with back-end loan remission. All BC student grants were eliminated in the 2004 provincial budget but were partially restored in 2005 for students from very low-income families through a program funded by the Canada Millennium Scholarship Foundation.

The changes to the rules of the game could not have occurred without the support, and even encouragement, of the public PSE system. Leading the way was the TUPC, which utilized the ideological predispositions of the government to create new opportunities for the universities. As noted earlier, the TUPC, with the leadership of Jack Blaney and Martha Piper, previous presidents of SFU and UBC, respectively, had been transformed into a unified strategic policy instrument. The university sector was developing a new approach to collaboration and cooperation among and between its own institutions. This is illustrated with the Medical School and Doubling of Opportunity initiatives. The medical initiative involves a partnership between UBC, UVic, and UNBC. The numbers attending UBC have increased, and a new $102 million facility is under construction. In addition, teaching capacity and research capacity at both UVic and UNBC has been introduced, with a concentration on aging and geriatrics at the former and rural medicine and general practice at the latter. All students will get the same degree from UBC. The Doubling the Opportunity initiative grew out of discussion between industry and the deans of engineering and was subsequently sponsored by the TUPC. The result was an increase in the financial resources and the support for students and professors in the targeted areas of computer engineering, computer science, and electrical engineering, which fulfilled one of the government's 2001 election commitments.

The Liberal government's approach to accountability was paradoxical. On the one hand, the government freed the public-sector postsecondary institutions from historical constraints and created new markets for private institutions; on the other hand, by creating more rigorous accountability frameworks that privileged institutional performance in achieving government goals over the needs and wants of the PSE market, it constrained the ability of the public-sector institutions to fully exercise their new freedoms. This is explained to some extent by Premier Campbell's own paradoxical views on public- and private-sector accountability, but it is also explained by the tendency of bureaucracies to try to centralize power. This was resisted by the university presidents and faculty, who viewed the expansion of these accountability mechanisms as an encroachment on institutional autonomy. Although a certain amount of ground was conceded to the new accountability frameworks, it does not appear to be significant ground and it certainly goes nowhere near as far as do similar exercises in Alberta and Ontario, which led to funding mechanisms driven by key performance indicators.

The magnitude of the shift across the whole policy terrain raises questions about the determinants of policy and policy change. Naturally, one would expect to find familiar influences such as resource constraints, technological changes, and various kinds of pressure to deal with inadequacies in current policies and structures. A change of some kind to the tuition fee freeze, for instance, was quite predictable given the growing gap between PSE revenues and operating costs. As noted above, technological change was cited as a factor in the closure of OLA and the creation of BC Campus. According to the ministry, the new arrangement would also "reduce costly duplication within the system and improve efficiency for students (Ministry of Advanced Education, October 30, 2002). Efficiency was evidently an objective in other policy changes as well, as in the case of ITAC, where the government's planning documents cited long-standing and well-known problems with apprenticeship (Beatty 2002). No doubt, other inefficiencies and pressures could also have been found within the PSE system. Still, it is difficult to identify any obvious factor in the Liberal government's policy environment that would have been comparable to the trials suffered and overcome by previous administrations, such as the global recession of the mid-1980s, the structural adjustment of the early 1990s, or the reduction of federal support to education and training in 1995-96.

Indeed, it is difficult to avoid the conclusion that the Liberals' sharp turn does not reflect a particular change in the "external" environment so much as the government's own neoliberal ideology, which was given practical effect by an overwhelming legislative majority. The Liberals' commitment to free market ideals and public-sector downsizing is well enough established in the public record that it need not be demonstrated here, though a few examples illustrate its application to PSE policy. The principle that market forces guarantee fairness (and the implication that government regulations and public enterprise are morally suspect) was frequently invoked. For instance, as he repealed the NDP's fair wage legislation the minister of skills, training and labour argued that what wage and training requirements had imposed on contractors had amounted to a "restrictive practice" that unfairly limited their competitiveness and violated the principles of a competitive marketplace (*Hansard*, 16 August 2001). Similar arguments were invoked in relation to the elimination of the Training Accord and PPSEC, and the introduction of the Degree Authorization Act. Market competition in the education sector would also have the benefit of bringing a competitive stimulus and discipline to an inefficient public sector. University Canada West was the first new private institution to be granted degree-granting powers and university status under the act. The muted public response to the end of the tuition fee freeze, like the absence of protest over ITAC's elimination, suggests that the Liberals gambled well. Similarly, although tens of thousands took to the streets in February 2002 to protest the Black Thursday cuts, the organized opposition soon dissipated, much as it had in the aftermath of the Kelowna Labour Accord of 1984. Five years later, ideology appeared to be less powerful, at least on the surface of the electoral promises. The short-term vicissitudes of parliamentary electoral politics cuts against ideological principles.

POLICY THEMES AND THE POLICY-MAKING PROCESS

The review of changes in the policy environment and policy directions in British Columbia reveals that they had many different causes: the influence of powerful individuals and ideas, of macroeconomic conditions, of demographic and technological change, of interest group pressures, of policy ideas imported from elsewhere, and of collective bargaining pressures and fiscal constraints. It also draws attention to how the actual policy-making process influenced the rules of the game. We now highlight the four key policy themes and conclude with an analysis of the policy-making process.

Policy Themes

As noted in the Introduction, the major policy themes are accessibility, vocationalism and skills, accountability, science and technology, and marketization. These themes are presented in the order of their priority as we look across the whole period of our study. It follows that by far the most important policy priority in the development of PSE policy since the mid-1980s is the desire to create more access to the system. We define accessibility as participation and retention in, and graduation from, the postsecondary system by all willing and capable persons regardless of age, gender, socio-economic status, race, culture, religion, and geographic region. The emphasis has varied between different governing parties, but a consistent aim has been to increase access for both full- and part-time students to degree-granting programs outside the Lower Mainland and Victoria.

Accessibility as a priority overlaps with the constant pressure towards "academic drift" in the system, a trend that has been propelled by both professionals within the system and successive provincial governments. Another major policy priority that is often inseparable from accessibility is access to vocational education and training and, in a more general sense, life-long learning. This theme became particularly important during the NDP administrations. While we discuss some of these vocational policy initiatives under the heading of accessibility, the major focus on "skills" is covered as a separate priority.

The 1988 PAC report established accessibility as the key policy priority for PSE in British Columbia. Through a series of major reports and legislation, this priority was further translated into action by the Socred government. Actions, for example, like the creation of the first university outside the Lower Mainland and the establishment of university colleges came to have a clear impact on the structure of the PSE system. During this period, there was a strong focus on generating access to degree programs outside the Lower Mainland and in densely populated areas that, up to that point, had not been adequately served by universities. At this stage affordability was not an issue that received much attention either in the PAC report or in the Socred's discussions on accessibility. This is not surprising as, at this time, student fees in British Columbia, as in the rest of Canada, had remained relatively stable and low.

When the NDP government took office in 1991, it made the Socred's Access for All policy the foundation of its integrated reforms in academic PSE. The general ambition of increasing access got translated into institutional expansion and diversification and low tuition fees. As discussed above, the increasing demand for academic qualifications was addressed by conferring degree-granting powers on a wider range of institutions and by building more (and more specialized) universities.

We can identify some fundamental differences between the Socred's and the NDP's approaches to accessibility. The Socred government was primarily interested in increasing the opportunity for traditional forms of PSE, particularly in areas outside the Lower Mainland. The NDP government, while continuing this ambition, also gave more attention to the underrepresentation in PSE of minority groups, especially Aboriginal youth. To address the concerns of the latter, public Aboriginal institutions were created; furthermore, the NDP government focused on new forms of vocational-oriented PSE offerings.

Towards the end of the NDP reign, student fees had started to increase rapidly in some provinces, particularly Ontario. In order to assist cash-strapped universities the government was under severe pressure to follow the same route. However, concerns that such a move would reduce affordability and therefore threaten the accessibility strategy convinced the NDP government to freeze student fees.

The Liberal government, while maintaining a focus on accessibility, drastically changed the approach it took to the realization of this goal. Having introduced a three-year spending freeze on education and health but still expecting the PSE system to increase enrolment by eighty-five hundred seats over the period between 2002 and 2005, the Liberal government allowed institutions to fill the funding gap with increased fees. A vastly improved fiscal environment and political considerations, in conjunction with the upcoming election, resulted in a fundamental reversal of the Liberal's fee policy. The 2005 Throne Speech re-regulated fees and stipulated that any further increase be limited to the rate of inflation. This signalled a reversal – a move back to the accessibility policy of the Socred era. The second Liberal government's implementation of the special purpose, teaching universities, the substantial expansion of total student spaces in public PSE, and the introduction of graduate internships and scholarships confirmed this reversal.

As noted earlier, a defining characteristic of the NDP administrations during the period between 1991 and 2001 was their commitment to vocationalism and skill training. The underlying theme was the idea that academic education had received most of the attention in previous decades and that now it was the time to rectify this unevenness. Through a series of reports and legislation, successive NDP governments increased both economic and institutional resources for non-academic and applied education.

The roadmap for the NDP's skills agenda was set by a series of reports during the early 1990s. The grand aim was to dramatically reduce structural unemployment. To achieve this aim the government launched the Skills Now initiative, which outlined an integrated plan to increase the amount of vocational education in the PSE system, in tandem with an activist labour policy that promoted the employment of skilled workers and implicitly protected organized labour. What followed was a massive expansion in the number of vocational spaces as the new funding mechanisms took effect. Apprenticeship programs expanded and "sixteen training and enterprise centres" were established, along with a series of advanced technology courses. In parallel with federal efforts, the government created a provincial labour force development board and – also in step with federal developments – disbanded it after only two years in operation.

The renewal of the NDP's mandate in 1996 under Glen Clark (British Columbia 2002) saw a continuation of its vocationalist approach to PSE. The case for a coordinated and smoothly integrated vocational/skill strategy had been made in successive policy papers, including the 1996 *Charting a New Course*. In 1997, the government established ITAC, aiming to revitalize and expand the moribund apprenticeship option, in part by giving the system's key stakeholders greater autonomy in its governance.

On assuming power in the early summer of 2001, one of the Liberal government's first priorities was to expunge the influence of organized labour from the vocational training system. Measures included the repeal of the Skill Development and Fair Wage Act as well as other laws and regulations requiring trades workers to hold formal certification. In 2003 the Industry Training Authority was created on the skeleton of the former ITAC but with two fundamental differences: its governance was placed under an all-employer board, and its founding legislation avoided all mention of employers' responsibilities in workforce training. British Columbia's "New Model" was indeed novel: a workforce training system now entirely dependent on public resourcing and yet governed exclusively by private interests.

The new government also acted quickly to annul the Training Accord, which had facilitated the colleges' access to government training contracts, and to dissolve the associated CTMS. This was followed by a major overhaul of the skills training system. By March 2003, sixteen regional offices had been closed, which meant the dislocation of 115 apprenticeship counsellors and other staff. A "New Model for Industry Training" was introduced that removed government from its direct involvement with apprentices, gave business a dominant role in the governance of the training system, and introduced a system of "flexible," modular training courses that could be adapted to suit the needs of specific employers and delivered by private trainers (Ministry of Advanced Education 2002). In another institutional change, the government announced in February 2002 that the recently formed TechBC would be dissolved and its assets and operations taken over by SFU.

An underlying but consistent theme has been the commitment by successive governments to make the connections between educational spending and useful outcomes more transparent and understandable to the general public. Commitments to accessibility and to vocationalism are good examples of the ways governments have attempted to make the PSE system more accountable to the public. Located within these policy initiatives are more specific attempts, particularly in the college sector, to make institutions directly accountable in their planning and student outcomes. While the NDP took this direct approach during the 1990s, the Liberals have adopted a different definition of accountability. Accountability has come to mean both quality assurance in the most general sense and a blurring of the boundary between the public and the private sectors. In the latter case, this is direct political accountability to the capital interests that are the main backers of the Liberal Party.

Before leaving office the Social Credit government introduced legislation in 1990 to establish an independent PPSEC to replace the government office that had performed that function. As an independent agency with industry representation, PPSEC gave the private training industry greater control over its own governance and introduced stronger consumer protection measures in the wake of several high-profile bankruptcies and complaints over educational quality in the sector. The commission continued to operate through the NDP years but was eliminated once the Liberals took power.

In addition to the skills accountability agenda, the NDP also made inroads into the university sector. The New Programs Committee, which later became the Degree Program Review Committee, while ostensibly a response to the rapid expansion of degree programs in the university colleges and the institutes, became the gatekeeper for all new degree programs. For the first time, government had a role in monitoring the academic community. The monitoring process was closely tied to the emergence and spread of applied degrees across the PSE sector. Finally, the creation of university colleges, TechBC, and RRU, increased the permeability of the boundary that had separated the university and the non-university sectors. As the vocational orientation of the system increased the NDP was achieving its underlying goal of making the system more responsive to the government's agenda and, thus, in the eyes of the government, more accountable.

As noted earlier, the Liberal government adopted a very different approach to accountability. At every point, the three-year planning exercises that each ministry undertook included accountability language. Yet their specific actions aimed at dismantling what the NDP had put in place to promote its version of accountability. As noted in previous sections, the government eliminated ITAC, PPSEC, CEISS, and the Degree Program Review Committee as well as OLA and TechBC. The argument so well rehearsed in Alberta and Ontario was that free market competition was the best means for making institutions accountable. In other words, accountability to the marketplace was the best means of making the system accountable to the public.

Where new regulatory mechanisms like the Private Career Training Institutes Agency, the Degree Quality Assessment Board, and the Industry Training Authority were created to replace the NDP versions of these bodies, the new governing boards were decidedly more business-friendly and their mandates were more explicitly tied to fulfilling what business determined were the priorities for the province. More generally, the government steered the public institutions by providing targeted funding for particular occupations and professions and by leaving institutions with little choice but to increase tuition fees in the face of government decrees that more students were to be educated without an increase in funding.

The Liberal government that took office in 2001 was explicit in its commitment to market ideology and to the reduction in the size of the public sector. Bill 15, the Degree Authorization Act, 2002, set out criteria under which new institutions, including private and public institutions from outside the province, would be authorized to offer degree programs and to grant degrees in British Columbia. In addition, the bill allowed public colleges and institutes to offer "applied baccalaureate degrees" and university colleges to offer "applied master's degrees" (*Hansard*, 11 April 2002). In a move that reflected the spirit of Bill 15 but that was not directly related, the Liberals established Sea to Sky University (now Quest University).

Liberal reforms of PSE governance seem to reflect similar objectives, a signal example being the privatization of governance in the trades training system under the New Model (*Hansard*, 16 August 2001, 23). Citing the need for greater responsiveness to market opportunities, the government restructured the board of Royal Roads University along corporate lines in June 2002. Finally, the deregulation of fees was a clear attempt to create a quasi-market in the PSE system. Perhaps the best measure of this government's commitment to neoliberal ideology is the inverse relationship between changes in the sources of university operating revenues in British Columbia between 1995 and 2005. The proportion coming from government decreased from 74 to 57 percent, while the proportion coming from student fees increased from 18 to 32 percent (CAUT Almanac 2006, figs 1.2 and 1.3, p. 3).

Policy-Making Process

The policy documents and interviews point to the importance of looking at the actual policy-making process, particularly as it relates to interest groups involvement, as an important element of the policy environment. Our work suggests that differences in the policy-making process reflect particular government interests and can be seen as an attempt to influence the rules of the game through the structuring of the public policy process.

From the middle of the 1980s through the 1990s governments, regardless of political ideology, encouraged public input into the policy-making process through the appointment of broadly representative committees. During his time as minister of advanced education, Stanley Hagen appointed several committees to study financial need, and this would have a significant impact on the structure of the PSE system. The policies as well as the policy process seemed to spring from two related yet distinct sentiments: on the one hand, recognition of the inherent and/or instrumental benefits of education and, on the other, a commitment to educational access as a democratic right. In line with the "human resources" theory of the day, the government's Access for All initiative addressed the issue of social inclusion not by directly redistributive means but, rather, by investing in public PSE as a spur to economic growth and general prosperity.

In many ways, the NDP's ten-year mandate reflects strong continuities of the policy direction under the late Social Credit era and a further strengthening of the consultative process. A distinguishing feature of the NDP's governing style, especially in the early years of its mandate, seemed to be a preference for using broadly participatory processes and forums as vehicles for both defining and articulating its policy directions. On the downside, it is arguable that the NDP's appetite for dialogue and experimentation also created space for internal clashes of stakeholder interest and the constant risk of policy incoherence.

The consultative approach to policy making was evident in the work leading up to the influential *Charting a New Course: A Strategic Plan for the Future of British Columbia's College, Institute and Agency System* (Ministry of Education, Skills and Training 1996). This process has been credited with achieving a broad acceptance within the college system of a new funding formula and accountability measures and has brought a more conciliatory and inclusive tone to the skills policy discourse. Yet, while the civil servants felt they had a clear role, and the stakeholders were glad to be consulted, administrators at the institutional level were sometimes uncomfortable with the egalitarian approach and the inclusive relationship that characterized the policy environment.[19]

Charting a New Course as well as NDP policies like *Skills Now* reflect a somewhat technocratic understanding of education as a policy area crucially important to economic competitiveness and general prosperity and social cohesion. On this point, NDP policy was consonant with the directions taken under Social Credit since the mid-1980s. The practical importance of getting the policy "right," as well as the high profile of education and its dominance of the budget, encouraged broad stakeholder participation in policy generation and governance structures.

The particular approach to system building during this period was also influenced by the NDP leadership's ideological commitment to using policy, in PSE and in other areas, to build the foundations of a more social-democratic society. Central to this approach was a vision of European-style cooperation among equally legitimate "social partners," including business, labour, and civil society groups, in the policy process.

The same principles were evident in other high-profile policy initiatives of the time. For instance, the government's Forest Renewal policy responded to structural adjustment in the forest industry by providing a wide range of supports for retraining and economic development activities in depressed rural communities, with joint management by community organizations, unions, and employers. All of these initiatives relied on a vision of local community development based on collective endeavour and consensus, ideally channelled through formal community organizations and trade unions.

The emerging BC tradition with broadly constituted committees addressing significant policy issues came to an abrupt halt when the Liberal government took office in 2001. Our review of the Liberal "New Era" reforms suggests a radical rupture with the former pattern of PSE policy making in British Columbia. Within the Ministry of Advanced Education, civil servants looked back to the period between 1995 and 1999 when *Charting a New Course* was being developed and defined it as a "refreshing, exhilarating, exciting and frustrating time when they [the civil servants] felt they had a part in building a perspective on the non-university side of PSE."[20] The new model created a certain amount of angst for both the civil servants (who bemoaned their loss) and the stakeholders (who felt they were now excluded). This was particularly the case for the non-university sector, which no longer had a body representing all its interests. As the university colleges separated themselves and voiced their aspirations to become universities the united front presented through the Advanced Education Council of British Columbia (AECBC) was broken. On the other hand, the TUPC was able to convince government that the universities should be treated separately and that research was important. As one commentator put it: "There is much more willingness to see differentiation in the system and much more willingness to appreciate that certain institutions in the postsecondary system have distinctive roles to play."[21]

Plausibly, the Liberals' aggressive policy reforms represent a sincere belief in markets and a neoliberal view of social process. Not only in PSE policy but also across the whole policy-making process, the Liberal's record seems to presuppose a polity of distinct groups with specific and conflicting interests, where the role of public policy is to arbitrate in a zero-sum competition for resources and to allocate costs on a "user-pay" basis.

Arguably, the Liberals actively shaped their own "policy environments," whether intentionally or not, through their approach to public consultation and communication. Although, like their predecessors, the Liberals set up a number of advisory groups on specific policy issues, it often seemed that their purpose was neither to produce "objective" information on policy issues nor to generate democratic consensus but, rather, to articulate the positions of the government's partisans. An example is the BC Progress Board, which was established by Premier Campbell in July 2001 to advise on economic and social policy and was composed of fourteen business leaders plus the president of UBC. In December 2002, it released a report recommending comprehensive reforms to the education system (BC Progress Board 2002). Similarly, the government's consultation process for the overhaul of the apprenticeship system involved, first, synthesizing the recommendations of several business lobby groups (British Columbia Chamber of Commerce 2002; Coalition of BC Businesses 2001) into a "draft" plan and then, around the province, holding a series of regional discussion forums hosted by employer groups (Ministry of Advanced Education 2002). Meanwhile, the minister of advanced education admitted in the Legislature that no consultation of any kind with faculty members, unions, students, employers, or institutional board members had preceded the government's introduction of Bill 28, which over-rode educators' collective agreements (*Hansard*, 27 January 2002, 973).

FUNDING

While the development of PSE policy is dependent on changes in the policy environment, clearly the major way governments transmit policy is through funding decisions. In this sense, PSE has consistently been a policy priority, regardless of which party formed government. In this section we try to assess whether these pronouncements were merely rhetoric or whether they were based on a deeper commitment to increased access. As evidence we look at the changes in funding allocation to the PSE sector. First, does government funding of PSE actually increase? Second, do increases in funding simply mirror a rise in enrolment? Third, how well has PSE done over time in comparison to policy areas such as health?

The analysis starts with mapping changes in provincial expenditure on PSE and training over the last twenty-four years (see figure 2.1, with 1986–87 as reference year). The comparisons are made in 2002 dollars. In 1986–87, the sector received approximately $721 million in operating grants from the provincial government. Funding for PSE increased rapidly during the latter part of the Socred period, and in 1991–92 the sector received 29 percent more funds in operating grants from the provincial government than it had in 1986–87. The increase in these grants continued during the first four years of the first NDP mandate but started to decline in 1996–97. This is most likely related to the sharp cuts in 1995–96 to the Canada Health and Social Transfer (from the federal government to the provinces), which substantially reduced resources for PSE. The decline was short-lived as the economy improved, federal transfers were partly restored, and funding increased sharply. During the last three years of the NDP era (1998–99 to 2001–02) these grants increased by 22 percent. The increase came to a halt when the Liberal government took power in 2001, and, over the next three years, the resources for PSE decreased by approximately 9 percent. During Campbell's second term the economy improved significantly, which can explain why PSE operating grants increased by a dramatic 38 percent from 2005–06 to 2009–10.

Examining changes in the operating grants from the province going to each sector during the period 1986–87 to 2001–02 (see figure 2.2),[22] we can see that, apart from the small dip in the mid-1990s referred to above, all three sectors experienced substantial increases. Given the emphasis on vocationalism and skill training during the NDP years, one might have expected the increases to have

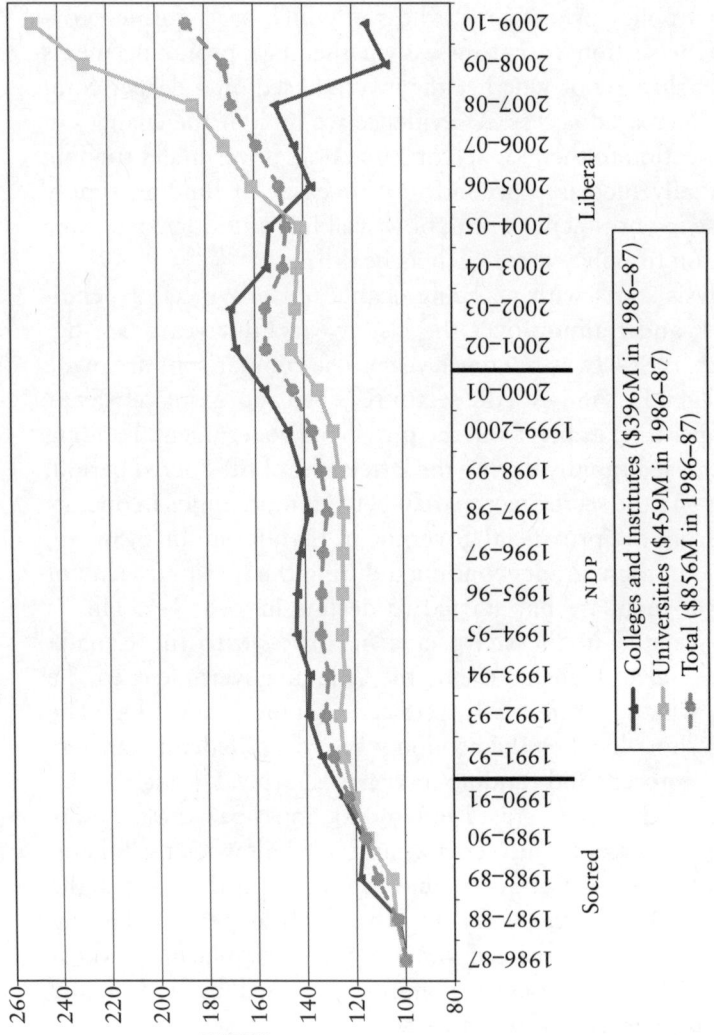

Figure 2.1
Changes in provincial operating grants for BC college and institute, university/college and university sectors, and total postsecondary education, 1986–87 – 2009–10 in constant 2002 dollars, 1986–87 = 100.

Source: Ministry of Advanced Education, BC.

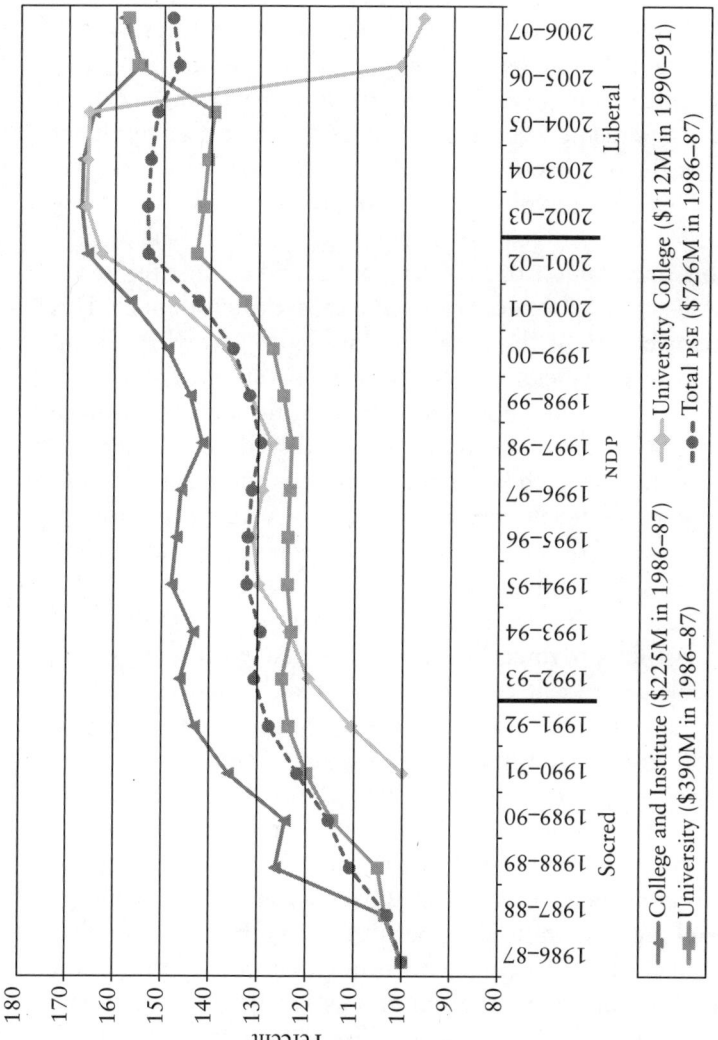

Figure 2.2
Changes in provincial grants for BC college and institute, university college, and university sectors and total postsecondary education, 1986–87 – 2006–07 in constant dollars (2002 dollar), 1986–87 = 100.

Source: Ministry of Advanced Education, BC.

gone mainly to the colleges and institutes, and university colleges rather than to the universities. Yet, while the university colleges did receive increases amounting to around 10 percent between 1991–92 and 1997–98, the other two sectors experienced a slight decrease over the same period. All three sectors experienced quite dramatic growth during the latter years of the NDP era. Between 1997–98 and 2001–02 the provincial operating grants going to the university colleges, the colleges and institutes, and the universities increased by 38, 25, and 21 percent, respectively. Since the Liberal government came to power the only sector to experience an increase has been the universities. This can be explained by changes to the system that saw university colleges being reclassified as regional universities.

A common complaint from public postsecondary institutions is that funding has not kept pace with the increase in enrolment. This claim is supported by the data presented in figure 2.3, which documents changes in provincial grants towards operating expenditures (constant dollars) per funded FTE for colleges and universities from 1986–87 to 2009–10. In 1986–87 colleges received $8,000 per FTE and the universities received $11,000. During the Socred era the provincial grant per FTE for universities and colleges followed a similar pattern. At the end of the era the grants had risen somewhat, slightly more for colleges than universities.

The dip in grant per FTE to colleges in 1989–90 was due to a modest increase in provincial transfers coupled with a 5 percent increase in college student enrolment that year, which is one year after the implementation of Access for All. During the NDP regime the provincial grant per funded FTE for universities consistently decreased until 1999–2000, when it started to rebound somewhat. In 1999–2000, universities received close to 17 percent less per FTE than they did in 1990–91. This shows that funding per FTE had not kept up with enrolment increases in university education. Colleges saw a marked increase in funding per FTE in the first NDP budget, which most likely can be explained by an expansion of FTE in the university colleges and the initiation of a skills agenda and, specifically, the Skills Now initiative. This is followed by a decreasing trend that, surprisingly, is sharper than it was in the university sector. By 1999–2000, colleges were receiving 19 percent less per FTE than in 1990–91 and 22 percent less than in the peak year of 1992–93. At the end of the NDP era there was an increase in funding per FTE for colleges but at a somewhat lower level than in the university sector.

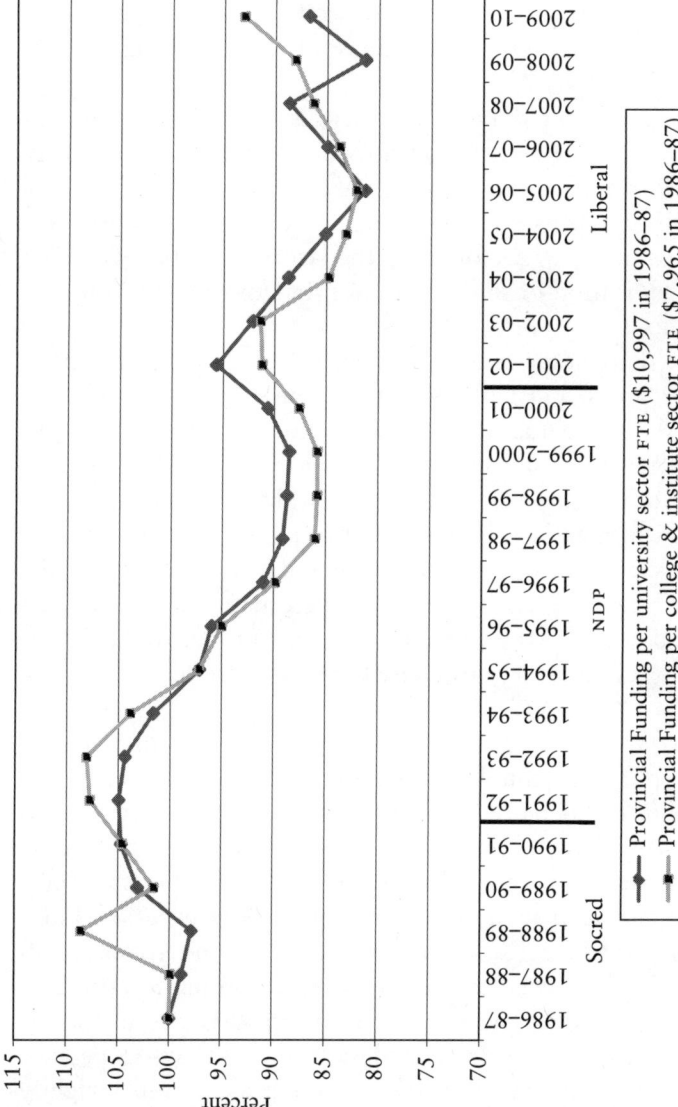

Figure 2.3
Changes in provincial grants per funded FTE for BC college and institute and university sectors, 1986–87 – 2009–10 in constant 2002 dollars, 1986–87 = 100.
Source: Ministry of Advanced Education, BC.

The high level of funding per FTE for colleges was mainly unchanged during the first two years of the Liberal government, and then, after a one-year increase in 2004–05, it declined to the lowest level in any of the last twenty years, partly as a result of structural changes to the system. The funding per FTE for universities decreased dramatically during the first Liberal term but started to rebound during the second term.

The analysis presented in figures 2.1, 2.2, and 2.3 is limited because the changes in transfer do not address the relative priority of the sector. As a complement to the data presented in figures 2.1 and 2.2, table 2.1 focuses on the share of public expenditure allocated to different policy sectors over the last twenty-six years. This provides an indication of the importance the government in power has given to PSE.

Clearly the share going to PSE has been relatively low in comparison to other areas, particularly health. The relative funding for health started to accelerate during the second NDP government and has continued to do so during the Liberal government. In 1986–87, 28.6 percent of the expenditures went to health, and, by the end of the Social Credit mandate, it had risen to 32.6 percent. It remained at around this level during the first NDP mandate but rose during the second NDP mandate and reached 38 percent in 2001–02. This trend continued under the Liberal government, and, by 2011–12, health care expenditure was estimated to have risen to a staggering 45.4 percent.

In contrast, the share of resources being earmarked for PSE has, with the exception of a couple of ups and downs, remained relatively stable. During the Socred government the proportion that went to PSE rose sharply in the 1987–88 budget year, when it went from 6.4 percent in the year before to 7.8 percent in 1987–88. This is the largest year-over-year change in the entire twenty-six-year period. Interestingly, this change precedes the announcement of the Access for All initiative, which happened in March 1988. According to table 2.1, the relative expenditure on PSE did not increase as a result of this initiative but, in fact, went down slightly from the 1987–88 peak.

During the first NDP mandate the PSE initially received a slightly lower share than during the last years of the Socred era. Following the Skills Now initiative, the NDP priority seems to have changed and, in 1995–96, the share going to PSE had increased to 8.1 percent. This policy continued during the second NDP government, and

Table 2.1
Expenditure – budget plan 1986–87 to 2011–12 in percentage of total expenditure

	Year	Postsecondary education training	Education	Health	Rest of government
Socred	1986–87	6.4	12.3	28.6	52.7
	1987–88	7.8	13.4	31.1	47.7
	1988–89	7.3	16.7	33.1	43.0
	1989–90	7.4	16.5	31.9	44.1
	1990–91	7.4	19.8	31.5	41.4
	1991–92	7.5	19.9	32.6	40.1
NDP 1	1992–93	7.2	20.0	33.0	39.9
	1993–94	7.1	19.3	32.6	41.0
	1994–95	7.9	19.3	32.7	40.1
	1995–96	8.1	19.8	32.9	39.2
	1996–97	–	–	33.7	38.1
NDP 2	1997–98	8.1	20.2	35.7	36.0
	1998–99	8.1	20.8	35.3	35.8
	1999–2000	8.3	20.7	36.7	34.3
	2000–01	8.5	20.3	37.1	34.0
	2001–02	7.9	19.7	38.0	34.4
Liberal	2002–03	7.4	19.0	40.0	33.5
	2003–04	7.6	19.4	40.8	32.2
	2004–05	7.6	19.6	42.2	30.4
	2005–06	7.3	18.9	42.5	31.4
	2006–07	7.5	19.0	44.5	28.6
	2007–08	7.6	18.8	43.9	29.7
	2008–09	7.2	18.1	43.8	30.9
	2009–10*	6.5	15.3	43.3	34.8
	2010–11**	6.3	15.3	43.9	34.6
	2011–12	5.7	15.1	45.4	33.7

Source: British Columbia Ministry of Finance and Corporate Relations, budget document "Health" includes "Health Innovation Fund" and "Healthy Living and Sport," where applicable.

* Used September update of the budget

** From 2009–10 to 2010–11, "Advanced Education" was changed to "Advanced Education and Labor Market Development." However, in 2011–12, it was changed back to "Advanced Education."

in 2000–01 PSE and training accounted for 8.5 percent of the public expenditures, the highest it ever reached during the twenty-six-year period. In its last budget the NDP government reduced its share to 7.9 percent. During the Liberal era the relative allocation to PSE has been going down, first gradually and recently more dramatically, and it is estimated to have shrunk to 5.7 percent in 2011–12.

The major relative increase to PSE under the Socreds took place not as a result of the report from the Access for All initiative but, in fact, at the time the task force was formed. Thus, the increase and the creation of the task force better speak to the importance given to PSE by the Socred government than does what happened after the report was published. We suspect that this might be quite typical of the way reforms occur in the public sector. During the NDP era there seems to have been a somewhat better correspondence between the policy rhetoric, stressing the centrality of PSE and training, and the share of public resources being allocated to this policy area. We can further note that the Socred government put more priority on K-12 education, which saw its share increase dramatically between 1986–87 and 1991–92. However, it is worth noting that K-12 continued to be a priority area during the NDP government but that it has gradually received a smaller share since the Liberal Party came into power in 2001.

Faced with insufficient government funding to meet major enrolment increases, postsecondary institutions have increasingly adopted a market approach and focused on increasing revenue from sources other than government. Figure 2.4 documents the relative share of revenue coming from (1) transfers from different levels of government and (2) revenue generated from different sources by the institutions. The data show the dramatic change that has occurred over the last two decades in the funding of PSE in British Columbia. In 1988–89, government transfers accounted for 71 percent of the total revenue of postsecondary institutions, while only 29 percent came from revenue raised by the institutions. Hereafter followed a period of steady decline (which accelerated somewhat during the NDP'S time in government) in the proportion of revenue stemming from government transfers and a growing dependence on outside funds. By 2000–01 government's relative contribution was down to 58 percent of the total revenue, with the other 42 percent being raised by the institutions. The downward trend continued during the first Liberal mandate, and, by 2004–05, the relevant proportions were

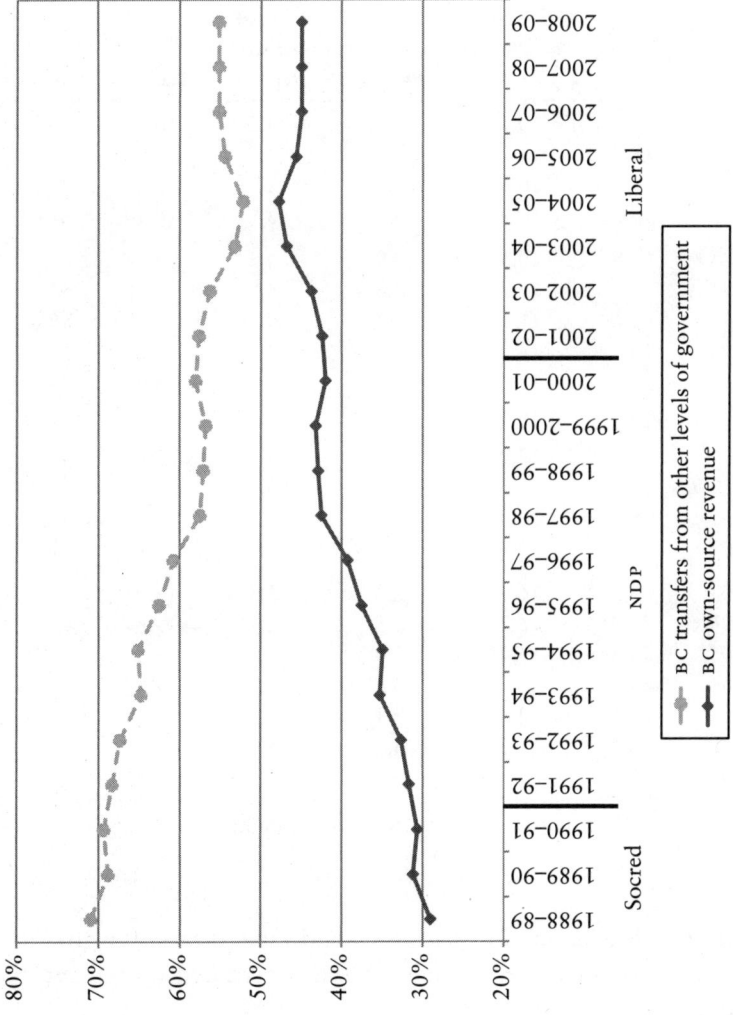

Figure 2.4
Proportion of revenue from own-source revenue and government funding, British Columbia, 1988–89 – 2008–09.

Source: Statistics Canada, CANSIM, table 387-007.

Table 2.2
Funding sources as a percent of total funding: BC postsecondary education, 1988–89 to 2008–09

		Own source revenue				Government transfers	
		Tuition fees	Other sales of goods and services	Investment income	Other own-source revenue	Federal	Provincial
Socred	1988–89	13.0	10.7	2.2	3.2	6.3	64.6
	1989–90	13.7	10.7	3.1	3.7	10.0	58.8
	1990–91	13.7	10.0	3.1	3.9	7.2	62.1
	1991–92	13.8	10.0	4.0	3.8	6.9	61.4
NDP 1	1992–93	13.9	10.5	3.9	4.3	6.8	60.5
	1993–94	15.2	13.3	2.6	4.2	6.6	58.1
	1994–95	15.6	11.7	2.2	5.4	6.6	58.4
	1995–96	16.1	14.2	3.1	4.2	5.2	57.1
	1996–97	17.0	15.2	2.5	4.6	5.0	55.5
NDP 2	1997–98	17.2	17.9	2.7	4.7	4.7	52.6
	1998–99	17.9	17.9	2.5	4.6	5.2	52.0
	1999–2000	18.6	15.5	3.3	5.3	6.0	50.8
	2000–01	18.3	15.8	2.5	5.3	6.0	52.0
	2001–02	17.0	17.8	1.7	6.0	6.8	50.8
Liberal	2002–03	18.9	16.6	2.3	5.8	8.0	48.2
	2003–04	22.0	16.2	2.5	6.1	7.6	45.6
	2004–05	23.3	15.7	2.4	6.3	8.5	43.7
	2005–06	23.1	13.7	3.0	5.7	9.1	45.3
	2006–07	23.3	12.8	3.1	5.7	8.0	46.9
	2007–08	23.3	12.8	3.1	5.7	8.0	46.9
	2008–09	23.3	12.8	3.1	5.7	8.0	46.9

Source: British Columbia Ministry of Finance and Corporate Relations, budget documents.

52 percent and 48 percent. During the second Liberal term the government proportion increased somewhat and constituted 55 percent in 2008–09.

A closer look at revenue sources (see table 2.2) reveals that the decrease in government transfer is entirely related to a decrease in the share of provincial transfers to the PSE institutions. At the end of the Socred mandate provincial transfers constituted 62.1 percent of total revenue. Towards the end of the first NDP mandate this figure had dropped to 55.5 percent and continued its decline under the second NDP mandate, when it reached a low of 50.8 percent. Under the first Liberal era it continued to decline so that, by 2004–05, it was down to 43.7 percent. During the second Liberal mandate the trend changed, and by 2008–09 it had risen to 46.9 percent. The federal contributions going directly to the postsecondary institutions (which have always formed a very small share of the total revenue) have not shown the same degree of variation. They were mainly stable during the late 1980s and early 1990s but declined in 1995–96 and remained low until 1998–99, when they started to increase. This trend has continued and reached a peak in 2005–06, when it reached 9.1 percent of total revenue. Thereafter this proportion has declined slightly to 8.0 percent. Turning to the institutions own source of revenue, tuition came to be responsible for an increasing share of revenue during the first NDP administration, when it went from 13.7 percent in 1990–91 to 17.0 percent in 1996–97. For the period of the tuition freeze, the percentage rose slightly to 18.3 percent in 2000–01. As a result of the Liberal deregulation of tuition fees, the proportion increased substantially to 23.3 percent in 2004–05 and has remained at this level during the second Liberal era. The other main source of own funding comes from "other sales of goods and services."[23] The income from this source rose from around 10.5 percent during the Socred era to a high of 17.9 at the end of the second NDP era. Since the Liberals took office the share of income from this source has declined sharply and constituted only 12.8 percent of total funding in 2008–09.

OUTCOMES

In this section we examine indicators of accessibility, participation, and the level of commitment to research and development.

Accessibility

Two measures of accessibility are analyzed in this section: (1) average university tuition fees by program and (2) average tuition fees as a proportion of after-tax average income. Figure 2.5 illustrates two major interrelated developments during the period: (1) a dramatic

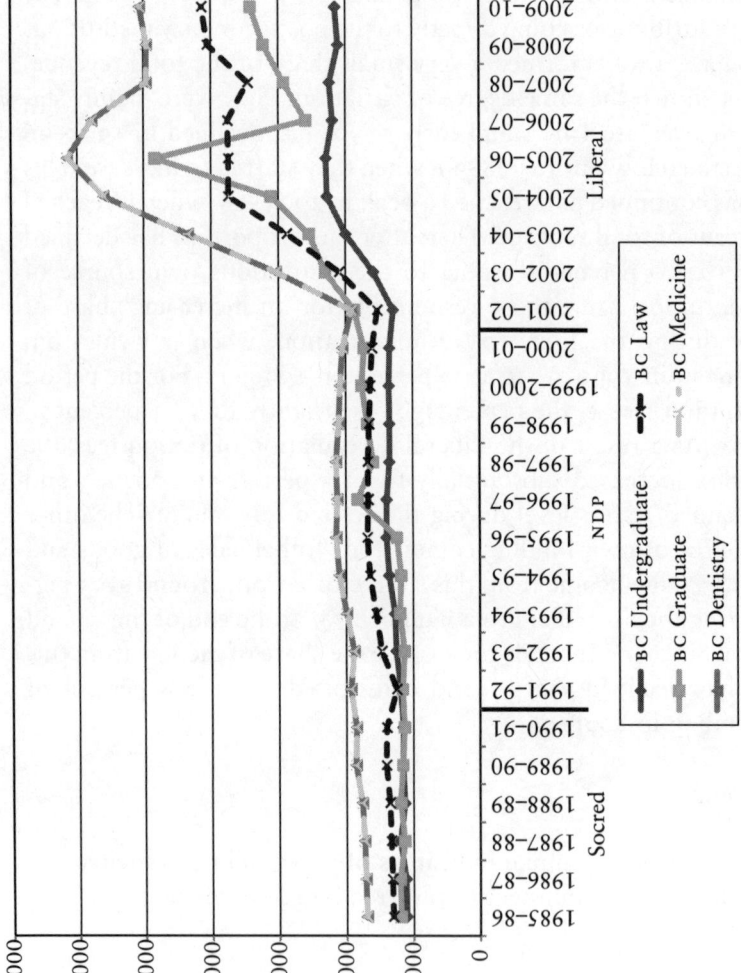

Figure 2.5
Average university tuition by brogram in BC, 1985–86 – 2009–10 (2002 dollars).
Source: Statistics Canada. TLAC, table 08E.

increase in tuition fees that was spread unequally between programs and (2) the election of the Liberal government. Tuition fees rose for all full-time university students.

During the second NDP era, the fees in all programs but graduate studies remained relatively flat in constant 1992 dollars. This reflects the commitment of this government to accessibility not only to undergraduate programs but also to professional programs. When the Liberals took office this position changed, and, in accordance with its market philosophy, the fees were allowed to increase rapidly. Between 2001–02 and 2005–06, fees for all programs rose dramatically. This was particularly the case for medicine and dentistry, where the cost rose by a massive 300 percent from $3,230 to $13,078. Since then the peak fees for medicine and dentistry have declined somewhat and stood at $11,356 in 2009–10. Law has continued to rise during the last decade, with an increase of approximately 200 percent from 2001–02 to 2009–10. The average fees for graduate programs rose from $3,324 in 2001–02 to reach a peak of $10,279 in 2005–06 and thereafter dropped sharply before slowly increasing again to stand at $7,668 in 2009–10. Average undergraduate program fees rose by close to 90 percent during the first Liberal mandate but remained basically unchanged during the second Liberal era, reflecting the government's changed policy, which, since 2005, has only allowed fees to increase at the rate of inflation.

The second indicator of accessibility is average undergraduate university tuition fee as a proportion of after-tax average income (1986 dollars) that is divided into quintiles. The variation in this indicator, as we move from 1986–87 to 2004–05, shows the lowest quintile experiencing the most change and the highest quintile the least (figure 2.6). During the Socred years (1986–87 to 1991–92) no group experienced any significant change. Over the course of the first NDP administration the only group to experience a significant upward change was the lowest quintile, which recorded a change of 5.1 percent between 1990–91 and 1995–96. While this evidence certainly raises questions about the success of the NDP's policy of tuition freezes leading to more equitable access across socioeconomic groups, we do see the impact of this policy during the second NDP administration. All five quintiles remained remarkably stable during these years and even experienced a slight decline. Given the trends recorded in the previous sections it is predictable that, between 2001–02 and 2004–05, this proportional statistic would

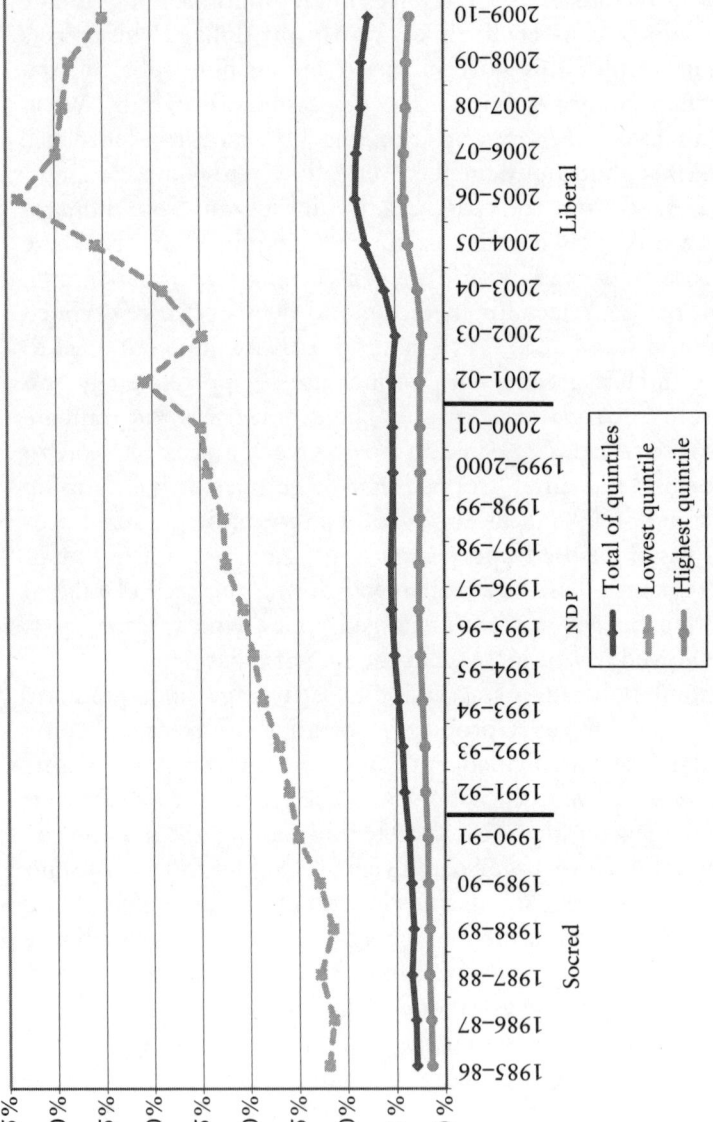

Figure 2.6
Average undergraduate university tuition fees as a proportion of selected after-tax average income quintiles British Columbia, 1985–86 to 2008–09 (constant 2002 dollars).
Source: Statistics Canada, Tuition and Living Accommodation Costs, Survey 3123.

change upward. The lowest and the highest quintiles rose by 5.9 percent and 1.6 percent, respectively. In 2004–05, average undergraduate tuition fee as a proportion of after-tax average income quintiles was 3.7 percent for the highest quintile and 21 percent for the lowest quintile.

Affordability is dependent not only on the level of student fees but also on the level of loans that are available (see chapter 5).

Participation and Choice

Traditionally, the participation rates for 18- to 24-year-olds in British Columbia have been lower than the Canadian average. However, the concerted effort from the late 1980s and through the 1990s to expand the system has improved the situation. and the figure is now above the Canadian average. Between 1986–87 and 2001–02, the participation rate, using FTE enrolment figures, rose from 26 per cent to 40.7 per cent (figure 2.7). Thus, the system moved from being "elite" through a "mass" phase to finally becoming "universal (Trow 1973; Scott 1995). The increase was particularly rapid during the Socred Liberal era, when the rate rose from 25.8 percent in 1985–86 to 34.0 percent in 1991–92. Since 2002–03, there has been a slight decrease followed by small changes up and down, and in 2009–10 the participation rate was 41.8 percent.

Similarly, between 1986–87 and 2006–07, the participation rate for the 18–29 age group rose from 14.9 percent to 25.1 percent. By 2009–10, the rate had decreased slightly to 24.3 percent.

Figure 2.8 suggests that there is variation in how participation has evolved in the different programs over time, trends that become even more apparent when we examine participation rates by program.

In figures 2.9 and 2.10 and table 2.3 we plot the changes in participation rates, using FTE enrolment figures, in adult basic education (ABE), vocational programs (apprenticeship and career/technical), academic/bachelor and graduate programs (master's and doctoral) between 1985–86 and 2004–05 for the 18–24 age group. Table 2.3 shows the percentage distribution for the same grouping of major programs for the same time period.

Given the previous analysis, we would have expected the rise in participation rates during the 1990s for ABE, apprenticeship/vocational and career/technical combined to rise more rapidly than the combined academic rates. Certainly the NDP was insistent that

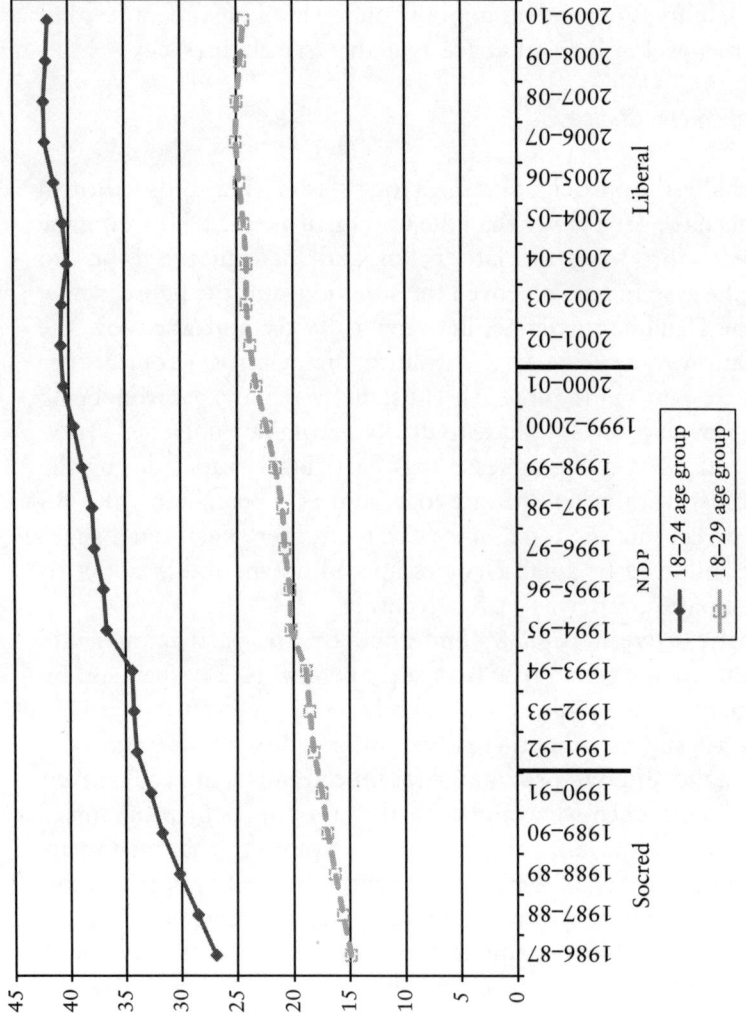

Figure 2.7
Postsecondary education and participation rate, 18–24 and 18–29 age groups in British Columbia, 1986–87 – 2009–10.

Source: Ministry of Advanced Education, BC.

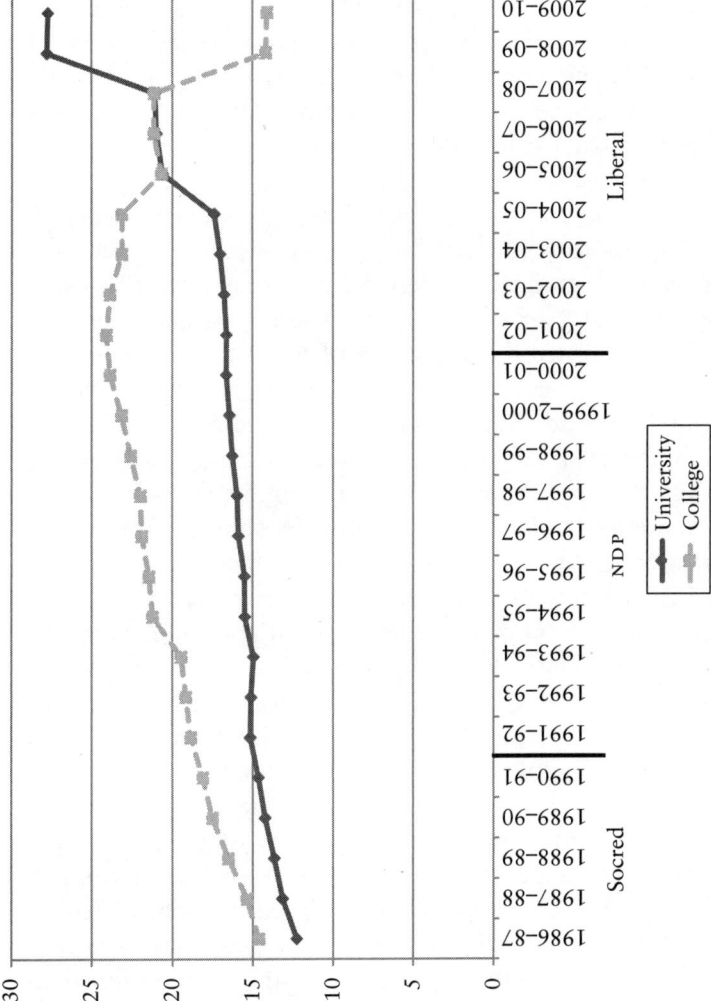

Figure 2.8
Postsecondary education participation rate (18–24 age group) by sector in British Columbia, 1986-87 – 2009-10.

Source: BC Statistics; Ministry of Advanced Education, BC.

vocational programs be given more priority than had been the case under the Socred governments, and between 1991–92 and 2001–02 the combined participation rate did expand a little from 12.5 percent to 14.0 percent. But, as noted earlier, the total participation rate was also climbing during this time, so the combined academic participation rate rose from 15.5 percent to 26.0 percent. The expansion of the academic participation rates speaks to the power of academic drift throughout the system and the increasing demand from students for degree programs. This same division of emphasis is evident in the participation rates by combined programs between 2001–02 and 2004–05.

Figure 2.10 provides a better picture of how these same participation rates changed through time by program. Both academic programs (bachelor and graduate) experience consistent upward growth during the period 1985–86 to 2004–05. The largest gains for academic programs came in the latter part of the 1980s and from the mid- to late 1990s. The least growth for these programs occurred during the first NDP administration. ABE and the career and vocational programs receive a significant boost starting in the early 1990s, only to decline to those earlier levels after the Liberals took power.

The distribution of FTE by program provides some slight evidence that the vocational/ABE programs gained during the 1990s. The ABE proportion moves up substantially from 7 percent to around 9 percent in the mid-1990s and then stays at that level until the Liberals take power. Between 1991–92 and 2001–02, the proportion of FTE allocated to the Vocational/ABE programs rose from 35.5 percent to 37.5 percent and then dropped to 33.9 percent in 2004–05 (table 2.3). Yet the differences are so small they are hardly significant. All the evidence in this section suggests that all governments during the period from 1985–86 through to 2004–05 were strongly committed to increasing access to the system. Yet while on the surface the higher education policies of the three parties were different, particularly with respect to vocationalism, the outcomes were very similar. The academic/graduate part of the offerings continued to account for about two-thirds of the total FTE allocation and as a share of the total participation rate for both the 18–24 and 18–29 age groups. If anything, the vocational commitment was slightly higher in 1985–86 than in any later year. Just as colleges wished to be more academic, so successive governments were committed to increasing access to programs leading to degrees in the Interior.

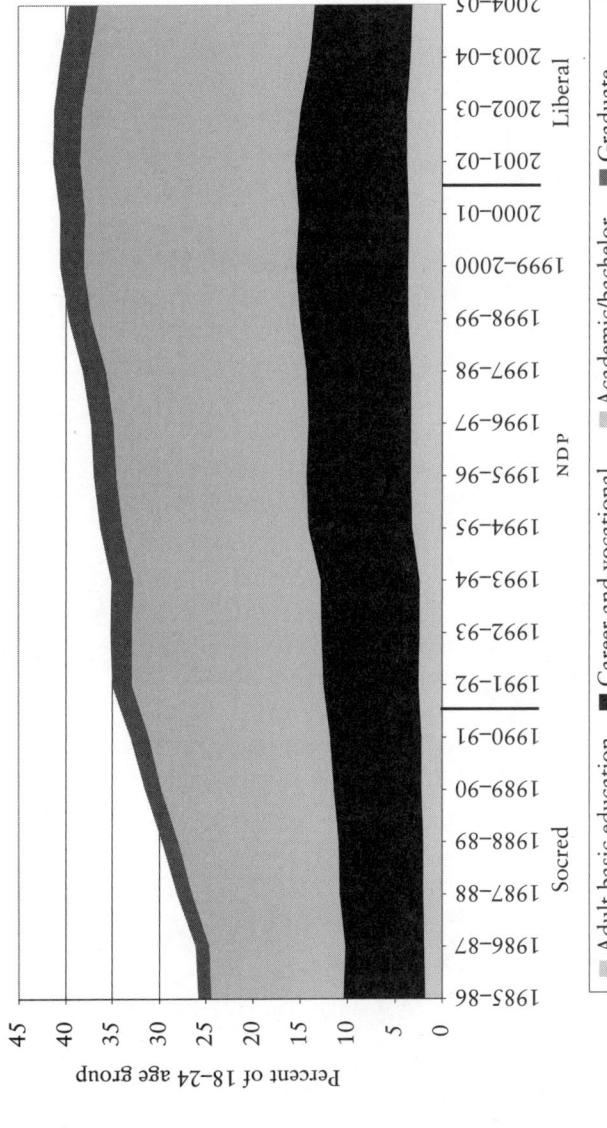

Figure 2.9
Postsecondary education participation rate (18–24 age group) in adult basic education, career/vocational, academic/bachelor and graduate (masters and doctoral) programs in British Columbia, 1985–86 – 2004–05.

Note: Data after 2004–05 not available.

Sources: BC Statistics; and Ministry of Advanced Education, B.C.

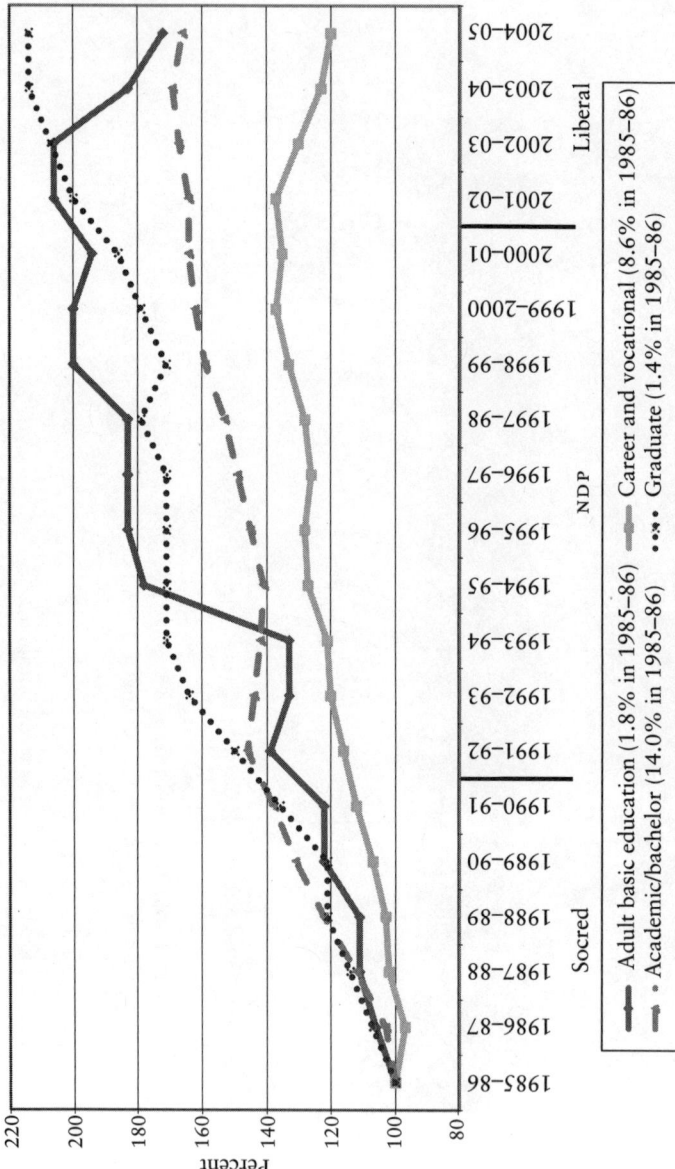

Figure 2.10
Changes in postsecondary education participate rate (18–24 age group) in adult basic education, career/vocational, academic/bachelor and graduate programs in British Columbia, 1985–86 – 2004–05.

Sources: BC Statistics; and Ministry of Advanced Education, BC.

British Columbia   111

Table 2.3
FTEs by grouped major programs 1985–86 to 2004–05 in BC, percentage distribution

	ABE	Career/ Vocational	Academic/ Bachelor	Graduate	Total
1985–86	6.8	33.4	54.2	5.6	100
1986–87	7.4	31.9	55.1	5.7	100
1987–88	7.1	31.3	55.8	5.8	100
1988–89	6.7	30.2	57.6	5.5	100
1989–90	6.8	29.3	58.5	5.5	100
1990–91	6.6	29.1	58.4	5.8	100
1991–92	7.0	28.5	58.3	6.1	100
1992–93	6.9	29.1	57.4	6.6	100
1993–94	6.9	29.4	56.8	6.8	100
1994–95	8.9	29.8	54.6	6.7	100
1995–96	9.0	29.6	54.8	6.6	100
1996–97	8.7	29.0	55.8	6.4	100
1997–98	8.7	28.8	56.1	6.4	100
1998–99	9.0	28.8	56.0	6.2	100
1999–2000	8.8	29.0	56.0	6.1	100
2000–01	8.7	28.5	56.5	6.3	100
2001–02	9.0	28.5	55.8	6.6	100
2002–03	9.0	27.1	56.7	7.2	100
2003–04	8.1	26.2	58.3	7.4	100
2004–05	7.9	26.0	58.5	7.6	100

Sources: University College and Institute enrolment data. Custom tabulation prepared by the Funding and Analysis Branch, Ministry of Advanced Education. University enrolment data, table 4.1, on the University Presidents' Council website, http://www.tupc.bc.ca/facts_figures/index.html.

"Useful and Relevant" Research Development

Gross expenditures on R&D as a percentage of GDP in British Columbia remained relatively stable during the 1990s. After a brief dip in the mid-1990s, this ratio increased steadily from 0.91 percent in 1997 to 1.45 percent in 2004 (figure 2.11).

Except for two years at the beginning of the 1990s, the most important source for these expenditures has been business (figure 2.12). Since 1992, the proportion of the gross expenditures on R&D funded by business has hovered in the 40 to 50 percent range. Following a slight dip in 1996, the proportion rose steadily to reach

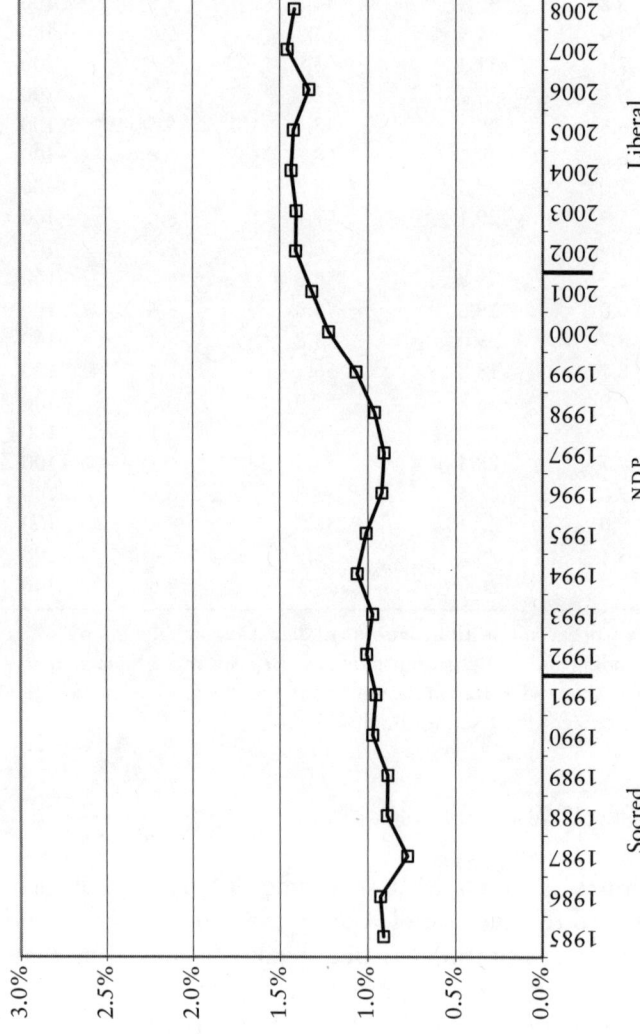

Figure 2.11
Gross expenditures on research and development for British Columbia as a proportion of gross domestic product, 1985–2008.

Source: Statistics Canada, table 385–007.

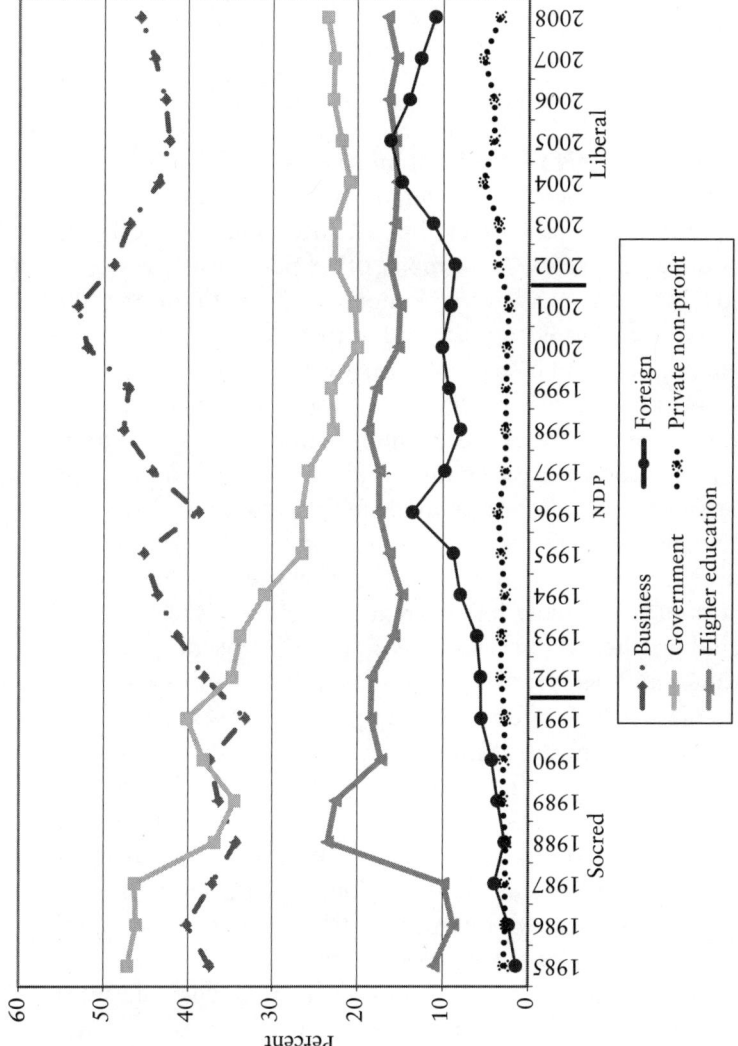

Figure 2.12
Proportion of gross expenditure on research funded by business, government, higher education, foreign and private non-profit funders for British Columbia, 1985–2008.
Source: Statistics Canada, table 385-007.

a peak of 53 percent in 2001. Thereafter it declined to a low of 41 percent in 2004. The proportion funded by government has declined from a high of 40 percent in 1991 to a low of 21 percent in 2004. PSE remained relatively stable in the 15 to 19 percent range, while foreign sources increased substantially from 4 percent in 1990 to 17 percent in 2004.

CONCLUSION

This chronology has highlighted a number of developments in different, overlapping dimensions of higher education policy as it has evolved in British Columbia over the last forty and, especially, the last fifteen to twenty years. As in many other parts of the world, in British Columbia PSE has seen phenomenal growth during this period, both in terms of enrolment and in terms of its profile on the government policy agenda. As elsewhere, this evolution is marked by some key features (mass participation, economic utility, growing standardization, and centralized administration) and seems to be have been influenced by some common factors (the global economy, public demand for access, and limited public resources). Laid over this basic framework are many local peculiarities that give British Columbia's experience a unique cast. The province's historical position as a resource producer had a great influence on social institutions, including the labour movement, political parties, and the cultural values and perspectives of various groups. Individuals such as Hagen, Harcourt, Miller, and Campbell have left their own imprints on policies and institutions, some more enduring than others. Over time, PSE policy has gained prominence, whether because politicians and civil servants have seen it as the important denominator among many other policy issues or because public demand made it impossible to ignore. Political ideology has also supplied concepts and terminology for interpreting these demands and articulating various imperatives for the PSE system.

Nor do these variations in policy necessarily align with our intuitive or common-sense expectations of the environment. For instance, greater expansion in British Columbia's PSE system was initiated under a nominally small-"c" conservative government. In contrast, notable shifts towards vocational "relevance" and managerialist accountability in PSE policy were introduced by social democrats (and the highest-educated governing caucus in BC history). Divergent trends and developments not only reveal the complexity of the policy environment but also license different theoretical perspectives as the real drivers of policy change. While presenting a narrative about the evolution of PSE in British Columbia, this chapter also strives to bring to the surface some of the socio-theoretical assumptions and value orientations employed by participants in and observers of this evolution. It seems reasonable to point, if not to a continuous evolution in PSE policy in British Columbia, at least to several fairly distinct phases and sets of influences over the last two or three decades. Still, these apparent continuities are offset by enough unexpected turns, strange alliances, and counter-intuitive developments to inspire theoretical caution.

The balance between equality of opportunity and the common good, on the one hand, and labour market responsiveness and economic development, on the other, has altered during the period since the Second World War. Since the mid-1980s, the role of education in wealth creation has come to dominate the policy discussions on education in British Columbia regardless of the government in power.

Collectivism has been an underlying principle in the debates over differentiation, coordination, and centralization throughout the period. A binary system of colleges and universities emerged first, but, with the creation of four-year university colleges and the expansion of degree-granting status to almost all public institutions, the boundary lines separating strata have been blurred. The overwhelming power of academic drift means that the university system is differentiated into three layers, which are separated by the level and type of degree the institutions offer: (1) full universities (whole range of degrees); (2) teaching-intensive universities and BCIT (full range except non-applied master's degrees and doctorates); and (2) colleges and provincial institutes (up to bachelor's degrees). This does not take into account the private institutions that offer degrees and other credentials either directly or at a distance. This group clearly occupies a fourth strata and a new fault line between public and private provision. This process is a result of policy decisions taken mainly in response to demands to increase access.

Alongside the move to decentralize is an increasing emphasis on accountability. The international literature reports how various governments have attempted to extend accountability through techniques like performance indicators and performance-based funding into the realm of personal autonomy. Yet so far this has not been the case in British Columbia. Despite frequent references by government to the need for institutions to become more accountable, particularly during the Liberal era, no government has introduced accountability regimes of the kind that are in place in, for example, the United Kingdom or Australia. Nor has there been any serious consideration of introducing any elaborate form of performance funding. However, this is not to deny there is a growing internal discussion, particularly in the research-intensive universities, of the need to develop performance indicators in order to better situate the university in the competition for external funding. Accountability has also come to mean recognition of the dominance of market ideology. In the past, when universities only served the elites in society, the academic tradition that emphasized autonomy and independence protected universities and academics from explicit interference from external forces. More recently, governments have encouraged postsecondary institutions in British Columbia to be more responsive to the economy and to create alliances with the private sector

The history of PSE policy in British Columbia seems to reflect changes not only in the "environment," conventionally understood, but also in policy makers and policy-making mechanisms. Our study suggests that government institutions and policy-making processes do not simply telegraph external signals onto public policies but also exert their own influences on the environment and, in turn, on future policy. In our narrative we have focused mainly on how aspects of the external environment seem to have influenced governments' decisions regarding PSE. Apart from noting some coincidences between such things as tuition subsidies and enrolment rates, we have said almost nothing about the reciprocal relationship: how public policy has affected the outside world. Given the costs involved, and the bottomless faith that governments and publics seem to place in the instrumental power of PSE to benefit individuals and society, more careful study is needed to associate education policy in British Columbia with such benefits as economic growth, industrial innovation, and social cohesion (Rubenson 2003; Wolf 2002).

Looking across the two periods of dramatic change, the 1960s and the 1990s, we can identify four long-term trends. First is the expansion of the system both in terms of students and institutions. Second is the diversification of the system as it evolved from a "university-dominated" model through a "binary" stage to the current "diversified," or "stratified," system. In the Scott typology, British Columbia's system is clearly a mixed category situated somewhere between the binary and the stratified. Third is academic drift. This begins with the creation of the colleges, which incorporated the existing vocational schools but also, from the beginning, served an academic transfer function. It continues with the emergence of a new research university and the transformation of five of the colleges into university colleges and then, latterly, teaching-intensive universities. In addition, most other institutions have sought and gained degree-granting status.

Alongside academic drift, we have the continuing emphasis on linking education and work. This was particularly noticeable in the 1990s as the private sector expanded and we saw the creation of two niche universities, TechBC and RRU. This trend has been heightened by the granting of university status to two for-profit private institutions that offer narrow vocational programs (and the subsequent rescinding of that status from one of them). Inevitably, these trends both reflect and have been driven by a set of underlying principles. For the last twenty years, PSE has been and will continue to be a government priority. The public's perception that a good education is the passport to personal prosperity, coupled with the popular notion that an educated citizenry is a necessity for a nation's prosperity, drives this policy priority. As long as the public continues to demand more PSE, any government, regardless of its political ideology, will accede. While funding has not always been generous, particularly in comparison to that for health, the budgets for education and PSE have often been spared when other areas have suffered deep cuts during economic downturns. In its attempt to cure the structural deficit and to balance the provincial budget by 2004–05, the Liberal government protected the budgets of education and PSE while cutting the budgets of other ministries.

The BC case provides some insights into the interrelated impact of political ideology, financial conditions, and economy on government funding for PSE. Figure 2.13 illustrates the connection through time between political ideology, specific policies, and the changes in provincial funding for the three sectors. The most dramatic changes came in the last five years between 2002–03 and 2006–07 as the Liberal government de-emphasized the vocationalism championed by the NDP and, thereby, reduced the funding to the college and

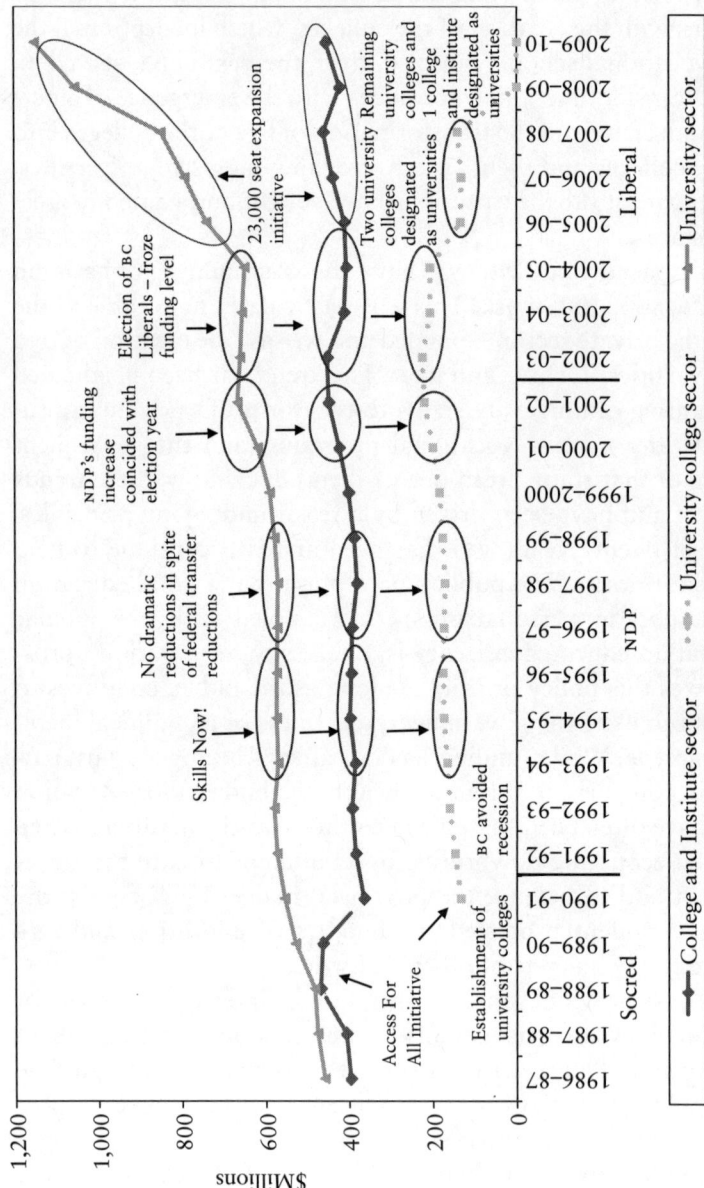

Figure 2.13
Provincial operating grant for BC college and institute, university college, and university sectors (in constant 1992 dollars) and postsecondary education policies, 1986–87 – 2009–10.

institute sector. Further, with the change in the status of two university colleges, we see the transfer of funding from that sector to the university sector.

The BC case also exemplifies the complex relationship between the state of the economy and allocation of funds for PSE. To illustrate this, figure 2.14 presents the yearly changes in GDP and the percent change in operating grants for PSE. If there were a simple direct link between the economy and the allocation of funds for PSE we would expect the lines to be more or less parallel. This was partly the case during the Socred era, when early sharp increases in allocation of funds for the sector were very much in line with its ambitious access goals (set by the government and very strong growth in GDP). However, the Socred government continued to increase the funding during years when the GDP increase was substantially lower. In assessing the developments during the NDP era, one has to account for the sharp decline in federal transfers that took place during the mid-1990s. This is reflected in a reduced increase to PSE in the years 1994-95 to 1997-98. During the second NDP mandate the allocation to PSE grew continuously and can be partly, but not fully, accounted for by increases in GDP. What occurred during the first Liberal mandate differs from what happened under Socred and NDP governments. Despite substantial GDP increases for the period 2002-03 through 2005-06, the increases to PSE continuously became smaller and smaller so that there was actually a decline in 2005-06. Thus, while PSE did well in comparison to all other sectors but health during this period, the increases to education did not follow GDP increases, which had been the case during the Socred and NDP governments.

The policy environment set by successive provincial governments has, until recently, been remarkably stable. Socred and NDP administrations have been committed to "access" and vocationalism. The pressure for academic drift has come from within the system and from Interior communities who wanted more access to degree-granting programs outside the Vancouver and Victoria conurbations. Most recently, the operation of ideology can be recognized in the contrast between the NDP's freeze on student fees versus the Liberal's initial program of deregulation. Similarly, the new regulatory mechanisms, such as the Private Career Training Institutes Agency and the ITA, which were created to replace the NDP versions of these bodies, had governing boards that were decidedly more

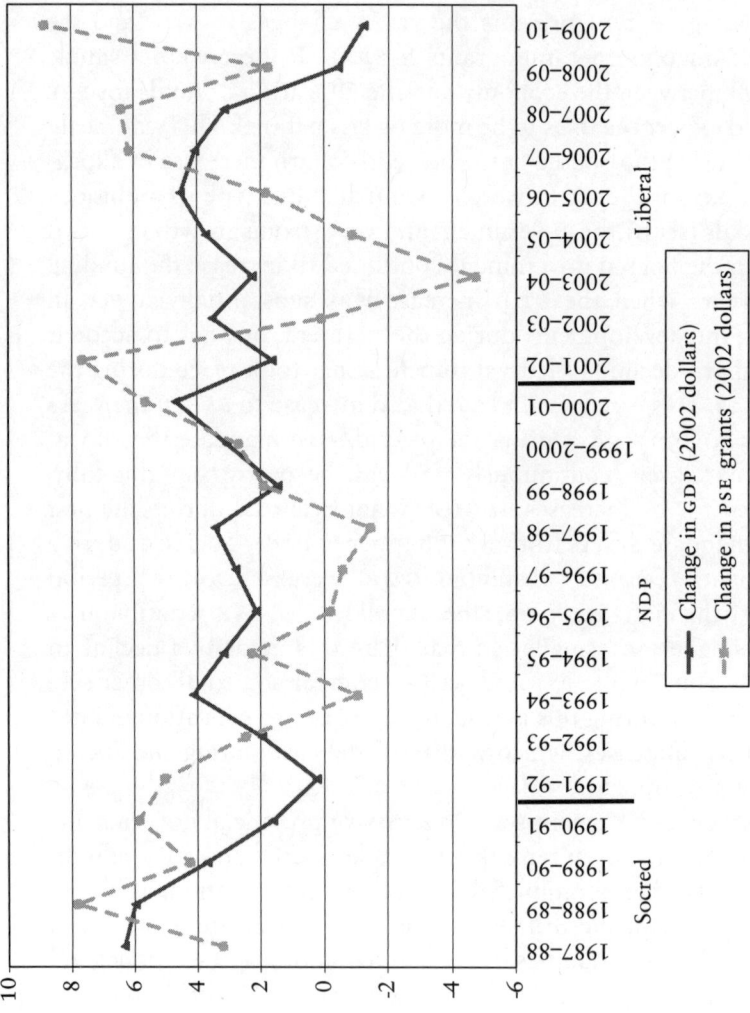

Figure 2.14
Percent change in gross domestic product and postsecondary education operating grants, 1987–88 – 2009-10

Sources: Ministries of Finance and Advanced Education, BC and CANSIM Table 384–0002

business friendly, and their mandates were more explicitly tied to fulfilling what business determined were the priorities for the province. So while no government since the mid-1980s has been able to ignore the importance of the market, in 2001 the Liberal government was the first to enthusiastically support this approach to governing. However, the re-regulation of fees by the Liberals in 2005 can be seen as an indicator that the citizens of British Columbia will not support a far-reaching neoliberal agenda.

3

Contradictory Trends in PSE Policy in Ontario

THERESA SHANAHAN, GLEN JONES,
DONALD FISHER, AND KJELL RUBENSON

INTRODUCTION

This chapter presents a profile of Ontario's PSE policy during the period from 1985 to 2010. A review of major government policy initiatives during this period reveals that successive provincial administrations employed various strategies to enhance key postsecondary themes, including accessibility, quality and accountability, affordability, research and innovation, as well as labour market relevance. These efforts emerged within the changing political economy complete with economic booms and economic recessions. The result is a story of contradictory trends in Ontario PSE: years of structural stability followed by rapid policy changes that altered government's approach to regulation, increased spending followed by dramatic retrenchment and then massive reinvestment, rationalization followed by system expansion, and expansion of the private sector and market presence in PSE at the same time that governments expanded mechanisms of control over system coordination.

Our analysis of data was informed by the conceptual framework employed by the AIHEPS project as described earlier in this book. Our central objectives were: (1) to identify the policy trends within each administration and place them within their political and economic context, (2) to characterize the policy process in Ontario PSE during each administration, and (3) to identify how the policy developments influenced structural arrangements of the postsecondary system. Recognizing that PSE systems operate in very different policy environments influenced by constitutional status, political culture, and federal research and development policies, the focus of this profile is on the relationships between policy priorities and system design, performance, and fiscal arrangements.

The rest of this chapter is divided into six sections. First, we address system coordination arrangements for PSE in Ontario, including the components and governance of the system as well as the funding mechanisms. Second, we trace chronologically the evolution of policy across the four administrations in power between 1985 and 2010, and place these policies within a political-economic context. Third, we identify the major recurring policy themes across administrations, such as accessibility, accountability, developing a competitive economy, and marketization. This section ends with a brief analysis of the policy-making process. Fourth, we trace fiscal policy and the financing of the postsecondary system. This leads into two sections that provide a summary of the impact of the policy themes and the aligned fiscal policies on system design and organization and on a range of outcomes. Here we pay special attention to accessibility, participation and choice, and R&D. Finally, we draw some conclusions about the relationship between the policy environment, system design, and outcomes in Ontario.

CURRENT SYSTEM DESIGN AND FUNDING MECHANISMS

In the centre of Canada geographically, Ontario is Canada's most populous province. The population in 2010 stood at 13.21 million, which represented 39 percent of the total population of Canada.[1] Between 1986 and 2010, the total population of the province grew from approximately 9.4 million, or by approximately 40 percent. Growth has been remarkably even through this period, ranging between a low of 100,000 to a high of 250,000. Over the same period, the province's 18- to 24-year-old population slowly decreased over the first ten years and then very gradually grew beginning in 1997. The 18- to 24-year-old population had, thus, recorded a very small increase from 1.19 million in 1986 to 1.29 million in 2010. In 2010, the 18- to 24-year-old population of Ontario, as a proportion of the total Canadian 18- to 24-year-old population, was 39 percent and, therefore, consistent with the overall population ratio. The pattern for the 18- to 29-year-old population is quite similar to that for the 18- to 24-year-olds in that the numbers are remarkably stable. Over the same period, the province's 18- to 29-year-old population increased for the first three years and then declined gradually from

1989 to 1998. From then through to 2010 the population gradually increased to a level slightly above that in 1986. The 18- to 29-year-old population recorded a small decrease from 2.06 million in 1986 to 2.21 million in 2010. In 2010, the 18- to 29-year-old population of Ontario as a proportion of the total Canadian 18- to 29-year-old population was 38.5 percent and, therefore, was consistent with the overall population ratio.

COMPONENTS OF POSTSECONDARY EDUCATION

Ontario's postsecondary system consists of universities, colleges of applied arts and technology (CAATs), agricultural colleges, and colleges of health sciences and of art, a military college, privately funded degree-granting institutions, and registered private career colleges. Historically, it has been referred to as a binary system because the two dominant sectors, publicly funded universities and publicly funded CAATs, are distinct and run parallel to one another. Further, the two sectors were divided along degree-granting lines.

Recently, however, Ontario has seen changes that have expanded degree-granting authority and resulted in new arrangements between universities and colleges. With the passage of the PSE Choice and Excellence Act, 2000, organizations wishing to offer a program leading to a degree or to advertise as a university must have the consent of the minister of training colleges and universities (MTCU) or obtain this authority under an act of the Legislative Assembly of Ontario. As a consequence of this act, limited degree-granting authority has been expanded to the colleges and to out-of-province public and private institutions upon consent of the minister. By 2010, eleven out-of-province public and private institutions and nineteen in-province public and private institutions were offering programs leading to a degree under a ministerial consent.[2] Consequently, it is becoming more difficult to neatly classify Ontario as a strictly binary system broken down along degree-granting lines.

PUBLICLY FUNDED INSTITUTIONS

Universities

Ontario has twenty publicly funded universities, including nine French-language and bilingual universities.[3] Each university offers undergraduate (bachelor's) degrees, and most offer graduate (master's and doctorate) degrees. Each institution operates independently and determines its own academic and admissions policies, programs, and staff appointments. The MTCU provides funding to the universities and gives them degree-granting authority, originally under the Degree Granting Act, 1983, and currently under the PSE Choice and Excellence Act, 2000.[4] Each publicly funded university in Ontario operates under its own distinct provincial charter (an act of the provincial legislature) as an independent not-for-profit corporation.

The Colleges of Applied Arts and Technology

In 1965, the Government of Ontario created the Colleges of Applied Arts and Technology (CAATs). CAATs are publicly funded institutions. The MTCU approves programs offered by these colleges and is responsible for their overall governance. The goal of CAATs, as originally conceived, was to be a distinct sector from the universities but of comparable quality and status. The central objective of CAATs is to serve the needs of the labour market. The occupational education function is generally regarded as one of the most important functions of a community college. Unlike hierarchical relationships between community colleges and universities found elsewhere in North America, with the former serving as feeder institutions for the latter through a transfer process, in Ontario the founders of CAATs explicitly rejected the transfer model. Instead they envisioned CAATs as being first-rate technical institutes and adult education centres offering a comprehensive applied curriculum. The decision to not include a university transfer function was a controversial issue in the establishment of CAATs and in the history to follow. Difficulties surrounding articulation arrangements and transfer functions between CAATs and the universities have resurfaced repeatedly over the last forty-five years in Ontario. The need for better coordination between the two sectors has been called for in numerous government commissions and reports.

In 2010, there were twenty-four publicly funded CAATs in Ontario. Many CAATs have more than one campus location across the province. Two colleges are French-language colleges. When created, CAATs initially offered only diplomas and certificates under the Ministry of Colleges and Universities Act, 1971. However, with the passage of the new PSE Choice and Excellence Act, 2000, applied degree-granting status has been extended to some CAATs, and the government has created new hybrid institutions that combine elements of a university and a CAAT. Five CAATs had been designated, but, by 2010, only three were using the title Institute of Technology and Advanced Learning (ITALS).[5]

PRIVATELY FUNDED INSTITUTIONS

Institutions with Degree-Granting Authority

Under the Degree Granting Act, 1982, seventeen privately funded institutions had been granted restricted degree-granting authority by an act of the Legislative Assembly of Ontario (See appendix 3). All are bible colleges or small religious-affiliated institutions. All but two (Institute for Christian Studies and Redeemer University College) are restricted to granting "religious" degrees. The Institute for Christian Studies has the authority to grant master's degrees in counselling, and Redeemer has the authority to offer secular degrees such as a BAs, BEds, and BScs in addition to theological degrees, though the act is somewhat restrictive in its language. By 2009, under the new PSE Choice and Excellence Act, 2000, nine new ministerial consents were granted to private (in-province and out-of-province) institutions in a variety of degree program areas. Six of these new consents were given to institutions that already had limited degree-granting authority in Ontario in other disciplines and that were seeking to expand their offerings.[6]

Non-Degree Granting Institutions

By 2010, six hundred private career college campuses were registered in Ontario. Private career colleges have been a part of PSE for many years, several having recently celebrated their one hundredth anniversaries. Although some colleges offer training in a variety of occupations, the majority focus on courses that will prepare students for clearly defined occupations. Private career colleges are privately owned and are operated as commercial enterprises. Any PCC offering vocational training must be registered under the Private Career Colleges Act, 2005, administered by the MTCU, and their programs must be approved by the superintendent of PCCs. Registration of a college under the act means that it has met the minimum requirements set out in Regulation 939 regarding curricula, teacher qualifications, advertising, and refund policies.[7] A number of registered PCCs are eligible to participate in various government financial assistance programs for students. Normally, this assistance applies only to courses that are of twelve weeks duration or longer and that require Grade 12 or equivalent standing for enrolment.

PROVINCIAL COORDINATION OF PSE

Prior to the 1960s, the provinces took an institutional approach to coordination of the postsecondary system, which meant that the government dealt with institutions on an individual basis. However, as in other provinces, in Ontario the pressure to expand the system and to increase access led first to the creation of CAATs in 1965 and then to the move towards sector coordination in the early 1970s for both the universities and CAATs. Although universities and colleges operated under the same ministry in Ontario, each was a distinct sector, with distinct roles and regulatory mechanisms. Consequently, policy discussions in PSE in Ontario have typically revolved around the particular sector rather than around the totality of the system (Cameron and Royce 1996; Jones 1997b; Jones, Skolnik, and Soren 1998).

Almost every province experimented with some form of intermediary governing body focused on university-sector policy. Ontario created the Committee on University Affairs and then, in 1974, the Ontario Council on University Affairs (OCUA). Both incarnations were advisory bodies to the Ontario minister responsible for universities and did not have executive decision-making authority. OCUA was dismantled in 1996 by the Progressive Conservative (PC) government. In 2005, the Ontario government created an independent agency, the Higher Education Quality Council of Ontario (HEQCO), to advise the government on the best ways to measure quality in the system and to conduct research on quality, participation, and accessibility (Shanahan and Jones 2007). However, currently no buffer institution is in place. Consequently, universities in Ontario deal with the provincial government, either individually or collectively, through the Council of Ontario Universities (COU).[8]

In the university-sector, structural arrangements have been characterized by a high level of institutional autonomy for universities, the strict regulation of degree granting by government, and the equal treatment of institutions with regard to the distribution of provincial grants within the university sector (Jones 1997b). Historically, the government controlled expansion of the university sector by strictly controlling authority to grant degrees. Originally, this was accomplished by giving funding only to secular institutions, then, in 1983, the Degree Granting Act was passed, legally securing the provincial government's monopoly over degree granting by limiting expansion of the sector and regulating out-of-province institutions offering degrees in Ontario (Jones 1997b; Skolnik 1987). In 2000, the PSE Choice and Excellence Act (PSCE Act) was passed to replace the Degree Granting Act, 1983. The new act expanded degree granting to the colleges, out-of-province institutions, and the private sector, albeit under certain conditions and only if authorized by an act of the Legislative Assembly of Ontario or with the consent of the minister of training, colleges and universities.

The Postsecondary Education Quality Assessment Board (PEQAB) assesses applications for ministerial consent referred to it from the minister of training, colleges and universities under the PSCE Act and makes recommendations to the minister based on national and international academic quality assurance standards. Since PEQAB's inception in 2001 up to 31 March 2010, 351 applications to offer degree programs have been submitted from a total of sixty-one institutions (private, public in-province, public out-of-province, and CAATs). Of the 351 applications received, 316 have been completed, seventeen are still under review, and eighteen have been withdrawn. In 2009–10 alone, thirty applications were received (these included applications for consent to offer undergraduate or graduate degrees, or renewal/amending existing consents). Sixteen of these applications were from seven CAATs, thirteen were from six public organizations and one was from a private organization. As of 31 March 2010, seventeen applications remained under review (seven from CAATs, six from private organizations, and four from public organizations (see table 3.1).

The intermediary role between CAATs and the government was formerly assumed by the Ontario Council of Regents for Colleges of Applied Arts and Technology. The council was a provincial agency established under the Ministry of Colleges and Universities Act, 1971, to provide advice to the minister responsible for the college sector. Recent changes to CAATs governing legislation – the Ontario Colleges of Applied Arts and Technology Act, 2002, and Regulation

Table 3.1
Applications submitted to PEQAB 2001–10

Type of institution	Institutions	Completed applications	Withdrawn applications	Applications under review	Total applications received
Private	25	31	10	6	47
Public in-province	6	79*	2	1	82
Public out-of-province	9	29	4	3	36
CAAT	21	177	2	7	186
Total	61	316	18	17	351

Source: PEQAB Annual Report, 2009–10, 9.

* The public in-province applications include seventy-five applications from the University of Ontario Institute of Technology, which were reviewed by the board prior to the university receiving its degree-granting authority in legislation (in 2007). Similarly, Algoma University does not have full degree-granting authority under its act (passed 2008) and must seek ministerial consent for all new degree programs.

34/03 – have transformed this body into the Colleges Compensation and Appointments Council (CCAC) and provided the colleges with more autonomy and responsibility for their programs.[9] In addition, the revised act created an oversight body for the college's self-regulatory mechanism for quality assurance and improvement called the Ontario Colleges Quality Assurance Service (OCQAS). The OCQAS implements two mechanisms for quality assurance: the Credentials Validation Service (CVS) at the program level and the Program Quality Assurance Process Audit (PQAPA) at the institutional level (Colleges Ontario 2006, 2007). The council's responsibilities are fourfold: (1) providing advice and/or strategic planning, (2) appointing college boards and dealing with governance issues, (3) collective bargaining and human resource management, and (4) other roles and responsibilities assigned by the minister.

CAATs are governed by individual boards. Some elements of system governance are highly centralized: the CCAC appoints governors to the college boards across the province and the provincial government approves curricula.[10] Under the Colleges Collective Bargaining Act, 1990, the council has the authority to act as the agent for the employers (the provincial government) in negotiating collective agreements with academic and support staff at the colleges who are members of the Ontario Public Service Employees Union (OPSEU). The council is also responsible for making recommendations to the minister regarding salaries and terms and conditions of employment for administrative staff.[11] Interview data suggested that recent changes to the CAATs' charter legislation had indeed increased the Governing Board's powers and diminished the council's role in collective bargaining and board appointments. The legislation underpinning the new college charter changed the relationship between CAATs and the government from "a command and control model, to an accountable for results model" (Charles 2011, 278). The new governance arrangements and organizational forms set out in the legislation for CAATs allow for greater responsibility and flexibility; however, they are still subject to the minister's directives, and final executive decision-making authority still resides with the minister. Therefore, it is unclear whether these changes have led to more overall autonomy for CAATs.

Fiscal Arrangements

The largest source of revenue for the public postsecondary system comes from provincial operating grants. Provincial funds for PSE are drawn from the general revenue of the province (which includes any federal government transfers and provincial tax revenue). While part of the annual provincial government's budget is set aside for education, other provincial ministries outside of education have, on occasion, been involved in initiatives that have benefited education.[12]

Over the past two decades, provincial governments in Ontario have utilized a variety of mechanisms to determine operating grants to fund the postsecondary system. These include General Purpose Operating Gants (GPOG) and Special Purpose Operating Grants (SPOG). To determine the share of general operating grants allocated to each institution, Ontario has used enrolment-based funding formulas. The provincial government determines the overall level of grant available to each sector, and separate formulas for universities and colleges are used to determine the size of grant given to each institution. In general terms, both formulas focus on enrolment by program, and different program weights are used in order to account for the variable costs of delivering more expensive programs, such as medicine (Alberta 2005).

A number of commissions have advised the Ontario government to consider alternative funding models (such as a student-driven funding system) to replace some or all of the government's grants to the colleges and universities. One initiative for universities – the corridor funding negotiations – was implemented between 1986 and 1990. With this mechanism, funding corridors and negotiated enrolment benchmarks were combined with the existing enrolment-based funding formula in order to meet system-level needs. Institutions negotiated enrolment and funding activity levels with OCUA, and increases or decreases in enrolment were "planned." The result was stable funding shares of operating support as long as institutions did not go beyond their planned targets plus or minus 3 percent of the formula enrolment calculations. The corridor system was designed to allow universities to plan by decreasing the impact of modest fluctuations in enrolment (Royce 1998; Jones 1997b).

The college funding model during this time period was also based on student enrolment, but it was much more responsive to changes in enrolment than was the university formula. Colleges that increased their share of provincial enrolment by growing faster than their peers received a larger share of the provincial grant. The formula led to a competition between the colleges for more students to maintain their share of operating grants.

In addition to the GPOG, special funding programs have been created at different junctures over the last two decades by different administrations to address special purposes (e.g., supporting access for underrepresented groups such as students with disabilities and Aboriginal students) and to support grants for bilingual programs and northern and rural projects. Other special purpose grants include Differentiation Grants, which explicitly support differences among institutional missions, thus enabling institutions to develop their own mandates.[13] Additionally, various governments have created envelopes of funding that are targeted (or tied or matched) to enrolment growth in certain programs.[14] Since the mid-1990s, Ontario governments have toyed with connecting funding to performance. In 1998, key performance indicators were introduced in both the universities and CAATs sectors. In 2000–01, the government announced performance funding attached to indicators in two envelopes (one for accessibility and one for performance) to which institutions could gain access if they met the benchmarked performance indicators. Although the amount of funding attached to them was small (approximately 2 percent of provincial operating grant support), this was the first time in Canada that funding was attached to performance indicators.

Elements of the operating grant allocation formulas were modified to encourage system expansion in the early 2000s. Following detailed negotiations, the province agreed to provide additional support to encourage the expansion of undergraduate enrolment, which was required in response to the double-cohort of 2003, and similar modifications were introduced to encourage enrolment growth in graduate programs a few years later.

In 2005, the provincial government introduced yet another funding approach, multi-year accountability agreements (MYAAs), whereby significant investment in PSE was accompanied by performance agreements for each institution. The MYAAs were instituted as three-year, bilateral agreements starting in 2006–07 and were in force until the 2008–09 academic years, at which time they were extended to 2009–10 to allow for transition into a redefined accountability framework that reflected new directions for the next three-year cycle.[15] The agreements outline the government's commitment to stable funding as well as each institution's commitment to accountability, quality improvements, and the measurement of results, and they "*tie*[*d*] ... [government] commitments to [institutional] results" (HEQCO 2009a, 1). In a Letter of Advice to the MTCU minister, HEQCO chair, Frank Iacobucci, states: "The agreements define goals and system-wide measurements alongside institution specific 'Action Plans' of indicators and quantifiable targets" (ibid.).

The government funding for this initiative is contained in an envelope known as the Quality Improvement Fund (QIF). The MTCU provides QIF funding *after* institutions have demonstrated they have met their targets.[16] Where an institution fails to meet its targets, the minister withholds a portion of its QIF funding until satisfactory completion of a "Report Back" review confirms that it is back on track for meeting its commitments and provides evidence that an improvement plan, approved by the MTCU, is in place.

Although QIF funding is supposed to be dependent on institutions making their targets in identified areas, in the first generation of MYAAS (2006–09) even HEQCO was concerned that "the link between reporting and funding is unclear" (HEQCO 2009a, 2). While there is evidence that many institutions engaged in the report back process, suggesting they may have failed initially to reach their goals, it is less clear if any institution ultimately lost funding.[17]

The MYAAs augment existing performance, accountability, and funding arrangements. They retain existing key performance indicators (KPIs) and add others, including student retention and the results of the National Survey on Student Engagement (NSSE) and the Canadian Graduate and Professional Student Survey (CGPSS) (See Alberta 2005; HEQCO 2009b; OCUFA 2006a, 2006b, 2007a; York University 2006a). In addition to provincial grants, student tuition fees are an important source of funding for postsecondary institutions. In 2008–09, 52 percent of total college revenue came from provincial operating grants. Tuition fees made up approximately 22 percent of college revenue. The remaining amounts came from various sources, including federal, municipal, and provincial grants; international student fees; adult training and ancillary and other fees; and the private sector (Ontario Colleges 2010, 3–4).

In the university sector in 2004–05, provincial grants made up 56 percent of operating income while tuition made up 36 percent of operating revenue. Other sources of income – including municipal and other government grants, bequests, donations, sale of products, investment income, and federal government grants such as SSHRC, CHST, NSERC, CIHR, and other grants – made up 8.1 percent of university operating income (Council of Ontario Universities 2007, 15). By 2009–10, government grants and contracts accounted for 52 percent of total income for universities from all sources. This proportion remained fairly constant over the five-year period between 2005 and 2010, at just over 50 percent of total revenue from all sources. Tuition accounted for 29 percent of total income from all sources in 2009–10. Investment and donation income stood at 7 percent and 4 percent, respectively, of total income from all sources for universities. Investment income in actual dollars and in percentage of total income increased significantly in 2009–10 over the previous two years.[18]

POLITICAL ECONOMY AND PSE POLICY: 1985–2010

Political Context

Ontario's political context has been shaped by its geographical size, its multicultural population, and its rich resources. Ontario is the second largest province in Canada, spanning more than 1 million square kilometres (more than France and Spain combined), with a population of 13 million. Approximately 80 percent of the province's people live in urban centres around the Great Lakes. English is Ontario's first language, although French language rights have been extended to the legal and educational systems. Francophones in Ontario make up 4.8 percent of the population. Approximately 240,000, or 2 percent, of Ontario's people identify as Aboriginal, including peoples from thirteen North American First Nations, Métis, and Inuit peoples. This means that approximately 20 percent of Canada's Aboriginal people live in Ontario. Additionally, half of Canada's annual immigration (approximately 250,000) chooses to live in Ontario, making it a very culturally diverse province.[19]

Ontario is rich in natural resources: water, forests, fish/wildlife, minerals, energy, parks, and protected areas. However, Ontario's economy leans more towards manufacturing, finance, and business, especially service sectors, and less towards agriculture, forestry, and mining. In 2010, Ontario's northern economy depended upon natural resources, while its southern economy was more industrialized. Ontario makes up approximately 40 percent of Canada's total employment. Although Ontario's place in Canada's economy is central, over the past thirty years it has evolved from being "Canada's heartland," according to which its interests and Canada's were seen to be aligned, into a North American "region-state" whose interests are now more connected to, and influenced by, the continental economy (Courchene and Telmer 1998). Over recent years, Ontario's relationship with the Canadian economic union has become more strained. Tensions revolved around preferential federal equalization payments that redistribute wealth to disadvantaged provinces. Successive governments have argued that Ontario contributes a disproportionate amount to this program as well as to others.

Ontario's political system, like Canada's, is a parliamentary system based on the British system of government. Elections are held every four to five years, and three major parties dominate the political landscape: the New Democratic Party (NDP), the Liberal Party, and the Progressive Conservative Party (PC). Between 1985 and 2010, Ontario had four different political administrations: the Liberals under David Peterson (1985–90), the NDP under Bob Rae (1990–95); the PC under Mike Harris (1995–2002) and then Ernie Eves (April 2002–October 2003); and the Liberals under Dalton McGuinty (October 2003–2010).[20]

The Liberals: 1985–90

In June 1985, the PC minority government led by Frank Miller received a vote of non-confidence in the provincial legislature. A coalition government, led by Liberal leader David Peterson with the support of the NDP led by Bob Rae, assumed office. The coalition government continued until 1987, when an election was called and Peterson's Liberals won a strong majority government.

In taking power in 1985, the Peterson Liberals not only toppled a forty-three-year Tory dynasty but also brought in a new socio-economic era referred to as Ontario's "quiet revolution" (Courchene and Telmer 1998, 70). In part, their victory was due to the Liberal-NDP Accord, which subsequently dictated much of the Liberal government's policy in Peterson's minority government. The Liberals assumed leadership when Ontario was in "full economic bloom." A strong economic climate continued throughout their administration, and this is described as a "golden era" for Ontario (5). In its postwar history, this was a period of unparalleled economic growth for Ontario. The combination of a strong economic climate and a social policy agenda driven by the Liberal-NDP Accord resulted in increased government spending and the advancement of Ontario's social policy agenda. During this period, Ontario emerged as a social policy leader in Canada.

Ontario's economic policy agenda at this time was geared to ensure Ontario's international economic competitiveness, focusing on the key areas of human capital and the information/technology revolution. With the establishment of the Premier's Council on Technology in 1986, which provided $1 billion in provincial funding over ten years to steer Ontario to the forefront of technological innovation, Peterson's was the first Ontario government whose economic policies attempted to respond to globalization and the knowledge/information revolution.[21] To accomplish its goals in this area, the government actively intervened in the economy. However, the economic agenda never superseded the social policy agenda of this administration.

The booming Ontario economy proved incapable of financing the expensive revolution in spite of the successive tax hikes that took Ontario from one of the lowest tax jurisdictions to one of the highest during this administration. The tax-and-spend approach of the Liberals proved insufficient to support the social agenda and left little room to generate much needed revenue through further hikes. Eventually, the economic bubble burst in Ontario in late 1989 and early 1990. At the same time as the economic downturn, Ontario's social assistance spending was set to expand under a newly legislated program. Additionally, the federal government's 1990 budget imposed a cap on the Canada Assistance Plan, which was applicable only to the wealthy provinces, and this further exacerbated the financial strains in Ontario. However, it was the newly elected NDP government (1990) that was met with these challenging fiscal problems.

Funding PSE was a concern for the Liberal government. Jones (1997b) explains that, during this period, the government's two most important goals were accessibility and reducing/stabilizing the level of government funding. The Liberal government focused on funding and, particularly, the mechanism for allocating operating grants in PSE. Its priorities may have been set in part by the burgeoning participation in and demand for PSE, which went beyond all predictions, for both the university and college sectors (Cameron and Royce 1996).

During the Liberal Party's reign a new corridor funding mechanism was introduced in the university sector and new targeted funding envelopes were created (OCUA 1988).[22] In addition, an $84 million accessibility fund was created by the Liberal government in 1987–88 to fund unexpected and significant enrolment growth. This fund provided additional revenue for institutions beyond their corridor entitlements. However, in doing this, Royce (1998, 189–90) points out the government actually undermined the effect of the corridor funding: "This special funding program effectively over-rode the intended enrolment insensitivity of the corridor system and resulted in a formula that was highly sensitive to enrolment."[23]

Funding and governance were key issues for CAATs during this time period. Operating grant support was determined by an enrolment-sensitive formula rewarding growth,[24] which resulted in increased competition between CAATs for enrolment. Labour relations in CAATs were also contentious. At issue were workloads, salaries, collective bargaining, and the relationship between the Council of Regents (as management) and the colleges in the collective bargaining process. Province-wide strikes occurred in 1984 and again in 1989. In 1985, Walter Pittman, then executive director of the Ontario Arts Council, was appointed to advise the minister on "the current governance structures of Ontario's college system." Pittman's report is entitled *The Report of the Advisor to the Minister of Colleges and Universities on the Governance of the Colleges of Applied Arts and Technology*. It recommended structural changes to the governance of CAATs, establishing an advisory council on the colleges, and shifting of functions and responsibilities away from the Council of Regents to the college level. The government did redefine the role of the Council of Regents and modified the composition of college boards after the release of the report, but substantial changes were not made to CAATs' governance arrangements (Cameron and Royce 1996).[25]

Although the Liberals did not attempt any major structural changes to the overall PSE sectors, they did attempt to link PSE policy to the province's economic agenda. Ontario's PSE policy at this time was focused on economic globalization, strengthening the province's science and technology infrastructure, and stimulating university-industry research partnerships (Lang et al. 1999). The largest initiative was the December 1987 creation of Ontario Centres of Excellence based on recommendations from the Premier's Council on Technology. These publicly supported research corporations linked universities and industry and were meant to stimulate advanced research, to train and develop researchers, and to encourage technology transfer to industry.[26] They were partly funded through the Premier's Council Technology Fund and the University Research Incentive Fund (URIF).[27]

The Premier's Council also released a major report entitled *People and Skills in the New Global Economy* (Government of Ontario 1990). This report made recommendations with respect to postsecondary coordination and planning. It suggested viewing Ontario's PSE as a continuum allowing for life-long learning opportunities, viewing the community colleges and universities in a "postsecondary context" instead of as two discrete sectors, and establishing credit transfer arrangements between colleges and universities. The report called for a co-coordinating council to deal with transferability and continuity across the system (i.e., admission requirements, program standards, degree requirements, and transfer of credits). As the decade drew to a close the lack of formal interaction between the two sectors, including problems associated with credit recognition when students transferred between the sectors, was a point of contention among constituents in PSE.

In 1988, the Ministry of Colleges and Universities asked the Council of Regents to review the Ontario CAATs to develop a vision for the year 2000. Charles Pascal, chair of the Council of Regents at the time and subsequently the deputy minister of education under the NDP government, organized the task force. The final report was released in 1990 as *Vision 2000* (Ontario Ministry of Colleges and Universities 1990). It affirmed the original mandate and role of CAATs. It recommended increased cooperation between the universities and CAATs, increased student mobility between sectors, and the development of an "institute without walls" to facilitate the coordination of arrangements between universities and colleges. These recommendations led to the eventual development of a government transfer guide (in 1994 during the NDP administration) and an increase in articulation arrangements between individual universities and colleges. However, this report did not ultimately resolve the issue of university/college relations because nobody transcended both sectors. One of its major recommendations was that CAATs should have periodic program reviews and reviews of system-wide quality standards. This led to the creation of the College Standards and Accreditation Council (CSAC).

Another recommendation was the call for a task force to examine how the province could meet its advanced training needs. Walter Pittman returned to the sector to chair this task force which released a final report entitled *No Dead Ends: Report of the Task Force on Advanced Training to the Minister of Education and Training* (Task Force on Advanced Training 1993). Published in 1993 (during the NDP administration), the report addressed the challenges of the technologically dominated economy. Recommendations included system changes to link colleges, universities, businesses, and industry and to design advanced training. It also recommended the development of credit transfer policies and practices. Steps taken in response to the task force's recommendations included, in 1996, the creation of the College University Consortium Council (CUCC), a voluntary consortium designed to promote college-universities cooperation.

Other concerns for the Liberals included the need for French-language postsecondary programs for franco-Ontarians, addressing the special costs associated with postsecondary programs in the North, and developing mechanisms to support postsecondary research overhead costs. Three CAATs, in which French was a primary language of instruction, had been added to the system by 1993 to address the needs of franco-Ontarians. A cost-sharing agreement with the federal government made the establishment of the three new French-language colleges possible (Cameron and Royce 1996; Jones 1997b; Royce 1998).[28]

The New Democratic Party: 1990–95

Bob Rae's NDP government inherited the Liberal's legacy when David Peterson was unexpectedly defeated in the 1990 election. The

NDP was elected on the platform "Agenda for the People," which continued the social agenda of the Liberal/NDP Accord. The agenda included new taxes for the wealthy and corporations, tax relief for the poor, increased funding to public schools, and a myriad of other promises, including government-run auto insurance, employment equity and other employment protection plans, increased social assistance, environment protection initiatives, and resources to improve conditions in Ontario's North. Patrick Monahan (1995, 16) observes, "Running through the agenda was a single theme: resources should be allocated by state planners rather than by private markets, to redistribute wealth rather than create it."

Most of the agenda did not survive the economic downswing of the early 1990s, the only significant exception being employment equity. The NDP entered office during the worst recession in Ontario since the 1930s. In fact, the 1990 recession triggered such dramatic revenue collapses that Ontario thrice qualified for stabilization payment during Bob Rae's mandate. However, the federal government had altered the program by this time and had limited the maximum payout. The changes detrimentally affected Ontario's benefit from the program.[29]

This administration was mired in debt and deficits flowing from the expansion of the welfare system, the federal government's transfer cuts in the 1990s, and the 1990 recession. Its first budget exacerbated the situation by enacting further increases in welfare benefits, which were to take effect on 1 January 1991. By 1992, the NDP was forced to retrench the system and introduced the "STEP down" initiative. Other NDP initiatives, such as the social contract and employment equity (both continuations of Ontario's quiet revolution),[30] proved unpopular to some and further challenged mainstream party support.[31]

During its administration the NDP increased Ontario's debt by $60 billion over and above the $42 billion debt it had inherited from the Liberals. It also progressively increased taxes to make Ontario one of the highest taxed provinces. Courchene and Telmer (1998, 6, 141) argue that this effectively set the successor government's fiscal direction: the next government would have to "place fiscal conservatism at the core of its platform" and the province's economic circumstances "invited a dramatic retrenchment."

The NDP government followed the Liberals lead in terms of employing PSE policy to build upon university and industry linkages and to increase industrial and technological developments, but with a greater emphasis on equity and social mobility (Lang et al. 1999). Two issues dominated postsecondary policy decisions during this era: (1) accessibility in light of restrictive funding levels and (2) improving university accountability.

Accountability had become an issue as a result of the provincial auditor's audit of three universities between 1988 and 1990 (Cameron and Royce 1996; Royce 1998). Comprehensive provincial audits were subsequently recommended. In 1991, William Broadhurst, a member of the Ontario Council on University Affairs (OCUA), was asked by the minister to chair the Task Force on University Accountability, which focused on accountability at the institutional level and the role of governing boards. In 1993, the Broadhurst Report, *University Accountability: A Strengthened Framework* (OCUA 1993b), recommended an institutionally based accountability framework with the responsibility for demonstrating accountability assigned to the governing board of each institution. In addition, it was suggested that an independent external agency located within OCUA should be set up to monitor accountability (Royce 1998). Although the report was accepted, the external monitoring body suggested by the task force was never established. In part, this was because it lacked a system perspective and focused narrowly on accountability within each institution in isolation rather than on how well all the institutions together as a system were meeting the public's needs (Cameron and Royce 1996; Royce 1998; Skolnik 1994).

At the same time as the Broadhurst task force, Minister of Colleges and Universities Richard Allen asked OCUA to provide advice on how to establish a system of program review for academic quality for universities. OCUA's response was controversial in the postsecondary community.[32] It recommended the establishment of a province-wide systemic quality review process at the undergraduate level (noting that, for graduate programs across Ontario's universities, the Ontario Council on Graduate Studies had had an appraisal process in place since the late 1960s). Royce (1998, 208) suggests that this was a "monitored self-regulation" approach to accountability for program quality. This would take the form of a publicly appointed, independent body, which would audit institutions to make sure policies and processes were in place for reviewing the quality of undergraduate programs.

In essence the OCUA recommendations on accountability were not new or even radical; rather, they were similar to the Broadhurst Report recommendations (OCUA 1994b). However, they advocated further government intervention in universities in a political environment in which the government was retrenching. University reaction to the OCUA recommendations, especially as they related to establishing another oversight body, was unfavourable. The recommendations were deemed unworkable and the government did not respond. Instead, in 1995, the ministry approved the Education Quality and Accountability Office (EQAO), which was initially contemplated as having responsibility for addressing issues of educational quality and accountability in the elementary/secondary and postsecondary sectors. However, the postsecondary role of the EQAO did not materialize. OCUA went ahead and began the process of establishing its own undergraduate program review process, which was supposed to commence in 1997. However, the government fell, and OCUA was dismantled by the new PC government in 1996 before the first of these reviews could take place. In 1997, the COU subsequently established its own undergraduate program review audit committee for the review of undergraduate program quality (without the external monitoring body recommended by the Broadhurst Report). This COU review continues today.

Tensions between OCUA and the COU were exacerbated in 1993 amid worsening economic conditions. After a cabinet shuffle the new minister of education and training (a combined super ministry), Dave Cooke, asked OCUA to undertake another review of the funding system for universities in Ontario, with the focus on accountability in the context of a resource allocation review. This time OCUA recognized that, in the absence of a system-wide master plan, funding mechanisms had become the government's primary instrument for influencing institutional behaviour. OCUA called for greater flexibility and responsiveness from universities with regard to government policy priorities. It recommended the use of funding mechanisms to make the universities more accountable to government.[33] The new recommendations were seen as making universities instruments of government policy and as challenging university autonomy. The entire exercise linking funding to accountability "was received at the outset with scathing hostility on the part of universities," which argued that institutional autonomy and the independence of intellectual inquiry were essential to the public interest (Royce 1998,

222). By the time OCUA delivered its report in late 1995, the new PC government had taken over, and it deemed the recommendations too complex and disruptive to universities that were dealing with the new government's $400 million budget cuts to the PSE system.[34]

Rae's employment equity legislation and social contract legislation affected the PSE sectors in Ontario. Universities and CAATs were considered part of the broader public sector and were affected by its arrangements and obligations.[35] The University Restructuring Steering Committee, co-chaired by Dr Bernard Shapiro (deputy minister of education) and Colin Graham (then chair of OCUA), was established in 1992. Its mandate was to develop long-term strategies for making the university sector responsive to continuous life-long learning and the needs of the modern economy and, at the same time, to assure the NDP government's access and equity agenda in a time of financial constraint. The committee could have reshaped the postsecondary sectors in Ontario. However, by 1993, the government was making further funding cuts and had shuffled the cabinet. A new "super ministry" (Ministry of Education and Training) was created, integrating elementary, secondary, and PSE. As a result of fiscal developments, the new minister buried the steering committee's report (Royce 1998).

The severe and sudden fiscal constraints facing universities in the 1990s led to a number of developments within institutions across the province. Royce (1998) suggests that the government began to move unilaterally to address these issues, breaking with the tradition of broad consultation with the universities and OCUA.[36] Fiscal restraint was facilitating the rationalization and planning of the system.

During this decade, a number of institutional changes took place. Nipissing College, which was affiliated with Laurentian University, requested independent degree-granting status as early as 1988 during the Liberal government. Royal assent finally came in December 1992 through a private member's bill.[37] Similarly, Ryerson Polytechnic Institute sought to become a polytechnic university during this period. Royal assent was granted in 1993.[38] In 1994, the complete integration of the independent Ontario Institute for Studies in Education (OISE) with the University of Toronto was proposed as the former was under intense financial strain. A complete merger was approved in 1995 by Minister of Education and Training Dave Cooke, with the significant involvement of his deputy minister, Charles Pascal (Royce 1998).

Throughout the 1990s, a major theme of commissions and reports continued to be the need for greater coordination and planning between and within sectors of the postsecondary system. Emphasis was placed on credit-transfer between the sectors so as to facilitate life-long learning. The *Report of the Commission of Inquiry on Canadian University Education* (Association of Universities and Colleges of Canada 1991), led by Stuart L. Smith at the request of the Association of Universities and Colleges of Canada, expressed these concerns and called for greater cooperation within PSE, noting, in particular, the problem of credit transfer between universities. At the suggestion of Smith's 1991 report for national leadership on this issue, in 1995 the CMEC issued a document entitled *Pan-Canadian Protocol on the Transferability of University Credits* (CMEC 1995). This document called on degree-granting institutions to provide a national transferability of credit for first- and second-year university courses. This group of provincial education ministers had no national authority in Canada, but in Ontario OCUA approved the CMEC protocol. Since 1996–97, the CMEC protocol pertaining to the transferability of year one and year two credits among universities has been in force, and all postsecondary institutions in Ontario have complied (Royce 1998). In 1992, the *Transfer of Undergraduate Course Credits among Ontario Universities: Report and Recommendations*, also known as the Baker Report after its chair Donald Baker (vice-president academic of Wilfrid Laurier University), was released and also recommended policies and procedures with respect to transfer of credits among Ontario universities (COU 1992). As a result of the Baker Report, the COU moved towards making credit transfer practices among universities more consistent, and, in 1993, the Ontario universities agreed to a general policy for credit transfer.

The Progressive Conservatives: 1995–2003

The Harris PCs were elected in June 1995, winning eighty-two of 130 seats and 45 percent of the popular vote. They swept to power on a platform known as "the Common Sense Revolution" (CSR) and, within eighteen months, had implemented every tenet of their platform. This government had two foci: (1) to address the province's fiscal situation and (2) to implement a massive municipal and institutional restructuring. Almost immediately it cancelled or reduced nearly all the initiatives of the Liberal-NDP accord, including rolling back welfare benefits by approximately 20 percent, introducing workfare for able-bodied recipients, and abandoning employment equity (Bill 79), labour relations and employment reforms (in the pro-labour Bill 40,) and the Social Contract (Bill 48). The Harris government privileged the economic agenda over the social agenda. It advocated for a smaller, less intrusive government, reduced taxes, privatization, and institutional restructuring (i.e., reorganizing delivery of health care, especially regarding hospitals; reworking provincial and municipal financial arrangements; municipal amalgamation; school board consolidation; and the creation of the Toronto mega-city).

The primacy of the market infused Harris's political agenda. During his government's administration the economy recovered. In 1997, the PC administration enjoyed the lowest interest rates, the lowest inflation rates, and the most competitive economy since the Robarts era of the 1960s (Courchene and Telmer 1998, 47).

The postsecondary agenda for the PCs emerged from a document created by the PC caucus in 1992 entitled *New Directions II: A Blueprint for Learning in Ontario* (Ontario Progressive Conservative Caucus 1992).[39] Through advocating for a smaller role for government in university affairs and financing, increased partnership funding, and increased contributions to PSE on the part of students, the government, and the private sector, the *Blueprint for Learning* foreshadowed increased tuition fees, an expanded student loan program, income-contingent loan-repayment schemes, and an increase in institutional scholarship and bursary programs. It also suggested greater private-sector support for PSE research and development. For the PCs, institutional competition and productivity were recurring themes. Postsecondary institutions were encouraged to diversify, specialize, and capture niche markets in either graduate or undergraduate studies. The *Blueprint* proposed public accountability through value-for-money audits of universities and promised to lift the restrictions on the ability of private institutions to grant degrees.

Shortly after taking power, Minister of Finance Ernie Eves announced a $400 million cut from postsecondary operating grants. This was followed by the new minister of education and training's decision to review government postsecondary policy, specifically calling for "universities ... to restructure and rationalize ... [a]nd planning for major change, fundamental change, in the way you work. It [would] mean downsizing, rationalizing, even eliminating in some areas" (Royce 1998, 237 quoting remarks of the Honourable John Snobelon, 8 November 1995, to the Board Chairs of Ontario Universities), restructuring, rationalizing, eliminating, and cutting on a scale never before seen in the postsecondary system (Royce 1998). A "blue ribbon committee," known as the Advisory Panel on Future Directions for PSE (also known as the David Smith Commission), was struck. This was the first commission since 1972 that examined the postsecondary system as a whole (other committees and reviews had focused only on the university or college sectors). The panel was given an extremely short time frame of five months within which to research and release its report. The report, entitled *Excellence, Accessibility and Responsibility*, was released in December 1996. It affirmed the principle of institutional autonomy within a strengthened accountability framework but also called for a less regulated PSE environment. The thrust of the report emphasized: the restoration of public funding; assigning greater responsibility to governing boards of institutions in order to demonstrate accountability; a larger role for governing bodies of colleges and universities; differentiation among institutions; stronger student financial aid; tuition deregulation; stronger support for research and innovation; and focused incentives to encourage private-sector support and partnerships with universities and colleges.[40] The panel affirmed the basic binary structure of Ontario's postsecondary sectors, endorsing the structural status quo. However, it recommended establishing a body on postsecondary matters covering colleges and universities in order to produce research and to oversee institutional accountability but not to undertake system coordination and planning. The panel placed the task of postsecondary quality assurance in the hands of the governing boards of institutions. It rejected the approach of British Columbia and Alberta, which treated postsecondary sectors and institutions as components of an integrated system. The panel supported a parallel system of differentiated colleges and universities and endorsed the continuing work and funding of the CUCC.[41] The report is significant for its broad review of the PSE system in Ontario and its acceptance of Ontario's ad hoc approach to policy coordination and planning.

Soon after taking power the PC government began advocating for a system of postsecondary accountability that included reporting on key performance indicators (KPIs) in addition to meeting the existing reporting requirements of academic senates and governing boards as well as the quality reviews undertaken by the COU.[42] In addition to announcing the creation of the Public Sector Accountability Act, which requires public-sector organizations (including universities, colleges, hospitals, municipalities, schools boards, and social service agencies) to account for their budgets, business plans, and so on, the Ontario government required all colleges and universities to report on a set of KPIs for each program as an expression of their commitment to increased accountability to stakeholders in education. The full set of KPIs for colleges and universities was first reported in 1999. Colleges reported on graduation rates, graduation employment rates six months after graduation, graduate satisfaction rates, employer satisfaction rates, and student loan default rates. Universities reported on graduation rates, graduation employment rates six months after graduation and again at two years after graduation, and student loan default rates.

At this point KPIs were mandated for reporting purposes only. After initial funding cuts to universities, the PC government slowly began to reinvest. The new operating funding was delivered in envelopes and tied to enrolment growth and university performance.[43] By March 2000, a small portion of postsecondary funding (approximately 2 percent of total operating support) was linked to key performance indicators through the performance funding envelope. As noted earlier, while the amount of funding attached to performance indicators was small in relation to total grant support, it was a significant change and was a harbinger of the direction of future policy.

Further increases in operating grants to universities and colleges came in the 2001 budget to accommodate increased enrolment anticipating the "double cohort."[44] In addition to increases in operating grant support other funding came in the form of ongoing special purpose grants connected to the Access to Opportunities Fund (ATOP) and increases in northern grants.[45] The Ontario Ministry of Education and Training had first announced the ATOP program in May 1998. In response to lobbying from the information technology and communications sector, led by Nortel, the 1998 Ontario budget provided $150 million over three years to double entry-level enrolments at universities in computer science and high-demand areas of engineering by September 2000, and to increase entry-level enrolments in related college programs by 50 percent.

In addition to these funding envelopes the government provided each participating university or college with one-time program expansion funding on a "matching" basis (up to defined maximums based on actual enrolment). The government would match dollar-for-dollar private-sector cash and/or in-kind contributions towards eligible one-time expansion costs. Every eligible dollar contributed by the private sector meant two dollars to the university or college.[46]

The Super Build fund was created by the PCs in 1999. Under this program the government and partners provided capital to the colleges and universities that was directed at expansion, upgrades, and renovations of existing buildings as well as at building new residences. Subsequently, this fund was extended to assist institutions to create new student spaces and to make new hires to support the expanded enrolment of the double cohort as well as new learning resources and tools.[47]

During the PC administration tuition fees were deregulated for graduate and certain professional programs (e.g., tuition was deregulated in business/commerce, dentistry, law, optometry, pharmacy, and veterinary medicine). Fees for undergraduate engineering and computer sciences programs were deregulated following ministerial approval of each university's plans to double the number of entry-level spaces in these programs by September 2000. Undergraduate arts and science programs, as well as other selected professional programs (such as education), continued to be regulated.

The government tuition policy at this time was to balance funding for colleges and universities by bringing tuition fees back to 35 percent of the cost of providing university and college courses. A five-year cap at 2 percent on tuition fees was introduced for most programs over the maximum allowable levels set in 1999–2000. Caps extended over the years when enrolment would be affected by the double cohort. During this administration, average overall student university tuition fees increased more than 60 percent between 1995 and 2001–02.[48]

At the same time, funding for student assistance was increased to maintain accessibility, and universities and colleges were required to set aside 30 percent of tuition increases for need-based student aid. The PC government placed a greater emphasis on matched private-sector funding and increased university spending on student assistance and discipline-specific scholarships instead of enhancing the Ontario Student Assistance Program (OSAP). In 2001, the provincial government created tuition scholarships called Aim for the Top Scholarships, whereby $35 million was invested annually in tuition scholarships. Additionally, through an agreement with the federal government, the Canada Federal Millennium Scholarship Foundation guaranteed that Ontario's share of the Millennium Fund would reflect its population – approximately $113 million a year. Ontario Graduate Scholarships were increased in number and value from $11,859 to $15,000 over three terms, though universities were asked to contribute one-third of the total value of these scholarships, and five hundred of them were awarded annually in science and technology. The Ontario Student Opportunity Trust Fund was created in 1997 to establish a permanent trust fund with a total value of $600 million. This was created through private- and public-sector contributions and was to be distributed by colleges and universities to provide aid for students in need. Funding for the Work Study Program was doubled in the 2000 budget, and $4 million was allocated to free tuition for medical students who agreed to practise in rural and Northern Ontario.

The general thrust of reforms in this area was to deregulate tuition fees in order to increase the role of the market in specific programs areas, especially engineering, information technology, and the professions of law, medicine, and dentistry. Universities and the private sector were asked to play a much larger role in student financial assistance – the universities through allocating need-based support as required under the new deregulated tuition framework and the private sector through new leveraged fund-raising mechanisms (such as the Ontario Student Opportunity Trust and the modified Ontario Graduate Scholarships initiative).

However, at the same time the government's student loan regulations were tightened (tougher credit screening, eligibility requirements, reassessment procedures, and default rate threshold), which translated into fewer recipients of student aid. Government expenditures on student support dropped from $400 million in 1995–96 to $310 million in 2000–01.[49] Also during this period, the Ontario government signed an agreement with the federal government to harmonize loans under the Canada Student Loans Program with loans under provincial student assistance programs.

In September 2000, the government struck the Investing in Students Task Force in response to the double cohort and rising concerns about increasing tuition and fears that the overall cost of PSE would undermine access and quality in universities and colleges.[50] The task force recommended creating a seamless transfer system within PSE and encouraged differentiated missions for postsecondary institutions and supporting institutions to achieve their missions through investment (e.g., polytechnic and other specialized institutions could foster advanced training and skills). It also recommended the establishment of a new college charter by 2003, whereby colleges would continue their evolution as non-profit corporations and generate revenue through new partnerships. The task force further recommended that college boards be fully responsible and accountable for governance; that a clear accountability framework for publicly funded institutions be established, and that each institution make an annual public report on its mission, key strategies and accomplishments, outcomes on performance indicators, student benefits, and audited financial statements.

Once again, greater cooperation between universities and colleges was a theme that emerged from many key government reports on PSE in Ontario during this period. The PC government encouraged credit transfer and joint degree programming. Some Ontario colleges lobbied for degree-granting powers, while the COU opposed college degree granting and argued instead for credit transfers between the two sectors. In May 1999, an Ontario college-university degree completion accord was signed by the college and university sectors. Within a voluntary framework this accord set out principles for developing degree completion arrangements between colleges and universities.

Although the government did not allow for the creation of new private secular postsecondary institutions in its first mandate, this was clearly envisioned in its policy direction document.[51] The government's own Advisory Panel on Future Directions for PSE (1996) recommended the establishment of privately financed, not-for-profit universities under strict conditions developed by an advisory body on PSE. In addition, this panel recommended that "the award of secular degrees should continue to be a responsibility of universities at this time. It should be possible, however, for a college to transform to a polytechnic degree-granting status and from there to a university." In April 2000, the government acted on this advice and passed new legislation for degree granting and operating a university in Ontario entitled the PSE Choice and Excellence Act, 2000.[52] This new degree-granting act permitted organizations to offer programs leading to a degree or to operate a university, either with the consent of the minister of training, colleges and universities or by an act of the Legislative Assembly of Ontario. The act also permitted the Ontario colleges to offer degrees in applied areas subject to the approval of government following recommendations from a new advisory body established under the act.[53] PEQAB was created as a new advisory board to the MTCU and was assigned a number of key roles in assessing applications to offer degree programs in Ontario.[54] All applications for ministerial consent were referred by the minister to PEQAB for recommendation. PEQAB evaluates programs offered in the Province of Ontario by out-of–province institutions and new free-standing institutions. However, existing Ontario degree-granting institutions (except the UOIT) were exempt from PEQAB assessment.[55]

The number of institutions offering degrees in Ontario slowly began to expand following the passage of the PSE Choice and Excellence Act as a number of colleges and out-of-province institutions applied for ministerial consent to offer applied degrees or academic degrees. The government approved legislation to provide degree-granting authority to the Ontario College of Art and Design (OCAD) in July 1991. In addition, in the May 2001 budget the government announced plans to build the University of Ontario Institute of Technology (UOIT), a technical university created in partnership with Durham College and having as one of its purposes the support of the automotive and power industries in the Durham region. On 4 October 2002, the minister of finance and the minister of training, colleges and universities, along with the new UOIT president Gary Polonsky (who was also president of Durham College), announced the first entirely new university to be created in Ontario in almost forty years. The government provided $60 million to establish UOIT through the Super Build Fund.[56] The proposed university was to integrate its campus, administration, and services with Durham College, and it was to link university and college curricula, offering a number of market-driven programs ranging from manufacturing to nuclear technology and safety. By 2007, UOIT offered a range of programs that went beyond this focus, including graduate degrees and its first PhD degree. Moreover, the merging of governance structures and the integrating of financial and administrative mechanisms between UOIT and Durham College created serious accountability concerns that later had to be untangled. By 2007, UOIT had hired its own president (separate from Durham College) and was continuing to work towards achieving independence between Durham College and UOIT's governance and management.⁵⁷

The Liberals: 2003–10

The Liberals, led by Dalton McGuinty, were elected with a majority government in November 2003 on the tide of disenchantment with the PC agenda. They came to power with a plan called Strong People, Strong Economy, which emphasized both social and economic priorities. Education, health, and the economy were the three key priorities. The Liberals inherited an economy that was growing and competitive, with continuing low interest rates and low inflation rates. However, they also inherited a $5.5 billion deficit from the PCs. Shortly after taking office the province experienced a period of slower economic growth that was affected by a weakening US economy, record high oil prices, and a strong Canadian dollar. Nevertheless, the Liberals invested significantly in health care, PSE, and infrastructure and set about reducing the deficit. They proceeded to eliminate the previous government's deficit and then delivered three consecutive surplus budgets between 2004 and 2007.⁵⁸

Throughout the Liberal administration the strength of the US economy, fluctuating oil prices, and fluctuations in the strength of the Canadian dollar continued to affect the Ontario economy. In 2008, the sub-prime mortgage crisis hit the US economy and sent global markets into decline, triggering a worldwide recession that lasted into 2009. The Canadian dollar and stock markets spiralled, as did the Canadian auto industry. Ontario was dramatically affected as revenues collapsed. In 2008, Ontario projected a $500 million deficit and had qualified for an equalization payment for 2009 as a "have-not province" – for the first time in its history. By the fall (2009) budget, the Ontario government was forecasting a deficit of $24.7 billion for 2009–10. The actual 2010 deficit for Ontario came in at $19.3 billion.⁵⁹

Although the Liberals positioned themselves as the party to roll back some of the PC retrenchment initiatives, the unexpected deficit and their emphasis on a strong economy prevented them from entirely doing so. Instead, they took advantage of the deep cuts in government spending and institutional restructuring that the PCs had implemented in the mid-1990s and set about infusing support for social initiatives – to this end spending increased, particularly in the areas of health, education, and welfare. However, they also employed market and audit-type mechanisms to achieve their social objectives. Support was targeted and attached to performance and accountability mechanisms.

An excellent PSE system was a critical element in the Liberal Party's Strong People, Strong Economy platform. In its first budget in 2004, the government acted by announcing a major review of the design and funding of Ontario's postsecondary system (known as the Rae Review and led by the former NDP Ontario premier Bob Rae). The review's mandate was to advise government on strategies to improve PSE by providing recommendations within the context of a publicly funded system offering services in both official languages. The mandate recognized that postsecondary curricula must build both a skilled workforce and promising scholars, and that the system must be integrated, articulated, and differentiated to meet the diverse learning needs of Ontarians. Funding was to be cost-effective and, at the same time, enough to support an accessible, affordable, and quality system. The Rae Review was explicitly asked to consider the appropriate sharing of costs of PSE among government, students, and the private sector and to identify an effective student assistance program that promoted increased access to PSE. Strengthening accessibility was a key concern for policy makers, especially accessibility for groups traditionally underrepresented in Ontario's postsecondary system.[60]

Until the review was completed and recommendations on cost-sharing could be vetted, the Liberals froze tuition fees for two years, announced funding for twenty thousand new spaces in PSE, and announced funding to establish Northern Ontario's first medical school – the Northern Ontario School of Medicine – at Lakehead University (Thunder Bay) and Laurentian University (Sudbury), expanded enrolment in nursing programs, and created a fund to provide additional support for students in PhD nursing programs.

After reviewing and revising existing legislation, the Liberal government proclaimed the new Ontario Colleges of Applied Arts and Technology Act, 2002, which allowed for more diversity in college programs. In turn, in 2004–05, it reviewed the Private Career Colleges Act, which had not been updated for thirty years, and ultimately passed the new Private Career Colleges Act (PCC) to provide more protection for students against financial loss. Some of the key components of this act included: improving access to Ontario student loans for PCC students, establishing the Training Completion Assurance Fund (TCAF), establishing a credential framework, developing key performance indicators for this sector, and improving protection for international students.[61] In 2009–10, the government made further changes to the PCC's regulation, including introducing financial penalties for career colleges that break the law. The government also doubled the number of inspectors from six to twelve, appointed a provincial offences officer, and began to develop a qualifications framework for the career college sector (MTCU 2010).

In February 2005, *Ontario: A Leader in Learning* (the Rae Report) was released. The report made numerous recommendations under five headings: (1) accessibility, (2) quality, (3) system design, (4) funding, and (5) accountability. The Liberal government systematically set about implementing the majority of the recommendations. In the 2005 budget the government formally announced its response to the Rae Report with the multi-year, $6.2 billion *Reaching Higher Plan*.[62] The plan was the largest multi-year investment in PSE that the province had seen in forty years. The government promised substantial investments that would represent a 39 percent funding increase by 2009–10, compared to 2004–05 funding levels. Improved access to colleges and universities, increased quality and accountability, and better facilities were identified as key priorities for PSE. Within two years (in 2007) the government had announced an additional $390 million for postsecondary education to help with infrastructure improvements and rising enrolments.[63] In May 2007, the Liberal government announced plans to introduce legislation to establish an independent Algoma University, further expanding the PSE system and access opportunities for people residing in Ontario's North.[64]

Specifically, the *Reaching Higher Plan* aimed to increase access and participation through outreach and enrolment of underrepresented groups, including Aboriginal students, students with disabilities, and francophone students. The plan included new programs, targeted support for bursaries for students in need, in addition to funding to support additional services. For the first time in Ontario's history, targeted government support was directed at "first-generation" students – students from families that had no history of university or college education ($65 million by 2010). Overall, during the period from 2002–03 through 2009–10 enrolment in colleges and universities increased by 120,000, well exceeding the promised seventy-four thousand FTEs – the greatest increase in demand for PSE education in Ontario in thirty years and representing a 31 percent increase over 2002–03 enrolment levels (COU 2007, 2011a; MTCU 2009, 2010).⁶⁵

According to the COU (2013), support was given to increase graduate enrolment from about 25,000 in 2002–03 to 37,000 in 2008–09, an increase of about 12,000 spaces. Additional funding was provided for another 2,000 students in 2009–10, and a further 1,300 spaces were funded to be phased in by 2011–12, totalling the graduate enrolment increases to over 15,000 between 2002–03 and 2011–12 (COU 2013), which were supported by new government investments of $220 million annually by 2009–10. This represented a 61 percent increase in planned graduate enrolment just between 2002–03 and 2009–10. Further funding supported the increase of one hundred new first-year medical education spaces – an increase of 38 percent over the 2005–06 level. In 2009–10, the first class of doctors graduated from the Northern School of Medicine. Apprenticeship program enrolment was increased by sixty thousand between 2003 and 2010. Northern and rural colleges were targeted for new funding that was to increase access in their communities ($20 million by 2007). A new community-based nursing program was piloted in Northern Ontario. As well, a strategy was implemented to attract international students and to encourage study abroad for Ontario students. General enrolment growth at colleges and universities was supported by special one-time increased funding of $75 million in 2005–06 and by another $155 million in 2009–10 (MTCU 2010, 4).

Another dimension of access – namely, student assistance, was also addressed in the plan. Base funding levels in OSAP were doubled between 2004–05 and 2009–10. Conditions of loan entitlement were improved and expanded to assist more low- and middle-income students as well as single students. The Ontario Student Opportunity Grant program reintroduced up-front grants and continued to limit student debt annually to $7,000 per academic year. Additionally, new grants were offered for first-and second-year dependent students, some in cooperation with the federal government's Canada Millennium Scholarship Foundation. New Ontario Graduate Fellowships were endowed with over $132 million in 2005 to support graduate students plus another $10 million in 2008–09 (MTCU 2010, 22).⁶⁶ A significant dimension of the approach to student assistance involved the college and university institutions. The government provided $50 million annually to match funds raised by colleges and universities to establish endowments for student financial assistance. The Ontario Trust for Student Support (OTSS) was established to provide allocations for smaller institutions with limited fund-raising capacity.

At the same time, the government signalled its intention to deregulate tuition fees as recommended in the Rae Report. The tuition freeze continued until September 2006, when a new tuition framework was put in place. A regulated tuition framework was instituted under which each institution would be held to an *average* overall increase of 5 percent per year and would be required to demonstrate improvements in access and quality. Under this plan, average tuition increases for 2006–07 would be approximately limited to an average of $100 per year for almost 90 percent of college students and about $200 per year for university students.[67]

Improved quality in PSE was another priority set out in the Rae Report. The Liberals intended to address this priority by increasing faculty at colleges and universities to accommodate expanded enrolment targets and to improve student success, though most of the funding increases were directed at expansion and accessibility with few new funds available for quality enhancement. While the rate of provincial operating grants per student was relatively stable or in decline, total operating revenue from *all* sources remained stable or increased slightly over the period as tuition increases and variable soft monies, which included federal grant money, made up for the loss in provincial operating funds. Capital support was provided to ensure medical and graduate schools could accommodate their enrolments. Deteriorating infrastructure was addressed with funding over five years in the amount of $200 million. The Facilities Renewal Program helped institutions repair and maintain facilities, including making them accessible. The 2005 budget also announced new funding in the amount of $5 million to assist in the internationalization of Ontario's postsecondary system.

The Liberal approach to quality included strengthening the student experience. Integral to this dimension of quality was the government's desire to improve pathways for students to move efficiently through Ontario's PSE system. This meant increasing the collaboration and coordination between colleges and universities. Although the government did not tackle formal university-college articulation arrangements by altering the binary structure of postsecondary education, clearly transfer mechanisms between institutions and between sectors were an issue.

Significantly, in the *Reaching Higher Plan*, the government had explicitly signalled its intention to hold institutions accountable for achieving access, participation, and quality goals. One of the government's strategies to improve quality, increase access, and strengthen accountability was to attach accountability mechanisms to the new financial support and expansion of PSE. To achieve this goal, the ministry linked accountability agreements to significant amounts of funding. The *Reaching Higher Plan* promised that, by 2009–10, total base operating grants to colleges and universities were to be increased by $1.2 billion (a 35 percent cumulative increase over five years) to support seventy-five thousand new spaces.[68] Government documents suggest the actual spaces in colleges and universities during 2003–10 increased by 120,000. In 2009–10, government operating funding reached $3.2 billion to universities and $1.3 billion to colleges – a 62 percent increase over 2002–03 levels (MTCU 2010, 23).

Approximately 44 percent of the new funding to PSE was contained in an envelope known as the Quality Improvement Fund. In order to receive funding from this envelop, institutions were required to sign multi-year accountability agreements with the government. Within these agreements institutions self-identified and committed to enrolment targets, quality improvements, public reporting, and student support. Institutions were to articulate and justify capital and educational support for proposed student enrolment growth, estimating in advance of receiving the financial resources required. These agreements augment rather than replace performance, accountability, and funding arrangements already in place. Existing KPIS are now accompanied by reporting on student retention, the results of the NSSE and the CGPSS (Alberta 2005; OCUFA 2006a, 2006b, 2007a, and 2007b; Shanahan 2008; York University 2006a and 2006b).[69]

Another strategy employed by the Liberals to improve PSE quality, accessibility, and accountability followed the Rae Report's recommendation to establish a research council with a specific mandate to monitor quality, accessibility, and accountability in the system and to advise the ministry. In 2005, the legislation was passed to establish the Higher Education Quality Council of Ontario, a council that advises and coordinates research priorities with a view to raising Ontario's profile as an international research centre.[70] HEQCO's mandate is to monitor and report on accessibility to the government and Ontarians, to create a quality framework, and to advise on system planning and competitiveness, including advising on targets and time frames that should be set to improve PSE (KPIs). The creation of this council represents a move back to the use of an intermediary body to monitor the system and to provide the government with policy advice. Indeed, under the terms of the Multi-Year Accountability Agreements, in order to receive QIF funding institutions must work with HEQCO to develop system and institutional indicators (Shanahan 2008; York University 2006b).

The Liberals introduced other accountability mechanisms to control and regulate the system. They brought universities under the provisions of the Freedom of Information and Protection of Privacy Act. This legislation mandates that institutions provide access to information under certain conditions, and it also holds institutions accountable for ensuring that private information is protected (Shanahan and Jones 2007). In June 2005, the Ontario government passed the Accessibility for Ontarians with Disabilities Act (AODA), which increased institutional accountability for accessibility. The act requires that all institutions receiving public funding (including colleges and universities) report annually on their efforts to make their institutions accessible to persons with disabilities as a precondition for receiving funding for facility maintenance and upgrading under the Facility Renewal Program. Finally, the Liberals extended the scrutiny of the auditor general (provincial auditor), who has been given broad scope to audit the postsecondary system.

The Liberals clearly viewed a strong postsecondary system as an instrument of the economy and targeted labour market training and integration as a priority throughout their administration. The dual priorities of accessibility and economic integration are evident in the numerous initiatives focused on increasing enrolment in apprenticeship programs and increasing access and economic integration for internationally trained immigrants. For example, the government designed the One Stop Training and Employment System, a service program that aids in access and increases the number of apprentices and skilled immigrants working in trades or professions. The 2004 budget also announced several new initiatives to increase entrants into the apprenticeship programs by seven thousand, to reach a total of twenty-six thousand annually by 2007–08. By 2009–10 this increased to twenty-eight thousand (MTCU 2010). The program included scholarships for high school leavers who return to complete high school and enter apprenticeship programs and an apprenticeship tax credit to encourage employers to hire more apprentices in the skilled trades. Additionally, the ministry provided the Apprenticeship Enhancement Fund Program (AEF), which awarded $10 million to community colleges in 2005–06 – $3 million in direct funding (reflecting the number of apprentices trained at the colleges) and $7 million in a competitive process rewarding colleges for enrolling apprentices. The Ontario Youth Apprenticeship Program (OYAP) also increased enrolment in apprenticeship programs.

In 2005–06, the Ministry of Training, Colleges and Universities signed the historic Labour Market Development Agreement (LMDA) and Labour Market Partnership Agreements (LMPA) with the federal government, allowing the ministry to integrate labour market programs in Ontario and to expand programs to provide more training, apprenticeship, and labour market services. The LMDA transfers federal training and employment programs to Ontario, along with federal funding, to provide employment programs, information centres, staff, and administration to support the transferred programs. Further federal funds are attached to the LMPA to enable Ontario to administer initiatives in six priority areas for investment.[71] These agreements, while common in other provinces, were late in coming to Ontario.

Labour market integration was also behind the government's investment of $9.5 million in 2004 (to reach $12.5 million in 2005–06) to work with professional regulatory bodies to increase access, remove barriers, and improve information on employment opportunities for internationally trained individuals. The Liberals also committed to report annually on progress on removing the barriers to the internationally trained.[72] In June 2006, Bill 124, the Fair Access to the Regulated Professions Act, was introduced to ensure internationally that trained individuals have fair and transparent access to Ontario's regulated professions. This was followed in 2007 by the creation of Ontario's first-ever fairness commissioner, who works with regulatory bodies to ensure that the credentials of internationally trained professionals are evaluated fairly and transparently.[73] Subsequently, the Ontario Bridging Partnership Assistance Program was created, which provides bursaries for foreign-trained professionals to secure employment in their field. Economic integration of immigrants fuelled the creation of the Colleges Integrating Immigrants to Employment Program in 2010, providing internationally trained professionals access to programs and services in CAATs across Ontario.

Even after the economic downturn of 2008–09, the Liberals continued to increase spaces in PSE and to invest in employment and training services. In 2009–10, $1.6 billion was provided through the Ontario Second Career Program for workers laid off by the recession (Ministry of Finance 2009). Skills and literacy training also figured prominently in the Liberal investments, including announcing the Ontario Green Jobs Strategy in 2009, which provided opportunities to train in the emerging green energy sector. In 2009, the MTCU (2010) announced the government's plan to establish a college of trades to modernize and build the profile of the trades in Ontario. The Ontario government passed the Ontario Labour Mobility Act, 2009, which allows professional and skilled workers to move across Canada and to work in Ontario. Thus, individuals certified in another province no longer have to complete additional training, examinations, or gain further experience to be certified in the same occupation in Ontario (MTCU 2010).

As part of their commitment to research and innovation and a strong economy, the Liberals created the Ministry of Research and Innovation in 2005. Initially, it was led by Premier McGuinty himself and attached to his office. It funds innovative research as well as infrastructure to support research and innovation, and it showcases Ontario's efforts nationally and internationally. Through this ministry funds have been channelled through the Ontario Research Fund (ORF) to establish research projects at various institutions. Additionally, the Ministry of Research and Innovation has invested $1.8 billion over four years to support both research and commercialization through both public and not-for profit research and development institutions. These funds are in addition to the Reaching Higher budget.

By 2009–10 the *Reaching Higher Plan* for PSE in Ontario was completed. In the Throne Speech for the 2010 budget, the Government of Ontario announced the *Open Ontario Plan*, which laid out its intention to focus on the economy and to support new jobs through investment in schools, colleges, universities, and skills-training. The *Open Ontario Plan* aims to raise PSE attainment in the province from 62 percent to 70 percent by 2020, add twenty thousand new FTE spaces in 2010–11 (according to the 2010 Government of Ontario budget this commitment was made, and funds to support it,

$310 million, were set aside), improve OSAP, create the Ontario Online Institute to increase PSE online opportunities for students, and increase international student enrolment by 50 percent (from 37,000 to 74,000 students) within five years (2015) (MTCU 2010).

POLICY THEMES AND THE POLICY-MAKING PROCESS

Our research findings suggest that the substantive policy directions taken by government and the policy-making process of each administration from 1985 through to 2007 have been influenced by different philosophies, individuals, and economic conditions. However, we found that all four administrations were consistent in that they all treated PSE policy as an instrument for economic development. Within this commonality, each administration placed varying emphases on social, equitable, educational, and economic goals. This is evident in each respective government's focus on the elimination of the deficit, balancing the budget, and the increased role of the market. Within these varying emphases, each administration has employed a range of fiscal, accountability, and accessibility mechanisms to achieve its goals – in some cases continuing and extending the previous administration's initiatives, with the general trajectory in Ontario leading to increased market and private-sector presence in the postsecondary system. In the following sections we highlight the four policy themes and offer an analysis of the policy-making process in Ontario.

Policy Themes

The major postsecondary policy themes emerging in Ontario during this time frame are: (1) accessibility; (2) accountability; (3) developing a competitive economy through vocationalism, skills development, and research (especially, science and technology); and (4) marketization. Analysis of these themes inevitably reveals their interconnection. In particular, in Ontario successive governments have increasingly employed market principles and mechanisms to achieve their postsecondary objectives. That is to say, marketization has been both a policy objective and a policy tool for achieving other objectives. The theme of marketization is threaded through the following analyses of postsecondary accessibility, accountability, and vocationalism/skills and science/technology research priorities.

Young (2002) describes marketization in Ontario PSE policy in terms of the introduction of market mechanisms, not precluding or increasing government control but, rather, changing government's approach to reform and changing the nature of its control over the system in order to induce institutions to adopt government-identified priorities. This policy priority is reflected across social policy in Canada through retrenchment measures, which began with the federal government (i.e., the Progressive Conservative Party) in the late 1980s and continued into the 1990s (with the federal Liberal government). The federal measures had provincial consequences and resulted in cuts, restructuring, the introduction of performance-based funding, and reinvestment through targeted initiatives. In Ontario, as a result of this, the province saw: the reorganization of local government, the consolidation of the provincial government's control over K-12 education (through a massive amalgamation of school boards), massive cuts in social spending, and an overall reduction in the size of government accompanied by cuts in corporate and individual taxes (Courchene and Telmer 1998). The shift towards the market was apparent in the opening up of the private sector in previously public-dominated areas, deregulation, downsizing, and rationalization. The Harris government employed matching grant strategies to lever increased private-sector support for, and involvement in, a range of areas, including its initiative to expand enrolment in engineering and increasing endowment support for student financial assistance – essentially increasing the role of the market in these areas (Jones and Young 2004). An increase in the number of industry partnerships is particularly evident in the area of R & D, where there has also been an increase in investment both provincially and federally. The overarching government approach towards the market over the last two decades has been to utilize financial incentives to achieve policy objectives. Market mechanisms have been employed to increase market activity, presence, and priorities in the sector. This context sets the stage for postsecondary policy development

Accessibility has been a strong priority of all the governments over the past two decades. However, each government expressed this priority in various ways and adopted different mechanisms to achieve it. We define accessibility broadly as participation and retention in, and graduation from, the postsecondary system by all willing and capable persons, regardless of age, gender, socio-economic status, race, culture, religion, and geographic region. Further, we contend that any discussion of accessibility in Ontario's postsecondary system must recognize that, historically in Ontario, degree-granting has been strictly controlled by the government and public universities through their monopoly on granting degrees. In the past the private postsecondary sector was small and inconsequential. Moreover, the university and college sectors lacked integration, even though CAATs had repeatedly lobbied (unsuccessfully) for a transfer function. As demand for participation increased, these inherent characteristics of Ontario's postsecondary system became challenges (and, arguably, hindrances) for successive governments as they attempted to achieve the goal of accessibility.

Early attempts during the Liberal administration (1985–90) to address accessibility focused on reducing and stabilizing levels of government funding in order to accommodate the burgeoning demand for PSE. This was accomplished by introducing corridor funding and targeted funding envelopes and by creating an accessibility fund for unexpected and significant enrolment growth. In addition, the Liberals attempted to increase accessibility by integrating the system linking universities and CAATs. Evidence of their vision for a continuum for PSE can be found in successive reports from that period, including *People and Skill in the Global Economy* and *Vision 2000*. However, their efforts at integration were largely unsuccessful because no co-coordinating body had responsibility for system-wide planning, and the government made no attempt to introduce structural changes. Accessibility was improved during this era primarily by overall expansion of the number of postsecondary institutions and the introduction of postsecondary bilingual programs and, specifically, the creation of CAATs, where French was the primary language of instruction, in order to meet the needs of franco-Ontarians.

Between 1990 and 1995, accessibility continued to be a concern for the NDP. However, this was within a very different economic context: namely, a deep recession and restrictive funding. The NDP government maintained the policy objective of linking the universities and CAATs through encouraging articulation and credit transfer arrangements. Credit transfer issues between universities were the theme of three major reports during this period: the Smith Report (1991), the *Pan-Canadian Protocol on the Transferability of University Credits* (1995), and the Baker Report (1992).

The PC government (1995–2003) took another approach to accessibility, departing from Ontario's long-standing, tightly controlled approach to degree granting. This administration moved the system closer to the market by opening it up to the private sector, expanding degree-granting authority, and increasing competition among publicly funded universities (Jones and Young 2004).[74] These changes were justified in terms of increasing accessibility and choice for students. This approach has, arguably, resulted in the most dramatic change in system organization, moving Ontario's postsecondary system out of a strict binary typology and into a hybrid arrangement whereby sectors are no longer distinguished by degree-granting authority (Jones 2004). Its success in increasing accessibility and choice for students, however, is contested.[75] In part, this is because of the increase in tuition fees and that tightening of student assistance that came along with it. PC student assistance policies emphasized greater matched private-sector funding and greater university spending on student assistance.[76] PC government policy (1995–2003) moved away from assistance in the form of government-guaranteed loans through OSAP and towards government-created scholarships.[77] Student loan regulations were tightened, and the amount of government funding going towards student aid decreased, as did the total number of recipients of government loans.

By contrast, the Liberals' (2003–10) approach to accessibility was to freeze tuition fees and then to regulate them, allowing increases according to a framework. They increased student assistance, enhanced and expanded loan entitlement and repayment provisions, and increased grants. Total government expenditures on student aid and the number of recipients increased. However, we note that, across all four administrations profiled in this chapter, changes in tuition and student assistance policy suggest that Ontario governments are moving away from supporting students. In this policy area it is clear that Ontario is transferring the cost of education to students and their families, universities, and the private sector. Underpinning this approach is the belief that individual students obtain a private benefit from PSE and that they should pay a larger share of the costs of their education. Another tenet of the Liberal government's (2003–10) approach to accessibility has been to expand system funding and enrolments. It has invested in training and apprenticeship programs, at-risk youth, and foreign-trained professionals. It has increased undergraduate and graduate enrolments and professional school enrolments for nursing and medical school. Groups that have been traditionally underrepresented (Aboriginals, persons with disabilities, francophones, and first-generation students) have been targeted for support and outreach programs at the undergraduate level. Rural and northern communities have also been targeted for special support.

Accountability is a second policy priority that has emerged in PSE in Ontario. This is evidenced by institutional accounting for public funds and institutions demonstrating achievements according to prescribed indicators. By contrast, system-level accountability mechanisms have been more difficult to implement in Ontario because of the lack of system-level planning.

Improving postsecondary accountability emerged as a major policy concern for the NDP between 1990 and 1995 after audits of three Ontario universities raised alarms. The NDP recommended comprehensive provincial audits, an accountability framework that rested with the governing boards of each institution, and an external monitoring system (which was never established). The NDP government was the first of the four administrations profiled to tackle institutional accountability, even considering mechanisms that challenged university autonomy. Although it was not entirely successful in implementing a novel model of accountability, it highlighted the issue and began discussions that were to continue throughout successive administrations.

The PC government (1995–2003) also identified accountability and quality as a major thrust of its PSE platform. For the first time in Ontario, this government brought in KPIs for colleges and universities and institutional targets to address accountability concerns. A small portion of funding was attached to KPIs to further influence institutional behaviour. This performance reporting was in addition to existing reporting by CAATs, academic senates, and governing boards of universities.

The Liberals (2003–10) used legislation to accomplish their accountability goals, such as the Freedom of Information and Protection of Privacy Act as well as the Accessibility for Ontarians with Disabilities Act, which have built-in accountability reporting requirements linked to funding for the sectors. The Liberal approach to accountability continues the trend towards the use of KPIs. The difference in the Liberal approach appears to be that the Liberals are increasingly marrying accessibility goals to funding and accountability agreements, all rolled into one. Institutions and governments are negotiating agreements on an institution-by-institution basis, leveraged with attached funding. Institutions themselves are defining the targets that they must meet under these contracts in order to obtain new funding.

The Liberal approach of using performance funding and collapsing system-level accessibility, accountability, and funding goals into one mechanism in the form of multi-year accountability agreements may have strengthened the influence of government priorities on institutional behaviour. Another dimension of the Liberal Party's approach to accountability and quality assurance has been its return to using an intermediary body that monitors the system and develops performance indicators, as seen in the creation of HEQCO.[78] Overall, the Liberals have emphasized more targets, more reporting, more transparency in the use of funds and implementation of processes, and more mechanisms of control to achieve their accountability goals.

Over the last three decades, provincial governments have consistently linked Ontario's PSE policy to economic development and the province's competitiveness in a global economy. This has been reflected primarily in two ways: (1) through an emphasis on vocational and skills training and (2) through an emphasis on R&D (especially science and technology). A distinct shift in emphasis in Ontario's PSE system has occurred, moving it away from a liberal education and towards a vocational, technical education; away from basic, curiosity-driven research and towards applied, market-driven research. The use of funding mechanisms towards tied and matched private-sector funding has moved the system towards the market and has placed a greater emphasis on vocational training, meeting labour market needs, and increasing market-oriented R&D.

The Liberal government (1985–90) was the first in Ontario to address the implications of the globalized economy and advances in technology. It clearly supported increased university–industry partnerships, and it funded science and technology research. This support is contained in the report of the Premier's Council, *Competing in the New Global Economy* (Government of Ontario 1988b), and was made clear with the creation of the Ontario Centres of Excellence, the largest publicly supported initiative linking university and industry research corporations. In fact, Ontario led in this area, and the federal government followed suit and subsequently created the national Networks of Centres of Excellence. This provincial government also established the Council of Technology (1986), providing $1 billion towards technological innovation. The University Research Incentive Fund also aimed at developing research capacity and encouraged technology transfers from university to industry.

The NDP (1990–95) approach followed this lead and built upon university-industry linkages, the aim being to increase technological and industrial developments at the same time as advancing the government's equity agenda. The University Restructuring Steering Committee was established to develop long-term strategies that would make the university sector responsive to continuous life-long learning as well as to the needs of the economy. However, the committee's efforts to reshape the postsecondary sector were buried as a result of the negative fiscal developments in the economy during this period.

The PCs (1995–2003) clearly favoured market principles in linking PSE and the economy. This government's postsecondary policy emphasized education as serving the economy, often at the expense of social and equity needs. Emphasis was placed on vocationally oriented programs and market-oriented research. For example, the first new university created in forty years in Ontario under the new degree-granting legislation was the University of Ontario Institute of Technology, which emerged with strong administrative linkages to the neighbouring Durham College of Applied Arts and Technology. The mission of this publicly funded university explicitly includes serving the private-sector needs of the surrounding labour market (the automotive and power industry in the neighboring region).[79] The PCs also employed targeted, tied, and matching funding mechanisms to steer postsecondary research and programming towards strengthening the labour market. They advocated for greater private-sector involvement in, and support for, PSE, and they encouraged institutional competitiveness, productivity, diversification, and marketization.

The Liberals (2003–10) continued the use of targeted, tied, and matching funding mechanisms to steer the system's research and programming direction towards a competitive economy. However, they have heightened the emphasis on skills training by targeting labour-market training (especially in trades and apprenticeships) and the labour-market integration of internationally trained persons. They have also funded science and technology research and supported the innovation and commercialization of knowledge (knowledge transfer) beyond the postsecondary ministry – that is, they have structurally created a new ministry of research and innovation.[80] The use of new audit and accountability exercises, leveraged by funding, also marks the Liberal approach and has given this government an additional measure of control over the direction of the system, enabling it to financially reward certain institutional behaviours (such as meeting enrolment targets explicitly crafted to serve Ontario's economic needs).

In summary, there has been an overall trend in Ontario's PSE policy over the last two decades towards encouraging postsecondary-industry partnerships. At the same time, government has decreased operating grants to universities and colleges,[81] while adopting funding mechanisms that encourage private-sector support. Ontario governments have increasingly employed targeted funding mechanisms and matching funding programs to achieve their policy goals (of vocationalism and skills, research, science and technology) and to induce postsecondary institutions to embrace its priorities, leading to increased interactions between universities and the private sector.[82] This varied use of funding mechanisms to accomplish policy objectives has enabled Ontario governments to steer the system towards its economic goals, but these policies also create problems by disadvantaging smaller rural postsecondary institutions that lack a fundraising and partnership base.[83]

Policy-Making Process

Historically, a distinctive aspect of Ontario's PSE policy-making process has been the absence of a systematic approach or system perspective (Royce 1998; Lang et al. 1999). Our interview data confirmed this finding. Participants agree that "no overarching policy framework or plan" and "no integrative holistic vision" was applied to the policy-making process during the period 1985–2010.[84] Although, historically, Ontario policy has been sector-specific (Royce 1998), our interview findings suggest that, even within postsecondary sectors during this time period, there was little direction, and "all kinds of discretion on the parts of battling (institutional) administrators" was evident.[85] This vacuum in leadership leaves open the possibility for individuals within government and within institutions to advance agendas that indirectly shape the system.

In the early 1980s, two major government commissions (the Commission on the Future Development of the Universities of Ontario, 1984, a.k.a. the Bovey Commission, after its chair, Edmund Bovey; and the Committee on the Future Role of Universities in Ontario, 1981, a.k.a. the Fisher Committee, after its chair, Harry Fisher, deputy minister of colleges and universities) attempted, with limited results, to address sector rationalization and institutional differentiation as a means of creating an appropriate fiscal and policy framework for universities (Jones 1997b, 1997c; Cameron and Royce 1996; Royce 1998). The approach has been to deal with Ontario's universities and CAATs as separate sectors with distinct missions and funding mechanisms.[86] Lang et al. (1999, 158–9) state:

> Even within these two sectors there is little evidence of policy designed to treat institutions as components parts of a network of complementary institutions. Even within the Ministry, policy development has tended to focus on one sector or the other. The conclusion that there is no such thing as an Ontario PSE "system," or even an Ontario university system, is far from new since it has been raised in a number of government reports and research articles, but there is little indication that the government is taking steps to even consider PSE policy in terms of a system.

Interviewees went further, suggesting that policy decisions in PSE have not been situated within a larger societal or system context but, rather, emerge from technocratic considerations and from the need to balance budgets.[87]

In the past, policy making in the PSE sector has been a broad, consultative process. At various junctures these consultations have included intermediary advisory bodies to the minister without executive decision-making authority that focused on the university or CAAT sectors (such as the Committee on University Affairs, followed by the Ontario Council on University Affairs, and the Ontario Council of Regents for Colleges of Applied Arts and Technology).[88] However, this pattern of consultation was discontinued in the early 1990s, when the NDP government began to (re)act unilaterally to sudden and severe fiscal constraints.[89] Notwithstanding this change to the policy-making process, the government continued to take an ad hoc approach to system planning and coordination, reacting to the fiscal realities rather than developing a master plan. Fiscal restraint began to drive the policy-making process. The PC government in the mid-1990s continued the movement away from consultation with the broader postsecondary sector by dismantling agencies and closing off points of entry into the policy community and decision-making process for society at large (such as consultation with constituencies, stakeholders groups, and advisory bodies). For example, OCUA was dismantled, and, during this administration, major policy decisions (such as the expansion of degree granting and the creation of UOIT) were announced with little or no sector-specific consultation, let alone wider public consultation. Furthermore, consultation and delivery of the Smith Commission's review of postsecondary education during the PC's first mandate was limited to five months, an extremely short time frame.[90]

Governments have preferred to deal directly with individual universities or collectively with sector institutions like the Council of Universities. While, historically, CAAT governance and decision making has been highly centralized, in the last two decades recent legislation has attempted to devolve some powers to the college boards. Across administrations, since the 1990s successive premiers have exerted considerable control over policy making, centralizing decision making within the premier's office but drawing upon a close circle of advisors (some unelected and some elected, including, especially, the ministers of finance, health, and education). There is also some evidence that, over the last two decades, provincial governments have been working to integrate policy making across ministries.[91]

Over the last two decades, change in provincial educational policy in Ontario (broadly conceived) has been significant, given Ontario's history of maintaining the status quo. But it is perhaps less dramatic compared to changes in PSE in other international jurisdictions. In Ontario, change has been accomplished, in part, through omnibus bills that incorporated massive amounts of new legislation, which were then implemented as new policies. The aim has been to achieve rationalization and reorganization, centralization of decision making and control (in elementary and secondary education particularly but not exclusively), delegation of services to local government, spending cuts, and the introduction of accountability mechanisms. All of which have had an impact on Ontario's PSE.[92]

At the same time, administrations during most of this time period (1985–2010) have had limited *internal* research capacity around postsecondary education. Interviewees suggest that, over much of the last two decades, Ontario's postsecondary ministry had "no capacity inside" and conducted little original research, preferring to look at other comparable national and international jurisdictions and to borrow from initiatives and directions employed outside Ontario.[93] The creation of HEQCO in 2005, whose mandate explicitly includes conducting research on PSE and advising the minister, addresses this gap. HEQCO has covered considerable ground in cultivating research in PSE in Ontario.

Through HEQCO, Ontario has also returned to the use of an advisory body to help coordinate the expanded and increasingly complex system.[94] In an effort to be consultative and transparent, HEQCO publishes an annual summary of its research agenda as a mechanism for soliciting feedback, and it publicly disseminates all of its commissioned research studies. HEQCO is thereby developing a considerable research database. The McGuinty administration sought input from stakeholders throughout the province in its review of the postsecondary system (the Rae Report), and, unlike what happened with other reports and commissions, which just sat on the shelf, the government set out to implement the recommendations with a particular emphasis on increased funding.[95] One informant suggested that this was courageous, given the lack of political capital that, in the past, has adhered to investments in PSE. However Clark and Trick (2006, 180) observe:

> The Rae Review benefited from political conditions that favoured stronger investment in postsecondary education, despite a difficult fiscal situation. The report also benefitted from a stakeholder community that was able to put aside most internal differences for the sake of a perceived common good. With this environment, the review created a highly focused process that involved extensive consultation, the support of expert panel members and frequent interaction with decision-makers.

We argue that, since the mid-1980s, PSE policies have served to blur the boundaries separating sectors within PSE (universities and CAATs) and, more generally, between public and private funding sources. These changes to the structure of PSE were to some extent unintended consequences of policies that had no explicit structural goals. Government commissions such as the Advisory Panel on

Future Directions for PSE (1996), on the one hand, endorsed the distinction between colleges and universities (the binary structural status quo) but, on the other, advanced principles that would change that structure, such as allowing polytechnic colleges to offer applied degrees, opening up degree granting to the private sector, increasing differentiation among institutions, introducing tuition deregulation, and providing incentives for private-sector support and partnerships with universities and colleges. Likewise, the Postsecondary Choice and Excellence Act, 2000, also opened up degree granting. All of these initiatives and policies have potential structural implications. Some of the policies were explicitly intended to move PSE closer to the market. It could be argued that this shifted the locus of control away from the government towards the market and that this had negative implications for university autonomy because it meant that, potentially, private donors and corporate funders could have an influence on university decision making.[96]

FUNDING

Changes in the allocation of funds to PSE are one indicator of a government's policy priorities. Government promises with regard to increasing access and improving quality may be rendered meaningless in the absence of resources to achieve these goals. To assess the commitment of governments to their stated policies we first analyze changes in the allocation of funds to PSE against PSE enrolment trends, and then we compare the allocation of funds to PSE with the allocation of funds to other policy areas (such as health and K-12 education).

The most recent provincial government (Liberals 2003–10) made a significant $6.2 billion investment in PSE as it implemented its *Reaching Higher Plan* between 2005 and 2012. In 2009, $4.42 billion in operating grants were allocated to the universities and colleges. Of this amount, $3.11 billion in operating grants went to the universities sector (a 63 percent increase since 2002–03) and $1.3 billion went to the college sector (a 60 percent increase since 2002–03). Since 2002–03, when the Liberals took power, per-student funding per FTE has increased in both university and college sectors. However, it still remains below 1994–95 levels. At the same time, university and college enrolments have steadily increased over the last two decades.[97]

Total revenue for the college system from all sources totalled $2.98 billion in 2009–10, while total expenses were $2.93 billion in 2009–10 (Colleges Ontario 2010, 2). Total income from all sources for universities was $12.2 billion in 2009–10, which included government operating grants and contracts (57 percent of total university revenue), sponsored research (21 percent of total revenue), ancillary funds (7 percent of total university income), and trust, capital, and endowment funds (15 percent of total university income) (COU 2011b, 3).

The changes since 1988–89 in provincial operating grants are illustrated in figure 3.1. The graph shows that increases in operating grants started to occur with the Liberals between 1985 and 1990 and continued into the early years of the NDP administration (1990–93). This pattern is consistent with the commitment by both administrations to increase access. However, this trend is short-lived as PSE funding declined drastically starting in 1993–94 in part due to the recession. Premier Rae initially tried to spend his way out of the recession before implementing restraint measures in 1992–93. In 1995, funding sharply declined again and then flattened out until early 2000, when slow increases were apparent. This decline in funding coincides with sharp cuts in the federal Canada Health and Social Transfer (described in the introduction to this book). It also coincides with the Harris Common Sense Revolution and the consequent partial withdrawal of the provincial government from social spending. The PCs slowly increased funding in small amounts in preparation for the double cohort and the 2003 election, which they lost to the Liberals. Recent history shows that operating grants to colleges and universities have increased by $1.7 billion since 2002–03, when the Liberal administration took power.

The story becomes more nuanced when looking at the figures for provincial operating grants per funded FTE in Ontario for colleges and universities (see figure 3.2). College funding per student (FTE student) fell from a high in 1992–93 to a low in 1997–98. In the decade 1992–2002, college enrolments increased by almost 16 percent, while provincial operating grants in real terms decreased by 17 percent. By 2009–10, operating grants per FTE in colleges were 7 percent lower than in 1994–95, while enrolments were 26 percent higher than in 1994–95. Essentially, provincial funding for most of the last two decades has not kept pace with college enrolment. At the same time, trends for college tuition fees show, since 1992–93, an increase by almost 70 percent in real terms (Ontario Colleges

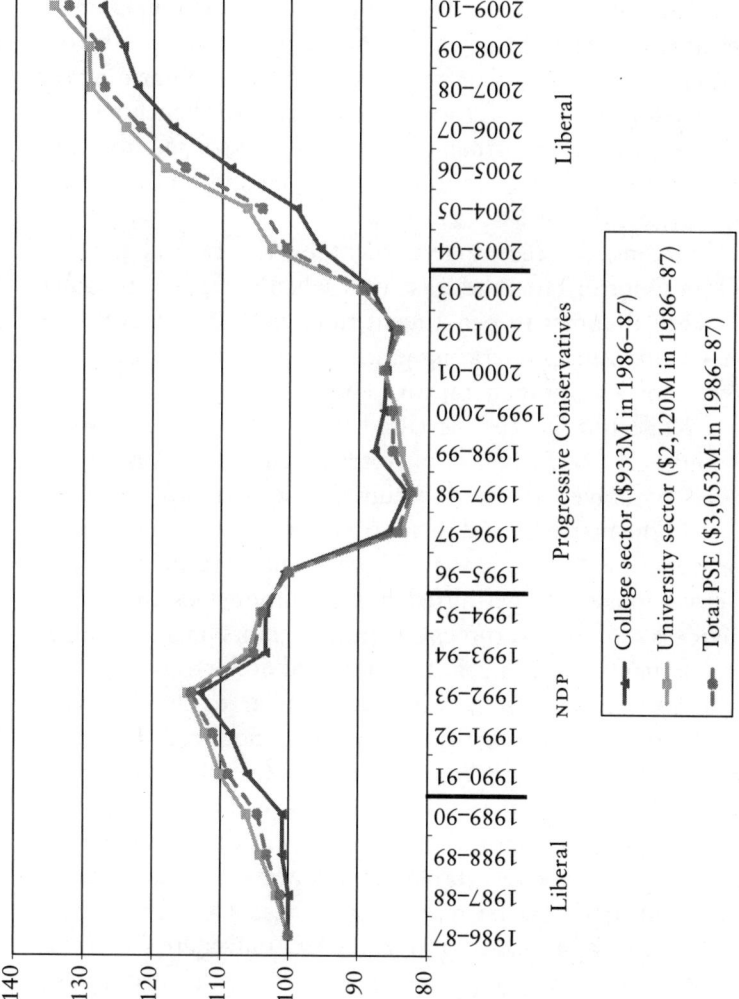

Figure 3.1
Changes in provincial operating grants for Ontario college and university sectors and total postsecondary education, 1986–87 – 2009–10 in constant 2002 dollars, 1986–87 = 100.
Source: Ministry of Training, College and Universities, Ontario.

2007, 54). The decrease in operating grants and the increase in tuition revenue signals a shift of the financial burden of college education from the state to the students. Although college tuition fees have increased, the combined revenue from tuition and operating grants is still lower than it was in 1992–93. Even with the new Reaching Higher investments, college revenue per student in Ontario from operating grants and tuition fees in 2010 continued to be the lowest among all the Canadian provinces (Colleges Ontario 2010, 6). In comparison to other sectors, the colleges have benefitted the least from government investments in PSE. By 2010, funding (per student) for Ontario colleges continued to lag behind the K-12 education and universities sectors (2).

Notwithstanding the recent investment by the Liberal government, PSE in Ontario fares the least well when compared to other provinces when it comes to per-student funding. Between 1987–88 and 2002–03, provincial operating grants per student, for universities, decreased by 3.9 but then improved by 6.2 percent over the next two years. While tuition fees increased by 136.8 percent between 1987–88 and 2003–04, when they were frozen until 2006, beginning in 1996–97 universities were required to set aside 10 percent of the increase in the first year and then 30 percent in subsequent years to use for student aid (COU 2007, viii; constant 2002 dollars). The Ontario government has permitted higher tuition fees than most other provinces so that government operating grants plus tuition per student has remained constant in CPI-adjusted dollars.

The funding trends for universities are similar to those experienced by the colleges, although they are less pronounced. The combined provincial operating revenue and tuition fees per FTE is only slightly higher in 2009–10 than it was in 1988–89 and 1992–93 and is lower than both if we factor in the tuition set aside for student aid (See figure 3.2; COU 2007, 3, table 1.2). However, the universities (unlike some colleges) have been able to gain access to other sources of funds. Between 1990–2000 and 2004–05, universities doubled their income from federal grants (mostly research grants) from $459 million to $941 million (COU 2007, table 1.6). In the same time period, they have also increased their income from non-governmental sources by 128 percent (COU 2007, table 1.7). However, over the last five years (2005–10), government grants and contracts, tuition, and miscellaneous fees continue to represent the largest source of income for universities (81 percent). Since 2005–06, government grants and contracts account for more than 50 percent of total university income (including grants from MTCU as well as other federal and provincial grants and contracts). Investment income (in actual dollars and percentage) has increased between 2007–08 and 2009–10 but remains constant with 2005–06 levels. Donor income has remained constant at about 4 to 5 percent of total revenue over the past five years (COU 2011b, 2). These funding trends occurred during a period (2002–03 to 2009–10) when overall PSE spaces increased by 120,000 (FTE) and undergraduate and graduate FTE enrolment grew significantly – the largest increase in enrolment in thirty years (COU 2007).[98]

When we examine changes in provincial grants per funded FTE for Ontario colleges and universities over the last two decades we find the trend has been mostly downward (see figure 3.2). Even with the recent government investments that reverse this trend, grants per FTE are still lower than 1992 and 1987 levels for colleges and universities, respectively. Although successive governments have claimed accessibility as a PSE priority (which has manifested most recently in dramatic enrolment increases), they have not allocated the necessary funds to support this goal. In fact, the decreasing funding per FTE could jeopardize not only their PSE accessibility goals but also their PSE quality goals. The implication here is that, in order to support the massive enrolment increases in PSE, the provincial government must make significant and sustained investments to achieve the access and quality objectives it has set as priorities.

To get a sense of the relative weight successive governments have given to PSE, we compare the share of public expenditures allocated to different policy sectors over the last twenty-five years (1986–87 to 2009–10). Table 3.2 shows that, over the last two decades, health dominates government spending throughout the period, sitting at a low of 31 percent and a high of 42 percent. Similarly, K-12 education increased steadily by almost 3 percent over the same period and accounts for 13 percent of total government expenditures by 2009–10.[99] In contrast, spending on PSE as a proportion of total government expenditures decreased over the same time period, dipping to its lowest during the first year of the McGuinty Liberal administration at 5.4 percent in 2004–05. By 2009–10 it was lower than 1986–87 levels.

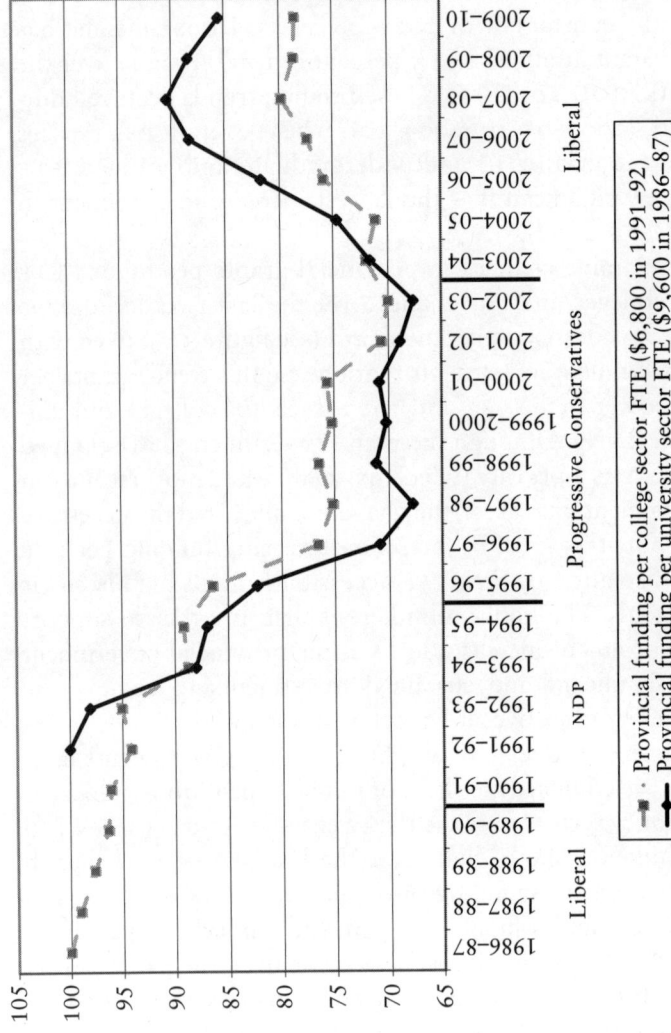

Figure 3.2
Changes in provincial grants per funded FTE for Ontario college and university sectors, 1986–87 – 2009–10 in constant 2002 dollars, 1986–87 = 100.

Source: Ministry of Training, Colleges and Universities, Ontario.

Table 3.2
Expenditure: Budget plan 1986–87 to 2010–11 in percentage of total Ontario government expenditure

Party in power	Year	Postsecondary Education	Education	Health	Rest of government
Liberal	1986–87	6.7	11.2	31.8	48.9
	1987–88	6.7	12.3	32.2	47.5
	1988–89	6.5	12.0	32.8	47.5
	1989–90	6.4	11.9	33.2	47.5
	1990–91	6.4	12.3	33.8	46.9
NDP	1991–92	19.6		36.4	44.0
	1992–93	18.5		34.6	46.9
	1993–94	19.5		35.1	45.5
	1994–95	17.1		33.7	49.2
	1995–96	17.2		33.9	48.9
PC	1996–97	6.9	9.6	34.4	49.1
	1997–98	5.8	10.6	35.5	48.1
	1998–99	5.9	13.1	34.2	59.9
	1999–2000	5.8	13.9	35.5	58.7
	2000–01	5.7	13.6	37.3	43.4
	2001–02	5.5	13.8	38.3	42.4
	2002–03	5.5	14.0	40.1	40.3
	2003–04	5.9	14.7	40.5	38.9
Liberal	2004–05	5.4	14.3	38.5	41.8
	2005–06	5.9	14.3	40.8	39.0
	2006–07	6.0	13.8	40.2	39.9
	2007–08	6.4	14.5	41.6	37.5
	2008–09	6.5	13.7	42.1	37.7
	2009–10	6.0	13.3	39.1	41.6
	2010–11	6.4	17.4	36.6	39.6

Source: Budget documents (various years), Ministry of Finance, Government of Ontario.

Note: Education includes the item "Teachers' Pension Plan (TPP)," "Health" includes "Health Promotion and Sport" and its related expenses under "other expenses." From 2009 onwards, Postsecondary education includes time-limited investments for colleges under "other expenses."

Despite the latest commitment to PSE by the McGuinty Liberal government, PSE across Ontario administrations has had a relatively low priority in budget allocations when compared to funding allocated to other sectors. The latest $6.2 billion investment over five years (2005–10) has scarcely made a dent in PSE's proportion of the total budget. While spending on K-12 education and health grew especially at the end of the PC administration and in the beginning of the Liberal administration, it is difficult to ascertain the specific trend during the NDP administration. As all the education funding was distributed by the super ministry we cannot document the trend for PSE. Yet it is notable that, during the NDP administration, the proportion assigned to education (combined K-13 as it was then and PSE) decreased by more than 2 percent.

In this economic environment it comes as no surprise that PSE institutions have sought alternative sources of revenue. We can get a sense of the financial strain placed on PSE institutions by focusing on the proportion of revenue coming from government sources. Between 1988–89 and 2009–10, the proportion of postsecondary revenue coming from (provincial and federal) governments has steadily decreased from 67 percent to 46 percent. Concomitantly, funding from own sources rose from 32 percent to 54 percent (see figure 3.3 and table 3.2). In other words, postsecondary institutions have sought out other sources of revenue to replace decreasing government funding in the face of increasing enrolments.

When we break down the two funding-source categories (government and "own source") into their component parts, we can see more clearly how the funding burden has been shifted from the state to individual students (see table 3.3). Provincial transfers to PSE (combining all sectors and as a percent of total funding) have steadily decreased from 61.9 percent in 1988–89 to 37 percent in 2008–09. All other sources of revenue for PSE increased during the same time period. Tuition fees as a percent of total funding have increased the most, going from 12 percent in 1988–89 to 26.5 percent in 2008–09. Notably, it was at the beginning of the PC era in 1995–96 that we saw the largest increase in tuition fees as a percentage of total funding and, similarly, at the end of the PC administration in 2003–04 that tuition fees were at their highest level (27 percent). In the same year, provincial transfers to PSE reached their lowest level as a proportion of total funding (36 percent).

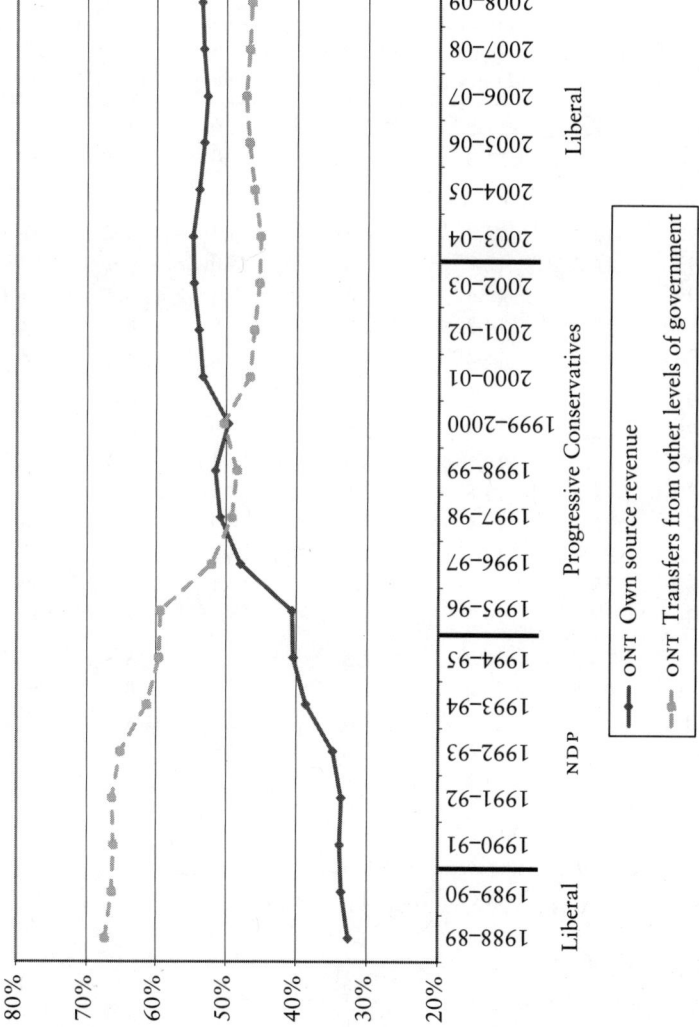

Figure 3.3
Proportion of revenue from own-source revenue and government funding, 1988–89 – 2008–09.
Source: Statistics Canada. CANSIM, table 385-0007.

Table 3.3
Funding sources percent of total funding: Ontario postsecondary education, 1988–89 – 2008–09

	Year	Own-source revenue				Government transfers	
		Tuition fees	Other sale of goods and services	Investment income	Other own-source revenue	Federal	Provincial
Liberal	1988–89	12.2	11.8	2.6	6.0	5.4	61.9
	1989–90	12.9	11.8	2.9	6.0	5.5	60.8
	1990–91	13.3	12.3	3.0	5.3	6.7	59.4
NDP	1991–92	13.6	12.2	2.5	5.4	6.4	59.9
	1992–93	14.8	12.7	2.4	5.0	6.6	58.4
	1993–94	16.3	13.4	2.6	6.4	6.9	54.4
	1994–95	17.3	14.2	2.0	6.9	6.7	52.8
	1995–96	17.7	13.2	2.6	7.2	6.7	52.7
PC	1996–97	22.0	14.8	2.8	8.3	6.6	45.3
	1997–98	22.9	15.5	3.5	8.9	6.2	42.7
	1998–99	25.0	14.1	2.3	10.1	6.2	42.1
	1999–2000	24.6	13.8	2.8	8.5	6.2	44.1
	2000–01	25.3	16.4	2.3	9.3	7.7	38.8
	2001–02	26.4	17.1	1.7	8.8	8.3	37.3
	2002–03	27.3	18.1	1.3	8.1	8.7	36.5
	2003–04	27.0	16.5	3.3	8.1	8.7	36.3
Liberal	2004–05	26.5	16.2	2.6	8.7	8.6	37.3
	2005–06*	26.5	16.2	2.6	8.7	8.6	37.3
	2006–07	26.5	16.2	2.6	8.7	8.6	37.3
	2007–08	25.8	15.0	3.6	8.9	9.0	37.4
	2008–09	25.9	15.4	3.5	8.7	9.0	37.3

(The series terminated after 2009)

Source: Statistics Canada, CANSIM, table 385–0007.

Note: The entries for 2005–06 and for 2006–07 are estimates.

OUTCOMES

In this section, using a selection of indicators, we examine the policy themes of accessibility, participation, and commitment to R&D in terms of system outcomes. This is not meant to be an exhaustive analysis of PSE performance indicators but, rather, a snapshot of system behaviour alongside the policy themes we have identified.

Accessibility

Affordability is an essential aspect of accessibility. To assess affordability we consider average university tuition fees by program and average tuition fees as a proportion of the after-tax average. Between 1993–94 and 2009–10 average university tuition fees increased for all programs (see figure 3.4). Yet the increases have not been equal and have been more rapid at some times than at others. The largest increases in law, medicine, and dentistry occurred shortly after the PCs took power in 1995 and follow from the deregulation of tuition fees in these professional programs. In 2003–04, tuition was frozen, and a regulated framework was introduced in 2006. Figure 3.4 shows the effect of these measures as tuition increases stabilize across most programs (except dentistry, which continues a slow climb).

The second measure of accessibility we consider is the average undergraduate tuition fees as a proportion of after-tax income (1986 constant dollars) by quintile (see figure 3.5). Between 1987–88 and 2008–09, the lowest quintile experienced the most change whereas the highest quintile experienced the least. The most dramatic change for the lowest quintile occurred during the PC era (1995–2003) and then plateaued during the Liberal administration (2003 and following). Over the two decades between 1987–88 and 2009–10, the lowest quintile experiences over 25 percent change in tuition fees as a proportion of after-tax income, whereas the highest quintile experiences a change of less than 5 percent. This raises concerns about the effectiveness of accessibility policies across socio-economic groups and, in particular, the relative impact of tuition policies on different socio-economic groups. Increasing tuition fees represents a larger proportion of after-tax dollars for those individuals with the lowest wages and salaries. Furthermore, while the greatest increase occurs during the PC era, the upward trend clearly begins with the NDP administration from 1990, notwithstanding the social equity platform the NDP government espoused but understandable given the deep recession it faced. In summary, PSE has not become more affordable in Ontario, and tuition increases have disproportionately affected lower-income students.

Participation and Choice

We have considered a range of selected data to reflect various aspects of participation, including: participation rates by institution type,

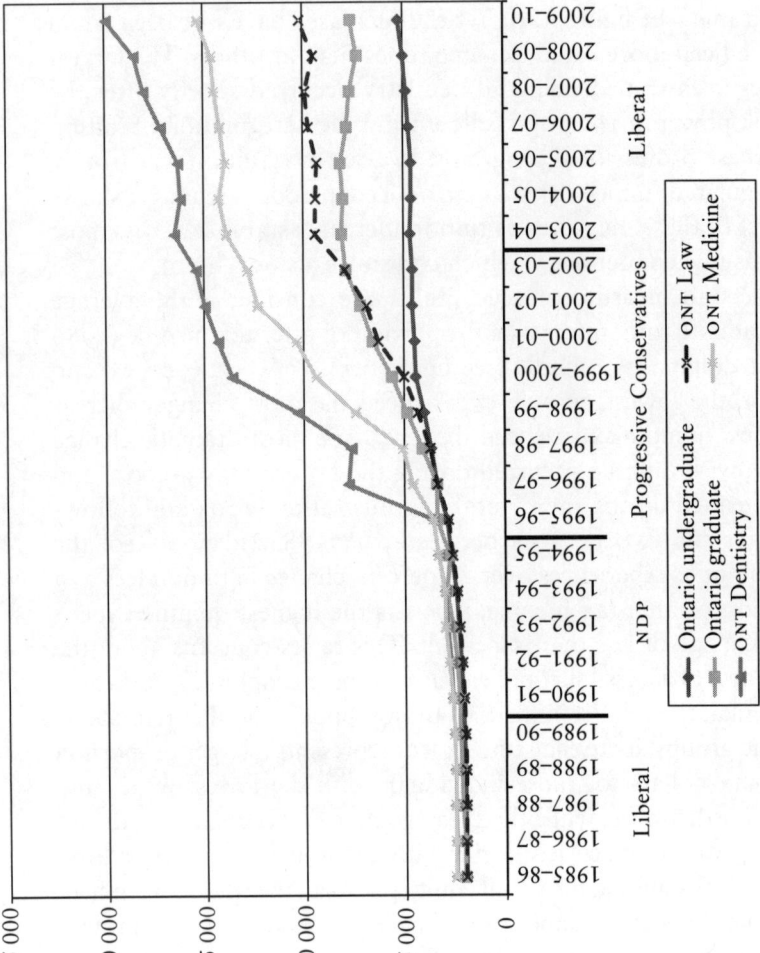

Figure 3.4
Average university tuition by program in Ontario, 1985–86 – 2009–10 (constant 2002 dollars).

Sources: Statistics Canada, TLAC, table 08E.

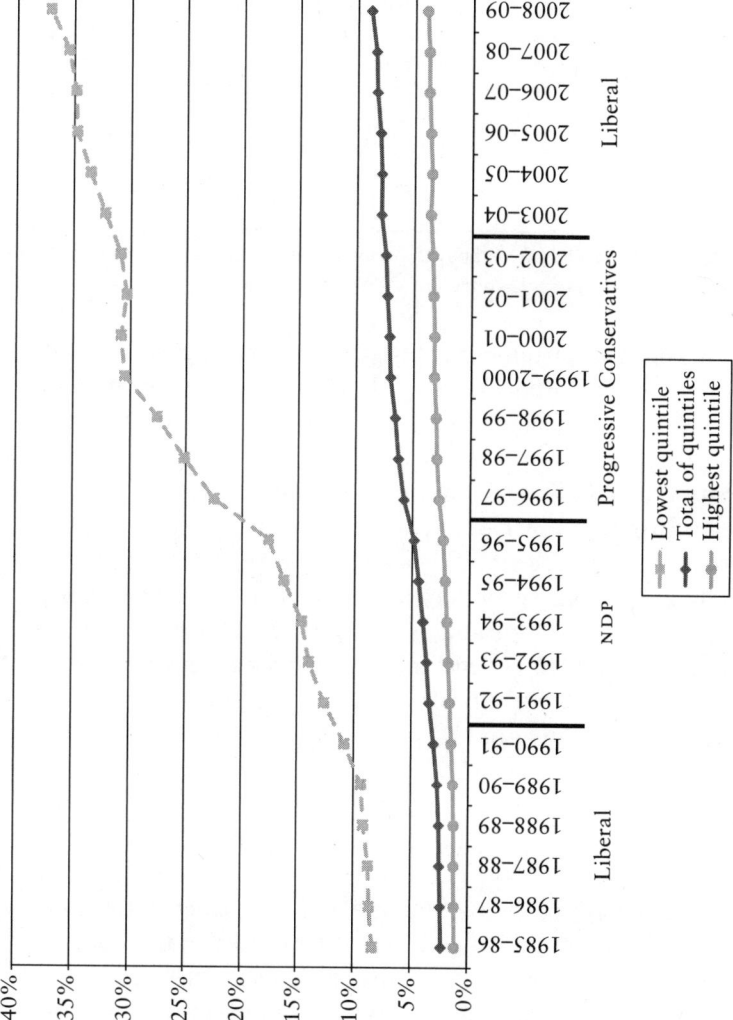

Figure 3.5
Average undergraduate university tuition fees as proportion of selected after-tax average income quintiles, Ontario – 1985–86 to 2008–09 (constant 2002 dollars).

Sources: Statistics Canada, tuition and living accommodation costs, Survey 3123.

Table 3.4
Postsecondary participation rates of young adults aged 24–26 by December 2005, by province and type of institution attended

	Percentage attended postsecondary education	Percentage attended university	Percentage attended college/CEGEP	Percentage attended other postsecondary institution
Canada	79	40	42	26
Ontario	83	43	43	17
British Columbia	80	38	27	45
Quebec	79	38	64	23

Source: Youth in Transition Survey, Statistics Canada, adapted from table 1 in Catalogue No. 81–595–M No.070 (retrieved 17 November 2008).

university headcount enrolment rates, and university participation rates of the traditional student groups (18- to 24-year-olds and 25- to 29-year-olds) as well as highest level of schooling and postsecondary degree production.

Participation by adults, aged twenty-four to twenty-six, in college and university, by December 2005, is evenly split between universities and colleges at 43 percent, with a substantial percentage (17 percent) attending other postsecondary institutions taking, for example, apprenticeship or trade programs (see table 3.4). Ontario is ahead of the national average in college and university participation rates of this cohort of adults, but it trails the national average in terms of participation in other vocational types of PSE.

Undergraduate enrolment rates in Ontario's universities vary significantly between part-time and full-time students (see table 3.5 and figure 3.6).[100] Between 1992–93 and 2008–09, full-time undergraduate enrolment increased by 56 percent. The most dramatic increases occur after the passage of the PSE Choice and Excellence Act, which expanded PSE in the province and into the early Liberal mandate. By contrast, undergraduate part-time enrolment decreased by 25 percent during the same time period. The greatest decreases in part-time undergraduate enrolment began during the NDP era between 1992 and 1998, with the onset of an economic recession, and continued into the PC administration, a period of fiscal retrenchment. Part-time undergraduate enrolments increase slightly between 1999 and 2003 during the end of the PC administration at a time

Table 3.5
University headcount enrollment undergraduate – level instructional programs, 1992–93, 1998–99, 2004–05, 2008–09

	1992–93	1998–99	2004–05	2008–09	% Change 1992–93 to 2008–09	1998–99 to 2008–09	2004–05 to 2008–09
CANADA	677,157	633,495	785,757	822,501	21.46	29.84	4.31
Full-time student	480,306	484,734	631,956	662,610	37.95	36.70	5.03
Part-time student	196,848	148,758	153,804	159,891	-18.77	7.48	1.45
ONTARIO	266,454	241,947	339,030	361,425	35.64	49.38	6.61
Full-time student	199,947	197,382	290,736	311,799	55.94	57.97	7.24
Part-time student	66,510	44,562	48,294	49,626	-25.39	11.36	2.76

Source: CANSIM, table 477–0013 (retrieved 1 June, 2011).

when the postsecondary system was expanded with the passage of the PSE Choice and Excellence Act, 2000. However, they dip again after the Liberals take power in 2003, despite investment in PSE and prominent accessibility goals, and then flatten. In 2008–09, part-time undergraduate participation rates remain below 1992–93 levels. Table 3.5 demonstrates that, historically, part-time and full-time undergraduate enrolment rates mirror changes at the national level but with more pronounced increases in full-time enrolments and greater decreases in part-time enrolments in Ontario. The data taken together suggest a movement towards mass education for full-time students, but they also indicate a participation gap between full-time and part-time students.

The pattern on graduate-level headcount enrolment rates for universities is similar to the undergraduate picture (see table 3.6). Between 1998–99 and 2008–09, full-time graduate enrolments in Ontario increased by 71 percent, while part-time enrolment counts increased by about 25 percent. Both rates increased substantially between 2004–05 and 2008–09, which coincides with the Liberal's graduate enrolment targets set out in the *Reaching Higher Plan* and the use of the multi-year accountability agreements, which tied funding to meeting enrolment targets. At the graduate level, Ontario enrolment patterns for part-time students diverge from the Canadian pattern. At both the graduate and undergraduate levels Ontario's enrolment patterns reflect an accessibility gap for part-time students

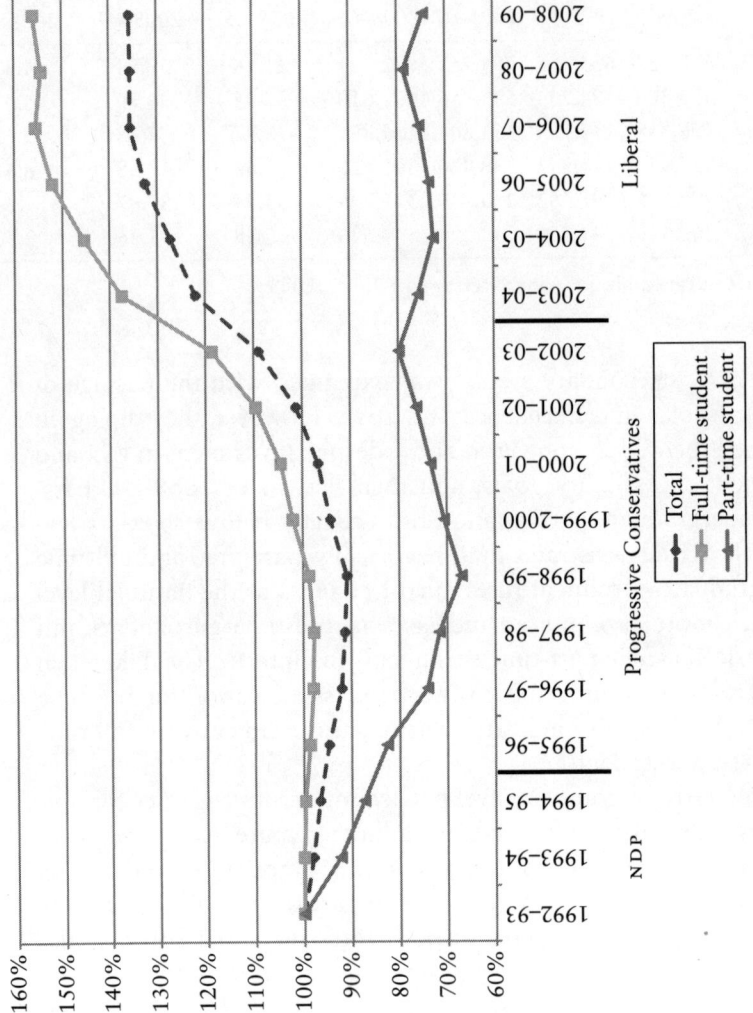

Figure 3.6
Change in headcount enrolment for Ontario universities, undergraduate, 1992–93 – 2008–09.
Source: Statistics Canada, CANSIM, table 442-0013.

Table 3.6
University headcount enrolment graduate-level instructional programs, 1992–93, 1998–99, 2004–05, 2008–09

	1992–93	1998–99	2004–05	2008–09	% Change 1992–93 to 2008–09	% Change 1998–99 to 2008–09	% Change 2004–05 to 2008–09
CANADA	109,494	113,481	148,776	170,076	55.33	49.87	12.52
Full-time student	71,706	78,828	105,645	127,527	77.85	61.78	18.35
Part-time student	37,788	34,653	43,131	42,549	12.60	22.79	-1.94
ONTARIO	38,304	37,665	48,450	60,441	57.79	60.46	24.76
Full-time student	27,021	28,668	38,262	49,158	81.93	71.47	28.48
Part-time student	11,283	9,000	10,185	11,283	0.00	25.37	10.78

Source: CANSIM, table 477–0013, (retrieved 1 June, 2010).

that, since the early 1990s, has gone largely unchecked in terms of effective policy. Part-time enrolment rates for graduate students, despite recent increases, remain at the 1992–93 levels in headcount numbers and reflect a 0 percent rate of change over the time period.

Overall university participation rates increased by approximately 5 percent between 1992–93 and 2008–09 for both age groups (18–24 years and 18–29 years) (See table 3.7). Again, these changes followed the national pattern (see figure 3.7). The enrolment and participation rates for undergraduate and graduate students remain stable in the mid-1990s under the PC government throughout a period of tuition increases and restructuring of student assistance programs (especially around tightening of eligibility criteria). Increases in total university enrolment and participation rates (as a percentage of the population aged 18–24 years and 18–29 years) over the Liberal administration (2003–04 to 2008–09) have been slight (less than 5 percent in both age groups), notwithstanding the Liberals' massive investment in PSE, the MYAA enrolment targets with funding attached, the tuition freeze, and a regulated tuition framework. This suggests that these policy mechanisms, whose purpose was to increase accessibility as reflected in *overall* participation and enrolment rates, have been only marginally successful. Conversely, the increases in tuition and the tightening of student assistance did not have a dramatic negative impact on the *overall* aggregate enrolment and participation rates. An analysis of enrolment and participation rates broken down by demographic groups

Table 3.7
Ontario total university enrolment and university participation rates (18–24 years and 18–29 years). Selected Years: 1992–93, 1995–96, 1998–99, 2001–02, 2004–05, and 2008–09

	1992–93	1995–96	1998–99	2001–02	2004–05	2008–09
Total university enrolment numbers	304,758	289,947	279,612	311,157	387,480	421,866
University participation rates, proportion of the population aged 18 to 24 yrs	28.23%	27.74%	26.95%	28.18%	32.75%	35.50%
University participation rates, proportion of the population aged 18–29 yrs old	15.09%	15.39%	15.14%	16.29%	19.37%	19.83%

Source: CANSIM 477–0013 and CANSIM 051–0001.

would reveal a more nuanced understanding of accessibility for groups traditionally underrepresented in PSE.[101]

We offer data on highest level of schooling and degree production to capture a broader notion of participation so as to include not only enrolment but also ongoing attendance, retention, and graduation rates. Table 3.8 suggests the proportion of Ontario's population with some PSE (a trade or college certificate/diploma, or university degree or higher) has increased steadily since 1991. In 2006, 51 percent of the population over fifteen years had some postsecondary education as their highest degree or certificate. Between 1986 and 2006, the proportion of the population with some PSE increased by almost 20 percent, suggesting a general upward trajectory of attendance, retention, and completion rates in postsecondary education. At the same time, 49 percent of the population over fifteen years had a high school graduation certificate or less. In the two decades from 1986 to 2006, the percentage of the population in Ontario with university as their highest degree has almost doubled, followed closely by college certificate or diploma. Similarly, the proportion of population over fifteen years with a master's degree also doubled in the same two decades (1986 to 2006) but still remains a small proportion of the total population (4 percent). However, the proportion of the population with a vocational trade certificate/diploma as their highest degree has remained constant over the last two decades

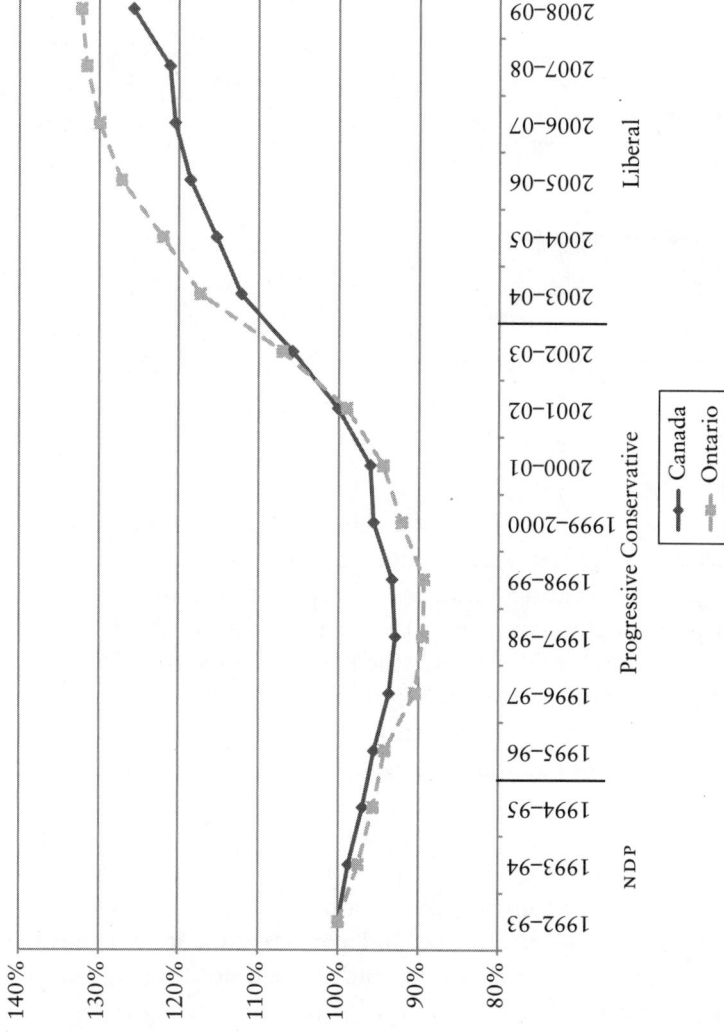

Figure 3.7
Change in university participation rate, Ontario and Canada, 1992–93 – 2008–09.
Source: Statistics Canada, CANSIM, table 447–0014, CANSIM, table 051–0001, and CANSIM, table 477–0013.

Table 3.8
Highest degree, certificate, or diploma attained for population 15 years and over. Ontario, 1986–2006

Year	1986 (%)	1991 (%)	1996 (%)	2001 (%)	2006 (%)
No degree. certificate, or diploma	46	39	35	32	22
High school graduation certificate	21	25	24	24	27
Trades certificate or diploma	9	10	9	9	8
College certificate or diploma	11	12	15	16	18
University certificate or diploma below	2	2	2	2	4
University degree	11	13	15	18	20
Bachelor's degree or higher	7	8	10	11	13
University certificate above bachelor	1	2	2	2	2
Medical degree	0	0	0	1	1
Master's degree	2	2	3	3	4
Earned doctorate	0	0	1	1	1
High school graduation certificate or less	68	63	59	55	49
Postsecondary education	32	37	41	45	51

Source: Canadian Census Data 2006, 2001, 1996, 1991, 1986.

(1986 to 2006). This could mean that the policy mechanisms intended to increase vocational training have been less successful. Or it could mean that vocational training is being taken up in the workplace and is not culminating in a certificate/diploma. Or it could mean that vocational training is not the highest degree for individuals who are obtaining university degrees or college certificates in addition to obtaining trade certification.

Similarly, degree production (degree, diplomas, and certificates) at both the graduate and undergraduate levels has steadily increased across administrations (see table 3.9). These trends suggest some success in the policies directed at expansion of degree granting and in those aimed at retention and completion

In summary, overall enrolments and participation in PSE have increased, although not for part-time students and not for all groups across all programs of study, especially traditionally underrepresented groups (see Jones et al. 2007). Further, increasing enrolments are accompanied by increasing tuition, which has disproportionately affected lower-income students. Increasing enrolments have also been accompanied by decreasing government funding. Altogether this translates into a less affordable system of PSE, especially for those in need.

Table 3.9
Degree production, Ontario 1992, 2008–09

Year	Graduate degrees, diplomas, and certificates granted	Undergraduate degrees, diplomas, and certificates granted
1995–96	10,269	56,448
1996–97	10,593	56,940
1997–98	10,218	55,206
1998–99	10,599	55,149
1999–2000	10,989	54,534
2000–01	11,115	55,950
2001–02	11,328	56,805
2002–03	12,060	58,527
2003–04	13,122	62,613
2004–05	14,097	66,042
2005–06	14,520	69,507
2003–04	13,122	74,286
2004–05	14,097	86,454
2005–06	14,520	69,507
2006–07	14,763	74,286
2007–08	15,426	86,454
2008–09	16,881	82,218

Source: CANSIM, table 477–0014 (retrieved 1 June, 2010).

'Useful and Relevant' R&D

Gross domestic expenditure on R&D (GERD) as a percentage of GDP has climbed since 1990, irrespective of which government has been in power (see figure 3.8). The sharpest increase took place between 1999 and 2001. However, figure 3.9 illustrates that the largest proportion of gross expenditures on R&D funded by business in 2008 was about 50 percent – the same rate as 1985. Similarly, the proportion of GERD funded by government in 2008 was at 1985 levels (about 20 percent), notwithstanding rhetoric about the importance of R&D in a competitive economy. The decline in the rate of expenditures on research funded by government is especially evident throughout the NDP and the PC administrations during the 1990s and may be associated with the recession in the early 1990s as well as the climate of restraint that followed the 1995 federal budget.

We observe in figure 3.9 that the proportion of expenditures on research by private non-profit funders has remained at 1985 levels and has been relatively constant throughout the last two decades. The proportion of expenditures on research by foreign funders

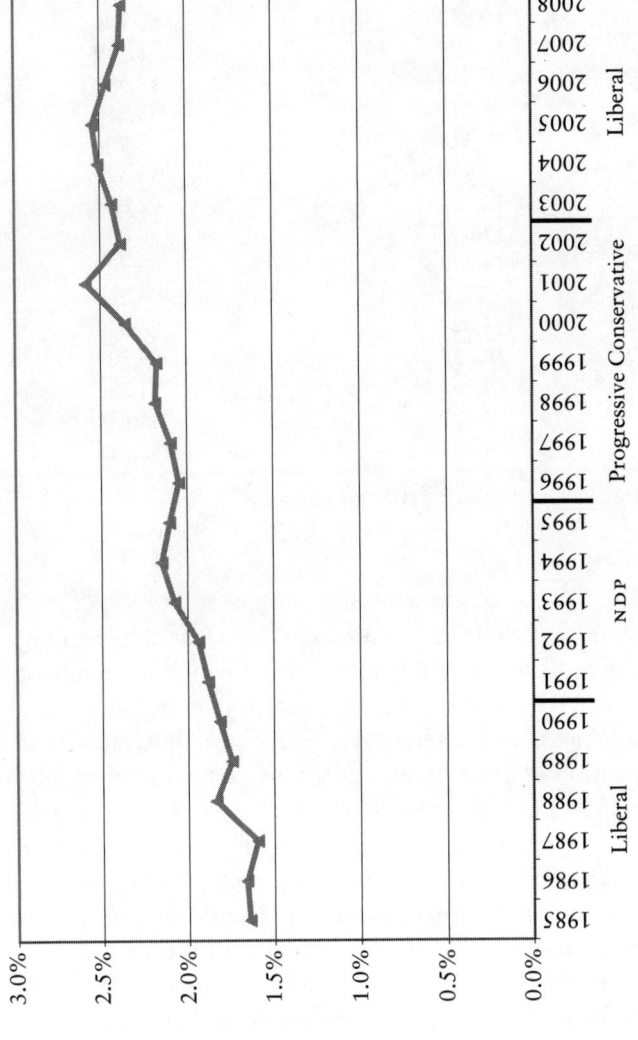

Figure 3.8
Gross expenditures on R&D for Ontario as a proportion of gross domestic product, 1985–2008.

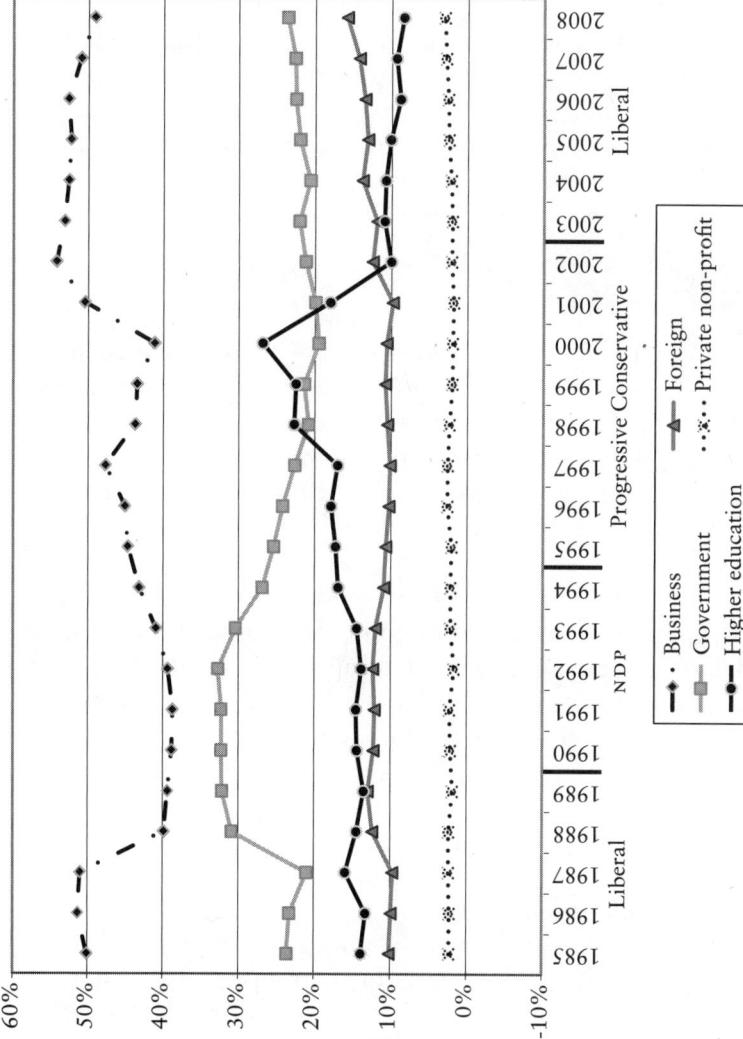

Figure 3.9
Proportion of gross expenditure on research funded by business, government, higher education, foreign and private non-profit funders for Ontario, 1985–2008.
Source: Statistics Canada.

slowly increased until 1997, peaked in 2000, and then dramatically fell to below 1990 levels. This pattern inversely mirrors business expenditures in the period from the late 1990s to 2004. While foreign expenditures were peaking, business expenditures were dipping in 2000. When foreign expenditures fell between 2000 and 2002, business expenditures rose sharply during the same period. The proportion of gross expenditures in research funded by higher education has increased slowly and slightly over the last two decades by about 5 percent to a high of about 15 percent in 2008. In summary, these data suggest that, while the Ontario provincial government has prioritized R&D in its policies, it may not have created the conditions for increasing investment from all R&D funders.

CONCLUSIONS

This chronology has identified various developments in postsecondary policy in the last two decades in Ontario that have contributed to a structural shift in the province's PSE. Our analysis of the evolution of PSE in Ontario began by identifying the defining characteristics of the postsecondary system. We conclude by revisiting and redefining these characteristics.

To understand the evolution of PSE in Ontario it is useful to return to the four broad types of PSE systems first developed by Clark (1983) and later discussed by Scott (1995), which we identified in chapter 1. As noted earlier, Ontario's postsecondary system consisted of universities, CAATs, agricultural colleges, colleges of health sciences and of art, a military college, privately funded degree-granting institutions, and registered private career colleges. Universities and CAATs have comprised the dominant sectors since 1965 (when the latter were created), running parallel to each other, distinct and lacking integration. Hence, PSE in Ontario has been referred to as a binary system.

However, during the period from 1985 until 2010 we see dramatic changes that have created new institutional arrangements. We argue that Ontario is moving out of the binary type and into a new type that is perhaps not captured by the Clark/Scott typology. Various policy themes, including increasing accessibility, enhancing accountability, improving skills training, and expanding capacity for R&D have contributed to this evolution. However, not all of these policy themes have been implemented with equal success. To summarize the trends, over the last two decades we have witnessed an expansion and opening up of the system to the private sector, the expansion of degree granting, increasing competition, and an effort to increase accessibility through increasing institutional diversity and student choice. Successive provincial governments have placed greater emphasis on meeting labour market needs through curricula and R&D in the postsecondary system. Connections with the private sector have been encouraged through postsecondary partnerships with industry. Government has shifted funding of postsecondary institutions, adopting market mechanisms to allocate resources and generate revenue, introducing KPIs attached to funding, and employing targeted and matching private-sector funding schemes. Greater emphasis has been placed on demonstrating accountability and quality through audits and adopting performance funding embedded within institutional contracts. Governments have also changed their approach to student tuition and assistance by implementing partial deregulation of fees in certain programs and adopting a tuition framework in others that increases tuition according to an agreed-upon schedule. Additionally, we see a shift in the form of student assistance away from government grants/loans and towards government scholarships as well as an emphasis on matched private-sector funding and greater university spending on student assistance. We also see a shift towards students and their families contributing more to the cost of their PSE.

Although these policy directions have been employed with different measures of success, taken together they have had structural and governance consequences for Ontario's PSE system. For example, the expansion of degree granting has created the potential for academic drift. Universities are no longer the only sector to offer degrees. By 2010, thirteen (out of twenty-five) Ontario publicly funded CAATs and two Ontario private colleges were offering applied degrees under ministerial consents.[102] With these developments, some CAATs are moving within what had previously been viewed as the "university territory" of research and degree granting (albeit *applied* research and degree granting). Additionally, a myriad of new program arrangements between colleges and universities has emerged (e.g., Guelph University at Humber).[103] Similarly, out-of-province, public, non-profit, and private for-profit institutions are applying for degree-granting status for mainstream programs already offered by Ontario universities. These institutions no longer need to seek out niche program areas that Ontario universities are unable or unwilling to offer.

By 2010, there were nine out-of-province institutions offering degrees in Ontario with ministerial consent. Increasingly, the binary structure of PSE in Ontario is becoming blurred and stratified by the range and number of competing institutions that have been given the authority to grant degrees. Academic drift can also be seen as resulting from the government's prioritizing of research, which has led to universities becoming more like each other by all engaging in adopting research-intensive missions. At the same time, the government has emphasized institutional diversification in order to address accessibility goals. The push and pull between academic drift and institutional diversity is playing out in Ontario. It is not clear if the system will flatten and homogenize or stratify and diversify. It is clear, though, that the system is no longer neatly classified as "binary." The policy directions taken by governments have started to change how the components of the system relate to each other.

Furthermore, the introduction of market principles into Ontario's PSE policies takes place within a particular historical context. Ontario does not have a systematic approach to coordination and policy making in PSE. It does not have a coordinating body for the whole system. The process of policy making has been characterized by an ad hoc and sometimes reactive approach to decision making. Over the last two decades, the policy process has, at some times, been marked by unilateral philosophically and ideologically driven decisions and, at other times, by pragmatics, influenced more by individual personalities and politics than by rationality and the application of the "rules of the game." Figure 3.10 provides an illustration of this, capturing the intersecting influence of political ideology, the economy, and the influence of personalities on government spending.

To compound matters, the Ontario government has historically demonstrated a limited capacity to conduct its own in-house research – research tailored to the Ontario postsecondary landscape and culture and so able to ideally inform policy decisions. Rather, our findings suggest that, over the past two decades, successive Ontario governments have looked to other jurisdictions inside Canada (i.e., Alberta and British Columbia) and outside of Canada (i.e., certain states in the United States, such as New Jersey) and have imported policies, principles, and approaches without regard for differences in educational, economic, cultural, and political contexts. The Ontario

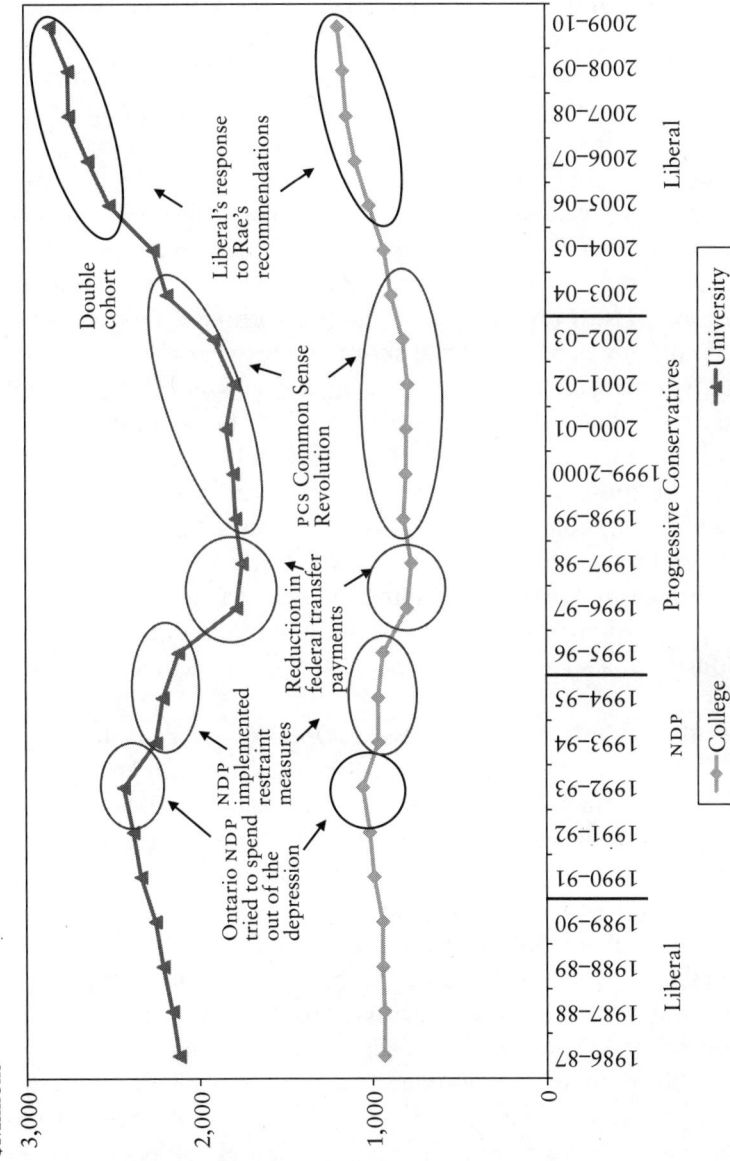

Figure 3.10
Provincial operating grants for Ontario college and university sectors (in 2002 dollars) and postsecondary education policies, 1986–87 – 2009–10.

government's policy research capacity has been increasing in recent years, following the creation of HEQCO.

Government consultation with postsecondary constituents has alternatively expanded and contracted over the last two decades, depending on the government in power. However, even in periods of consultation it is unclear whether the consultation has been meaningful or effective either in influencing the policy direction taken by the government or with regard to the functioning of the system.

Into this postsecondary policy and co-coordinating vacuum, market dynamics have been introduced in order to provide direction and even to produce changes in the organizational arrangement of the system. Ontario governments over the last two decades have used funding mechanisms to steer the system but without articulating an overall vision of where the system should go or what it should look like. One interviewee suggested that PC fiscal policies (1995–2003) were used to deliberately "shake up" the system rather than to provide needed coherence and direction. This causes some concern, especially for those critical of the market paradigm operating in what was once a public sphere. It also represents a significant divergence in recent years for Ontario PSE, which has been, historically, primarily public and structurally stable. More than any other time in its history, Ontario requires a clear vision for coordination and planning, along with a strong policy process in order to achieve this end in PSE.

Our findings confirm that successive Ontario governments have generally announced and pursued postsecondary policy themes of accessibility, accountability, linking PSE to the economy/labour market (through skills-training and R&D), and the implementation of marketization/privatization schemes, without necessarily providing the requisite support and funding to achieve success in these areas. Ontario governments link postsecondary policy to economic competitiveness, and yet, in order to be competitive, adequate support is needed. Ontario has fared poorly with regard to its financial support of PSE over the last two decades, raising concerns that system expansion and reform are exceeding operating support. This discrepancy is short-sighted and ultimately threatens the success of government policy priorities.[104] We do not assert a direct causal link between the policy decisions taken over the last two decades and postsecondary system measures – largely because of the policy vacuum within which Ontario PSE has operated over this period. Rather, we observe that, overall, fiscal policies, especially in times of restraint, have had an impact on the direction, arrangements, and functioning of PSE. This is especially so because Ontario has lacked an informed policy vision.

The case of Ontario also offers us an example of how significant structural change can be accomplished through strategic policy initiatives and without massive legislative system reform. While this approach has affected system organization by increasing the diversity of institutions; increasing the potential for degree granting; and moving the system closer to the market, where, historically, degree granting has been a public endeavour, it is less clear from the outcome data reviewed in this chapter whether these changes have significantly improved PSE when measured against stated government policy priorities. In other words, it is not clear whether accessibility and affordability has improved, whether the participation of certain underrepresented groups has improved, and whether participation in vocational and skills training has increased. Nevertheless, compared to other international and Canadian jurisdictions, Ontario has a large, relatively accessible system with high overall aggregate participation rates. It has dealt with, and even survived, recent government decreases in financial support, albeit at the expense of students and having turned to the private sector to make up losses.

Finally, Ontario does not fit the assumptions underlying the "bounded rationality" model of state planning and coordination, whereby policy decisions are the result of rules that are created and revised through a political process; individual actors are intentionally rational ("bounded rationality"); there are causal links between policy and performance; and "rules in use" ultimately determine the behaviour of the system (Richardson 2004). Rather, Ontario's postsecondary policy story is marked by the influence of local characteristics; unique cultural, economic, educational, and socio-political factors; along with political ideology. These have inevitably interacted with more common global trends in PSE – such as massification, the globalized knowledge economy, fluctuating public resources, and the quality assurance movement – to produce rapid change and contradictory trends in Ontario PSE over the last two decades.

4

PSE Policy in Quebec: A Case Study

CLAUDE TROTTIER, JEAN BERNATCHEZ, DONALD FISHER, AND KJELL RUBENSON

INTRODUCTION

This chapter presents the case study on PSE policy in Quebec. Drawing upon the analytical model that has emerged from the first stage of the AIHEPS Project (cf. chapter 1), our objectives are to reconstruct Quebec's PSE policy; place it within the environment in which it was developed; analyze the design, or structure, of the PSE system and its rules of the game; and study the relationships between system design in relation to its context. The system was completely restructured in the 1960s. Since then, successive changes have been introduced at the margin but have not modified its structure fundamentally.

The chapter is divided into six sections. First, we describe how the PSE system is designed, coordinated, and funded. Second, we cover the context in which the current system emerged in the 1960s and subsequently developed. Third, we reconstruct the main features of the decision-making process, what we have labelled as the "rules of the game." Fourth, we examine the system's four key policy themes and show how they are translated into its structure and fiscal, or funding, strategies. Fifth, we utilize a few quantitative system indicators as a means of connecting some outcomes to the stated policies. Finally, in the conclusion, we discuss the factors that helped to shape the system and the government's role in it.

PSE SYSTEM DESIGN

Quebec is located east of Ontario and covers an area of 1.7 million square kilometres. The population of 7.9 million people accounts for 23.2 percent of Canada's population.¹ French is the mother tongue for 79.6 percent of the Québécois, while English and "other languages" account for 8.2 percent and 12.2 percent, respectively (Office Québécois de la langue française 2008). The 108,430 self-declared Aboriginals in Quebec account for 1.5 percent of the total population.² First Nations peoples belong to ten Amerindian nations and the Inuit nation. They are spread out over fifty-five communities. Inuit live in fourteen northern villages and Amerindians generally live in reserves or in settlements administered by a band council.³

Between 1986 and 2010, the total population grew from approximately 6.7 million, or by 18 percent. Yearly growth was slow and uneven, ranging between a low of five thousand to a high of ninety thousand. The province's 18- to 24-year-old population slowly decreased over eight years until 1994, then changed very little until the three years between 2008 and 2010, when we can observe a slight increase. Over the whole period, the 18- to 24-year-old population recorded a marked decrease from 828,000 in 1986 to 707,000 in 2010. The pattern for the 18- to 29-year-old population is similar, although the decline continues through until 2000. Henceforth, this age group increases marginally, yet still, by 2010, it had decreased from 1.48 million in 1986 to 1.24 million (16 percent).⁴

Constitutionally, the provinces have exclusive jurisdiction to legislate on education. This right is not absolute, however, because, as noted in chapter 1, certain federal laws and programs have a direct impact on PSE. Nowhere is the tension between the two levels of government on the PSE file more pronounced than in Quebec. While this chapter focuses on provincial policies, it makes reference to the importance of federal interventions in funding provincial systems as a whole, mainly through the Canada Social Transfer and Equalization Program, and their influence on provincial policies, especially in the field of R&D. Historically, jurisdiction over PSE has been one of the most sensitive issues facing the federal government in its relations with Quebec.

Since provincial governments are responsible for education, systems vary from one province to the next. In Quebec, there are four levels of education: elementary, secondary, college, and university. Children start elementary school at the age of six; there are six years, or grades, preceded by kindergarten. Students begin to attend secondary school at age twelve. The secondary program leading to a secondary school diploma (SSD) lasts five years. As a rule, students finish high school at age seventeen, although their obligation to attend school ends after sixteen years of age. The program is divided into two cycles. Cycle 1 (two years) is centred on a common basic curriculum, while Cycle 2 (three years) is diversified. The General Education Path and the Applied General Education Path leading to the SSD lasts five years. Students have access to the Vocational Training Path (two years) leading to the diploma of vocational studies (DVS) after the completion of the third year of the General Education Path. They may also opt for a vocational education program path after the completion of the SSD. Another path, the Work-Oriented Training Path for students with learning difficulties, is based on the cooperative education method and leads to either the training certificate for a semi-skilled trade or the pre-work training certificate. PSE in Quebec is divided into two stages: (1) college education and (2) university education. This model is unique in the Canadian context.

College Network

College education is divided into pre-university programs (two years) and career, or technical, programs (three years) and is characterized by a comprehensive approach. All students must take a number of courses in general subjects, some of which (humanities, languages and literature, second language, and physical education) are common to both pre-university and career tracks. Graduates are awarded a diploma of college studies (DCS), delivered by the Ministère de l'Éducation du Loisir et du Sport (MELS), or the Quebec Ministry of Education, Leisure and Sport, which is required in order to attend university. Since the college education reform at the beginning of the 1990s, students may choose a third path – the orientation and integration session. This one-semester path is for students who meet the requirements of the college but who want to strengthen their academic record to be eligible for the program of their choice, or who need to clarify their vocational orientation, or who just wish to explore the curriculum. They profit from supervision tailored to their needs. This path was designed to facilitate the transition from secondary school to PSE.

The college and the university sectors are not parallel but they are structurally complementary. These special features differentiate Quebec's PSE system from those of the other provinces, where students can go directly from high school to university (Doray et al. 2009). Most students in Quebec complete a pre-university program before they go to university. Although college career programs are designed to prepare students for the labour market, graduates can opt to go on to university (27.5 percent in 2009–10 [Gouvernement du Québec 2011b), subject to certain conditions.

The college network includes forty-eight Collèges d'enseignement général et professionnel (CÉGEPS) (forty-three of which are French, five of which are English), eleven institutions that come under a ministry other than education (Institut de technologie agroalimentaire, Institut de tourisme et d'hôtellerie, Conservatoires de musique), and forty-eight private colleges (twenty-five accredited for funding and twenty-three with permits only). Public colleges, or CÉGEPS, come under the General and Vocational Colleges Act and are administered by a board of governors made up of teachers, students, and community representatives. Private colleges are governed by the Act Respecting Private Education, which sets out the conditions for obtaining a permit to operate from MELS once the Commission consultative de l'enseignement privé (Private Education Advisory Committee) has been consulted. Private colleges are part of the same school system as are CÉGEPS. Some of them are accredited for government funding while others – most of which provide career training in specialized fields – only have a permit to operate.

In 2010–11, 217,674 students were attending college: 84.5 percent in regular programs and 15.5 percent in continuing education. Students of the English CÉGEPS represented 16.3 percent of the regular students and 19.1 percent of the continuing education students. In the regular programs, 45.5 percent of the students were enrolled in career programs leading to a DCS in career training or an attestation of college studies (ACS), whereas this was the case with 78.1 percent of the adult education students. In all, only 9.7 percent of students were enrolled in private colleges (35.4 percent in regular programs and 64.6 percent in continuing education), even though private institutions, many of which are small and specialize in career training, represent 50 percent of the college network.[5]

Pre-university education includes the following programs: natural science, humanities, liberal arts, music, dance, fine arts, science, liberal arts, history and civilization, and the international baccalaureate. The 128 technical training, or career education, programs leading to a DCS are grouped under five broad categories: (1) biological and agri-food technology, (2) physics technology, (3) human affairs technology, (4) business administration, and (5) arts and graphic communications. Since 1994, all programs leading to a DCS include four components: (1) general courses common to all programs, (2) general courses specific to the program chosen, (3) complementary general courses, and (4) courses specifically for the program chosen. These are Quebec government, not institutional, programs, and the diploma is awarded by MELS.

In order to attend college, a person must have a general SSD or a DVS. Many college programs are selective and have prerequisites beyond the minimum college admission requirements. This stratification of some college programs is linked to the university programs to which they lead, many of which have enrolment quotas.

The number of DCS-BA programs stemming from agreements between universities and CÉGEPs has increased in recent years. These programs aim to harmonize college career training and university training, and they allow the university covered by the agreement to credit career training as one year towards a BA. This enables students to get both a DCS and a BA in five or six years instead of six or seven, depending on the discipline. Other kinds of "bridge" arrangements allow students in career programs to be credited for certain college courses at university.

Colleges have also developed career certificate programs that lead to an ACS. These short specialization or retraining programs are designed for adults and can include anything from seven to thirty courses. They are geared towards meeting personnel training needs and do not include any general courses. These are institutional programs, and the ACS is awarded by the college and not MELS, as in the case of the DCS. To be eligible for one of these programs, a person must already have training/experience that the college considers sufficient and must meet one of the following general conditions: the candidate must have been out of school for at least one school year; she or he must be covered by an agreement concluded between the college and an employer or by a government program; or she or he must have completed at least one year of PSE. In 2005, more than twenty thousand (65 percent full-time) students were enrolled in a program leading to an ACS (Cormier et Nadeau 2006).

Adult education departments offer non-credit training that does not require MELS approval and does not lead to a diploma – although an attestation, or certificate, is provided by the college.

This is the case, for example, with customized training, whereby activities are developed specifically to meet the needs of the business concerned. These courses fit in with the obligations provided for in the Act to Promote Workforce Skills Development and Recognition, according to which all employers with payrolls of over $1 million must invest at least 1 percent in training.

University Network

Quebec's university network includes eighteen institutions (universities, vocational schools, and institutes), the only bodies that can offer university education under the Act Respecting Educational Institutions at the University Level. They have rights and powers with respect to admission requirements, program definition, hiring, collective negotiations, and degree requirements. They are therefore far more independent than colleges.

Quebec has four French-language universities, including the Université du Québec, which alone has six general education institutions, or campuses, in different regions; a scientific research institute (Institut national de la recherche scientifique); and two vocational schools, one specializing in public administration and the other in engineering. The network also includes three English-language universities (see appendix 5).

Prior to 1968, universities were created by charter. Each university was thus a private institution that nevertheless relied heavily on public funding. The Université du Québec, which was created by an act of incorporation, and its components – branches, professional schools, institutes, and so on – are public institutions and have the same rights and powers as have universities created by charter. Charter-created universities whose revenue mostly comes from public funds are subject to the same operating and accountability rules and the same tuition policy as the Université du Québec, which means that, in fact, all Quebec universities are public universities.

In the fall of 2010–11, 281,954 students were enrolled in university programs: 74.8 percent in French universities and 25.2 percent in English universities; 63.7 percent full-time and 36.3 percent part-time; and 76.7 percent as undergraduates, 18.1 percent in master's degree programs, and 5.2 percent in doctoral programs. Women represented 58.9 percent of undergraduates, 56.8 percent of the master's students, and 47.9 percent of the doctoral students.[6]

In 2009–10, 24,475 international students were enrolled in university programs (8.7 percent of the student body). This percentage was lower in the French-language universities (6.5 percent) than in English-language universities (14.3 percent). The country of origin was also different. Most of the international students in French-language universities were from France, North Africa, and West Africa, while, in the English universities, most were from the United States and Asian countries (Gouvernement du Québec 2008).

The three levels of university degree programs are bachelor's (undergraduate), master's, and doctoral. These programs are organized on the basis of activities for which students are credited. Undergraduate programs lead to a bachelor's degree (3 years/90 credits or 4 years/120 credits), which prepares students for the job market, or to a certificate (1 year/30 credits), which is frequently offered as initial training or, even more often, as continuing education. To be admitted to a bachelor's program, candidates must have a DCS (from a pre-university or career program) or education and experience that is considered equivalent. Master's programs lead to a master's degree (2 years/45 credits), which confers a specialization or prepares students for research or a master's diploma (1 year/30 credits) focusing on a specialization. Doctoral programs lead to a doctorate in a specific discipline or field (3 to 5 years/90 credits).

System Coordination

Coordination of the education system is chiefly the responsibility of MELS.[7] MELS is in charge of implementing most laws and regulations concerning PSE. In addition, the Ministère du Développement Économique, de l'Innovation et de l'Exportation (MDEIE), or Ministry of Economic Development, Innovation and Export (Trade), is for the most part responsible for research and knowledge transfer support in conjunction with economic development. This ministry's "valorization-and-transfer" subsector coordinates knowledge transfer initiatives and is involved in the activities of technology transfer and liaison centres, university-business liaison offices, and university entrepreneurship centres.

In contrast to other Canadian provinces or American states the government has not delegated powers over PSE to any autonomous or semi-autonomous regulating agencies. To a certain extent, the

Conseil des universités, or the Council of Univerities, which was created in 1968, played this role for the universities, but it was abolished in 1993, at the same time as the *Conseil des colleges*, or the Council of Colleges. However, the system does have many regulating, consulting, evaluation, and accounting agencies.

At the system level there are two coordinating bodies. First is the National Assembly Culture and Education Commission (made up exclusively of members of the National Assembly [MNAS]), which has the mandate (among other things) to study the directions, activities, and management of government education agencies for all school levels. For example, since 1995, universities have been obliged to submit an annual report to the commission and to appear before it at least once every three years.

Second is the Supérieur de l'éducation (CSE), or the Superior Council of Education, which is an advisory agency. It was created at the same time as the Ministère de l'Éducation in 1964 but by a separate law that confirmed its autonomy. The CSE's mandate is to advise the minister on the government's educational mission, to ensure the education system keeps pace with developments in society, and to indicate what changes should be made. The 1993 abolition of the Conseil des collèges and the Conseil des universités confirmed the scope of its mandate. The CSE is made up of several bodies or agencies, in particular the Commission de l'enseignement collégial (CEC), or College Education Commission, and the Commission de l'enseignement et de la recherche universitaires (CERU), or University Teaching and Research Commission, whose mandates are to prepare recommendations on various aspects of PSE for the CSE. The Comité consultatif sur l'accessibilité financière aux études (CCAFE), or Advisory Committee on the Financial Accessibility of Education, established in 1999, also reports to the CSE but acts independently, and its briefs are not subject to CSE approval.

At the college level there are four coordinating bodies as well as various associations representing students and teachers.[8] First is the Commission d'évaluation de l'enseignement collégial (CEEC), or College Education Evaluation Commission, created in 1993. It is an independent government agency whose mandate is to evaluate program implementation, college policy relating to learning and program evaluation, and colleges' strategic plans. This commission took on some of the responsibilities of the Conseil des collèges (which was created in 1979) when it was abolished. The other part of the Conseil des collèges mandate was entrusted to CEC, which comes under the CSE.

Second is the Fédération des CÉGEPS, created in 1969, which is a voluntary federation of the province's forty-eight CÉGEPS. It defends their interests, promotes collaboration and expertise exchange, and represents them during collective agreement negotiations. Third is the Association des collèges privés du Québec (Association of Private Colleges of Quebec), which groups together those private colleges in Quebec accredited for subsidization (i.e., that qualify for partial government funding by MELS) and plays a role analogous to that of the Fédération des CÉGEPS. Fourth is the *RéseauTrans-tech*, which groups forty-six college centres for technology transfer (CTTCS) afiliated with CÉGEPS. The mandate of these centres is to perform applied research activities and to provide business assistance and information in support of regional development and innovative technology projects, with respect to a specific field linked to their career training expertise. Fifth is CÉGEP International, which groups the CÉGEPS and supports them in the elaboration and the implementation of their strategies of internationalization (projects of international cooperation, student mobility, recruitment of international students).

At the university level there is one major coordinating body as well as four bodies concerned with research and development. In addition, there are several agencies, organizations, and associations that are either part of the system or have links with its regulating agencies, as well as federations representing professors and students.[9] The Conference of Rectors and Principals of the Universities of Québec (CRÉPUQ), created in 1963, is a private umbrella organization for all university institutions. It represents them, plays an important role on their behalf with respect to government, and, since the Conseil des universités was abolished in 1993, has been the only non-governmental body for consultations and collaboration on university matters, especially regarding program evaluation and student mobility within the Quebec system and abroad.[10] In parallel to the federal system, Quebec has three independent government research funding agencies: (1) Fonds de recherche du Québec – Nature et technologies (Quebec Nature and Technology Research Fund), (2) Fonds de recherche du Québec – Société et culture (Quebec Society and Culture Research Fund), and (3) Fonds de recherche du

Québec – Santé (Quebec Health Research Fund). The boards of directors of the three funding agencies are chaired by the chief scientist. According to the law that created this new position in 2011, the chief scientist's mandate is to advise the minister of economic development, innovation, and exportation on the development of research and science; to work to enhance Quebec's position and influence in Canada and internationally; to coordinate efforts pertaining to issues that are common to the three funds as well as intersectoral research activities; and to be responsible for administering the funds' human, physical, financial, and information resources.

Funding Mechanisms

According to the budgetary rules for CÉGEPs for 2010–11,[11] the resources allocated come from two sources: (1) the operating fund (regular programs, continuing education, and self-financed services), taken directly from appropriations voted by the National Assembly, and (2) the investment fund (asset maintenance, computer equipment, and capital expenditure), financed by long-term loans. Decisions regarding investments come under a three-year plan put together with the institutions, but it is MELS that makes these decisions.

The operating fund includes:

1 fixed allowances that guarantee minimum funding for regular and continuing education, whatever the size of the CÉGEP, and an envelope to support its own initiatives regarding, among others things, measures to promote student success and services, research, and the facilitation of its development;
2 pedagogical activities and allowances regarding the expenses associated with teaching (except teachers' salaries);
3 building allowances (maintenance, energy, security, insurance);
4 teachers' salaries' allowances – the main item of the operating fund – which are calculated in a very technical manner (the budgetary rules concerning their task and compensation take into account the agreement negotiated with unions and include, in particular, a measurement of teachers' activities based on the number of class/periods/week for a given term);
5 specific allowances for carrying out objectives defined by MELS regarding, for example, measures to support work-study programs,

student success initiatives, research on teaching and learning, technological research, college technology transfer centres, accessibility of handicapped persons, members of Aboriginal and ethnic communities for college education, sport-study programs, in-service training programs, etc.

According to the Act Respecting Private Education and the Régime budgétaire et financier des établissements privés d'ordre collegial,[12] the funding of private colleges accredited for subsidization is inseparable from that of public colleges. The ministry ensures that the ratio of subsidies granted to accredited private colleges in relation to those granted to CÉGEPs remains stable, assuming that the parameters of the two networks remain the same (number of institutions, client-bases, surface area, etc.). To this end, "changes in funding in these networks must have the same variation rate for each fiscal year" (Ministère de l'éducation, du loisir et du sport, 2006, 7 [our translation]). Subsidization of private institutions solely involves operations (not investment) and is based on five factors: (1) the student-year number, regardless of the program taken; (2) the type of program in which a student is enrolled; (3) the rental value of buildings considering the "theoretical" surface area required for students; (4) part-time education; and (5) special MELS-supported activities associated with private college educational development (e.g., equipment, in-service training, research).

Up to 2000, operating grants were allocated to universities on a historical basis as the basic operating grant from the previous year served as a benchmark for calculating annual funding. This method was criticized for its lack of transparency as well as for its lack of regulating mechanisms with regard to funding activity classification and was, therefore, changed. That same year, the government adopted the Quebec Policy on University Funding (Gouvernement du Québec 2000), which was based on two principles: (1) the government's responsibility for determining its overall contribution and distributing resources among institutions and (2) respect for university autonomy. As in the case of CÉGEPs, operating expenses are financed directly from annual appropriations voted by the National Assembly, and capital expenditures are financed through loans that are reimbursed through debt service. Universities have more leeway, however, when it comes to using the funds they receive. Investment expenditures are authorized under a five-year plan. Some subsidies are recurrent and are granted, according to a standard framework, for new equipment and furnishings or new initiatives. Others are granted for specific purposes – property expansion, for instance. Investments in infrastructure are strongly regulated. Any investment of more than $1 million must be approved by MELS, according to the Loi sur les investissements universitaires.

In accordance with the budgetary rules for operating grants, operating expenditures have two components: (1) general funding and (2) specific funding.[13] The general funding component allows institutions to assume recurrent teaching-related costs, based on a measure of educational activities for a given year; teaching and research support; property maintenance (land and buildings); and special missions of institutions recognized for funding. The "teaching" part includes expenses linked to teacher compensation. The method takes into account 100 percent of the variation in the number of students measured in terms of full-time equivalency. The budgetary allowance for this component is distributed among institutions in proportion to the average number of students for the previous three years, weighted in accordance with education level and discipline group. In 2006, new scores were assigned after consultation with CRÉPUQ regarding types of programs (BA, MA, PhD) and discipline groups based on an analysis of actual costs. The scores of MA and PhD, medical sciences, and engineering programs in particular have increased considerably. This new approach has had an impact on the internal dynamics of the institutions. "Teaching and research support," including fixed and variable allowances, is for the operation of libraries, computer and audiovisual services, and administration. The "land and buildings" allocation is for spaces used for purposes other than research. Since 2008, the exclusion of spaces used for research from this envelope represents a change in relation to previous years and stems from Quebec's new indirect research cost policy (adopted in 2004) and the decision to fund these spaces via investment expenditures. Indirect research costs are now mainly supported by various programs covering the cost of the researches subsidized by the federal (for research supported by the federal government) and provincial agencies that provide direct research funding or by the private enterprises that enter research partnerships with universities. In conjunction with the "special missions" component, MELS recognizes that some institutions have a special mission (or, in the case of universities located in outlying areas, a particular mission regarding accessibility, regional development, and community services), and it grants them additional funding.

The specific funding component of operating expenditures is connected with special adjustments and grants awarded in trust. Special adjustments are numerous and refer to targeted needs, many of which correspond to orientations in the Quebec Policy on Universities. They refer, for example, to allowances of $500, $1,000, and $7,000, respectively, for the completion of a BA, MA, or PhD in relation to the policy concerning accessibility (not only to institutions but also to a grade or diploma). Special aduljstments also provide support for indirect research costs ($43.6. million in 2011); research conducted in small institutions; medical teaching of interns in affiliated hospital centres; a student's transition from university to the labour market; libraries; student services; a health insurance plan for graduate students; the integration of handicapped students and immigrants trained abroad; Aboriginal students; the international mobility of students; a work-study program for foreign students; collaboration between CÉGEPs and universities; a program for attracting professors of high calibre in the fields of engineering and administration; continuing education of school personnel; projects with partner groups to answer social needs; and endowment funds and university foundations' "matching" contributions ($0.25 for every dollar collected, up to a maximum of $1 million per institution).

The budgetary rules also include the policy on tuition and other compulsory fees as well as the management of allowances, including the payment ($228 million in 2011) conditional on a balanced budget, the transmission to MELS of the annual financial report and of standardized information about the number of FTEs (and its verification), research, personnel, and premises. The highly specific nature of these budgetary rules is illustrative of the kind of control MELS exerts on universities.

In addition to these resources allocated through operating grants, in the 2010–11 budget the government announced the decision to implement the University Funding Plan (Government of Québec 2011a), a six-year plan that will give universities annual access to additional revenues that will reach $850 million in 2016–17 ($320 million to take into account inflation and changes in the student population and an additional $530 million gradually allocated to support specific initiatives or programs). This additional funding will be allocated for the following purposes: 50 to 60 percent for the quality of teaching, 15 to 25 percent for the quality of research, 10 to 20 percent to ameliorate the competitive positioning of the universities, and 5 to 15 percent to improve administration and management. More than half the additional funding will come from the government, 31 percent from the students, and 18 percent from donations and other university revenues.

Tuition fees – the second source of additional funding – will be raised gradually regardless of the discipline by $325 per year beginning in 2012. Over five years they will rise by $1,625 to $3,793 in 2016–17, compared with $2,168 in 2011–12, and then they will be indexed. Thus the student contribution to the total university revenue will be raised to 16.9 percent in 2016–17 compared to 12.7 percent in 2008–09. However, the Loans and Bursaries Program will be modified. All the bursary students will be compensated in full for the increase in tuition fee. The students who are eligible for the maximum student loan, but not a bursary, will be able to obtain an additional loan with advantageous terms. Moreover, the tax credit for tuition fees (20 percent) and the Deferred Payment Plan that is available to former students who have difficulty repaying their student loans will be improved, and the contribution from the parents or the spouse of a student that is included in the calculation of the awarded amount of a loan or bursary will be reduced.

The third source of additional funding comes from the universities and government through Placements Universités, a new lever introduced by the government to encourage more donations from individuals and business. As mentioned previously, there was already a specific government fund concerned with "matching" contributions from endowment funds and university foundations ($0.25 for every dollar collected, up to a maximum of $1 million per institution and $10 million for all the universities). Placements Universités will now have a budget of $40 million as the global $10 million ceiling has been eliminated. The government has also set a fund-raising growth objective for each university for each of the next five years. They are asked to organize fund-raising campaigns aimed at increasing funds collected by 8 percent per year relative to the average donations they actually received from 2004 to 2009. Finally, universities will have to launch new initiatives to boost their other revenue sources (research revenue, revenue from certain continuing education services, and revenue from ancillary services). In 2010–11, this source of revenue accounted for 15.6 percent ($583 million) of the university operating revenue. Universities are expected to make an additional effort and to increase their other revenue sources by 1 percent per year beyond the growth rate of 1.7 percent observed over the past six years, for a total growth of 2.7 percent per year between 2012 and 2016 – an increase of $101 million.

Because the government wants to make sure that the additional revenue will be used in conformity with the criteria set out in the Quebec University Funding Plan, the universities will have to conclude partnership agreements aimed at improving their overall performance. The agreement may contain optional commitments concerning issues related to the situation of each institution. They will also have to account for the use of the additional revenue, make public the commitment contained in the agreement, and include in their annual report (tabled in the National Assembly) information on the implementation of the agreement. In order to determine the extent to which the goals identified in each institutional agreement have been met, the government has defined precise targets and indicators of performance concerning the quality of teaching and student services, the quality of research, the competitive positioning of universities in Canada and abroad, and the administration and management (see appendix 6).

EMERGENCE AND EVOLUTION OF THE PSE SYSTEM, 1960–2011

The current configuration of the PSE system dates back to the 1960s. The objectives of this section are to reconstruct the conditions under which it emerged; show how it was consolidated, and its development planned, during the years from 1970 to 1985; describe its subsequent evolution; and go over the main features of the decision-making process – that is, the rules of the game. In terms of our analytical model, we both (1) pinpoint aspects of the social, economic, and political environment in which the system emerged and developed and (2) put its orientations, structure, funding, and dynamics into perspective.

Emergence of the Current System, 1960–70

With the end of the "reign" of the Union Nationale Party in Quebec, a vast reform movement got under way sanctioned by the Liberal government of Jean Lesage (1960–66): this was known as the Quiet Revolution (see appendix 7). Although the term "Quiet Revolution" may seem like a contradiction in terms, it is not: it refers to rapid but orderly change by favouring state intervention in social and economic development and state participation in public affairs. This approach to social change has been referred to as the "Quebec model" (Hamel et Jouve 2006). Modernization and catching up were the objectives of the Quiet Revolution, which advocated reform and the assertion of national identity. Numerous initiatives led to this model of development.

One reform involved modernizing the education system by putting it under government control and making accessibility its top priority. This reform "was carried out in the name of a nationalist ideology geared towards catching up economically, according to which a higher level of education would lead to greater productivity, prompt more intensive development of Québec society, and enable Québec to have more control over its economy and development" (Bélanger et al. 1975, 219 [our translation]). This reform is the most well known symbol of the Quiet Revolution. It represented an affirmation of Quebec's own culture, which was in the process of breaking with Roman Catholic, French-Canadian culture. It meant a commitment to social change associated with the transfer of responsibility for and control over education from Church to State (i.e., the province) as well as massive government intervention in this jurisdiction, along with promotion of French-speaking Québecois (Ferretti 2000).

Before 1960, the education system was under-funded and lacked coordination. Only 63 percent of French-speaking students completed elementary school. The system was mostly managed by the Church and financed by the government and local authorities. The government's responsibilities were scattered among a few ministries. Private "classical" colleges, run by the dioceses or religious communities, were, for the overwhelming majority of francophones, the only way to PSE. French-language universities were Catholic institutions.

In 1959, the Union Nationale government introduced a change in direction with the settlement of the federal-provincial dispute on university funding and the increase in grants to school boards, colleges, and universities. The most important changes, however, were elicited by a set of laws put together subsequent to the Royal Commission of Inquiry on Education in the Province of Quebec (the

Parent Report), which was instituted in 1961 under the new Liberal government. This legislation proposed a complete reorganization of the education system based on the role that education should play in a democratic industrial society through the provision of equality of access (Gouvernement du Québec 1963–66).

In this context the Ministère de l'Éducation (MEQ) and the CSE were created in 1964; a network of secondary schools grew up in all of Quebec's regions; programs and curricula were redefined; a new level of PSE was created; teacher training was switched from "Normal Schools" to universities; and a number of steps were taken to ensure the education system's development.

Four important changes occurred at the postsecondary level. First, in 1967 the first institutions in the college network were built on the foundations of the classical colleges, technical and career colleges, and Normal Schools. They were supposed to solve several problems: the scattered and compartmentalized nature of first-level postsecondary institutions; the irrelevance of the extremely selective private classical colleges (whose curricula were mostly centred on Greco-Latin humanities and philosophy, paying little attention to science) and the fact that they were just about the only way to gain access to university; the shortcomings of the institutes of technology (whose general programs and basic science programs were inadequate); structural inequity in terms of education for francophones, who, due to the structure and curriculum of the classical program, had to complete fifteen years of education before they could go to university (compared to twelve or thirteen years for anglophones) (Conseil supérieur de l'éducation 1988). These intermediate colleges introduced a two-level PSE system (colleges and universities). The goal was to create comprehensive institutions offering courses common to pre-university and career programs, to promote access to PSE in outlying areas, and, through career training, to more adequately address societal needs for specialized/skilled personnel.

The other three changes involved the creation of a loans and bursaries program based on the needs of college and university students, its purpose being to remove obstacles to accessibility; the creation in 1968 of the Université du Québec, with campuses in different regions; and the creation of the Conseil des universités. The Conseil's mandate was broader than that of other advisory committees as it acted as an intermediary between universities and the government until 1993, when it was abolished.

At the university research level, the Parent Commission had proposed the creation of a council that would be responsible for supporting basic research. During this period, university research was perceived as being conducted within a "republic of science," which was in charge of its own decisions (Gingras et al. 1999, 21). Not until 1969 were the proposed bodies and agencies finally created, although not in the form of a council. To support research, the government set up a researcher training and concerted action program known as the Formation des chercheurs et action concertée (FCAC). That same year, it supported the creation of a new Université du Québec institution, the Institut national de la recherche scientifique (INRS), or Quebec Scientific Research Institute, dedicated chiefly to research.

SYSTEM CONSOLIDATION AND PLANNING, 1970–85

From 1970 to 1976: Consolidation of System and Increased Effectiveness

This period coincided with the first two terms of Robert Bourassa's Liberal government (1970–73, 1973–76). The Quiet Revolution continued with this government's major health care reforms, the introduction of the legal aid program in 1973, the proclamation of French as Quebec's official language in 1974, and the creation of the Quebec Charter of Human Rights and Freedoms in 1975. Faced with the economic repercussions of the oil shock in the early 1970s, the government instigated huge public investment programs to promote economic development – in particular, the construction of hydroelectric dams, highways, and public buildings.

This period was marked by political upheaval, notably during the October Crisis in 1970 when a British diplomat was kidnapped and a Quebec government minister killed by members of the Front de libération du Québec (FLQ), or Quebec Liberation Front. Social tensions grew after that, with the radicalization of the unions, the imprisonment of union leaders, and activism on the part of groups located on the far left of the political spectrum.

As far as education was concerned, the agencies and bodies created during the preceding period continued to do their work. The issue of access to the system remained crucial, but questions were raised about the operation of CÉGEPs. Efforts were made to finish implementing the PSE system, consolidate it, and plan for its development in order to increase its effectiveness. As early as 1971, the Rocquet Report raised a number of questions regarding the orientation and pedagogical organization of CÉGEPs. The CSE (Nadeau Report) (1975) analyzed the college network and made recommendations designed to consolidate it and to introduce institutional evaluation.

At the university level, the Conseil des universités launched an initiative regarding the general objectives of PSE and the broad orientation of its institutions. It published four reports (Conseil des universités 1973), which were designed to lay the groundwork for system planning in order to increase access, to introduce greater program specialization, and to recognize both university teaching and research as instruments of formation. Providing "services to the community" was approved as one of the university's missions, and universities were compared to a pool of expertise in the service of society. The Conseil recommended the creation of a decentralized network, with every university having to plan its own development while, at the same time, participating in system planning.

Regarding research, the first scientific policy in 1971 confirmed the central role played by universities but failed to mention the contribution of business. As Gingras et al. (1999, 74 [our translation]) note: "For all intents and purposes, university researchers are the only ones in charge of the orientation, choice and evaluation of research activities and therefore have maximum autonomy with regard to external demands, whether they be economic, political or social."

From 1976 to 1985: Social Democratic Project and Planning

This period covers the two terms when the Parti Québécois, led by René Lévesque, was in power (1976–81, 1981–85). The first term was characterized by the government's desire to demonstrate that it could govern well and not be solely concerned with organizing a referendum on Quebec sovereignty. With its social-democratic orientation, the government adopted progressive legislation on financial contributions to political parties, strike breakers, and automobile insurance. The 1977 Charter of the French Language (Bill 101) asserted the supremacy of the French language in Quebec and regulated the language of the workplace, signs and notices, and education – notably making it mandatory for the children of immigrants to attend French elementary and secondary schools while maintaining freedom to choose the language of instruction at the postsecondary level. It also launched a cultural development debate (Gouvernement du Québec 1978). Socio-economic summits were held, promoting collaboration between the government and social and economic partners and illustrating a style of governance that made room for civil society participation. Finally, in 1980, the government asked the people to vote in a referendum on its proposal for sovereignty-association with the other Canadian provinces. The proposed arrangement was rejected by 59 percent of the vote.

The Lévesque government was returned to power in 1981. Its second term was marked by major problems linked to the economic recession, high unemployment, and its unpopularity due to the measures it adopted in response to the recession – especially cutbacks in civil servant salaries. Added to this was disillusionment over the sovereignty issue, which was exacerbated by the adoption of the Constitution Act, 1982, subsequent to the federal government's decision to repatriate the Constitution according to terms and conditions that ran counter to Quebec's wishes.

Education was vital to the government's orientations, and it had to take stock of the problems caused by the PSE system's rapid growth. Education was part of the cultural mission upon which it placed a great deal of importance and continued to be perceived as a tool for social, economic, and political development, just as it had been at the time of the school reforms in the 1960s. From its first term in power, the Parti Québécois placed the Ministry of Education under the supervision of a cultural development "super ministry." It published a Green Paper on primary and secondary education (MEQ 1977) as well as a policy statement (MEQ 1979). During its second term, it proposed reforms based on decentralization to the schools (MEQ 1982).

With respect to PSE, the government set up the Commission of Inquiry on Universities in 1978 to analyze indicators that would enable it to define the choices available (Gouvernement du Québec 1979). This decision bore testimony to the government's efforts to plan and consolidate the system. The proposed orientations made the mission of universities more hierarchical. Training and research were considered to be the fundamental orientations, and services to the community were seen as an extension thereof.

In 1981, the minister of education submitted orientations for consultations preliminary to the development of a policy on universities (Laurin 1981). This novel approach did not come to anything until twenty years later, when the Parti Québécois government formally adopted the first Quebec policy statement on universities in 2000. According to the minister, during the 1960s and 1970s, the government had mostly concerned itself with elementary, secondary, and college education. Initiatives at the university level were isolated and were made without any explicit reference to an overall vision for university development. While recognizing the universities' autonomy and freedom, he justified his actions by stressing that the state funded the lion's share of their costs and that they were a network of public services. He reconfirmed their educational and cultural mission and planned to make it the basis for gauging their productivity. He recognized that the accessibility objectives were still valid, and he proposed initiatives to consolidate educational activities at the undergraduate level, to give education at the master's and doctoral levels a boost, to better recognize the universities' function of providing services to the community, and to open them up to inter-university dialogue and collaboration. He also reasserted Quebec's jurisdiction in matters of PSE and asked the federal government to withdraw from this arena and consent to tax transfers as compensation. In addition, the Conseil des universités instigated a series of sector-based studies aimed at taking stock of specific sectors, and it published the first study dealing with the engineering sector (1984), which was geared towards meeting Quebec's social and economic needs.

With regard to research, according to a Green Paper on scientific research (Gouvernement du Québec 1980), the aim of university research was to advance knowledge. Universities were asked to participate more in regional development. The publication of an economic policy (Ministère d'état au développement économique 1982) stressed the relevance of developing closer ties with business. In 1983, the Act to Promote the Advancement of Science and Technology in Quebec was adopted.

During its second term, the Parti Québécois continued with its efforts to consolidate the system that had grown rapidly under the Liberal Party. The aim was to improve the effectiveness of the components that had been put in place during the previous term. Since education and PSE were among the foundations of the culture and identity of the people of Quebec, the Parti Québécois government wanted to include the development of PSE in its social-democratic blueprint for society and to better plan it. What is more, at the time of the recession at the beginning of the 1980s, budget cutbacks were legitimized by arguing the need to streamline the PSE system and turn it into more of a network than it had been in the past, thus making it more effective. The government also emphasized the importance of linking teaching and research more closely to business needs, while reaffirming the cultural mission of universities.

Evolution of the System under the Liberals, 1985–94

The Liberals were returned to power in 1985 and led by Robert Bourassa (1985–89, 1989–94) and Daniel Johnson Junior (1994). Their time in power was notable for the economic recovery that occurred under them. In 1987, the political agenda was dominated by the talks surrounding the Meech Lake Accord. With the election of a federalist party in Quebec and a new Progressive Conservative government in Ottawa (1984), constitutional talks had resumed on a new basis. However, the Meech Lake Accord – whose goal was, among other things, to get Quebec to adopt the Canadian Constitution repatriated without its consent in 1982 – was not ratified as required by all the provincial parliaments.

The Liberal government proposed a neoliberal policy realignment. Committees on privatization, the reform of government agencies, and deregulation challenged the state's role. According to Paquet (2002), the Liberals advocated a philosophy founded on the principle of subsidiarity, according to which the government should only be in charge of matters that the private sector or the community could not do just as well. They created a ministry for the privatization of public corporations, but Robert Bourassa remained politically cautious and did not venture very far along this road.

Regarding PSE, one of the government's first decisions (1985) was to split up education-related responsibilities. MEQ was put in charge of primary and secondary education, and the Ministère de l'Enseignement supérieur, de la Science et de la Technologie (Ministry of Postsecondary Education, Science and Technology) was put in charge of college and university education as well as research and scientific development. By the following year, the "technology" component had already been transferred to a ministry dealing with economic matters, the Ministère du Commerce extérieur (Ministry of External Trade) and the "science" component to the Ministry of Postsecondary Education and Science. The Conseil des universités continued to conduct sector-based studies. Its studies of the education (1987) and social science (1990) sectors stressed the need to clarify the orientations of programs in relation to the labour market.

The Liberals' second term in power coincided with the recession in the early 1990s and, in 1994, the negotiation and ratification of the North American Free Trade Agreement (NAFTA). At the political level, the failure of the Meech Lake Accord led the government to pull out of all constitutional talks. It took until 1990 for these talks to resume, and they culminated in the Charlottetown Accord, which, like its predecessor, was also rejected when it was subjected to a Canada-wide referendum.

Most of the neoliberal-leaning ministers of the Liberal Party's first term were, in the second term, no longer part of Cabinet. They had either quit politics or had not been re-elected. The new economic state of affairs opened up the North American market to business and was characterized by policies that were more interventionist and geared towards collaboration in response to increased competition.

Four noteworthy decisions on PSE were made during this period. First was an increase in university tuition fees. In 1986, the report on government agency reforms proposed that tuition fees be increased by anywhere from 272 to 345 percent. That same year, a parliamentary committee concluded that PSE was under-funded and also recommended an increase in tuition fees. Even so, it took three years before a decision was made. The fees increased from $540 in 1989–90 to around $1,700 in 1994–95 (215 percent).

The second noteworthy decision on PSE was the adoption of the Loi sur les établissements d'enseignement de niveau universitaire (Act Respecting Educational Institutions at the University Level) in 1989. The objectives of this framework law were (1) to determine which institution had the power to confer grades, diplomas, certificates, or any other attestation of university studies; and (2) to use the word "university" to designate an institution or to qualify an instructional program (or to advertize such a program) provided by an educational institution at the university level. Despite the recommendation of the 1979 Commission on Universities, no such law had been instituted previously. This law was adopted within a context wherein some institutions/groups/individuals were endeavouring to acquire the authorization to confer university degrees or diplomas. This was the case, for example, with the Collège militaire royal de Saint-Jean (then affiliated to the University of Sherbrooke) and with the Bishop of Montreal (who wanted to create the Institut catholique de Montréal for the training of catholic teachers) (Proulx 2009).

The third noteworthy decision involved the revitalization of college education. The Conseil des collèges had continued on with its review, prompted by the Nadeau Report, and the evaluation of the college network was a constant concern for successive governments. Some groups even questioned the need for colleges. As a result of the 1992 publication of the Conseil des collèges (1992) report and a consultation initiative on the part of the Culture and Education Commission of the National Assembly, in 1993 the minister of higher education and science published a policy statement asserting that this intermediate level of education should be maintained and proposing ways of breathing new life into it (MESS 1993). The government therefore amended the General and Vocational Colleges Act and published its new regulations on the college education system in order to take the proposed changes into account. It abolished the Conseil des collèges and replaced it with the CEEC, thus confirming the Quebec college education model while at the same time making in-depth changes, in particular by giving institutions greater autonomy and reinforcing evaluation mechanisms.

The fourth noteworthy decision regarding PSE involved the abolition of the Conseil des universités and the transfer of some of its powers to the Conseil supérieur de l'éducation (CSE)and to two of its commissions (Commission de l'enseignement et de la recherche universitaire [CERU] et Commission de l'enseignement collegial [CEC]). Finally, in 1993, the government adopted Bill 198, an Act Respecting the Reduction of Personnel in Public Bodies and the Accountability of Deputy Ministers and Chief Executive Officers of Public Bodies. Its objectives were to reduce management personnel in the civil service and para-public organizations by 20 percent, to reduce personnel falling into other categories by 12 percent, and to make the people who run public agencies or bodies accountable to the National Assembly. This provision also applied to universities. Although this legislation was amended in 1995 and 1999, then rescinded in 2000, it was at the root of a set of measures designed to promote the accountability of the managers and directors of these institutions and bodies.

At the same time as these government initiatives, the CSE issued three statements indicating that universities should have closer ties with the labour market, echoing the three sector-based studies conducted by the Conseil des universités. In addition, CRÉPUQ adopted its periodic program evaluation policy at the beginning of the 1990s, which obligated all universities to evaluate their programs in terms of quality and relevance. A similar move was observed in university research. The desire to align it with business needs followed on steps taken by the federal government as early as 1987 to create a matching-funding policy for some of the research programs offered by its three national funding councils. This policy set the conditions for an increase in private-sector financial contributions to research and for the development of partnerships with businesses.

What one retains from this period, first and foremost, is the fact that the taste for neoliberalism was not as pronounced in PSE as had been anticipated. At the very most, the increase in tuition fees and abolition of the Conseil des universités might be linked to it. Even so, these decisions were not justified solely on the basis of neoliberal premises. The government adopted the Act Respecting Educational Institutions at the University Level. The college education reforms were implemented, and CRÉPUQ adopted its periodic university program evaluation policy. The government also introduced a formal accountability mechanism for the people in charge of university institutions. Finally, CRÉPUQ and the subsidizing agencies encouraged universities to develop closer ties with the labour market (in the case of programs) and with businesses (in the case of research).

In another vein, the Canadian political scene, with its constitutional talks, had much less impact on PSE policy than did the state of the economy. The recession in the early 1990s and its repercussion with regard to disposable fiscal resources at the federal level and, afterwards, the provincial level,[14] definitely influenced the Quebec government's decision to increase tuition fees. The free trade talks with the United States led the Liberal Party to rethink the state's role in the economy and to see it within the new context of international competition. This period, particularly during the second term of the Liberal government, can be characterized by the state acting as a partner rather than by neoliberal ideology.

Evolution of the System under the Parti Québécois, 1994–2003

Led by Jacques Parizeau, the Parti Québécois was returned to power in 1994. When Parizeau resigned in 1996, he was replaced by Lucien Bouchard, who finished the term and got the government re-elected in 1998. When Bouchard resigned in 2001, Bernard Landry took his place. This was a period of economic recovery and sustained growth, despite the problems encountered in the new technology sector. The favourable economic climate had a positive impact on reinvestment in PSE during Landry's second term, following on the drastic reduction in spending during the first.

Several important events occurred during this period: the second referendum on Quebec sovereignty (1995), the Commission for the Estates General on Education, the Summit on the Economy and Employment (1996), the Quebec Youth Summit (2000), and the adoption of Quebec's Public Administration Act (2000). In the second referendum, the sovereignty option was rejected by 51 percent of the vote, reflecting a sharp division in public opinion.

In 1995, the government held the Estates General on Education in order to take stock of the situation. After an initial round of consultations, the Commission for the Estates General on Education (1996) published a report, also submitted for consultations, which presented six priority projects concerning all educational levels. As though they wanted to protect their autonomy by avoiding the "eyes" of the commission, universities provided a muted response to the Estates General. The commission reproached them for this and invited them to "proceed with the reorganization necessary to meet the demand for mass higher education" while retaining their threefold mission. Several problems were highlighted, including the need to give more attention to the teaching component of their mission, the lack of program consistency, and the need to streamline training offerings. As far as research was concerned, the commission's report rejected the idea that certain universities should specialize in research, and it worried about the risk of drifting towards sponsored research or research too closely linked to industry needs. The commission asserted the need for universities to be accountable, for CRÉPUQ to introduce mechanisms for external evaluation, and for the government to ensure better coordination. In its final report, college education was only referred to in conjunction with the proposed plan of action regarding vocational and career training. The commission gave the impression that, before beginning another in-depth examination, it would wait until the 1993 college education reforms were sufficiently advanced. Still, the report insisted on the need for CÉGEP to establish a continuum regarding secondary school vocational and career programs.

Many initiatives were undertaken close on the heels of the Estates General commission. MEQ (1997b) introduced a reform in the shape of a plan of action focusing on high success rates. To demonstrate the system's effectiveness, MEQ argued that the democratization of education must favour not only access but also success. The objective was to see 85 percent of a generation of students with an SSD or a DVS by the age of twenty, 60 percent with a DCS, and 30 percent with a bachelor's degree: all this by 2010. The reform dealt specifically with the generalization of full-time kindergarten as of age four; a complete revision of elementary and high school curricula (MEQ 1997a); the creation of school boards based on language as opposed to religious denomination; and changes to how powers were shared between MEQ, the school boards, and the schools, the idea being to give more authority and autonomy to schools and to place greater importance on the education of children from low-income families and cultural communities.

In 1996, the Summit on the Economy and Employment brought together employers' stakeholders, unions and community organizations, and other lobbies to take stock of the post-referendum situation and, more specifically, of employment, public finances, and the government deficit. It was agreed to eliminate the annual $4 billion deficit over three years and to create a $250 million fund to combat poverty, which would be financed by workers, companies, and financial institutions. This decision led to a major reduction in spending across all areas of educational provision.

The same participants gathered together once more in 2000 at the Quebec Youth Summit; however, this time, young people played a more important role. Students' associations lobbied for better financial aid, maintenance of tuition-free college education, and a university tuition freeze. Consensus was reached on a number of points, in particular, the development of a policy on youth and the coordination of workers' actions based on this policy. In terms of education, there was a desire to give it high priority. This was demonstrated by the decision to prepare a school success plan for Quebec and to invest $1 billion in developing it. Since it had been decided to reinvest in universities, it was suggested that priority be given to hiring new professors, training, and basic research. This reinvestment coincided with the new performance-based approach, which resulted in allocating some of the operating grants to institutions via contracts.

The Public Administration Act, adopted in 2000, introduced a new management framework centred on outcomes and increasing accountability.[15] Responsibilities connected with improving services were passed on to the ministries. The regulatory framework was simplified and centred on a posteriori control and achieving predicted outcomes. Each ministry had to develop a strategic plan dealing with its mission, the context within which it evolved, its orientation and approach to intervention, targeted outcomes, and performance indicators. One part of the act dealt with the introduction of performance and accountability agreements that managers could conclude with the Conseil du Trésor (Treasury Board). In these cases, management evaluation was based on outcomes rather than on centralized process controls and production factors. This legislation had an impact on the regulation of PSE, particularly with regard to performance contracts between MEQ and the universities and the colleges' school success plans.

PSE DECISIONS AND ORIENTATIONS

In 1994, PSE was once more placed under MEQ's responsibility. During the subsequent period, hardly any new initiatives were undertaken with colleges. Intervention occurred mostly at the university level, drawing inspiration from the Estates General, the Public Administration Act, and the Quebec Youth Summit in order to streamline PSE.

At the college level, a ministerial plan of action for education reforms (MEQ 1997b) acknowledged that the revitalization measures implemented in 1993 needed to be given time to have their desired effect. However, the plan did provide for increasing the autonomy of institutions and making their administration more flexible. In 2002, MEQ amended the General and Vocational Colleges Act to provide for the colleges' obligation to implement a plan geared towards student success.

With regard to universities, the government's first decision was, in 1995, to amend the Act Respecting Educational Institutions at the University Level in order to make universities accountable for their management and outcomes not only to MEQ but also to the Culture and Education Commission of the National Assembly (much as were deputy ministers under the Public Administration Act). They were now obliged to attach to their annual financial statements a report on the salaries of senior management and the institution's performance, particularly regarding student success rates and steps taken to help and supervise students.

The government supported CRÉPUQ, which created the Commission des universités sur les programmes (CUP), or University Commission on Programs, and gave it the mandate to examine program relevance and complementarity and recommend ways to encourage collaboration. CRÉPUQ had insisted on leading the operation itself instead of its being assigned to an independent commission, as the Commission for the Estates General on Education had suggested. In three years, CUP (2000) studied all the programs and published twenty-four sector-based reports and a final report. A second updating phase got under way in June 2001. CUP considered that universities needed to take the choices made by other institutions into consideration and try to think in terms of the system, both at the level of the programs offered and at the level of the development of niche research areas.

MEQ adopted a policy on universities after submitting a statement for consultations in 1999. In the policy that was made public (MEQ 2000), there were three broad orientations: (1) access to university education; the universities' performance in terms of education quality, research excellence, and the system's efficiency; and (3) meeting the needs of society and being open to the world. A number of priorities stemming from these orientations were defined. Further, the "historical" approach to funding was dropped. The Quebec Policy on University Funding, which was also made public in 2000, aimed at ensuring transparency, equity, and consistency; maintaining a balanced budget; respect for university autonomy; and determining performance indicators.

In 2000, the government decided, in the wake of the Quebec Summit, to reinvest $600 million in universities over three years. Instead of distributing this amount according to the usual funding mechanisms concerning the operating and investment budgets described earlier, MEQ decided to allocate it according to priorities negotiated with the institutions. All of the universities had to conclude a performance contract with MEQ that corresponded to: a plan to define objectives for a three-year period, measuring the extent to which that plan had been realized, and reporting back. The main components of the plan referred to completion rates and ways of supporting students, the development and monitoring of programs, management efficiency, a balanced budget, and strategic development. Each institution had to negotiate an agreement with MEQ. The annual granting of the amounts provided for in the contracts was conditional on commitments being met, as assessed by the ministry. The plans were not implemented entirely; however, the ministry used this mechanism to intervene in the strategic development of the institutions and as an instrument of accountability. In 2003, the amount allocated for performance contracts ($250.7 million) represented 14.2 percent of the overall amount allocated to universities, and it varied between 7.2 percent and 20.1 percent, depending on the institution. This percentage was higher than that observed in US states in which this type of funding model was in place by between 1.0 and 2.0 percent, with the exception of Tennessee at 5.5 percent (Carrier 2001).

In 1999, with respect to university research, the government created the Valorisation-Recherche Québec, a not-for profit organization. Its objectives were (1) to contribute to the transformation of the research community in order to get university research teams to enter multi-disciplinary and multi-sector projects with governmental and business research teams; (2) to support four societies dedicated to the transfer of knowledge; (3) to increase the number of spinoff companies; and (4) to promote the marketing of the findings. This organization, which had invested $262 million, was abolished in 2006. In 2001, the government published its Quebec Policy on Science and Innovation (Ministère de la Recherche, de la Science et de la Technologie 2001), which referred to the demands of the "knowledge society" and a restructuring of its subsidizing agencies, which culminated in the three agencies already mentioned. Valorisation-Recherche Québec turned out to be a tool for implementing this policy, though it was criticized for allocating its grants not on the basis of the usual criteria of research programs but, rather, according to institutional demands. In 2002, the ministry also tabled a plan of action on intellectual property management (Ministère de la Recherche, de la Science et de la Technologie 2002), which sought, as the Bayh-Dole Act had done in the United States, to consecrate the principle of institutional ownership of university research despite the absence of consensus among university professors.

One cannot talk about these initiatives on the part of the Quebec government without mentioning those of the federal government and the role that it plays in regulating university research. While the Quebec government defined its orientations based primarily on the Quebec context, many of its initiatives were undertaken to complement federal government initiatives – sometimes in a climate of tension – so that Quebec's researchers could compete with other Canadian researchers. This is particularly the case for the Canada Foundation for Innovation.

From the start, the period from 1994 to 2003 was characterized by the call for greater accountability. Decisions were made within the broader context of reforms to be made to the entire education system subsequent to the Estates General on Education and the amendment of the Public Administration Act. PSE was to be streamlined and made more efficient. The universities were also asked to "think in terms of the system" when planning their activities and to take the choices made by other universities into account. Hence, all training programs were reviewed and, for the first time, an official policy on universities was issued. Institution managers could now refer to a new management framework that governed the whole government apparatus and that was oriented towards achieving measurable "outcomes." Finally, it was decided that Quebec's research initiatives, complementing those of the federal government, should contribute more immediately to economic development and innovation.

Changes to the System under the Liberals, 2003–11

In 2003, Jean Charest led the Liberals back to power. His federalist party was elected on a neoliberal platform to alter the government's role by limiting state intervention and cutting income tax. The beginning of this period was marked by sustained economic growth and a set of decisions by the new government, which was eager to show that it planned to carry out its promises.[16] The Liberal government embarked on a general attempt to redefine the role of the state, to reorganize government services (discussed in terms of "réingénierie de l'État" [re-engineering the state]), and to develop partnerships with private enterprises. At the beginning of its first mandate, its style of governance was less open to consultation practices than had been that of the previous government. Moreover, several decisions stirred up dissatisfaction. Among these was the government's intention to introduce major changes in the CÉGEP network and to modify the Loans and Bursaries Program; its decision to provide

100 percent of the financing for private Jewish schools; and its reorganization of the childcare services.

The Charest government attempted to counter this dissatisfaction by organizing the Forum des générations (Forum on Generations), which brought elected representatives and social and economic leaders together to discuss issues related to demographic change and the restructuring of public finance. It also drew back with regard to modifying the student loans and bursaries program and with regard to funding private Jewish schools. In February 2005, the premier also reshuffled his cabinet and appointed a new minister of education.

The Liberal government faced strong opposition on other issues, particularly with regard to three projects that were thought to have negative effects on the environment.[17] Other decisions were well received by the population, particularly the establishment of the Fonds des générations (Generations Fund) to refinance the public debt,[18] the refundable tax credit for child assistance, and the revision of the law on the protection of youth. The public also supported Charest's attempts to convince the Conseil de la Fédération (Council of the Federation) and Stephen Harper's newly elected federal Conservative government of the fiscal disequilibrium between the two levels of government (which Harper finally recognized) and to attempt to resolve it. What followed was the agreement between the provincial and federal governments to allow, under certain conditions, Quebec's participation in UNESCO, its adhesion to the objectives of the Kyoto Agreement, and the elaboration of a provincial plan to reduce greenhouse gas emissions (despite the resistance of the Harper government). Finally, in 2006, a collective agreement between the Charest government and the unions representing public-sector employees was reached regarding equal pay for men and women – something that had been mandated under the Pay Equity Act almost nine years earlier. By mid-2006, these decisions, inter alia, had contributed to a decrease in the level of dissatisfaction with the Liberal government. Were it not for the crisis of the softwood industry, which came about due to the dispute between Canada and the United States over the interpretation of NAFTA, and, to a lesser extent, the Quebec textile industry's place within a globalized economy (which culminated in very heavy job loss), the premier would have been tempted to call an early election in autumn 2006.

With regard to PSE, there were nine initiatives during Charest's first mandate. In 2003, the Liberal government gave the Comité consultatif sur l'accessibilité financière aux études (2003), or Advisory Committee on Financial Accessibility to University, the task of examining university funding from the angle of quality and accessibility. This parliamentary committee made thirty recommendations on quality issues and other considerations (e.g., the university's teaching role, research funding, recruitment of professors, indirect research costs, academic freedom, and institutional autonomy); and improved accessibility (e.g., financial aid, tuition fees, additional compulsory fees, international students, universities in outlying areas); financial soundness and management (e.g., the institution's financial means, variations in number of students, university diversity, planning, accountability, and federal government intervention). According to this committee, Quebec's universities, when compared to other Canadian universities, suffered from chronic under-funding, which it estimated at $375 million. This under-funding made Quebec's universities less competitive. Even though the committee recognized that this gap stemmed partly from Quebec's tuition fee policy, it did not take a stand on this issue.

The second initiative followed criticism of the efficiency of Quebec's college education model by the Quebec Federation of School Boards (FCSQ) (Bédard 2003), and it involved the minister of education organizing a forum on the future of college education. The debate was very lively. Regarding the first issue – whether to maintain the Quebec model of college education (CÉGEPs) – the forum participants, with the exception of FCSQ and CRÉPUQ, were in favour. They pointed out that college is an important place in terms of vocational orientation and reaching maturity (Rocher 2004). On the second issue, concerning the colleges' autonomy and decentralization of the college network, however, the Fédération des CÉGEPs disagreed with teachers' unions and students' associations. The federation called for decentralization of program management so that colleges could develop, alter, and evaluate their programs; issue their own diplomas; and decide on their own special admission requirements. The forum recommended that colleges equip themselves with a common procedure in terms of admission requirements, graduation requirements, and programs, and that a regulating agency be created to define this structure and to ensure system consistency. In return, it advocated outcomes-based accountability (Fédération des CÉGEPs 2004).

These recommendations, which reflected the call for modes of regulation centred on autonomy comparable to those found in universities, were not supported unanimously.[19] Detractors were worried that decentralizing college education would make it difficult to keep the network equitable and to ensure that quality was the same throughout Quebec. According to them, if more flexibility was required within the college network, this should be accomplished by restructuring MEQ's oversight. Finally, in January 2005, MEQ announced its intentions and it turned out that the changes proposed were relatively minor. They were received with a sigh of relief by those who had argued in favour of maintaining the Quebec model and against decentralizing the college network.

The third initiative of Charest's second mandate involved the loans and bursaries program, which had been changed many times during his first mandate. When the 2004 budget had been tabled, for example, the budgetary allowance, or "envelope," for bursaries was reduced by 30 percent and the allowance for loans was increased, with the result that students accumulated more debt. Since this financial aid is first distributed in the form of a loan (up to a given amount) then provided in bursary form, and since it is based on need and not merit, this decision hit poorer students the hardest. In response, Quebec's students staged a massive strike in the winter of 2005. The government responded by bringing the aid in bursary form back to its former level. This "reinstatement" was made possible by an agreement that MEQ concluded with the Canadian Millennium Scholarships Foundation and the Canada Student Loans Program, which agreed to allocate $40 million and $100 million, respectively, over five years.

Charest's fourth initiative, which occurred after the preceding educational controversies, involved the appointment of a new minister of education in February 2005. In addition, MEQ became MELS, and the Ministère du Développement économique et régional et de la Recherche (MDERR), or the Ministry of Economic and Regional Development and Research, became the MDEIE. However, this change in name did not result in any major changes in PSE policy, except that it accentuated a trend towards developing closer ties between business and university research.

The fifth initiative, in 2005, involved MELS adopting a new policy concerning indirect research costs. These costs have to do with the use of university services (library, computer, audiovisual, telecommunications and legal services, human resources management, bookkeeping, etc.) and spaces that are not directly related to research but that researchers need to use in order to conduct their work. MELS – a pioneer in this field in Canada since 1989 – assumes the totality of the costs of the projects and contracts financed by Quebec government agencies and part of the costs for those supported by organizations accredited by the Quebec government. Furthermore, the ministry demands that institutions impose indirect costs corresponding to a given percentage of the direct costs of research contracts with companies. It ensures that these amounts are collected, and, if they are not, it subtracts an amount equal to what they should have claimed from their annual operating grant. In addition, MELS decided that it would no longer finance space devoted to research activities out of the institutions' operating grants: the institutions would have to finance these out of investment programs and out of the amounts they received or collected to cover indirect research costs. The new policy was implemented gradually over a transition period until 2008–09, and a transition envelope was allocated to compensate the decrease of the previous MELS's grant for space.

Charest's sixth initiative entailed the government's not renewing the performance contracts for partial university funding when the three-year contracts expired in 2004. It did renew the $250.7 million grant, however, which had formerly been conditional on the performance covered by these contracts, although it did attach a new condition: balancing the annual budget.

Seventh, after a lengthy debate in 2005, the government decided to merge TÉLUQ with UQAM. The merger was so arduous that finally TÉLUQ disaffiliated from UQAM in 2012.

Eighth, a new university funding formula, in particular a new way of taking into account the relative costs of the various disciplines in the allocation of the operating funds, was negotiated between CRÉPUQ and the government, but it took time to implement. Despite the difficult fiscal situation in which all the universities found themselves, there seemed to be a consensus to apply the new funding formula only when the government decided to allocate more funds to PSE. Actually, the government decided, in December 2006, to allocate $320 million to PSE over three years, in addition to the previous operating funds ($240 million to universities and $80 million to CÉGEPs). The new formula was implemented with temporary measures for the year 2006–07 at the beginning of Charest's second mandate.

Finally, the government abolished the Valorisation-recherche Québec and launched its new strategy for research and innovation in December 2006 (MDEI 2006). This initiative followed up on the government's strategy of economic development (MDEIE 2005a). One element of this strategy involved raising R&D expenditures to 3 percent of the GDP and raising the proportion funded by business from 60 to 66 percent between 2005 and 2010. The first objective was to increase the quality of public research by improving research infrastructures, developing knowledge and technologies in key areas and targeted sectors in Quebec, and inciting researchers to participate in international research networks. The second objective was to support research and innovation in various enterprises, and the third was to strengthen the mechanisms of R&D in the various regions by supporting the regional constituents of the Université du Québec and the College Centres for Transfer of Technology. The government announced an investment of $888 million over three years to implement its strategy. Priority was given to the technological and economic innovation over social innovation, a component of the previous research policy that had almost disappeared. Concerns were raised about the highly instrumental conception of research underlying the strategy and the danger of neglecting fundamental research.

Charest's first mandate was notable for the review of policy relating to accessibility and funding, the loans and bursaries program, and the radical move of questioning the validity of the college network. Nevertheless, Quebec's college education model was unequivocally chosen once more, with only minor changes. The consultation-based decision-making process was also retained. The government changed its mind with regard to the loans and bursaries program, adopted a new indirect research costs policy, decided not to renew the performance contracts, allocated more funds to PSE, introduced changes in the allocation of operating funds to universities, and proposed a new strategy for research and innovation.

The Liberal Party of Jean Charest was re-elected for a second mandate in March 2007 but as a minority government. The party l'Action démocratique du Québec (ADQ), a rightist party with an electoral platform focusing on the autonomy of Quebec, formed for the first time the Official Opposition; and the Parti Québécois, the sovereigntist party with a leaning towards social democracy, became the third party. The first session of the Legislature was devoted mainly to the discussion and the adoption of the budget. The Liberal government survived its first budget with the support of the Parti Québécois.

Universities and colleges had expected the government to substantially increase the amount allocated to PSE as the federal Conservatives had transferred to the province nearly $1 billion as a result of its attempt to address the problem of the fiscal disequilibrium between the provinces and the federal government. This money did not materialize immediately; rather, the Liberal government chose to reduce income tax. It seemed as though the provincial government was waiting for the federal government to make a more explicit move to support PSE through transfer payments.

At the very beginning of its second mandate, the Charest government made two important decisions with regard to PSE. First, as it had indicated it would during the electoral campaign, it decided to increase tuition fees by fifty dollars per session for full-time university students over the next five years. During the election campaign, the ADQ had also favoured a thaw in tuition fees. By 2011–12, tuition fees had been raised from $1,668 to $2,168. Second, MELS modified the loans and bursary program to cover the increase of the tuition fees and had adopted other measures to improve the program (e.g., monthly indexation of the authorized expenditures, increase of the amount accepted for the reimbursement of the school furniture, reduction of the amount of student expenses to be covered by parents, etc.). Despite the relatively small increase of the tuition fees and the improvement of the program, student associations protested the thaw, and, in autumn 2007, some were considering, as in 2005, going on strike. The strike did not materialize, but student associations pressured the government to regulate the additional compulsory fees that institutions were inclined to increase. And, in 2008, the government adopted such a policy.

The government was compelled to intervene in a UQAM construction and urban development project that had become quite difficult to manage. The initial cost of the project ($226 million), implemented in partnership with a private enterprise, increased dramatically. As the university had guaranteed the loan and was unable to honour its obligations, it withdrew from the project in September 2007. Then the government took over UQAM's loan by setting up a $200 million fund in trust to alleviate the financial burden and to protect its credit rating until an agreement could be reached with the private enterprise. In return for this aid, the university has to adopt a hard recovery plan.[20]

This saga has had an impact on other government decisions concerning the entire PSE system and government agencies. The Liberal government redefined the rules regarding public investments, with some applying only to universities and others to all government departments and bodies. Some rules were imposed in response to specific problems regarding the management of large investments and projects, others followed from the political will to bring more transparency and a greater accountability to public administration. In December 2007, the Charest government brought in an amendment to the Public Administration Act, which established, among other things, a management framework for the financial resources of government departments, budget-funded bodies (including universities), and government enterprises. According to this amendment, these bodies cannot make important borrowings, investments, or financial commitments (determined by government regulation) unless they are authorized by the ministry responsible (MELS, in the case of the universities) and, in some cases, also by the Ministry of Finance. Moreover, according to a University Investment Act by-law adopted later in 2008, a university must declare to MELS all the projects of investment included in its five-year investment plan (even those that do not require public funding) and indicate for each project the proportion of public and private funds required for its realization. Finally, the government adopted the Act to Promote the Maintenance and Renewal of Public Infrastructure in reaction to problems the auditor general detected in the management of many infrastructure projects, including the extension of the Montreal subway and UQAM's urban development project. This act sets the conditions under which these projects can be conducted. The objective is to ensure that state investment in public infrastructures is in line with best management practices, that the process is transparent, and that the planning and monitoring of these projects is properly facilitated. The act compels institutions to authorize each step of their planning before engaging their own funds for these projects, even if they do not require public funding.

Charest called an early election in December 2008 and, this time, obtained a majority government. The Parti de l'Action démocratique lost its status of Official Opposition to the Parti Québécois, and one candidate of the Parti Québec Solidaire – a socialist and "sovereigntist" party – was elected for the first time. The election coincided with the financial crisis and the heavy loss ($40 billion) of the Caisse de dépôt et placement du Québec, which manages institutional funds primarily from public and private pensions and insurance. This third Liberal mandate was also characterized by a succession of controversies: (1) the implementation of the harmonized sales tax (federal and provincial); (2) allegations of political interference in the nomination of judges, which led to the creation of the Commission sur le processus de nomination des juges; (3) the exploration and extraction of shale gas in the Saint-Lawrence Valley; (4) allegations of corruption and patronage in the Quebec construction industry; and (5) the financing of political parties at the municipal and provincial levels. In education, the Charest government stirred up controversy when it introduced Bill 15 in response to a Supreme Court decision to find an alternative to a previous law (Bill 104) that had been found to be in violation of the Charter of Rights and Freedoms. The new bill granted students access to English schools after they had spent three years in a private non-subsidized English school. The act was perceived by many as a way of buying access to an English school.

With regard to PSE, we need to look at five initiatives that were undertaken during the third mandate of the Liberal government. First, in 2008, the federal government increased by $800 million the CSHT transfer to the provinces that was directed towards PSE. The Quebec government allocated its $187 million share by $112, $70, and $5 million, respectively, to universities, CÉGEPs, and private college accredited for funding. And it added $40 and $20 million more to universities and colleges, respectively. These funds were not simply included in the general funding of the operating grants. In the case of the universities, after consultation with CRÉPUQ, they were assigned to a program whose purpose was to attract high-calibre professors in the fields of engineering and administration, to provide teacher training and the training of immigrants, to ensure measures to enhance collaboration between CÉGEP and universities, and to facilitate the international mobility of students. To obtain these supplementary funds, and in accordance with the principle of accountability, each institution had to reach an agreement with MELS. In the case of CÉGEPs, some of these funds were used for specific projects of the institutions chosen in partnership with MELS and for infrastructure and maintenance of the buildings.

The second initiative was in reaction to UQAM's crisis and involved the Liberals' (1) supporting a study on the governance of the universities,[21] and (2) in 2008, tabling two bills (107 and 110) on the governance of CÉGEPs and universities, respectively.[22] These bills have to be placed in the context of the implementation of reforms inspired by the New Public Management approach to governance, which the Quebec government had initiated in the 1990s (Conseil du trésor 1999; Conseil supérieur de l'éducation 2009). These reforms aimed at improving the accountability mechanisms of the ministries and the Crown corporations (Gouvernement du Québec 2006a). The purpose of these bills was to apply the New Public Management approach to postsecondary institutions and, more particularly, to modify the composition, the functioning, and the responsibilities of the boards of governors of these institutions; to define rules concerning potential conflicts of interest; and to improve their efficiency, transparency, and accountability. The bills specify that two-thirds of the members of the board will be independent and only one-quarter will come from within the institution. The board will contain an equal number of men and women and the chair will be accountable to the minister. The boards are intended to cover major decision areas, including strategic orientations and plans for fixed assets, most of which were previously the prerogative of the members of the institution. The board will institute three committees: on governance and ethics, audit, and human resources, respectively. The bills also indicate what should be the contents of the annual report to the minister, including all the minutes of the board meetings and the results of the indicators defined by the minister, which should be made public on the institution's website. MELS' intention was to give more power to external members in governance and to introduce more transparency in the management of the system.

These bills were perceived by many as an attempt by MELS to exert greater control over the PSE institutions on the pretext of preventing the kind of financial problem observed in UQAM's construction and urban development project. The minister decided to modify its policy and, in 2009, tabled bills 38 and 44 under the same titles as the previous legislation. The main changes to the bill on universities concerns the proportion of independent members of the board (60 percent instead of 66 percent) and the adoption of strategic orientations. In the new bill on CÉGEPs, the proportion of independent members remains the same (64 percent) as it was in the first draft.

But the institutions no longer have to transmit to the minister the minutes of the board meetings, and the list of accountable indicators is shorter. Furthermore, a new section was added on the governance of the multi-campus regional CÉGEPS.

Despite these changes, both CRÉPUQ and the Fédération des CÉGEPS expressed their opposition to the bills during the public hearings of the Commission de la culture et de l'éducation in October 2009. CRÉPUQ (2009) agreed with the principle of good governance proposed in the bill on universities, particularly with the provisions concerning a majority of members of the board being independent and the creation of three committees (ethics, audit, and human resources). However, the conference did not think these objectives should be introduced by means of a new law that applied uniformly to all universities without taking into account the traditions and the organizational culture of each institution. Instead, CRÉPUQ suggested partnership agreements between MELS and each institution. The Fédération des CÉGEPS asked for major modifications of Bill 44. Apart from the high costs associated with the proposed changes, the Fédération did not think they should apply to all colleges without taking into account their diversity. The minister indicated that more modifications were possible when the parliamentary commission had had a chance to study the bill article by article; however, by February 2012, the minister still had not tabled them.

The third initiative involved the Liberals' 2009 adoption of a law concerning the recognition of professional skills.[23] This was in response to the length of time it was taking professional associations and educational institutions to recognize persons educated outside the country and in the context of the negotiations of the France-Quebec agreement on labour mobility. By virtue of this law, a commissioner of the office of the professions has the power (1) to examine complaints against professional associations concerning the mechanisms of recognition of professional skills and (2) to take action in order to "assure" collaboration between the educational institutions and the professional associations, in cooperation with MELS, so that training, when required by a professional association, may be effectively offered. Again, CRÉPUQ agreed with the objective of implementing programs of supplemental training for professionals educated outside Canada, but it concluded that the law would undermine university autonomy by intervening in the management of programs and admissions. Further, CRÉPUQ labelled the law superfluous because the conference was in the process of finalizing an agreement on additional university training with the Conseil interprofessionnel du Québec, in cooperation with MELS and other ministries. CRÉPUQ pleaded for changes that would lessen the constraining character of the law, but it was ignored and the bill was adopted.

The fourth initiative was put forward in the 2011 budget, when, in addition to its usual allocation of operating grants, the Charest government implemented a new university funding plan to give universities access to additional revenues of $850 million over six years. These new revenues are in addition to the gradual increases of the operating grants since 2003–04 ($2 billion in 2003–04 to $2.8 billion in 2009–10). At the end of the complete implementation of the plan in 2016–17, the total increase will reach $3.3 billion (Government of Québec 2011a). This plan comprises a built-in mechanism of accountability: university performance in the implementation of the plan will be monitored by means of a set of indicators defined by the government (see appendix 7).

The fifth initiative involved reorganizing the three research funds in the fields of health, natural sciences and engineering, and society and culture. In its attempt to reduce and control expenditures by abolishing or restructuring certain bodies and certain funds, the government had first thought to abolish the Conseil de la science et de la technologie and to merge the three Quebec research funds to create a single research fund, Recherche Québec, directed by the chief scientist. This new position, which was defined in a bill, created a controversy among researchers and research institutions. In the final version of the bill,[24] the government maintained its decision to abolish the advisory council on science and technology and to create the Commission sur l'éthique en science et en technologie to advise the minister of economic development and export trade. However, it changed its mind with regard to the three research funds, which, along with their boards of directors, are maintained under other designations (the Quebec Research Fund – Nature and Technology; the Quebec Research Fund – Health; and the Quebec Research Fund – Society and Culture).[25] The government created the position of chief scientist and appointed a scientific director to each fund on the recommendation of each board of directors. The three boards are chaired by the chief scientist, whose mandate is to coordinate efforts on issues that are common to the three funds, to promote inter-sector collaboration, and to advise the minister on the development of research and science.

The second and third mandates of the Charest government were notable for the softening of its neoliberal orientation (not unlike what the Bourassa government did at the end of the 1980s). In PSE, a number of issues have been controversial – namely, the slow growth of the universities' operating grants; the new rules regarding investments and the management of infrastructure projects; the adoption of the Quebec University Funding Plan, the two increases of tuition fees; the regulation of additional compulsory fees; the modification and improvement of the loans and bursaries program; the reorganization of the three Quebec research funds; the changes in the process of the recognition of professional skills; and the intention to introduce changes in the governance, monitoring, and accountability of the institutions.

MAIN FEATURES OF THE DECISION-MAKING PROCESS

In this section, we highlight four features that characterize the decision-making process for PSE in Quebec. The main decisions are made by the provincial government, especially MELS and, to a lesser extent, the MDEIE. However, the federal government intervenes in many ways, especially with regard to research. These interventions have clear consequences for the priorities of provincial policies and, as such, are part of the decision-making process, not just a source of tension or an element of the context (see chapter 1).

The first feature of the decision-making process is the predominance of public institutions. Both the universities created by charter and those created by an act of incorporation are subject to the same funding rules, including those concerning tuition fees and accountability, thus making the university network public. At the college level, there are truly private establishments, some accredited for funding and others with only a permit to operate. However, only 9.6 percent of college students (7.7 percent in regular programs) are in private institutions.

The private sector helps fund research not only through sponsorship but also in conjunction with partnerships linked to research projects funded by federal and/or provincial agencies. Furthermore, in the case of research contracts, businesses assume part of the indirect costs. Subsidizing agencies want universities to engage in these kinds of partnerships so that closer ties can be formed between research and the business world. By the same token, businesses are asked to support university foundations, are consulted when programs are being created or evaluated, and are encouraged to take on student interns. Professional corporations participate actively in the development of programs corresponding to their fields.

The second feature of the decision-making process is the nature of provincial government intervention. In terms of the typology referred to in chapter 1, the government's role is not limited to providing resources, regulating PSE, and ensuring that consumer interests are protected; rather, government plays a decisive, steering role. Unlike governments in other jurisdictions, it does not rely on university commissions or boards or on other semi-autonomous regulating agencies but, rather, on two ministries: MDEIE and MELS. MDEIE plays an active part in implementing the Quebec Policy on Science and Innovation (Gouvernement du Québec 2001) and in participating in federal R&D initiatives. While the federal government plays a major role and intervenes in a very direct way, this does not mean that MDEIE merely follows the federal lead. MDEIE's policy (Gouvernement du Québec 2001) and its strategy for research and innovation (Gouvernement du Québec 2006b, 2010) are designed to give Quebec a world-class innovation and research system, influence the provincial government's priorities, and update performance indicators (Gouvernement du Québec 2007). Even so, the state's preponderant role in PSE is best illustrated by MELS since it defines the budgetary rules for operating and investment funding.

In examining MELS' role we distinguish the college level from the university level. The administrative rules for the colleges are far more restrictive than are those governing universities. MELS is the authority with the most power. It governs all the programs leading to a DCS. Since collective agreements for the whole network are adopted at the provincial level, there is little room for labour negotiations at the institutional level. MELS is not the only centralizing element. As mentioned above, the teachers' unions and, to a certain extent, students' associations were opposed to more decentralization. In addition, the Fédération des CÉGEPS influences MELS on everything to do with program management and the general management of institutions and has ended up developing a strong working relationship with it. The teachers' unions have a considerable amount of say in labour relations, while the students' associations hold sway mainly on policy relating to tuition-free college education and the loans and bursaries program.

As its evaluation mandate covers most aspects of college education, the Commission d'évaluation de l'enseignement collégial has influence over programs and curricula as well as over institutional evaluation policies. This influence has increased since 2002, when its mandate was extended to evaluate administrative and academic planning and management, instruction and support services, and strategic plans. In addition, businesses have an influence over institutions, particularly with regard to career training and college technology transfer centres. And community groups have influence with regard to some of the institutions' cultural activities, especially in the case of CÉGEPS located in outlying areas. Two business representatives as well as two representatives of the socio-economic groups of the territory or district in which a CÉGEP is established are appointed to the college's board of governors. Although MELS is the actor with the most power over the college network, many joint advisory committees should also be taken into account. Within these committees, college representatives discuss such matters as funding priorities, new needs and the allocation of operating funds to each institution regarding teaching, buildings, teachers' salary, and specific activities.

In contrast to CÉGEPS, the universities develop and manage their own programs and award their own diplomas. However, new programs have to be approved by CRÉPUQ's New Program Evaluation Commission and then, for fiscal purposes, authorized by MELS' Committee of University Program. Moreover, current programs must comply with standards set by CRÉPUQ's Program Evaluation Review Commission. The institutions also negotiate their own collective agreements with their unions or employee associations based on (but not limited to) parameters set by the Conseil du Trésor for all government employees. For the past fifteen years or so, though, the trend has been towards a greater concentration of powers in the hands of the state, as seen in particular in the abolition of the Conseil des universités, the introduction of new accountability mechanisms (such as the obligation of each university to table an annual report with the National Assembly's Culture and Education Commission), and the use of performance contracts from 2001 to 2004. Accountability requirements aside, the implementation of clearly targeted budgetary rules – those concerning, for example, the indirect costs of research and the implementation of activities following from the new Quebec University Funding Plan – have had, as many interviewees have pointed out, the effect of decreasing the institutions' autonomy. This is due to the power inherent in the money controlled by MELS and other ministries.

This is not to say, however, that the power of these ministries is applied solely through coercion. This view does not correspond to the perception of PSE leasers, who have emphasized systemic consultation and collaboration. Basically, MELS does not attempt to impose its methods unilaterally but, rather, to develop them together with the institution in question. And, precisely because they are so different, the institutions can enlist their respective specificities and attempt to position themselves in a competitive environment within which decisions are very often backed up by a consensus (or at least by the majority).

With regard to the other actors in the university network, the teachers' unions or associations, even though they are grouped under a federation, are relatively fragmented since negotiations are carried out locally. The different university managers' associations are fairly low-key and focus on solving "in-house" problems. The students associations, grouped under two main federations (Fédération étudiante universitaire du Québec and Fédération étudiante collégiale du Québec) and one dissident association composed of local CÉGEP or university department student associations, which is critical of the two federations (Association pour la solidarité syndicale étudiante), have had a decisive influence on the long-term freezing of tuition fees, on the financial aid policy, and, to a certain extent (at the level of the institutions), on local issues. As far as businesses are concerned, they choose their targets and intervene in the form of partnerships or contracts. For the most part, they do not try to influence decisions at the MELS level (as one of the interviewees has indicated) but, rather, in connection with specific projects. For example, at the provincial level, they may intervene in the investment of risk capital and in research-based start-up companies, while at the federal level they focus on influencing their research programs by strengthening their links with technological innovation.

To sum up, this description of the provincial government's part in the decision-making process supports the image of a system in which MELS, MDEIE, and the Conseil du Trésor play a predominant role in the university environment. In addition, when one takes into account the configuration of other system actors and the process of consultation within the system, decision-making power is, to a certain extent, shared by different authorities and paradoxically appears relatively diffuse.

The third feature that characterizes the decision-making process for PSE in Quebec concerns the continuity that has existed since the 1960s. The broad brush strokes for the design of the current PSE system were made during the 1960s, when the whole education system was completely revamped. The system has not undergone major changes since then. The people in charge of the system continue to draw their inspiration from the basic orientations of the education reform of the 1960s. The system's design has therefore remained much the same throughout the past thirty years, regardless of which government was in power. In our opinion, there are four reasons for this continuity. First, according to the nationalist ideology embraced by all the political parties in power, which inspired the school reforms in the 1960s, education – and PSE in particular – was and continues to be perceived as a lever for promoting the development of a population that does not think of itself as merely a province within the Canadian federation but as a society in its own right and, moreover, as a nation. This ideology is associated with the nation-building process.

Second, the consultation approach has been a consistent element across governments (Donald 1997). The many permanent advisory agencies and bodies – not to mention the Estates General on Education, the summits, the forums, and the National Assembly Commission on Culture and Education – were all venues for collaboration, where points of convergence would appear and a consensus would be shaped beyond political party leanings and lobby interests. These consultation practices are not exclusive to PSE but, rather, characterize the education system as a whole and the "Québec model" of public management.

The third reason for PSE continuity in Quebec has to do with the province's "incremental" approach to developing policy, with policies being an extension of earlier activities that are gradually altered. This approach was developed in reaction to the "rational" paradigm, whereby policies stem only from rational analysis. With the "gradual" paradigm, the goal is to relieve problems (rather than to find an ideal solution) and to adjust policy objectives to fit the means at hand (Lindblom 1980). In the case of PSE policy, it is as though, at the time of the education reforms in the 1960s, an exhaustive analysis of these policies, born of "rational" policy development, had been performed but that the "incremental" approach gained the upper hand thanks to its more limited analysis and consultations, which culminated in gradual and successive changes.

Finally, demographic trends and the economy also had an impact on the development of PSE in Quebec. For example, the arrival of the baby boomer generation in Quebec's postsecondary institutions in the 1960s dictated a complete overhaul of the elitist system then in place. Likewise, at the economic level, the constraints imposed by the economic recessions of the beginning of the 1980s and the 1990s, and in 2008, along with economic globalization, proved to be important deciding factors when it came to PSE funding policy and research policies focusing on innovation.

Although the PSE system's design was not altered in major ways, this does not mean the system remained static. We have already indicated some changes: the decentralization of decisions concerning college education; a greater concentration of power in the hands of the state at the university level; changes in the allocation of disposable funds to universities; changes in tuition fees in 1993, 2007, and 2011; changes in the loans and bursaries program; changes in the organization and orientation of research funds; and changes in the process of accountability. Moreover, with regard to accessibility, access is no longer defined merely in terms of admission to institutions but, rather, in terms of "access plus success" – that is, the completion of programs.

The fourth feature that characterizes the decision-making process for PSE in Quebec concerns the tensions and conflicts in the system. We have already mentioned the quarrels between federal and provincial governments, the demands connected with decentralization at the college level, and the tensions over MELS's power at the university level. The increase in tuition fees was a constant source of conflict and mobilized students organizations, so much so that, between 1995 and 2007, no government dared to increase them. Students even went out on strike over the changes to the loans and bursaries program. In addition, the changes made to funding procedures, notably the introduction of performance contracts, caused tensions to build between the universities and the government, and between institutions. Not everyone approved of increasing links between training programs and labour market requirements, or of the federal and provincial governments' insistence on strengthening ties between research and business, or on the marketing of research. Two concepts stand in opposition to each other. On the one hand is a utilitarian conception of universities, which stresses vocationalism and the instrumentalization of research; on the other hand is the socially aware humanist conception, which stresses knowledge development and institutional autonomy.

POLICY THEMES

We now reconstruct the four broad PSE policy themes: (1) access, (2) accountability and efficiency, (3) strengthening ties between school programs and the labour market, and (4) development of "useful and relevant" research. We then show how they are translated into policy documents, system organization, and funding. Last, we report on how the interviewees perceived these priorities.

Access to PSE

This theme has been confirmed several times since 1993. At the time of the college reforms in 1993, it was recognized that Quebec had not caught up to the rest of Canada in terms of its population's education. While access to college remained a goal, gaining access was not enough in itself. Perseverance was required to complete programs and to obtain the diploma/degree in question. The emphasis is no longer only on access but, rather, on "access to success."

In 1995 and 1996, the Commission for the Estates General on Education made access its top priority, defining it in terms of access plus success. It proposed specific school completion objectives in order to facilitate accountability: 85 percent of these young people should receive their high school diploma before they turned twenty – 60 percent should receive a diploma of college studies and 30 percent a bachelor's degree. In a policy statement MEQ (1997a, 1997b) embraced this new way of defining access and adopted these school completion objectives. In 1999, the National Assembly amended the Act Respecting the Conseil supérieur de l'Éducation to create the Advisory Committee on the Financial Accessibility of Education. This committee was given the mandate of advising the minister of education on financial aid programs and fees (tuition and other compulsory fees).

Access was at the top of the government's list of three key orientations in the Quebec Policy on Universities, published in 2000. The objectives were to "ensure that the economic obstacles to access to PSE are reduced to a minimum; ensure geographical access to university education, particularly through the presence of the Université du Québec throughout Québec and the development of distance education; encourage students to remain in university, particularly by emphasizing support for undergraduates; and, at all levels of PSE, but particularly in graduate studies (master's and doctoral programs) facilitate the integration of students into research and teaching" (MEQ 2000, 17).

In 2003, the government entrusted the Culture and Education Commission with the mandate of analyzing university funding from the perspective of quality and accessibility requirements. Concerning access, it noted that remarkable progress had been made with regard to the socially underprivileged. It indicated, however, that many regions were far below the Quebec average in terms of the proportion of people with university degrees, that accessibility depended on the quality and relevance of program offerings, and that access concerns should not be limited to the bachelor's degree level but apply to the master's and doctoral levels as well.

TRANSLATING ACCESS INTO PSE ORGANIZATION
AND FUNDING

When the PSE system was reconfigured in the 1960s, accessibility was the top priority. Initially, the emphasis was placed on access to institutions. The implementation of a unified two-level system, development of the CÉGEP network in all the regions, and the foundation of the Université du Québec were aimed, among other things, at promoting geographical accessibility to PSE and reducing inequalities connected with gender and language of instruction. The loans and bursaries program was aimed at reducing inequalities stemming from socio-economic status. The creation of the Télé-université distance education university as well as the continuing education initiatives of the CÉGEPs and other universities were designed to favour adult access to PSE. In 1993, then again in 2005, the government reiterated its decision to have a two-level system in order to encourage access.

Many fiscal strategies aim at promoting access: tuition-free college education; allocation of a specific amount to implement school success plans (aiming at increasing the completion rates) to be integrated into CÉGEPs' strategic plans; university funding based on the number of students enrolled; regulation of university tuition and other compulsory fees;[26] loans and bursaries program; and university funding partly based on the number of degrees awarded. Others are of a more specific nature. For example, tax deductions for students or their parents, special funding for the Télé-Université and universities in outlying areas, and support programs for Aboriginal students, for integration of the disabled and the training of immigrants.

HOW INTERVIEWED PSE LEADERS PERCEIVED ACCESSIBILITY

The PSE leaders interviewed acknowledged that accessibility had been the key theme of the PSE system since the 1960s. Members of an inter-university consultative committee were of the opinion that there had been a consensus on this issue on the part of successive governments. According to civil servants from MEQ, this concern was the inspiration behind the creation of the Université du Québec and countless measures designed to favour access for various categories of individuals (e.g., people from low-income backgrounds, Aboriginals, the disabled, and part-time students). In their opinion, access policies had been extremely successful, even though there are still inequalities.

On the topic of school success, a former minister of education added a clarification. He said that the goal was for young people and not-so-young people to succeed, and that succeeding did not necessarily mean getting a diploma or a degree but, rather, acquiring the knowledge to which they aspired. A member of an inter-university consultative committee spoke along the same lines, linking accessibility with quality training and programs.

From the point of view of geographical accessibility, a member from a college students' association pointed out that one could definitely speak in terms of success for the forty-year period as a whole. This theme was embodied in the creation of the CÉGEP network. He emphasized the important role CÉGEPs played in regional cultural development. A CÉGEP director reiterated this statement, adding that they contributed to economic development as well. The president of a university professors' association considered that accessibility also entailed ensuring that universities in outlying areas have the resources that allow them to offer a wide range of programs.

Financial accessibility to education was a source of concern to many of the people interviewed. This was especially the case for a member of a university students' association (with regard to the government's changes to the student loans and bursaries program) and for the president of a university professors' association. Representatives from students' associations, by the time of the interviews, were afraid the principle of all public colleges being tuition-free would be challenged and were sceptical about the Liberal government's promise not to increase university tuition fees before the end of its first term in power. Later on, these representatives were very critical of the two increases of tuition fees in 2008 and 2011, during the Liberal Party's second and third mandates, respectively.

Accountability, Reporting, and Efficiency

The way that access has been redefined over the past decade (i.e., access to a diploma or a degree and not only to an institution) is an indication of a determination to get institutions to be really concerned about their effectiveness and efficiency. Accountability refers to the possibility of making organizations responsible for their actions. According to the CSE (1999, 24 [our translation]): "Accountability constitutes the 'moral framework' that is required in a democracy to exercise power ... It forces actors to assume their responsibilities and recognize that they have an impact on how well their institutions operate – that they have part of the power needed to change things." Efficiency is actually closely linked to it and emerged as a theme within the same context. It refers to the achievement of objectives at the lowest cost, to an organization's ability to meet these while reducing the effort required to do so, or choosing other options that are less costly (not exclusively monetarily) in terms of effort.

Concerns with accountability and its corollary, evaluation, are not limited to PSE: they affect the whole education system. The Estates General on Education in 1995 was possibly the most visible illustration of this. At the college level, many questions have been raised and countless reports written about the network, notably the Nadeau Report (Conseil supérieur de l'éducation 1975), which has affected and inspired different governments over the years. At the beginning of the 1990s, the idea of systematically evaluating the college network emerged and led to the creation of the Commission d'évaluation de l'enseignement collegial. In 2003, the same questions came up again. Following a new analysis of the network, the government decided once more to keep Quebec's college education format. At the university level, the concern with evaluation begins in the early

1980s, when the Conseil des universités began publishing its sector-based studies on engineering, social science, and education. But it was in its Policy on Universities that the Quebec government first clearly stated its accountability theme. Universities were to keep their autonomy and their power to organize their activities as they saw fit, and they were answerable to society and public authorities for their management of public funds (MEQ 2000).

As for the efficiency theme, it is part of the trend not only in PSE but also in general government. Quebec's Public Administration Act, adopted in 2000, introduced a new management framework focusing on outcomes, respect for the principle of transparency, and increased accountability. Likewise, according to the Quebec Policy on Universities, it is one of the principles on which government and university initiatives are based. Universities are supported financially by the state, and they must run their institutions efficiently by using the resources at their disposal optimally. The government defined principles of action and priorities for university performance in terms of education quality, research excellence, and the system's overall efficiency (MEQ 2000, 17).

TRANSLATING ACCOUNTABILITY, REPORTING, AND
EFFICIENCY INTO PSE ORGANIZATION AND FUNDING

At the college level, these themes are currently actualized chiefly through the CEEC. The CÉGEPs and colleges accredited for funding are also obliged to integrate a school success plan into their strategic plan. Each institution is given a grant to ensure its follow-up and that it reports to MELS. At the university level, the determination to make institutions accountable is reflected in their obligation to submit an annual report to the Culture and Education Commission. In addition, in 1989, the desire for accountability and the need to promote efficiency was translated into CRÉPUQ's New Programs Evaluation Commission and, in the early 1990s, into its policy concerning periodic program evaluation, which requires that universities evaluate all of their programs in keeping with quality and relevance requirements. The audit of this policy is the responsibility of the Program Evaluation Review Commission. In 1997, CREPUQ created the Commission des universités sur les programmes (CUP), a university commission on programs. In three years, this commission studied the complementarity and relevance of all programs.[27] After that, CRÉPUQ's academic affairs committee gave the program monitoring committee the mandate to bring the reports on various sectors of activity up to date. CRÉPUQ now follows up on CUP's recommendations. Furthermore, in conjunction with the Québec Policy on Universities, and with particular regard to efficiency, the government planned to monitor how all universities are managed, define a number of indicators in cooperation with these institutions on their management, and adapt these to fit the special features of each institution.

Concerns with accountability and efficiency have also been evident during the 1990s and at the beginning of the 2000s in four funding strategies (the last two of which have since been abandoned): (1) the obligation of colleges and universities to submit many different kinds of data regarding their management;[28] (2) the payment of a lump sum to universities for every degree awarded;[29] (3) university performance contracts covering the 2001–04 period; and (4) the failing grade "tax" in the CÉGEPS, whereby students were charged for every course they failed (except for the first one). In 2008, another strategy was to have both CÉGEPS and the universities reach an agreement with MELS on how to spend supplementary funds available since the government's reinvestment in PSE. More recently, the two bills on the governance of institutions also reflect the clear will of the government to improve the accountability of PSE institutions. Finally, as indicated earlier, the University Funding Plan, included in the 2011–12 budget for allocating additional resources ($850 million) to universities over a six-year period (2011 to 2017), fixes clear targets and precisely defines a set of indicators to make sure that the additional revenue will be used for specific purposes. Each university will have to conclude a partnership agreement with the government that specifies how new resources will be allocated with regard to four types of indicators: (1) quality of teaching and student services, (2) quality of research, (3) competitive positioning of universities in Canada and abroad, and (4) administration and management (see appendix 6). Further, universities will have to report annually to the National Assembly regarding the fulfilment of their commitments.

HOW INTERVIEWED PSE LEADERS PERCEIVED
ACCOUNTABILITY, REPORTING, AND EFFICIENCY

MEQ managers, acknowledging that accountability had become a priority, agreed that it emerged in the 1990s, in particular at the time of the abolition of the Conseil des universités.[30] In 1993, according to them, the provincial Liberal government was pursuing its objective of reducing PSE personnel (20 percent management and 12 percent other personnel categories). The approach adopted (Bill 198: an Act Respecting the Reduction of Personnel in Public Bodies and the Accountability of Deputy Ministers and Chief Executive Officers of Public Bodies) was to oblige university heads to account for their administration directly to the National Assembly, without going through the minister of education. The goal was, using the logic of accountability, to give universities a greater sense of responsibility. Universities had a long tradition of autonomy and were already practising accountability. A new link was established with the National Assembly, and universities, since they were experiencing the same personnel reductions, were subjected to the same rules as ministries. When these objectives were attained, Bill 198 was repealed, but the hearing mechanisms for heads of universities were readopted within the context of the Act Respecting Educational Institutions at the University Level.

According to members of an inter-university consultative committee, university accountability and autonomy went hand in hand. MEQ appreciated sharing the regulation of the university system with CRÉPUQ. This collaboration, or "give and take," began in the 1970s when universities sacrificed some of their autonomy by creating a CRÉPUQ committee to evaluate the "quality" of degree programming. However, MEQ, via its program committee, remained responsible for determining the "relevance" of programs before authorizing their funding. A committee made up of university representatives and civil servants had, since 1984, headed up a number of technical committees on various information systems to create data banks on student clientele, funding, human resources, research, and physical spaces.

Some of the PSE leaders interviewed took a critical view, however. A university president situated this theme in the international context. According to him, the OECD, the World Trade Organization (WTO), the International Monetary Fund (IMF), and the World Bank all had huge sums and means at their disposal, which enabled them to disseminate a structuring discourse, or philosophy, on accountability that was compatible with their interests and a close match with neoliberal precepts. The official ideology on universities drew its inspiration from this discourse, and it was transformed into organizational practices and behaviour in all spheres of activity. Resistance appeared to him to be stronger in the universities than in other sectors. A former minister of education believed that accountability was a trend that should be promoted but that, at the same time, we should continue to reflect on what needed to be integrated into this concept. He stressed the need to consider any given institution's specificity. For a college student leader, evaluation was not a bad thing in and of itself, provided that ways of achieving outcomes were evaluated and not just outcomes alone.

Strengthening Links between PSE Programs and the Labour Market

Even though this theme was expressed less frequently than the first two, the Charest government was unequivocal in its commitment. Strengthening links between PSE programs and business was articulated within the context of work organization changes, new technologies, increased productivity, and competitiveness requirements related to economic globalization. Quebec, it was argued, needed to adapt the structure of its economy, modernize its companies, and develop value-added light industry in technology sectors. For these changes to work, emphasis needed to be placed on training quality human resources, the fulcrum of economic development. The PSE system must ensure both initial training and upgrading to help people adapt to these changes. This goal entails collaboration with business and the forging of partnerships so that market requirements can be properly met. The CSE cautioned that the PSE system had to be careful not to be diverted either from its primary education mission or from the need to protect its institutional autonomy (CSE 2002). In addition, according to those who promoted this vision, because they would have to deal with people from other countries (or even work abroad), technicians, professionals, and management would have to learn more about internationalization.

At the college level, this theme was clearly expressed in the 1992 Conseil des colleges report that preceded the 1993 college reform policy set out by the Ministère de l'Enseignement supérieur et de la Science (Ministry of Higher Education and Science). This policy did not deal exclusively or even primarily with strengthening links between training programs and the labour market; rather, it confirmed "the comprehensive nature of college education, characterized by shared understanding around a common cultural core of general courses" (Ministère de l'enseignement supérieur et de la science 1993, 9 [our translation]). However, this position on the need to provide basic general courses and their contribution to career training is consonant with the theme of strengthening ties between programs and the labour market.

Three avenues for reforms were proposed by the minister in order to adapt career training to the labour market. First, reinforcing partnerships with the working world (focusing on creating a career program committee for Quebec, offering internships and co-op programs, appointing business representatives to college boards of governors, seeing that boards of governors participate in some of the initiatives of the Commission de l'enseignement collégial [which comes under the CSE]; creating ties between colleges and regional personnel development organizations; and developing technology transfer centres that could contribute to the development of the regions in which CÉGEPS are established). Second, introducing program revision according to a competency-based approach, which calls for designing programs in keeping with the competencies and skills that need to be developed for the career in question. Third, giving institutions greater leeway to develop their own career training programs, leading to attestations of college studies and therefore meeting requests for customized training more rapidly and with more flexibility.[31]

At the university level, the three sector-based studies on engineering, education, and social sciences conducted in the 1980s by the Conseil des universités highlighted the necessity of bringing programs and the realities of the labour market closer together (Conseil des universites 1984, 1987, 1990). In 2000, this theme was expressed very explicitly in the Quebec Policy on Universities, notably in the analysis of a series of policy issues: the globalization of the economy, interdependence between economic development and scientific and technological advances, the growing demand for research, the importance of universities to the fabric of society, the need to address society's requirements,[32] and the development of university-business partnerships. The CST shared these orientations, plus it insisted on a new dimension: innovation. Not only did university research and education have to keep close tabs on fluctuations in the needs of society and the economy but it also had to help effect timely changes by anticipating these fluctuations.

According to the policy on universities, quality training must also be relevant. In other words, it must enable students to acquire the competencies, skills, and tools they need to develop as individuals and to play their part in society. Training program content must be adapted to the needs of the people who will be entering the job market and to the requirements of society. In other words, it must meet general and cross-disciplinary needs as well as specific and occasional needs. Program content should be adapted with the help of partners. These competencies are not only acquired through specialized training programs. If training is to stand up to the test of time, it should be comprehensive so that people can evolve in their professional lives. It should include basic knowledge, specialized knowledge, and technical skills, but it should also offer generic knowledge that equips students to take up the challenges of a constantly evolving working life. Two of the policy themes to do with meeting society's requirements are specifically concerned with (1) strengthening ties between programs and the labour market and (2) creating strategies for the vocational integration of graduates (MEQ 2000, 26).

TRANSLATING STRENGTHENING LINKS BETWEEN
PSE PROGRAMS AND THE LABOUR MARKET
INTO ORGANIZATION AND FUNDING

At the college level, there are four dimensions to how this theme is actualized. The first involves a vocational and career education committee. This committee is composed of representatives from MELS, public agencies, employers, and union and association representatives, and it was created in 1994. Its mandate was to examine issues concerning the three education levels from the angle of education-employment relationships, to coordinate programs and place them in a continuum, and to avoid duplication. The second dimension concerns short vocational training programs of varying length that lead to an attestation of college studies. They are designed to rapidly meet regional requirements for customized career training, and they come under the authority of the institutions rather than MEQ. This enables institutions to rapidly adjust to training requests.

The third dimension of how one strengthens the links between PSE programs and the labour market involves support for co-op (work-study) programs. This educational strategy combines training in the school environment with industry internships and is aimed at "on-the-job" acquisition of the competencies targeted by the program, the transfer of competencies already acquired to real industry situations, and the gradual introduction of students to a career. The fourth dimension concerns one of the "ministerial orientations" defined at the beginning of 2005, and it deals with aligning training programs with training requirements. MEQ supports the collaborative efforts of the colleges, notably: the determination of courses common to related programs; the establishment of special admission requirements; program reviews in cooperation with professional corporations; the determination of intermediate sanctions, and so on. In addition, colleges will be able to develop specialized programs that expand on career programs for which they are already accredited.

At the university level, several committees and commissions have been charged with the task of evaluating programs from the point of view of their relevance. According to CRÉPUQ's program evaluation policy, every university must develop its own policy regarding the periodic evaluation of all its programs. This must be in keeping with scientific opportunity (recent progress in the discipline or field of study) and its criteria include the social and economic (e.g., labour market requirements), the systemic (e.g., comparable programs in Quebec), and the institutional (e.g., the institution's objectives, priorities, programs, and resources). For this purpose, as noted earlier, CRÉPUQ created the Program Evaluation Review Commission and the New Program Evaluation Commission, which looks at the reasons specific programs were created in relation to the establishment's orientation and development as well as its scientific, cultural, and socio-economic needs. Although these commissions are connected with evaluation, accountability, and efficiency themes, they also help to translate the theme of strengthening links between programs and the labour market into reality.

A number of clearly targeted funding initiatives also embody the aforementioned theme. At the college level, these initiatives fall into three categories: (1) those concerning institution and business promotion and support for co-op programs; (2) refundable tax credits for training, applicable to internships; and (3) support for entrepreneurship, designed to promote the development of an entrepreneurial culture. At the university level, specific funding with regard to student services ensures that part of the funding may be used to manage co-op programs, especially for foreign students. A budgetary allowance makes it possible to offer more internships as well as career guidance and placement services. Support is provided for developing short training programs (e.g., "bridge" arrangements between existing programs to facilitate career reorientation for people with university degrees, development of short programs requested by businesses, etc.). Funding is available for the continuing education of teachers, a fellowship program for master's and PhD students in nursing, and the training of immigrants. A program to support the internationalization of training and studies outside Quebec, including other Canadian provinces, has been implemented in the form of grants for short university study trips/stays.

HOW INTERVIEWED PSE LEADERS PERCEIVED THIS THEME
MEQ emphasized the importance of the Quebec Professional Code,[33] which gives professional bodies certain powers with respect to training. As a rule, these corporations have a training committee, including university representatives, whose mandate is to examine the qualifications required to practise their professions. They also observed: an increase in training length, reflecting steeper requirements; the incorporation into programs of courses on professional codes of ethics and ethical considerations; an increase in the number of internships being offered; and a greater desire to internationalize programs so that graduates would have access to more jobs.

Members of an education advisory body remarked that better preparedness for globalization was, in fact, one of their organization's priorities. According to them, MEQ has, with regard to its programs, an internationalization policy that aims to increase students' international mobility and to promote openness to different cultures; however, they did not see this policy reflected at the funding or structural levels.

A university president criticized CUP's systemic streamlining and its initiatives directed at greater program relevancy. According to him, universities live on autonomy and they should be left with the freedom to choose and orient their programs in accordance with the requirements of scientific development. By the same token, a member from a college consultative committee argued for greater institutional autonomy. However, a college student leader was reticent about giving colleges more autonomy to define programs because he feared that diplomas would no longer be of equal value.

A university student leader denounced the mercantilism of universities that proposed programs that were relevant in terms of the market but not necessarily adapted to their missions.

Development of "Useful and Relevant" Research

This theme is based on the principle that research must contribute more than before to the state's economic and social goals. The concept of "progress," which was generally associated with these goals, was replaced during the 1990s by that of "innovation." According to the Quebec Policy on Science and Innovation, it is by focusing more on inter-sector networks and partnerships that research will be able to truly contribute to innovation.

This orientation breaks with that of the Parent Commission report (Gouvernement du Québec 1963–1966), which placed the accent on basic research and the idea of the university as a "republic of science" in charge of its own decisions. It also emphasized that Quebec's researchers needed to catch up with researchers in the rest of Canada in order to be able to compete with them. Quebec is the only province that, as early as the 1970s, set up structures for directly supporting university research, and this was due, to a large extent, to its "catching-up" ideology.[34]

In 1971, the first science policy document recognized the central role played by universities in R&D, but it failed to mention the contribution of business. In a White Paper on Scientific Research published in 1980, university research was positioned in relation to government research and industry research. The aim was described as the advancement of knowledge. Universities were asked, however, to start concerning themselves more with research spinoffs and their effect on regional economic development. In the economic policy published in 1982 regarding the high-tech boom, or technological turning point, *Le virage technologique*, the need to develop close ties with business and to see that programs better addressed industrial training needs was emphasized. In 1983, the Act to Promote the Advancement Of Science and Technology in Quebec created the Conseil de la Science et de la Technologie (CST), whose mandate was to advise the Ministère de la Recherche, de la Science et de la Technologie (Ministry of Research, Science and Technology) on all matters relating to scientific and technological development in Quebec.

The Quebec Policy on Science and Innovation, published in 2001 by the Parti Québécois government, was based on a concept of the requirements of the knowledge society. University research was assigned an instrumental function: it had to be geared towards innovation. This concept referred to three different types of realities: (1) product technological innovation, which involved perfecting and marketing a product that was better than those already on the market; (2) process technological innovation, which entailed perfecting and adopting new or improved production and distribution methods; and (3) social innovation, which referred to any new approach, practice, or intervention – or any completely new product – developed to improve a situation or to solve a social problem in connection with institutions, organizations, or communities. By referring to the concept of social innovation in this way, the Quebec government distanced itself from the strict technological innovation marketing promoted by the OECD and governmental organizations (Dandurand 2005; Milot 2005). More specifically, this policy aimed to adapt the research support provided by Quebec's subsidizing agencies, to support companies ensuring knowledge transfer by recognizing and promoting the value of university research, and to harmonize universities' intellectual property policies so that they all recognized research accomplishments as institutional property. On the heels of this policy, the government then proceeded to restructure subsidizing agencies and tabled an action plan regarding intellectual property management.

As noted earlier, the concern for social innovation almost disappeared in the text of the Liberal government's *Stratégie de la recherche et de l'innovation* (MDEIE 2006), though the MDEIE still supports a program for social innovation and structuring projects in development and transfer. But the Charest government reaffirmed its will to support R&D so that, by 2010, it would reach 3 percent of the GDP,[35] and the portion of R&D funded by business would rise from 60 to 66 percent. The strategy also aimed at investing in those domains of research and technology that would have an impact on economic development and employment, to market the findings, and to promote careers in science and technology.

One cannot discuss Quebec's research policy without stressing how much it is regulated by the federal government, through its many councils, agencies, and programs. The federal government's heightened profile in this regard is in fact part of its strategy to better address the challenges of the knowledge society. Quebec's policies are within the sphere of influence of these federal policies, but they also distance themselves from them in certain respects, and sometimes even get ahead of them, as we saw when we discussed funding for indirect research costs.

TRANSLATING DEVELOPMENT OF "USEFUL AND RELEVANT" RESEARCH INTO SYSTEM ORGANIZATION AND FUNDING

At the college level, the research mission is far more defined and targeted than it is at the university level. The mission is limited to pedagogical research on teaching and learning, and to technology relating to economic sectors corresponding to career training programs. This technology research is mostly conducted in the forty-six college technology transfer centres (TTCs). Researchers are also associated with university teams supported by granting agencies.

At the university level, there are six examples of the major changes that have occurred since the beginning of the 1990s, when the "useful and relevant" research theme truly asserted itself. First, research and its funding no longer come under MELS but, rather, MDEIE. Second, in order to encourage businesses to invest in applied research, the government created a university research tax credit program. These tax credits range from 17.5 to 37.5 percent of eligible expenses based on the size of the corporate group.[36] Third, research investments and programs are increasingly targeted and oriented towards research subjects that are closely linked to the economic and social needs of the moment. For example, the concerted action programs, which associate public, para-public, and private subsidizing agencies; ministries; and organizations are designed to respond to research needs defined by governmental, community, cultural, and industrial communities. They favour the formation of partnerships between these organizations and researchers so as to ensure knowledge transfer and to maximize the usefulness of their findings. At the end of the 1990s, this trend was even more evident in Quebec than it was in the other Canadian provinces (Godin et al., 2000).

The fourth example of a major change since the early 1990s involves a new mode of research production that has gradually emerged to become the prevailing point of reference. Centred on the research topic, this mode is defined in terms of a knowledge application context and calls for a cross-disciplinary approach. Research subjects are no longer defined exclusively on the basis of academic and disciplinary interests but, rather, on the basis of topics linked to contemporary priorities (Lesemann 2003). Fifth, with regard to the institutional consequences of these changes, departments are being replaced by groups (teams, laboratories, centres, networks, etc.) as the research hub – the place where research is structured and where researchers are found. These groups are typically of an interdisciplinary, inter-university, or inter-sector nature. With respect to the inter-sector dimension, the government supported the creation and development of technology transfer and liaison centres (TTLCS) in the 1990s, which combine researchers from different universities and industry partnerships to facilitate strategic alliances, ensure technology transfer, and help train skilled personnel. Quebec's universities have responded to these expectations by creating autonomous units for liaising with businesses and communities, referred to as university-entrepreneurship centres (UECS) and university-community liaison offices.

The sixth example of a major change is that, since 1989, MEQ has been funding a portion of indirect research costs connected with services and space that universities place at researchers' disposal. As noted earlier, Quebec was a trail-blazer in this field. Its contribution varies, depending on whether projects are financed by Quebec government research funds and ministries or by organizations accredited by a joint CRÉPUQ-MEQ committee; depending on the field of research; and, in the case of health care research, depending on whether the research is conducted in a hospital or a university. Indirect costs linked to projects funded by a federal government agency are partly financed by the Canadian government's Indirect Costs Program.

HOW INTERVIEWED PSE LEADERS PERCEIVED THIS THEME
MEQ civil servants recognized that developing useful and relevant research is a theme in recent policies. Now that the research infrastructures have been created, they think the needs are being felt most at human resource and teaching resource renewal levels. Members of a university consultative committee noted that Quebec's universities go after their share from federal funding agencies. They thought that this was even more surprising when they considered that Quebec had proportionally fewer professors than did other provinces. They would like to see more funding going to the humanities,

however, and said that research was increasingly utilitarian, to the detriment of the humanities.

The president of a university professors' association emphasized the transformation of the teaching profession induced by the research instrumentalization movement. He lamented the fact that individualism and competition between professors have become commonplace. He also felt that far too much importance was placed on research and that this contributed to hierarchizing universities' missions. As a union official, he was inclined to defend the traditional university model, whereby teaching plays a central role and is inseparable from research.

A university president considered federal programs to be structurally influential and mentioned the "perverse effects" some people attributed to them. On the other hand, he said that, for an effect to be perverse, it must be undesirable in the eyes of its promoter, which was not the case with federal agencies. He regretted the federal programs' destructuring effect on Quebec's PSE system and saw this as a form of control that was on a far greater scale than anything the Roman Catholic Church had ever wielded over universities. Members of an education advisory body insisted that, from a social innovative perspective, it was important to avoid limiting research partnerships to industry and to build them with other social actors.

According to a CÉGEP director, there is far less research being done in the CÉGEPs than there is in the universities because research is not included in the teachers' task description. He complained, however, about college researchers' not having greater access to federal funding. He considered the research being done by TTCs extremely important from a regional development perspective.

Our reconstruction of policy themes was based primarily on existing public records. Generally speaking, our interviews with PSE leaders confirmed our wording of these themes. Yet two leaders, a university president and a former minister of education, while acknowledging the plausibility and relevance of our conclusions on these themes, preferred to distance themselves from them. Their perception of universities was much less utilitarian and focused more on "freer" development of knowledge and the need to make it accessible to everyone in the interests of having more informed citizens. They had a more socially aware, humanist vision of universities, seeing them as a public service. The university president concluded that it was important to protect the autonomy of universities and the collegial nature of decisions concerning their orientations. From this perspective, the under-funding of universities and highly targeted funding procedures reduced the leeway that universities should have to make decisions internally, in collegial fashion. In his opinion, the themes we described were not limited to Quebec's system; rather they fit with the trends extolled by large international organizations (e.g., the OECD, UNESCO, and the World Bank), whose discourse and influence he recognized in many countries.

FUNDING

To what extent was the importance of PSE reflected in its funding during the last thirty years? Did funding increase more than the rise in enrolment? How did PSE compare with other policy areas, such as health? In 2009–10, the provincial operating grants ranged around $4,563 million (61 and 39 percent, respectively, for universities and colleges).[37] Figure 4.1 presents the changes in the grants for the college and university sectors from 1986–87 to 2009–10 in constant 2002 dollars. At the beginning of this period, under the Liberal government of Robert Bourassa, funding increased steadily up until 1990–91, when the total allocation was 18 percent higher than it had been in 1986–87. The university sector saw a relatively larger increase than the college sector (20 percent versus 15 percent). During the last four years of the Liberal government, the allocation remained stable despite the economic crisis at the beginning of the 1990s, with a slight overall increase that nearly all went to the college sector (which was then in the process of revitalization). The first years of the Parti Québécois government in the mid-1990s coincided with the sharp decline in the Canada Health and Social Transfer to the provinces (more particularly, with the decision to end explicitly targeting its PSE component [Fisher and al. 2006]) and, later, with the decision of the Quebec government to suppress the deficit of the operating budget after the 1996 Summit on the Economy and Employment.[38] This decision has had an impact on a major reduction in government spending, PSE included. This is reflected in figure 4.1, where we can note a drastic decrease in the total provincial operating grants during a three-year period commencing with the 1995–96 budget. By 1997–1998, the grants for the university sector had declined by almost one-quarter, while the college sector faired a little better, "only" dropping by some 15 percent.

The trend was broken in the 1998–99 budget and during the remaining years of the Parti Québécois' reign as funding for PSE increased rapidly. In its last year in power (2003), the total expenditure had surpassed the previous high that occurred in 1994–95 by approximately 5 percent. Up until the last budget of the Parti Québécois in 2002–03, the changes in provincial operating grants for the university and college sectors have followed similar trends, with some minor differences. The 2002–03 budget ushered in a different pattern, with a sharp increase to the university sector accompanied by a decline in grants for the colleges. Under the newly elected Liberal government, the total operating grants declined slightly in 2004–05 and 2005–06 but increased sharply thereafter up until 2009–10 (a 22 percent increase) and almost equally for the two sectors. As for the years to come, with the adoption of the University Funding Plan (2011–16), included in the 2011 budget and described earlier, the proportion going to the university sector should continue to rise as there is no similar plan for the college sector.

Thus, provincial postsecondary funding seems to vary as much, if not more, in terms of the economic conjuncture than of the political party in power: it increased under both the Liberal Party and the Parti Québécois, remained static under the Liberals during the economic crisis of the beginning of the 1990s, decreased in the second half of the 1990s when the Parti Québécois government decided to curb the deficit, and increased again while it was still in power after this objective had been mostly attained, and then continued to grow under the Liberals. This is not surprising when we recall both the consensus on the role of education and of higher education with regard to the development of Quebec society and the consultation approach that characterized the Quebec model of public management.

Operating grants only reveal part of the story as changes in overall funding have to be seen in relation to variations in enrolment. To address this issue figure 4.2 documents changes in global provincial expense per FTE student in constant 2002 dollars for colleges and universities from 1986–87 to 2009–10.[39] From 1986–87 to 1994–95, under the Liberal government, the expense per university FTE student increased almost constantly by nearly 20 percent, while that for college students at first increased at the end of the 1980s, then decreased by 8 percent to rise again by 15 percent from 1992–93 to 1995. After the Parti Québécois rose to power in 1994, the pattern of FTE funding was at first relatively similar for the two sectors: it decreased by about 10 percent from 1995–96 to 1997–98. This drop coincided with the reduction of the federal transfers for

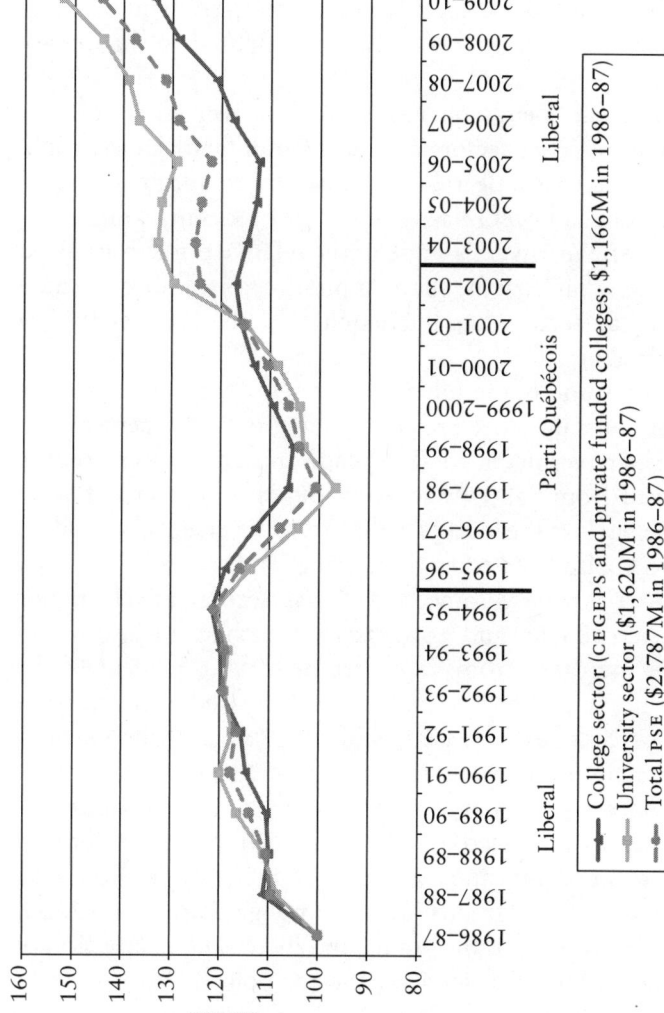

Figure 4.1
Changes in provincial operating grants for Quebec college and university sectors and total post-secondary education, 1986–87 – 2009–10 in constant 2002 dollars, 1986–87 = 100.
Source: Ministry of Education, Leisure and Sport, Quebec.

postsecondary education and the provincial government's decision to curb its deficit. Later on, the expenses per FTE university students increased rapidly under the Parti Québécois government and continued to grow almost constantly under the Liberals – a 40 percent increase from 1998–99 to 2009–10. During the same period, the expenses per FTE college students was characterized by minor fluctuations and remained relatively constant compared to the university sector.

What government spends on PSE has to be seen in relation to what it allocates to other sectors and the overall financial situation. Thus, it is possible that a decrease in expenditure during a specific year does not signal a lower relative priority of PSE but, rather, deteriorating finances. We can get a sense of the relative priority attached to PSE by focusing on how the share of public expenditure allocated to different policy sectors has fluctuated over the last twenty-five years (see table 4.1).

Three findings stand out in table 4.1. First, the share going to PSE in Quebec has constantly been relatively low (around 7 percent and 8 percent of the government total expenditure) and it decreased by only 0.6 percent from 1986–87 to 2007–08. However, in 2011–12, it almost came back at the level of 1986–87 (8.1 percent). Second, in comparison to health and "education, leisure and sports" (excluding PSE) and the rest of government, PSE has seen relatively minor shifts. Between 1986–87 and 2011–2012, the share of health and social services increased from 32.9 percent to 47.6 percent of the total expenditure (44.7 percent) and MELS decreased from 23.3 percent to 17.3 percent (25.7 percent) while the "Rest of the Government" decreased by 23.7 percent (from 35.5 percent to 27.1 percent). Third, judging from the data presented in table 4.1, the broad trends in policy themes, as expressed by relative allocation of expenditures, do not seem to be significantly affected by the party in power so much as by broader social trends such as, among others, demographics (declining proportion of the young and increasing proportion of the old), the cost of medical services, and the political propensity to reduce the size of the state whatever the party in power.

A common response from postsecondary institutions to increasing enrolment and decreasing funding per student at certain times has been to adopt a strategy known as academic capitalism (Slaughter and Rhoades 2004) and to compete with other institutions in order to diversify their sources of revenue and increase their own share.

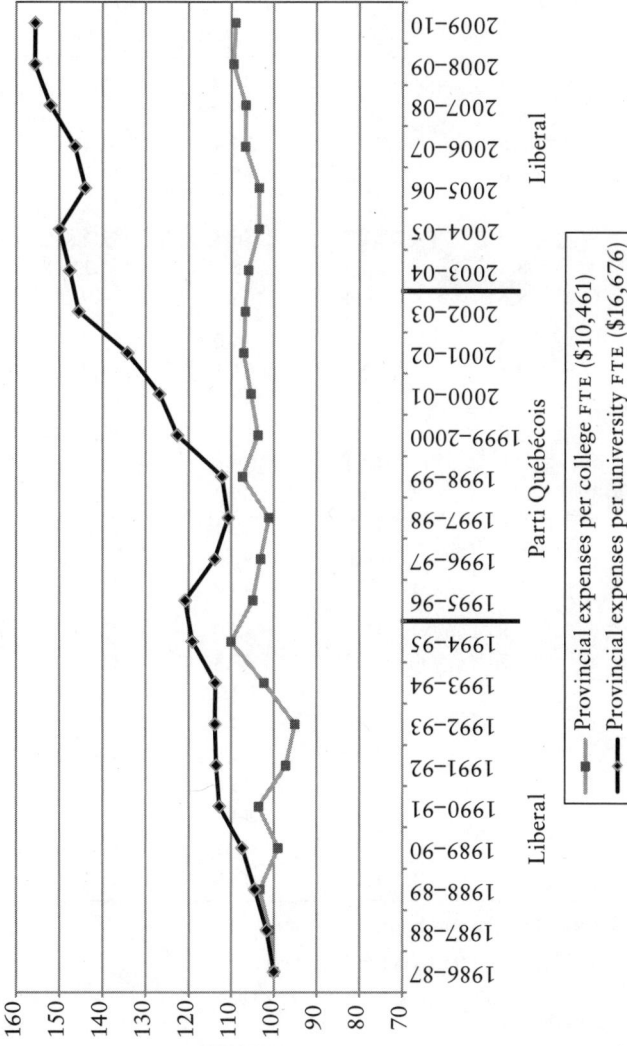

Figure 4.2
Changes in global provincial expenses per funded FTE for the college and university sectors in constant 2002 dollars, 1986–87 – 2009–10.

Source: Direction des statstiques et de l'information decisionnelle, Ministere de l'Education, du Loisir et du Sport.

Notes:

1. The global provincial expense refers to expenses related to operating grants and the immobilization of research.
2. The college sector refers to CEGEP and private subsidized colleges.

Table 4.1
Expenditure Budget plan 1986–87 to 2011–12 in percentage of total Quebec government expenditure (in million dollars)

Party	Year	Postsecondary education and training	Education, leisure, and sports (excl. PSE)	Health and social services	Rest of government
Liberal	1986–87	8.2	23.3	32.9	35.5
	1987–88	8.2	24.4	32.9	34.5
	1988–89	8.6	23.0	34.4	34.1
	1989–90	8.6	21.0	35.7	34.7
	1990–91	8.5	21.5	35.8	34.2
	1991–92	8.3	21.1	36.2	34.5
	1992–93	8.4	20.9	35.6	35.1
	1993–94	8.3	20.4	36.4	34.9
Québécois	1994–95	8.5	20.4	36.0	35.0
	1995–96	8.4	20.7	36.1	34.7
	1996–97[1]	8.5	20.7	37.2	33.7
	1997–98	8.0	19.4	37.2	35.4
	1998–99	7.9	18.1	39.4	34.7
	1999–2000	7.8	18.3	39.2	34.7
	2000–01	7.6	17.8	40.1	34.5
	2001–02	7.3	18.0	41.0	33.7
	2002–03	7.6	17.9	40.8	33.7
Liberal	2003–04	7.8	17.7	42.0	32.4
	2004–05	7.7	17.3	43.3	31.8
	2005–06	7.7	17.3	43.1	32.0
	2006–07	7.7	17.0	43.4	31.9
	2007–08	7.6	16.9	43.9	31.7
	2008–09	8.1	16.3	43.8	31.8
	2009–10	7.5	16.2	44.6	31.6
	2010–11[1]	7.9	16.9	45.8	29.3
	2011–12[2]	8.1	17.3	47.6	27.1

Source: Ministry of Education, Leisure and Sport.
1. The data for 1997–98 to 2009–10 refer to actual expenses.
2. Estimation.
According to the 2011–12 budget.

Figure 4.3 documents the relative share of Quebec universities and colleges' revenue coming from (1) transfers from different levels of government and (2) revenue generated from different sources by the institutions. The governments (provincial and federal) remain the main source of revenue despite some changes in the pattern of funding. Between 1988–89 and 2008–09, the change in the relative proportion coming from own-source revenue and government funding has been moderate. During this period the proportion of government funding has gone down from a high of 80 percent in 1988–89 to 70 percent in 1997–98. Then this proportion remained almost the same up to 2008–09. The decline in the proportion coming from federal and provincial governments coincided, at the beginning of the 1990s, with the economic downturn and the increase of tuition fees and, later in the decade, with the decision of the Quebec government to curb its deficit over three years.

A closer examination of revenue sources (see table 4.2) shows that there has been a steady decline in the share coming from the provincial government. In 1988–89 almost three-quarters of funding came from the provincial government, but by 2008–09 the figure had dropped to 59 percent. In contrast, during the same period, the relative allocation from the federal government increased from 5.8 to 10.2 percent.

The institutions own source of revenue has been boosted mainly through increases to what is labelled "other sales of goods and services" and to tuition fees.[40] The share of the first one passed from 7.9 percent to 11.9 percent, and that of the tuition fees increased by 3.4 percent. The major increase in the share coming from tuition fees occurred during the Bourassa government in the first part of the 1990s, when it went from constituting 6.2 percent of total revenue in 1988–89 to 9.8 percent in 1994–95. During the first years of the Parti Québécois government tuition increased slightly, despite its decision to freeze them, to reach a high of 10.5 percent. This is because, since 1997, out-of-province students (Canadian and foreign) have to pay a supplement, which has been taken into consideration by Statistics Canada in the calculation of the percentages. In 1999–2000 it started to decline, and by the last year of the Parti Québécois' time in power, 2002–03, student fees only made up 8.6 percent of total revenue. The downward trend came to a halt during the first years of the Charest government, when it increased slightly to 9.3 percent and then to 9.6 percent of total revenue.

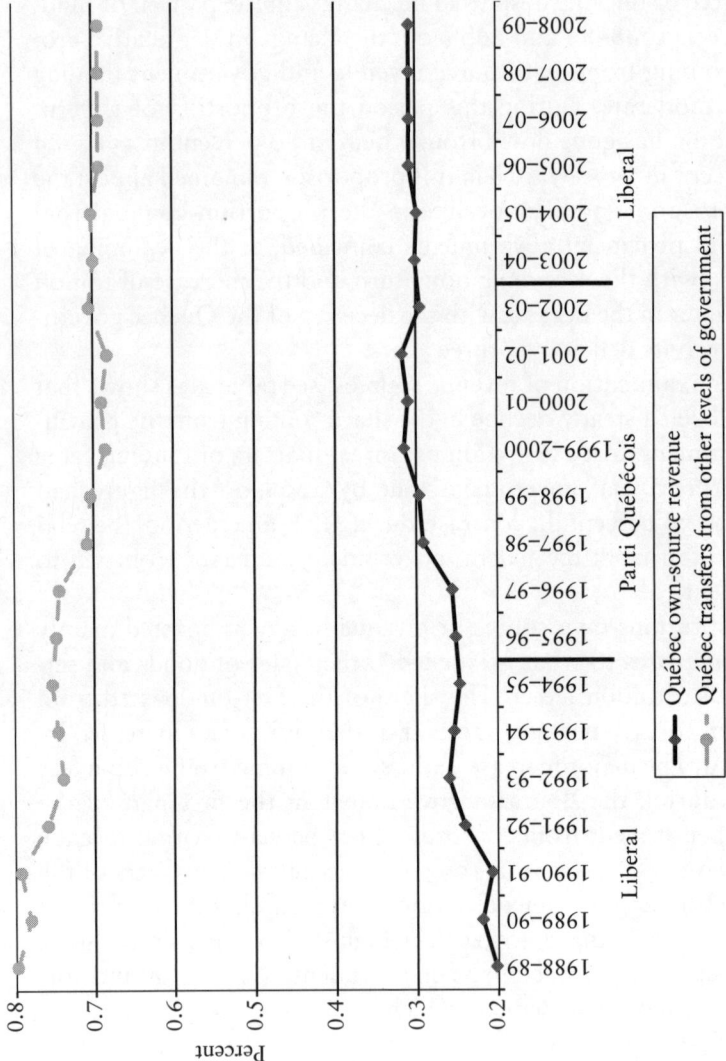

Figure 4.3
Proportion of revenue from own-source revenue and government funding in Quebec, 1988–89 – 2008–09.

Source: Statistics Canada, CANSIM, table 385–0007.

Table 4.2
Funding sources as a percent of total funding: Quebec postsecondary education, 1988–89 to 2008–09

Party	Year	Own-source revenue				Government transfers	
		Tuition fees	Other sales of goods and services	Investment income	Other own source Revenue	Federal	Provincial
Liberal	1988–89	6.2	7.9	1.2	4.9	5.8	74.0
	1989–90	6.5	8.4	1.3	5.7	5.8	72.2
	1990–91	7.2	7.5	1.7	0.0	6.2	73.1
	1991–92	8.6	7.6	1.3	6.5	6.0	69.9
	1992–93	9.4	9.4	1.2	6.0	5.7	68.2
	1993–94	9.9	9.1	1.2	5.2	5.7	68.9
Québécois	1994–95	9.8	8.1	1.9	4.9	5.5	69.8
	1995–96	10.5	8.4	1.3	5.0	5.6	69.2
	1996–97	9.6	9.3	1.3	5.5	5.4	69.0
	1997–98	10.5	10.3	2.0	6.3	5.0	65.7
	1998–99	10.4	10.6	1.7	7.0	6.1	64.2
	1999–2000	9.7	11.9	2.3	7.6	7.2	61.3
	2000–01	9.2	12.3	2.1	7.5	8.0	60.9
	2001–02	8.9	13.2	1.2	8.5	9.0	59.2
	2002–03	8.6	12.2	0.8	7.9	10.0	60.5
Liberal	2003–04	8.8	11.4	2.4	7.5	11.1	58.8
	2004–05	9.3	12.3	1.3	7.0	10.5	59.6
	2005–06	9.3	12.0	1.3	7.0	10.5	59.9
	2006–07	9.3	12.0	1.3	7.0	10.5	59.9
	2004–05	9.3	12.3	1.3	7.0	10.5	59.6
	2005–06	9.4	12.6	1.5	7.4	10.9	58.2
	2006–07	9.6	11.9	1.9	7.4	10.2	59.0
	2007–08	9.6	11.9	1.9	7.4	10.2	59.0
	2008–09	9.6	11.9	1.9	7.4	10.2	59.0

Source: CANSIM, table 385–0007.

OUTCOMES

In our analysis of policy themes, we limited ourselves to a description of the fiscal structure and the strategies illustrating them and to qualitative indicators. We now present a few quantitative indicators dealing with accessibility, rates of participation in PSE, and the development of useful and relevant research.

Accessibility

According to the National Centre for Public Policy and Higher Education, the ability of students and their families to afford educational costs is linked to the amount of tuition fees charged by the institution and to student assistance received from the government. Before analyzing how fees for a university education have changed over time, it is important to note that all Quebec's students have access to tuition-free college education in the CÉGEPs network. Thus, they benefit from one or two years of tuition-free postsecondary education, depending on whether they are taking a pre-university program or a career program.

It should also be emphasized that tuition fees are the same for full-time graduate and undergraduate students as they are for students of elite professional programs (medicine, dentistry, or law), except for foreign and Canadian students who are not Quebec residents.

The data presented in figure 4.4 reveal that, from 1972–73 (and even before) to 1988–89 tuition fees have been frozen and maintained for a long time at a rather low level ($500) without indexation. These fees were raised three times since then by different Liberal governments: by 270 percent in 1989–90, by 12 percent in 1994–95, and by fifty dollars per session over five years in 2007. Despite these augmentations, they remain the lowest in Canada ($2,415 compared to $5,138, the average undergraduate fee in 2011–12).[41] In other respects, as indicated in the section on funding mechanisms, a new five-year increase of tuition fees ($325 per year beginning in 2012), and indexation afterwards, was planned and was part of the University Funding Plan included in the 2010–11 provincial budget. This plan was repealed after the massive student strike in the spring of 2012 and the election of a Parti Québécois government in September of the same year.

For further evidence of changes in accessibility, we have examined how average undergraduate university tuition fees have changed in relation to after-tax average income for different income groups. Average undergraduate university tuition fees as a proportion of after-tax average income in constant dollars for the lowest and highest income quintiles for the period 1986–87 to 2008–09 are presented in figure 4.5. During the first four years of the Liberal government at the end of the 1980s, the proportion for the lowest quintile was 4 percent compared to 0.6 percent for the highest, but no change in affordability was observed for either group. This trend was broken in 1990–91 and during the Liberals' remaining time in power. The most vulnerable group experienced a sharp deterioration in affordability. Between 1989–90 and 1994–95, the average undergraduate university tuition fees as a proportion of selected after-tax income for this group rose from 3.9 to 14.4 percent. For the wealthiest group, the increase during the same period was modest, from 0.6 to 2.0 percent. The increase for those in the lowest income quintile continued during the first years of the Parti Québécois government, when the proportion rose to a high of 16.7 percent in 1997–98.[42] During the same period, those with the highest incomes experienced a change of only 0.1 percent in affordability. From 1997–98 and for the remainder of the Parti Québécois reign the situation improved slightly for both groups because of the non-indexation of the fees, and, in 2002–03, the proportion of fees to selected after-tax average income had declined to 14.1 and 1.8 percent, respectively. In 2008–09, it had increased again, under the Liberal government, by 2.5 percent for the lowest quintile and only by 0.2 for the highest.

In addition to tuition fees, affordability also depends on how much access students have to a needs-based loans and bursaries program. In 2009–10, 21.3 percent of college and 38.9 percent of university full-time students received financial aid from the Quebec loans and bursaries program. This auxiliary program aims at covering the difference between the admissible expenses and the contribution of the student and possibly her or his near relations. Among the university students, 32.3 percent obtained a loan only (mean amount $3,660), and 66.4 percent obtained a loan and a bursary (total amount $8,358), nearly half of which is in the form of a bursary.

From 1990–91 to 2009–10, the proportion of financial aid granted to university students in the form of a bursary has oscillated between 33.6 and 47.3 percent (Gouvernement du Québec 2011, table 4.3). The mean debt of Quebec baccalaureate, master's, and PhD students at the end of their studies in 2009–10 was, respectively, $12,923, $16,296, and $21,963. For those who were already on a loan at the college level, the mean debt rose, respectively, to $16,419, $23,735, and $33,602. According to the Ministry of Education, students' debts are much lower in Quebec than elsewhere in Canada because (1) the university tuition fees are lower, (2) the loans and bursaries program is more advantageous as a larger proportion of the financial aid is granted in the form of a bursary than is the case in the other provinces, and (3) the existence of CÉGEPs reduces the length

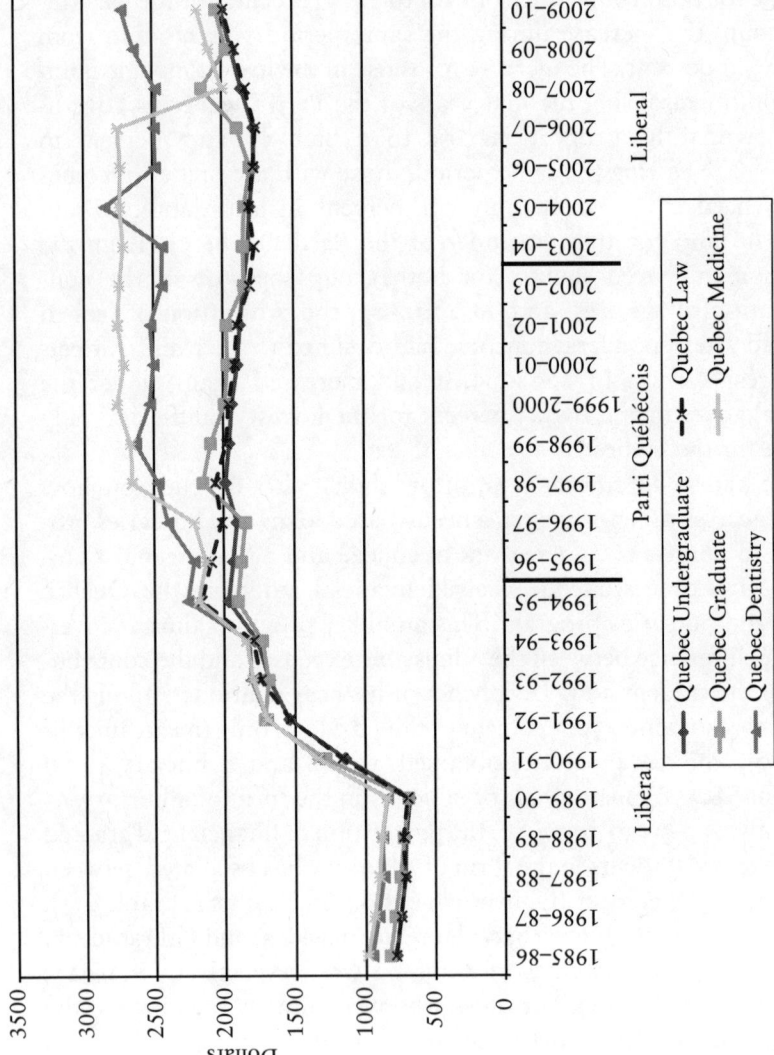

Figure 4.4
Average undergraduate tuition by program in Quebec in constant 2002 dollars, 1985–86 – 2009–10.
Source: Statistics Canada, TLAC, table 08E.

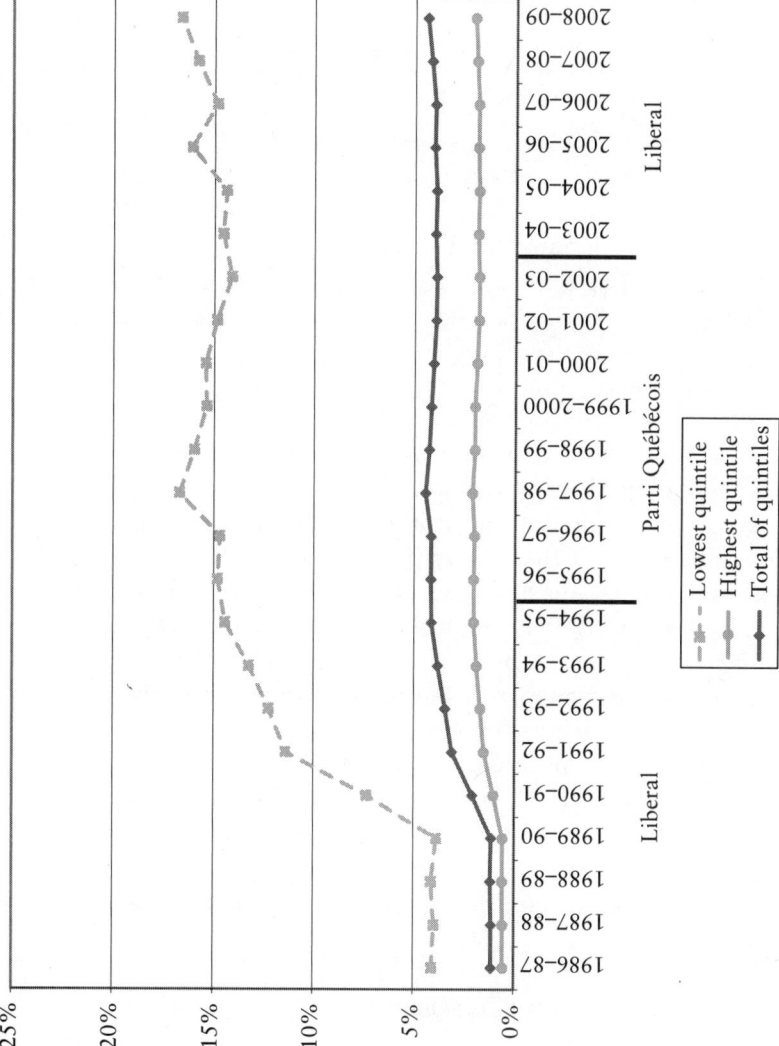

Figure 4.5
Average undergraduate university tuition fees as proportion of selected after-tax income quintiles, Quebec – 1985–86 to 2008–09.

Sources: Statistics Canada, Tuition and Living Accommodation Costs, Survey 3123.

Table 4.3
Proportion of financial aid to Quebec university students in the form of loan and bursary (%)

	1990–91	1995–96	2000–01	2005–06	2006–07	2007–08	2008–09	2009–10p
Prêt	59.4	66.4	59.3	61.2	55.4	55.3	54.6	52.7
Bourses	40.6	33.6	40.7	38.8	44.6	44.7	45.4	47.3

Source: MELS Indicators of education (2011).

Note: p = Provisional data.

of university studies and, as there is no tuition fee at the CÉGEP level. This is likely to diminish student debt.

Participation

In 2009–10, the participation rate in college programs leading to a diploma of college studies in regular education was 60.9 percent, 2.4 percent lower than the one observed in 1996–97, before the drop in the high school graduation rate and the tightening of the criteria for admission to CÉGEP. Enrolment in pre-university programs has decreased since 1990–91 (from 41.7 percent to 35.4 percent) while that in the career programs has decreased since 1996–97 (from 19.9 percent to 15.8 percent) and that in the orientation and integration path has increased from 6.6 percent to 9.7 percent (table 4.4).[43] In 2009–10, the participation rates in bachelor's, master's, and doctoral programs were, respectively, 42.9 percent, 12.3 percent, and 3.1 percent. Between 1990–91 and 1996–97, enrolment in bachelor's programs declined from 37 to 34 percent. Thereafter the rate began to rise, reaching 42.9 percent in 2009–10. With respect to postgraduate programs, enrolment rose steadily from 7.1 to more than 12.3 percent in master's programs and from 1.5 to 3.1 percent in doctoral programs.

"Useful and Relevant" Research Development

This theme may be illustrated by two indicators: (1) intramural R&D expenditures as a percentage of GDP (see figure 4.6), which is a conventional indicator of research efforts and (2) total R&D spending as a percentage by provider (see figure 4.7).

Between 1985 and 1994, the intramural expenditures on R&D as a percentage of GDP increased considerably, from 1.49 to 2.08

Table 4.4
Participation rates[1] in college education[2] and university programs

	1990–91	93–94	96–97	99–2000	03–04	06–07	08–09	09–10
College education	61.2	65.0	63.3	59.7	57.9	61.0	60.6	60.9
Pre-university programs	41.7	39.9	36.8	34.9	34.5	36.3	35.7	35.4
Career programs	19.5	25.1	19.9	19.2	16.2	16.2	15.6	15.8
Orientation and integration path[3]	–	–	6.6	5.6	7.2	8.5	9.3	9.7
Bachelor's programs	37.0	37.9	34.0	35.7	40.6	41.3	42.8	42.9
Master's programs	7.1	8.4	9.0	9.5	11.5	11.1	11.2	12.3
Doctoral programs	1.5	1.8	1.8	1.9	2.8	2.6	2.8	3.1

Sources: CRÉPUQ (2006), Le système universitaire québécois. Données et indicateurs, table 2.1 and DRSI, MELS, Indicateurs de l'éducation, éditions 2000, 2002, 2006b, 2009 and 2011.

Notes:
1. Proportion of a generation to be of an age to attend colleges or universities. University students enrolled in independent studies and programs of certificate are excluded.
2. Full- and part-time students in regular studies.
3. This new path was created in 1995 following the college education reform.

percent. It again increased sharply between 1997 and 2001 from 2.10 to 2.77 percent, despite the austerity measures adopted to curb the deficit in the mid-1990s. This rate was roughly maintained later, despite a slight decline to 2.61 percent in 2008. The rate was then about the same as in the United States (2.66 percent) but was lower than the percentage of the most advanced countries in that area (Sweden, 3.74 percent; Finland, 3.45 percent) (MDEIE 2009). We can identify two periods of rapid increase, the first between 1989 and 1993 under the Liberal government and the second between 1997 and 2001 under the Parti Québécois government, and then a period of stabilization with the Charest Liberal government.

The significant expansion of investment in research in Quebec has mainly been a result of business taking more responsibility (see figure 4.7). As a proportion of the total gross expenditures on R&D, the part provided by business rose almost yearly from a low of 43 percent in 1985 to a high of 57 percent in 2001. Thereafter, the rate dropped off slightly and stood around 54 percent until 2008. The proportion provided by government has not fared that well. In 1985, government's share was 37 percent; however, after a steady fall this had decreased to 17 percent by 1998. During the period from 1998

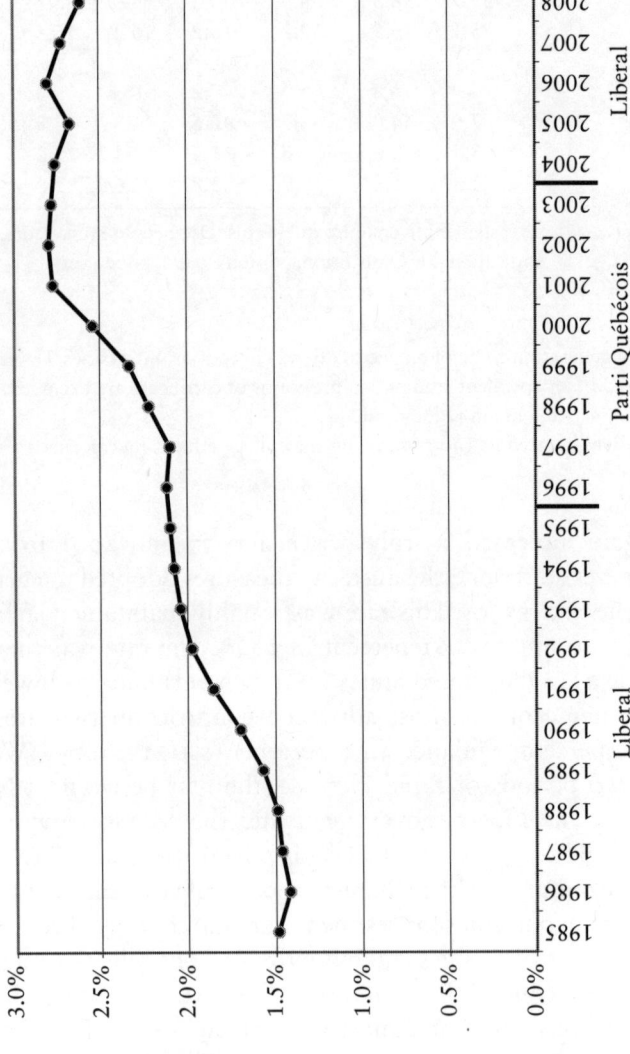

Figure 4.6
Gross expenditures on research and development for Quebec as a proportion of gross domestic product, 1985–2008.
Source: Statistics Canada, table 385-007.

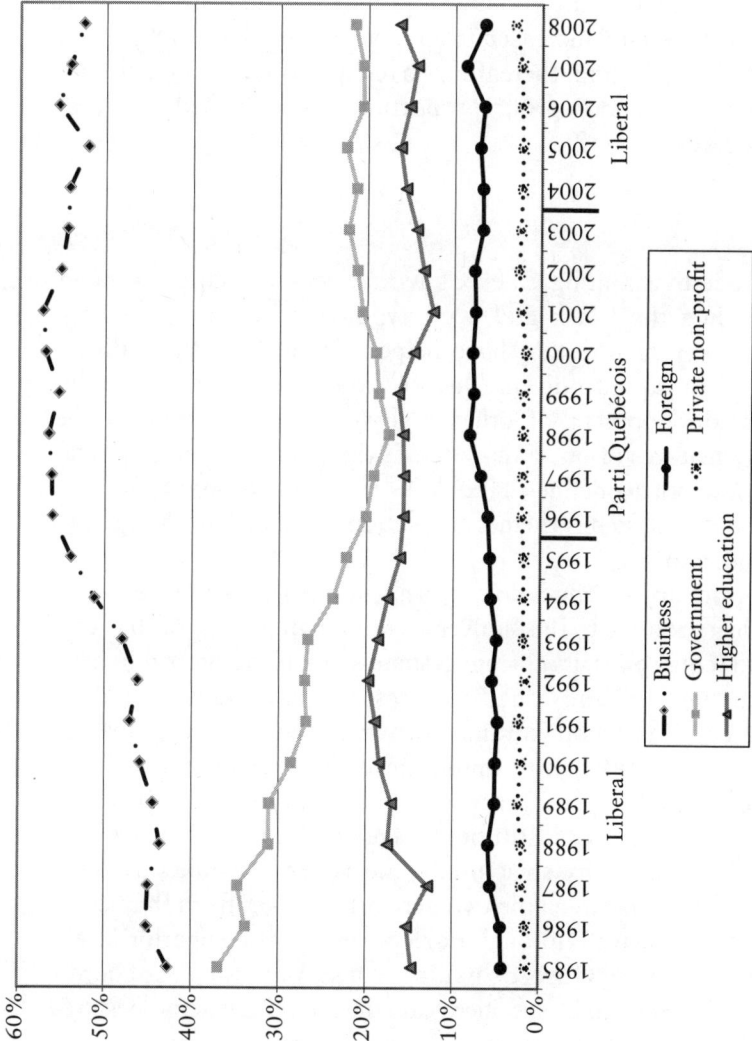

Figure 4.7
Proportion of gross expenditure on research funded by business, government, higher education, foreign and private non-profit funders for Quebec, 1985-2008.
Source: Statistics Canada, table 385-007.

to 2008 the government's share started to increase slightly, and it reached 22 percent in 2003, where it stayed until 2008.

The share of PSE increased from 15 percent in 1985 to 20 percent in 1992 but decreased significantly to 12 percent in 2001. Thereafter the proportion increased slightly and reached 16 percent in 2005 and remained there until 2008. The proportion funded by what is classified as "foreign" increased from 4 percent in 1985 to 8 percent from 1998 to 2002 and, thereafter, stayed at around 7 percent until 2008. The private non-profit proportion has remained stable at around 2 percent.

CONCLUSION

We conclude by situating Quebec's PSE system in relation to other systems, using the Clark and Scott typology (see chapter 1). We retrace the key factors that have helped shape the system, distinguishing those found only in Quebec from those that have influenced the development of other PSE systems. Since one of the distinctive features of our PSE system is the state's role in its regulation, we attempt to define that role as it relates to policy. We also review the PSE system's themes in relation to qualitative and quantitative indicators.

While prior to the education reforms in the 1960s Quebec's PSE system corresponded to the "university-dominated" type of the Scott typology (Scott 1995), its current system is, in our opinion, a hybrid, with both "unified" and "dual" features. The PSE system is unified in that it comprises both traditional universities and other institutions (mainly CÉGEPs) with important differences of status and is largely regulated by MELS (particularly the college sector). It is dual in that the two types of institutions have different missions (college comes before university structurally and is not a parallel avenue), and coordination between the two networks derives from their complementary character (although universities are at a superior level). This way of situating Quebec's PSE system may appear to be contradictory, but it attests to its specificity and the limited capacity of Scott's typology to reflect the diversity of contemporary PSE systems.

To the extent that Quebec's PSE system shares a number of the "dual" system's features, one might wonder if it does not show, as in other PSE systems, academic drift – namely, on the part of CÉGEPs, a propensity to claim the right to extend the scope of their mission by demanding greater autonomy and the privilege of offering university-level programs. The debate on the future of college education during the 1990s demonstrated that the Fédération des CÉGEPS had been making demands of this nature for a long time. Since then, these claims have been reiterated. But MELS has not responded favourably. In this case, while the propensity for academic drift existed, its promoters were unable to achieve their objectives.

Although Scott's typology enables us to classify systems in terms of their design and, in particular, the "division of academic labour" between different types of institutions, it does not cover other important aspects of PSE, in particular the relationship between the institutions and the state. It is important to take this into account because the state plays a decisive role in shaping the Quebec PSE system. Before we come back to this, though, we are going to piece together the various factors that helped shape Quebec's PSE system.

According to our analysis, the priorities of PSE systems, system design, and the rules of the game that govern them are shaped by a set of factors related to the demographic, economic, cultural, and political environment as well as by constitutional provisions and dominant political orientations. Four factors helped shape the system in the 1960s. First were the demographics associated with the wave of baby boomers that hit postsecondary institutions and brought with it the need to restructure the system. Second was the need to make sure the system could meet the high-skill personnel needs of an industrial economy. Third was the need to address the aspirations of the population, which was demanding greater accessibility to PSE. These demands were based on a concept of education as a means of promoting equal opportunity. An extremely elitist system seemed to be completely out of step with this idea and was ill-equipped to cope with the high number of young people who wanted to pursue postsecondary studies. Fourth was the political will to maintain the autonomy and cultural mission of the universities while entrusting them with a more explicit economic mission and giving them more sustained support from the government, which called on them to play a greater role than in the past.

Although these factors were not specific to Quebec and inspired PSE policy in other Canadian provinces and other countries, certain aspects do appear to be specific to Quebec. The state played an important role in education within the context of the Quiet

Revolution and its underlying ideology. The state directly intervened in the economy and social organization to ensure society's modernization and in the interests of promoting better socio-cultural conditions for francophones. The development of PSE was at the heart of the education reform of the 1960s and was seen as the centrepiece of the modernization of Quebec society. In the context of the knowledge society, the theme based on the assumption that PSE is a great asset was reaffirmed by the report of the Estates General on Education in the mid-1990s, and it was at the top of the government's key orientations when it published its PSE policy in 2000.

The Quebec government was far more inclined than the governments of the other provinces to resist federal government intervention in the field of education, which comes under provincial jurisdiction, while at the same time making accommodations. With regard to access, it implemented a student loans and bursaries program that was far more advantageous than were those of the other provinces. Further, it set up a system in which the English-speaking minority had its own universities and colleges without having to demand them (as French-speaking minorities had to do in some of the other provinces); and the government created provincial research funding agencies and programs to make up for lost time and to ensure that its researchers were in a competitive position to receive funding from federal agencies.

Another factor that affected Quebec's PSE policy concerns the role civil society played in policy development. Quebec's many consulting and collaborative agencies and organizations confirm the importance of this role. If this appears to be inherent to the management of PSE and can be found in most systems, then it has evolved particularly in Quebec and is characteristic of what has been referred to as the Quebec model of public management.

When we look at the situation over the past forty years, it is clear that many of the factors that helped shape the PSE system have continued to have an influence, although the point of reference has changed, at least in part. These factors do not only apply to Quebec.

The economy continued to put pressure on the system. Adjusting to the requirements of an industrial society was no longer in question; rather, the new demands of a knowledge-based global society took over. PSE was perceived as a way of increasing the competitive position of business. Two themes were reasserted more insistently: (1) strengthening the links between programs and the job market and (2) developing university research that was useful and relevant in terms of innovation. Reduced resources as a result of economic recessions, pressure on public finances, and the rise of neoliberalism all contributed to a more forceful reiteration of one theme in particular – the accountability of PSE institutions. Yet postsecondary aspirations and accessibility continue to be as important as they ever were, and the number of students has not gone down. However, accessibility objectives have been reworded in terms of access to educational success.

A number of new factors marked the development of the PSE system. These are not limited to Quebec but many of their features set them apart from those in other Canadian provinces. Quebec's tuition-free college has been maintained. Its student loans and bursaries program remains the most advantageous in Canada. Its PSE system is not as geared towards marketization as are those in the other provinces. There has been a trend towards the vocationalizing of programs, the instrumentalization of research, and the marketing of research findings. Universities compete for students, professors, and research grants. However, Quebec has no private universities and there is no explicit political will to create any. The Quebec PSE system is not as immersed in marketization as are those in Ontario and British Columbia.

The Quebec PSE system has not been influenced as much by the left-leaning or right-leaning inclinations of political parties as have the systems in other provinces. The Parti Québécois appears to be more social-democratic and to favour a style of governance that is more open to involving civil society in decision making than is the case with the Liberal Party. However, these differences have had very little impact on PSE policy. Since the 1960s, the system's configuration has mostly been characterized by continuity and consistency. We propose four factors that may help to explain this: (1) the divisions between political parties are not just the result of right/left tendencies but also of attitudes towards federalism/sovereignty; (2) to a certain extent, all parties share aspects of the nationalist ideology that spurred the school reform in the 1960s and that continues to colour political debate; (3) the consultation-based approach to public management has helped define a minimal ideological "corridor" within which the PSE system's agents tend to place themselves when they think of education policy; and (4) policy is developed incrementally. In our view, these factors help to explain why the popularity of neoliberal and marketization trends have not been as pronounced in Quebec as they have been in other provinces.

The propensity of college-level institutions to demand greater autonomy (i.e., academic drift) is far less pronounced in Quebec than in other provinces due to the design of the province's PSE system. In Quebec, academic drift exists more as a claim than as a reality. With regard to research, Quebec has had a slight inclination to develop an approach that differs somewhat from that of other provinces and countries. It refers to the concept of recognizing and promoting the value (i.e., "valorizing") of research findings and not just marketing them. In other words, the objective is not only to take initiatives geared towards technological innovation but also to include humanities-based social innovation. However, at the end of the 2000s, the Liberal government has put less emphasis on this approach.

Against this backdrop, we now attempt to define the Quebec government's role with respect to PSE, based on the Richardson et al. (1999) typology, which distinguishes four different types of roles: (1) the providing resources role, (2) the regulating role, (3) the consumer advocacy role, and (4) the steering role. These roles are not exclusive; while one might predominate in one province, another might predominate in another, depending on the PSE system design in place.

In Quebec, government plays a preponderant role in the management of the PSE system when compared to the role it plays in other systems. According to many of the interviewees, this is due to the "power of money" – the fact that the government assumes the lion's share of the funding in an environment of resource shortages. MELS plays a steering role not only through general policy statements such as the Quebec policy on universities (Ministère de l'éducation 2000) but also through funding mechanisms. The yearly budget rules for operating grants, as well as the targets it has determined and the indicators of performance it has defined in the recent University Funding Plan (included in the 2011 budget [appendix 6]), illustrate this kind of mechanism.[44]

However, the interviews we conducted enabled us to circumscribe the government's role in PSE management more clearly. First, although the government's management role is decisive, the decision-making process is dispersed and fragmented. Decision making is exercised at the provincial and federal levels of government (particularly with regard to research) and by different ministries within each level (i.e., MELS and MDEIE at the provincial level and the departments of industry and health at the federal level). Several other collaborative and reporting bodies participate in decision making. This is certainly the case with research funding agencies, which are relatively autonomous. Second, the decision-making process is fairly open thanks to consultation practices. Even though power is concentrated in the hands of the provincial government, consultation leads to power-sharing. Countless joint MELS-CRÉPUQ committees and the Fédération des CÉGEPS act as self-regulating bodies, despite the competition between institutions. Multiple provincial networks analogous with those described by Jones (1997a) all seem to have a hand in influencing policy making.

The government's steering role with regard to PSE policy appears to be more decisive in Quebec than it is in British Columbia or Ontario. In several sectors, through the province's ministries and corporations, this role has not changed since the Quiet Revolution – to the point where the government's practices have been identified as constituting what is referred to as the Quebec model. Yet, over the past fifteen years, the reasons given for government intervention have changed. Two predominate: (1) a desire to improve Quebec's competitive position within Canada and the global economy (including the global knowledge economy) and (2) the need for postsecondary institutions to be accountable (which contributes to reinforcing state controls or, at the very least, accountability and reporting mechanisms).

However, there are two paradoxes in connection with the state's role in PSE. First, the state's governance of PSE has not alleviated the competition between institutions and, to a certain degree, has even increased it: the rules of the game are such that, as far as system behaviour is concerned, the institutions compete to increase or maintain the number of students they have, to recruit the best professors, to obtain research funding, and to attract sponsorships from the private sector. The second paradox is that the government is more controlling than ever in how it regulates universities, while, at the same time, MELS is in the process of decentralizing elementary, secondary, and (to a certain extent) college education and is delegating more power to local institutions.

It is not easy to draw conclusions about outcomes. The objectives derived from pursuing Quebec's four PSE policy themes are complex. In some cases, they involve processes that are necessarily spread out over time or that cannot be measured in absolutes. How these objectives are met can also vary, depending on one's conception of them and the economic climate within which the PSE system evolves. The data at our disposal are not as complete as we would have liked. Moreover, how well objectives are met cannot be measured solely on the basis of quantitative data and statistical indicators. Indicators will never be anything more than tools for monitoring the system. For this reason, we can only partially answer the question.

The objectives stemming from some themes are easier to assess than others. With respect to the theme of strengthening links between training programs and labour market demands, the objective is in the process of being met. Many initiatives have been undertaken to this end, and the process is ongoing. Certainly, the objective itself is challenged by students and teachers' groups. And, even though its implementation can vary from one program area to the next, a corner has been turned. Policies and mechanisms for developing and evaluating programs attest to this.

We reached the same conclusion in the case of the theme of developing useful and relevant research. The orientations and decisions of the federal and provincial governments, as well as those of the subsidizing agencies, have clearly influenced research development in this direction, so much so, in fact, that now some groups are clamouring for more emphasis on basic and "free" research.

We had more difficulty determining how the objectives stemming from the accountability and efficiency theme had been met. In the case of accountability, the many reporting mechanisms set up allow us to conclude here, too, that the objectives are in the process of being met. It would appear to be harder to say the same for the efficiency theme. It is all a matter of degree.

For accessibility, we note that its definition has evolved over the past forty years and that the objective is no longer limited to improving access to institutions: it has been extended to include access to a diploma or a degree. This change in definition alters how the achievement of this objective is gauged. Without doubt, over a forty-year period, the system succeeded in promoting accessibility to institutions and in seeing that Quebec made up much of its lost ground in relation to other Canadian provinces. However, the participation rate of those attending universities is still lower than it is in Ontario, though the rate of those attending college is higher. Regarding affordability, the political will to make PSE affordable has been asserted and sustained. Quebec leads the other Canadian provinces in this respect. We wonder, though, about its scope and its effect on university competitiveness should the Quebec government fail to adequately compensate the amounts it would receive from tuition fees if they were as high in Quebec as they are in other provinces. Concerning access to full-time university studies, Quebec's participation rate is in the average range for Canada but is lower than those in British Columbia and Ontario. This seemingly counterintuitive outcome illustrates the complexity of trying to understand the interrelationship between all the factors that influence participation rates.

Inequality of access with respect to social background, gender, language, ethnic group, and region remain problems and should be documented. At the macro level, after the report of the Estates General on Education in 1997, Quebec set specific objectives for 2010: 85 percent of a generation of students should receive a secondary school or vocational studies diploma, 60 percent should receive a college diploma, and 30 percent should receive a bachelor's degree. On the basis of the completion rates at that time, the secondary school and college studies targets were ambitious. In 2009–10, the secondary school diploma completion rate was 74 percent among people younger than twenty, and the diploma completion rate for college studies rate was 39 percent. However, the bachelor completion rate (32 percent) exceeded the target (Gouvernement du Québec 2011b). In 2009, MELS reconsidered the target for the secondary school diploma rate and reduced it to 80 percent by 2020. Moreover, the expected rate could vary (67 to 88 percent) from one school board to another in order to take into account their percentage at the time the new targets were determined. Meanwhile, fiscal initiatives and strategies have been put in place to encourage institutions to improve supervision and to help them provide for their students.

It would be difficult, in connection with equality of access, to dodge the question that was at the heart of the debate on the Quebec PSE model at the forum on the future of college education. The question was: How well does the college education structure help Quebec make up for lost time in terms of PSE accessibility? The interviewees were clear that the current structure had helped Quebec catch up with regard to university attendance, even if it still has not reached the degree completion rates observed in Ontario and British

Columbia. However, it would be unrealistic to attribute all of these outcomes solely to the college education model. Many other factors have to be taken into account, in particular the creation of the Université du Québec and the student loans and bursaries program. Also to be considered (beyond the factors dealing with system design) are the internal dynamics of the institutions, what kind of student supervision and help they offer, and whether or not the students are getting any support from friends and family. Nevertheless, one must not lose sight of something that, fortunately, this debate has brought into relief. The college education system is nowhere near as inefficient as its detractors make it out to be. On the one hand, for students pursuing PSE at the college level, the diploma completion rate is higher in Quebec than anywhere else in Canada, despite the fact that the secondary school dropout rate is also higher in Quebec. On the other hand, one could wonder what the participation and completion rates at the college level would be if, fifty years after the education reform of the 1960s, tuition fee rates had been higher and if Quebec had adopted the predominant model of PSE in North America instead of the CEGEP model.

5

Trends across the Three Provinces: Similarities and Differences

DONALD FISHER AND KJELL RUBENSON

As noted in the introduction, our work is situated within the tradition of policy sociology, which is concerned with theorizing the nature of policy and its production and with illuminating the policy discourse (Gale 1999, 2001; Taylor et al. 1997; Rizvi and Lingard 2010). Our approach necessarily draws attention to the importance of power, control, and conflict in the policy-making process. We emphasize political economy and take into account the structural context and the social forces impinging on the system.

Again, as noted in the introduction, we decided to use a set of policy priorities as sensitizing concepts in order to document the changing policy environment and the "rules of the game." We used these concepts as a supplement to the AIHEPS model (see chapter 1, figure 1.1) and grouped the priorities under three overlapping headings: political, economic, and academic. This analytic grid was used to produce the three provincial case studies, which, in turn, provided the basis for the comparison that follows.

The rest of this chapter is divided into six sections. First is a section that compares funding patterns. This is followed by five sections that are devoted to the themes that dominated the PSE policy-making process. The five themes, in their order of presentation, are: (1) accessibility, (2) accountability, (3) marketization, (4) labour force development, and (5) research and development. In discussing these themes, we illustrate their impact on and within the three PSE systems in British Columbia, Ontario, and Quebec, respectively.

POLITICAL ECONOMY AND FUNDING

The financial relationships between the provinces and the federal government are complex and controversial. During the last thirty years the main story has been the change in emphasis on the part of the federal government. On the one hand, federal governments have drastically reduced the transfers for PSE to the provinces, while, on the other hand, the support for R&D has increased dramatically, particularly in the health, applied, and natural sciences. The federal government has used its spending power to reduce indirect transfers to PSE and to increase direct funding to universities for research, research chairs, research infrastructure, and the "indirect costs" of research.

The sharp decline over the last two decades in federal transfers to PSE has severely affected the provincial resources for PSE. Between 1988–89 and 2010–11, the total transfer (both cash and tax points) for PSE in 1988 dollars decreased from $5.084 billion to $3.5711 billion, or by 29.8 percent (Fisher et al. 2006, chart 6 and appendix 1).[1] When we compare changes in the total provincial operating grants for PSE over the period of our study (using 1986–87 as a reference year) we find that all three provinces record a decline in the mid-1990s (figures 2.1, 3.1, and 4.1), which we infer is in part a reaction to the sharp cuts in the total federal transfer that began in 1995–96. The decline in Ontario and Quebec is pronounced, while the one in British Columbia is very slight. Yet, beyond this similarity, the patterns of decline and expansion are quite different between the provinces. From around 2005 in all three provinces we can observe an increase in funding, a trend that was encouraged in 2008 when the federal government added $800 million to the CSHT and designated the increase for PSE.

In Ontario (figure 3.1), the PSE operating grant had already begun to decline in the early 1990s as the NDP government responded to the recession. The precipitous decline in the grant between 1995 and 1997, which took it well below the 1986–87 level, was the result of the combined impact on federal policy and the explicit neoliberal policies adopted under the Harris "Common Sense Revolution." The grant started to increase in the last year of the Harris period as the fiscal situation improved, but then, with the election of the Liberals in 2003, we see major increases in the total operating grant. By 2009–10, the grant had recorded an increase of over 40 percent. In contrast, during the 1990s, both British Columbia and Quebec maintained the total PSE operating grant at a relatively high level. While the total PSE operating grant in Quebec (figure 4.1) did decline substantially in the mid-1990s, it only dropped slightly below the 1986–87 level. The declining trend was broken in 1998–99, and the grants rose rapidly through to 2003 when the Liberals took over from the Parti Québecois. The grant declined slightly in 2005–06 but then recorded a sharp increase of over 20 percent by 2009–10. The record in British Columbia is very different (figure 2.1), in part because that province did not suffer an economic recession. At no time does the total PSE operating grant drop below the 1986–87 level. Even with the small decline in the mid-1990s, the grant level is continuously more than 30 percent above the reference level. The grant rises rapidly in the latter years of the NDP administration, and only with the election of the Liberal government in 2001 do the increases stop. At first the grant levels out and then, through the first Campbell administration, it declines. Since 2005–06, the grant has risen rapidly, recording an increase of almost 40 percent by 2009–10.

The differences in provincial expenditure on PSE become particularly apparent when we plot the changes through time using 1988–89 as the starting point (figure 5.1). We can observe the dip in spending in the mid-1990s, but this is most pronounced for Ontario and least apparent in British Columbia. Here we can see the contrast between the commitment of the BC NDP government to maintain the level of spending and the lack of commitment on the part of the Ontario Progressive Conservatives to do the same. These commitments are carried through the period. British Columbia is consistently above the starting point, recording the highest gain in the amount spent on PSE. Quebec maintains a relatively stable level of spending, while Ontario has for most of this period been below the starting level. In 2005–06, the grant rose above this level and it has continued to rise.

When we compare provincial operating grants by sector, again using 1986–87 as the reference point, we find that in British Columbia and Ontario the sectors (university, college and institute/college, university college) were treated relatively equally (figures 2.1, 2.2, and 3.1). In Quebec, the two sectors (university and college) were treated somewhat differently (figure 4.1). During the 1990s, while the two sectors followed similar trends the university operating grant was allowed to drop below the 1986–87 level. Since

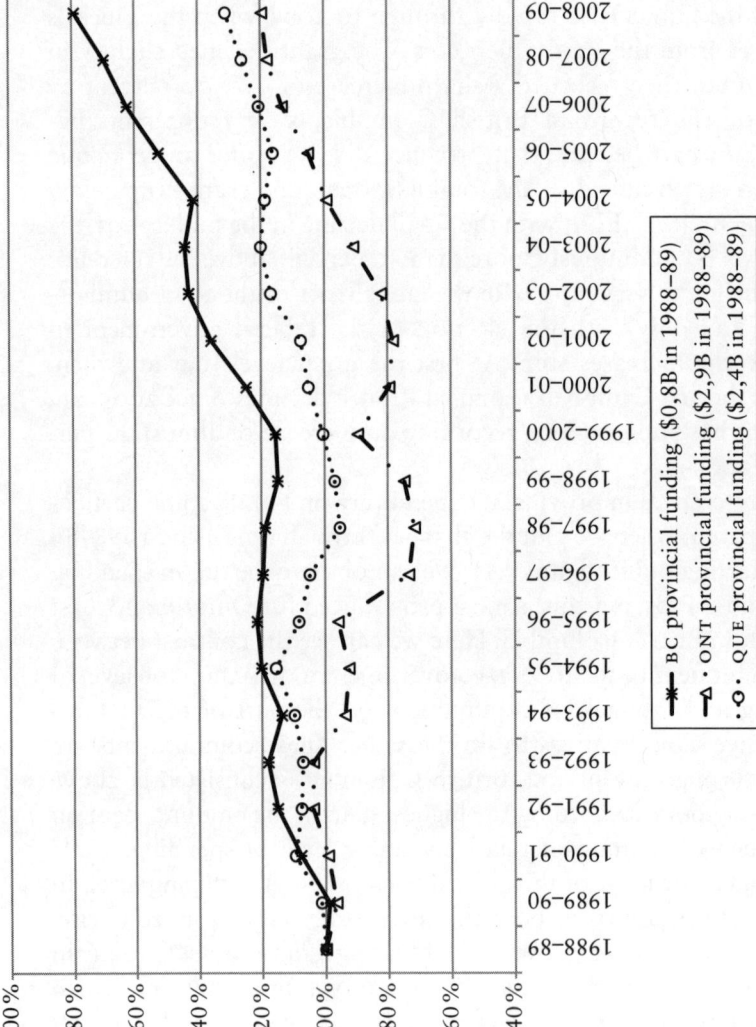

Figure 5.1
Change in provincial grants for postsecondary education in British Columbia, Ontario, and Quebec, 1988–89 – 2008–09 in constant 2002 dollars, 1988–89 = 100.

Source: Statistics Canada, table 385-007.

2002–03, when the Parti Québecois presented its last budget and the subsequent election of a Liberal government, the university sector has been privileged at the expense of the college sector.

Using Statistics Canada and Canadian Association of University Business Officers (CAUBO) as sources, CAUT (2005, 42, fig. 6.4; CAUT 2010–11 4, fig. 1.4) shows that total government spending as a share of university operating revenue between 1993 and 2008 declined in all provinces. The decrease was pronounced in Ontario, where the share went from 73 to 49 percent. The decrease was less but still substantial in both British Columbia and Quebec, where the share went from 72 to 58 percent and 81 to 70 percent, respectively. Over the same time period, tuition as a share of university operating revenue increased for all provinces (CAUT 2005, 42, fig. 6.3; CAUT 2010–11, 4, fig. 1.3). Ontario and British Columbia had by far the largest increases, from 21 to 42 percent and from 17 to 40 percent, respectively. Quebec registered by far the smallest increase, from 13 to 21 percent.

When we examine provincial transfers to colleges and universities per FTE student enrolments between 1993–94 and 2008–09 (2008 dollars), we can see some broad trends that cut across the provinces and also mirror changes at the national level. Four findings stand out in table 5.1. First, between 1993–94 and 1998–99, British Columbia registers a substantial decrease of -12.14 percent in provincial funding per FTE student enrolments, while both Quebec and Ontario remain relatively stable. Over the same time period, the national average increased by 10.66 percent. Second, between 1998–99 and 2003–04, the three provinces and Canada record decreases. Both British Columbia and Ontario record major decreases of -19.97 and -18.70 percent, which are not far behind the national average of -24.19 percent. Quebec is the exception, registering only a minor decrease (-3.61 percent). These decreases are probably a result, at least in part, of the dramatic reduction in the federal tax-point transfer that occurred in 2001–02. Third, between 2003–04 and 2008–09, the three provinces and Canada record increases. Ontario and British Columbia approach the national average of 25.16 percent, with increases of 23.93 and 18.31 percent, respectively. Quebec records a noticeable increase of 8.92 percent. Finally, when we compare the provincial funding per FTE student enrolments across the whole period from 1993–94 to 2008–09, we find that both Quebec and Ontario have remained stable, which is slightly behind the national

Table 5.1
Provincial government transfers to colleges and universities per FTE student enrolments, 1993–94 to 2008–09 ($2008)

	1993–94	1998–99	Percent change	2003–04	Percent change	2008–09	Percent change
British Columbia	$16,665	$14,642	-12.14	$11,718	-19.97	$13,863	18.31
Quebec	$12,534	$12,150	-3.06	$11,711	-3.61	$12,756	8.92
Ontario	$10,123	$10,154	0.31	$8,246	-18.79	$10,222	23.96
Canada	$12,839	$14,208	10.66	$10,771	-24.19	$13,481	25.16

Source: CAUT *Almanac of Post-Secondary Education*, 2010–11, figure 1.4, p. 2.

positive trend. Only British Columbia records a decline, from $16,665 to $13,863 (-12.49 percent).

As a means of measuring the relative priority of the sector we examined the share of public expenditure allocated to PSE. As table 5.2 illustrates,[2] between 1988–89 and 2008–09, the proportion allocated to PSE remained quite stable and low, particularly in comparison to health, where the proportion has risen substantially in all three provinces over the thirty-year period. Similarly, the proportion of expenditure going to education (K-12) rose somewhat in British Columbia and slightly in Ontario. On the other hand, the proportion going to "Education, Leisure and Sports" in Quebec decreased somewhat. The relative lack of commitment to PSE and the broad trends in policy priorities as expressed by the relative allocation of expenditures do not seem to have been significantly affected by the party in power but are likely a function of broader political economic trends and the priority given to health.

As noted earlier in this book, when faced with insufficient government funding to meet major enrolment increases postsecondary institutions have increasingly adopted a market approach and focused on increasing revenue from sources other than government. As table 5.3 illustrates,[3] the proportion of funding coming from government sources between 1988–89 and 2008–09 has decreased in all three provinces. The largest decrease occurred in Ontario (21 percent) followed by British Columbia (16 percent), so that by the latter year government sources accounted for 46 and 55 percent, respectively. While the decrease in Quebec (11 percent) was lower than that in British Columbia, government sources in 2008–09 still accounted for a very respectable 69 percent. Concomitantly, the

Table 5.2
Expenditure: Budget plan 1988–89 to 2008–09 in percentage of total government expenditure in BC, Ontario, and Quebec

	1988–89	1998–99	2008–09
BRITISH COLUMBIA			
PSE	7.3	8.1	7.2
Health	33.1	35.3	43.8
Education	16.7	20.8	18.1
ONTARIO			
PSE	6.5	5.9	6.5
Health	32.8	34.2	42.1
Education	12	13.1	13.7
QUEBEC*,**			
PSE	8.6	7.9	7.7
Health	34.4	39.4	43.4
Education, leisure and sports	23.0	18.1	17.0

* *Note*: Education includes the item "Teachers' Pension Plan (TPP)"; "Health" includes "health promotion and sport" and its related expenses under "other expenses." From 2009–10 onwards, postsecondary education includes time-limited investments for colleges under "other expenses."

** Data in the column 2008–09 are from 2006–07. Data on PSE, education, leisure and sports does not match budget data beyond that year.

proportion that PSE institutions were raising in Ontario, British Columbia, and Quebec had risen by 2008–09 to 54, 45, and 31 percent, respectively.

When we break down the two funding source categories (government and "own source") into their component parts we can see more clearly how the funding burden has been shifted from the state to individual students (see tables 2.2, 3.3, and 4.2). Between 1988–89 and 2008–09, provincial transfers to PSE (combining all sectors and as a percent of total funding) have steadily decreased in all three provinces. These decreases account for the great majority of the decreases in government transfers. All "own sources" of revenue for PSE increased during the same time period. Tuition fees as a percent of total funding have increased the most. In British Columbia, Ontario, and Quebec, the increases went from 13, 12.2, and 6.2 percent in 1988–89 to 23.3, 25.9, and 9.6 percent, respectively, in 2008–09. The increases were a direct response to provincial

Table 5.3
Proportion of revenue from own-source revenue and government funding as a percentage, selected years, 1988–89, 2003–04, and 2008–09 in British Columbia, Ontario, and Quebec

	1988–89	2003–04	2008–09
BRITISH COLUMBIA			
Government	71	53	55
Own source	29	47	45
ONTARIO			
Government	67	56	46
Own Source	33	44	54
QUEBEC			
Government	80	70	69
Own Source	20	30	31

Source: Stats Canada, CANSIM, table 385–0007.

government under-funding and, to some extent, were a reflection of the ideological perspective of the parties in power.

Accessibility

By far the most important priority in the development of PSE policy since the mid-1980s is the desire to create more access to the system. While the emphasis has varied between different governing parties, successive governments in all three provinces have developed a clear consensus on this issue. Accessibility as a policy theme in British Columbia and, to some extent, in Ontario overlaps with the trend towards "academic drift" in the system, a trend that has been propelled by both professionals within these systems and governments. Another major policy priority that is often inseparable from the accessibility theme is access to vocational education and training and, in a more general sense, life-long learning. While some of these vocational policy initiatives are discussed under the heading of accessibility, the major focus on "skills" is covered as a separate priority under "labour force development."

SYSTEM STRUCTURE

System structure has been a central policy instrument affecting access. Quebec, more than any other province in Canada, has made accessibility for all its citizens a top priority. In Quebec, where the strong commitment to accessibility harks back to the 1960s, access is tied to a reconfiguration of the PSE system and, to some extent, to the concern with nation building. Initially, the emphasis was placed on access to institutions.

The implementation of a unified two-level system, development of the CÉGEP network in the regions, and foundation of the Université du Québec were aimed, among other things, at promoting geographical accessibility to PSE and reducing inequalities connected with gender and language of instruction. The loans and bursaries program was aimed at reducing inequalities stemming from socioeconomic status. The creation of the Télé-université distance education university as well as the continuing education initiatives of the CÉGEPS and other universities were designed to favour access to PSE for adults. In 1993, then again in 2005, the government reiterated its commitment to have a two-level system in order to encourage access.

While on the face of things both British Columbia and Ontario have developed binary PSE systems, there are major differences between them. The key and most important difference is the connection between the two sectors. In British Columbia the colleges were, from the outset, designed to prepare a large proportion of their students for transfer into university degree programs. The British Columbia Council on Admissions and Transfer (BCCAT) was created to organize and facilitate these transfers and has been a major success story. In contrast to British Columbia, Ontario colleges were created as a completely separate sector with clearly defined non-degree functions. Only universities could award degrees. As transfer was not a goal, it follows that no intermediary body exists and that there are no mechanisms to facilitate this process. A consistent theme in the history of PSE in Ontario has been to undermine the boundary separating the two sectors.

While the creation of the college sectors in both provinces was regional and clearly designed to reduce regional disparities, there are again differences, which, as alluded to earlier, are part of the trend towards academic drift. In British Columbia, a consistent aim has been to increase access for both full- and part-time students to degree-granting programs outside the Lower Mainland and Victoria. Through a series of major reports and legislation this priority was further translated into action by the Socred government. Actions, for example, like the creation of the first university outside the Lower Mainland and the establishment of university colleges had a clear impact on the structure of the PSE system. During this whole period, there was a strong focus on generating access to degree programs outside the Lower Mainland and in densely populated areas, which, up to that point, had not been adequately served by universities. Most recently, degree-granting status has been granted to virtually all PSE institutions in a hierarchy of undergraduate and graduate applied and "pure" degrees. In 2011, the PSE public system contained eleven universities (divided principally by function: research or teaching), eleven colleges, and three institutes. The private sector contained four universities, two colleges offering baccalaureate programs, a number of foreign universities offering degree programs, and 350 institutions offering non-degree programs.

In contrast, despite numerous provincial and national reports recommending integration between the sectors, successive Ontarian governments have refused to make structural changes to the system. Accessibility was improved during this era by overall expansion of the number of postsecondary institutions and the introduction of postsecondary bilingual programs in CAATs, where French was the primary language of instruction, in order to meet the needs of Franco-Ontarians. In 2000, the PC government, as part of a package designed to increase choice, passed legislation to allow the CAATs to offer applied degrees as long as the applied degree program did not duplicate an existing program offered by a university and that it met strict conditions and standards developed by the Postsecondary Education Quality Assessment Board (PEQAB). As a result, a number of colleges and out-of-province institutions have received approval to offer degree programs. By 2007, three CAATs had changed their title to Institute of Technology and Advanced Learning. In addition, the government created UOIT, which is currently offering a range of degree programs that include graduate degrees and a PhD. In parallel to the Télé-université in Quebec, British Columbia and Ontario created similar institutional structures to promote distance learning and to serve the non-traditional learner.

The differences we can observe between the three provinces are to some extent a result of both political ideology and the economy. The foregoing chapters certainly demonstrate differential concern with affordability, with Aboriginal and other underrepresented groups, and with successful entry into the system and successful outcomes.

As noted earlier, Quebec has made accessibility for all its citizens a top priority. British Columbia, since the late 1980s, has made a concerted effort to increase its recruitment to PSE, while Ontario, on the face of it, seems to have reduced its responsibility for PSE. All three systems have expanded since 2005, at some points quite rapidly. In the next section we analyze how policies have affected recruitment to PSE.

A mainstay of Quebec policy over this whole period up to the election of the Liberal government in 2003 has been to make PSE financially accessible. This is housed in the concern with nation building (Berland and Lecours 2006) but also in the attachment of the Parti Québecios to democratic socialist principles. Many of the government's fiscal strategies were aimed at promoting access: tuition-free college education, allocation of a specific amount for the implementation of the school success plans to be integrated with the CÉGEPs' strategic plans, university funding based on the number of students enrolled, regulation of university tuition fees, loan and bursary programs, and university funding partly based on the number of degrees awarded. In addition, Quebec has created a system of fellowships for postgraduate students parallel to the federal programs. Others were of a more specific nature: tax deductions for students or their parents, special funding for the Télé-Université and universities in outlying areas, and support programs for members of Aboriginal communities and for integration of the disabled.

While not as extensive or pronounced, we can observe a similar trend in British Columbia during the 1990s. When the NDP government took office in 1991, it made the Social Credit government's "Access for All" policy the foundation of its integrated reforms in PSE. The NDP governments gave more attention to underrepresentation in PSE of minority groups, especially Aboriginal youth. To address the concerns of the latter, special Aboriginal institutions were created. Furthermore, the NDP focused on new forms of vocationally oriented PSE offerings and also responded to the unions' demand for expanding apprentice training. Significantly, despite the pressure to deregulate student fees, the NDP maintained its commitment to low fees by freezing them over the last five years of its mandate (1996–2001).

The election in Ontario of the PC government in 1995 saw the beginning of a very different approach to accessibility. The Common Sense Revolution translated into the deregulation of tuition fees and, thereby, the creation of a quasi-market in the public sector (Marginson 1997). Later, on the grounds that these measures would increase access and choice, the government opened up degree-granting status to the private sector by allowing for the establishment of not-for-profit universities. The Liberal government in British Columbia (2001) took up similar themes. Having introduced a three-year spending freeze on education and health but still expecting the PSE system to increase enrolment by eighty-five hundred seats over the period 2002–05, the Liberal government allowed institutions to fill the funding gap with increased fees.

The winds of political change had an impact on student fee policy in all three provinces. The election of Liberal governments in both Ontario and Quebec in 2003 brought a reversal of fortunes. In Ontario, the Liberals moved to re-regulate fees, while in Quebec the administration embarked on policies designed to decrease the amount of financial assistance and to deregulate fees. In British Columbia, a vastly improved fiscal environment and political considerations, in conjunction with the upcoming election, resulted in a fundamental reversal of the Liberal's tuition fee policy. The 2005 Throne Speech re-regulated fees and stipulated that any further increase be limited to the rate of inflation. As a result, the proportion of funding coming from tuition fees remained static at just over 23 percent during the second Liberal administration.

Finally, in contrast to the other two provinces, gaining access to PSE in Quebec has not been enough in itself. Perseverance has been required: the program should be completed and the diploma/degree in question obtained. In the mid-1990s, the government set completion objectives for high school diplomas, college diplomas, and bachelor's degrees. The goals were part of a general orientation towards enabling learners of all ages to succeed by acquiring the knowledge to which they aspired.

As alluded to above, behind the consensus on increasing accessibility there are major differences between political parties and across the three provinces regarding how this shall be achieved, particularly on issues relating to affordability, participation, and completion. In the next section we take a closer look at how these issues differ between provinces and political parties in power.

STUDENT FINANCIAL AID

According to the National Centre for Public Policy and Higher Education, the ability of students and their families to afford educational costs is linked to the amount of tuition fees charged and student assistance received from the government. Postsecondary studies are more affordable in Quebec than in Ontario or British Columbia. Quebec's students have access to tuition-free college education. They benefit from one or two years more of tuition-free education than do their counterparts, depending on whether they are taking a pre-university program or a career program. In addition, university tuition fees in Quebec have consistently been the lowest in Canada. This conclusion is abundantly clear when we compare "average tuition fees by programs" between 1993–94 and 2009–10 (see figures 2.5, 3.4, and 4.4). As table 5.4 illustrates, while Quebec has maintained very low undergraduate fees, the change in government policy in the mid-1990s in Ontario and then in 2001 in British Columbia, led to dramatic increases in the fees charged. With the election of a Liberal government in Ontario fees did become more stable, but then, between 2005–06 and 2009–10, they rose dramatically so that, in the latter year, Ontario undergraduates were paying the highest fees in the country. Similarly, in Quebec tuition fees were in the process of rising rapidly given the policy change in 2007.

Similarly, as table 5.5 illustrates, when we compare tuition fees for graduate programs and in dentistry, law, and medicine, the differences between Quebec and the other two provinces are equally stark. In Quebec, while each category of program does record an increase, they are relatively small. In each case the tuition fees in 1993–94 are in the $1,500 to $1,600 range and, by 2009–10, none had risen above $3,000. In contrast, over the same period, graduate program tuition fees in Ontario and British Columbia rose from the low to mid-$2,000 range to $6,256 and $6,230, respectively. The changes in dentistry, law, and medicine in Ontario and British Columbia are nothing less than astounding. In the former province each program was in the $2,000 range in 1993–94. By 2009–10, the tuition fees in these three program areas had increased to $22,639, $11,313, and $17,380, respectively. Similarly, in British Columbia, tuition fees in the three programs had risen from $2,700 to the mid-$3,000 range in 1993–94 to $11,356, $9,193, and $11,356, respectively, in 2009–10. As with undergraduate fees, the change in government policy in the mid-1990s in Ontario and then in 2001 in British Columbia lay behind these dramatic changes. The trend becomes even more obvious when we plot the changes in undergraduate tuition fees across the period 1986–87 to 2003–04 using 2002 dollars (see figure 5.2).

Table 5.4
Average undergraduate tuition fees, selected years: 1993–94, 1997–98, 2001–02, 2005–06, and 2009–10

	1993–94	1997–98	2001–02	2005–06	2009–10
Quebec	$1,550	$1,804	$1,843	$1,900	$2,309
Ontario	$2,076	$3,293	$4,492	$4,933	$5,985
British Columbia	$2,240	$2,518	$2,527	$4,867	$4,706

Source: Tuition and accommodation living costs for full-time students at Canadian degree-granting institutions (TLAC), Statistics Canada Survey, 3213.

Note: For undergraduate tuition fees, the fees for arts programs are used as the proxy for all non-professional undergraduate programs.

Table 5.5
Weighted average tuition fees for full-time canadian students by province and program in current dollars, 1993–94, 1997–98, 2001–02, 2006–07, and 2009–10

	1993–94 ($)	1997–98 ($)	2001–02 ($)	2006–07 ($)	2009–10 ($)
QUEBEC					
Graduate	1,519	1,950	1,935	1,950	2,443
Dentistry	1,600	2,243	2,471	2,703	2,986
Law	1,574	1,869	1,862	1,920	2,254
Medicine	1,617	2,410	2,702	2,989	2,501
ONTARIO					
Graduate	2,477	3,687	7,003	9,445	6,256
Dentistry	2,555	6,844	14,652	18,666	22,639
Law	2,026	3,347	6,697	10,581	11,313
Medicine	2,562	4,557	12,044	15,413	17,380
BRITISH COLUMBIA					
Graduate	2,109	2,974	3,660	10,409	6,230
Dentistry	3,501	4,000	3,740	12,491	11,356
Law	2,723	3,119	2,988	8,111	9,193
Medicine	3,501	4,000	3,740	12,491	11,356

Source: Tuition and accommodation living costs for full-time students at Canadian degree-granting institutions (TLAC), Statistics Canada Survey, 3213.

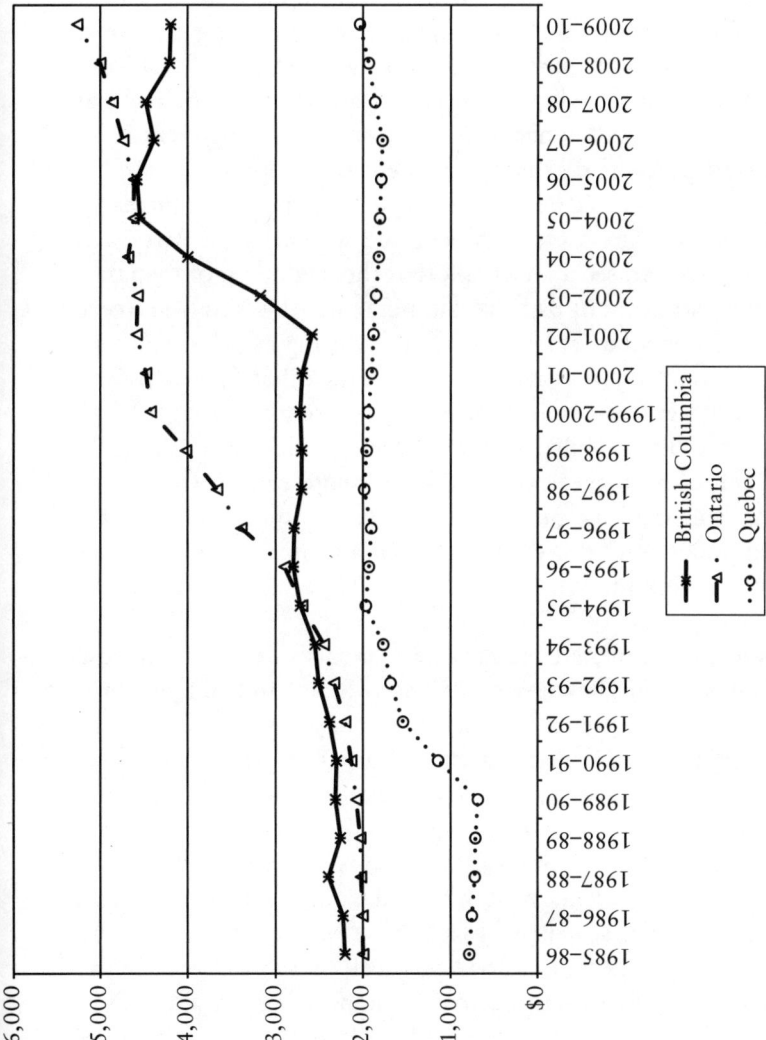

Figure 5.2
Average undergraduate full-time fees in constant 2002 dollars.
Source: Statistics Canada, annual tuition survey number 3123, weighted average domestic arts tuition fees by province.
Notes: Tuition adjusted using provincial CPI, Annual Average, 1986 = 100.

A second indicator of accessibility is the average undergraduate university tuition fees as a proportion of after-tax average income (constant 2002 dollars), which we divided into quintiles. Given the increase in undergraduate tuition fees it is predictable that the variation in this indicator in all three provinces as we move from 1986–87 to 2008–09 shows the lowest quintile experiencing the most change and the highest quintile the least (see figures 2.6, 3.5, and 4.5). Over this period, the highest quintile experienced an increase of between 1 and 3 percent, whereas the lowest quintile experienced an increase of 29 percent in Ontario, 23 percent in British Columbia, and 13 percent in Quebec. As one might predict, the major increases for the lowest quintile in Ontario occurred when the PC Party was in power, and we can see a levelling off at the beginning of the latest Liberal administration. In British Columbia, the NDP's tuition freeze only has some impact on the lowest quintile during its second administration in the latter half of the 1990s. Since the Liberals took power, the position of the least well-off in society worsened during the first administration but stabilized during the second administration. Finally, Quebec, with the lowest undergraduate tuition fees in the country, has put the least pressure on the lowest quintile. The average undergraduate university tuition fees as a proportion of after-tax average income for the lowest quintile has hovered around 15 percent since 1994–95.

In addition to student fees, affordability also depends on how much access students have to needs-based loans and bursary programs, and, in that regard, Quebec is far superior to the rest of Canada. Although this student assistance program was more profitable for students from less well-to-do backgrounds, there were still many questions regarding student debt and how parental contributions were calculated. In spite of these limits, the circumstances of Quebec's full-time students were more advantageous in 2001 than were those of students in British Columbia or Ontario, who were only eligible for a maximum of $260 a week or $275 a week in the form of loans or bursaries, respectively, compared to a maximum in Quebec of $416 a week for college students, $489 a week for undergraduate university students, and $512 a week for master's or doctoral students (table 5.6). By 2010–11, the discrepancy persisted, although British Columbia and Ontario had narrowed the gap slightly. Students in these two provinces were now eligible for a maximum of $320 and $360 a week, respectively. In Quebec, the

Table 5.6
Maximum provincial student loam (full-time, with no dependent, single, based on 34 weeks of study) and total maximum assistance for selected years: 2011 and 2011–12

	2001	2011–12
BRITISH COLUMBIA		
Maximum loan	$8,840/year	$10,880/year
Total maximum assistance including grants	$8,840/year ($260/week)	$10,880/year ($320/week)
ONTARIO		
Maximum loan	$9,350/year	$12,240/year
Total maximum assistance including grants	$9,350/year ($275/week)	$12,240/year ($360/week)
QUEBEC		
Maximum loan		
Total maximum assistance including grants		
COLLEGE STUDENTS		
Maximum loan	$2,005/year	$1,760/year
Total maximum assistance including grants	$14,152/year ($416/week)	$15,331/year ($451/week)
UNDERGRADUATE STUDENTS		
Maximum loan	$2,460/year	$2,440/year
Total maximum assistance including grants	$16,619/year ($489/week)	$18,592/year ($547/week)
GRADUATE STUDENTS		
Maximum loan	$3,255/year	$3,240/year
Total maximum assistance including grants	$17,414/year ($512/week)	$19,392/year ($570/week)

Source: Statistics Canada.

maximum per week had risen to $451, $547, and $570 for college students, undergraduate university students, and magistral or doctoral students, respectively. The maximum amount that Quebec's students could receive in the form of a loan in 2001 varied between $2,005 and $3,255 a year, while this amount was $8,840 and $9,350, respectively, for students in British Columbia and Ontario. By 2010–11, the range in Quebec was lower, beginning at $1,760 and going up to $3,240. In contrast, in British Columbia and Ontario the respective loan limits had reached $10,880 and $12,240.

In addition to the maximum loan amount, some of Quebec's students (11 percent of college students and 17.9 percent of university students) received a student bursary. The financial aid received by Quebec's students appeared to be even more advantageous because the monthly cost of living for single students who did not live with their parents was lower in Quebec ($805) than in British Columbia ($935) or Ontario ($914). In other respects, the average annual employment income for students was lower in Quebec ($3,100) than in British Columbia ($3,200) or Ontario ($3,700). Last, according to the Canadian Millennium Scholarships Foundation (2002), their debt at the end of their bachelor's degree was also a lot lower ($13,100) than in Ontario ($22,700), the western provinces ($20,300), or the Atlantic provinces ($22,400).

Changes were made to the Quebec policy on tuition fees in 2004–05; however, following the students' strike in 2005 the changes were reversed. So, as we see in table 5.6, the differences between the three provinces are still significant. Higher fees and less advantageous assistance programs in Ontario and British Columbia, one assumes, have a cumulative negative impact on the affordability of PSE in those two provinces. Two conclusions can be drawn from the data on student financing: (1) there is a clear link between student financing and the political ideology of the party in power and (2) access to PSE has been central to the Quebec nation-building program.

POSTSECONDARY PARTICIPATION RATES

Comparing participation rates across Canadian provinces is not easy because there is no uniform demarcation between secondary and postsecondary levels. In Quebec, elementary and secondary school combine for a total of eleven years, then postsecondary college education (two or three years) takes over. In British Columbia and Ontario, elementary and secondary school combined take twelve years (thirteen years in Ontario up until 2003), and students can go right from secondary school to college and university. While recognising this problem we can see that in all three provinces participation rates have increased during the 1990s for both the 18- to 24- and the 25- to 29-year-olds (see table 5.7).[4] Between 1990 and 2000, British Columbia and Quebec experienced similar gains of around 10 percent for the 18- to 24-year-old group, while Ontario gained 6 percent. British Columbia recorded the largest increase for the 25- to 29-year-old group at 7 percent, while Ontario and Quebec

Table 5.7
PSE participation rates by age (18–24 and 25–29) using full-time equivalent enrolment figures by province, British Columbia, Ontario, and Quebec

	1976	1990	1997	2000
BRITISH COLUMBIA				
Age 18–24	18.8	29.3	36.8	38.7
Age 25–29	7.7	7.2	14.4	14.6
ONTARIO				
Age 18–24	23.3	31.8	36.8	37.8
Age 25–29	8.5	9.8	11.5	11.9
QUEBEC				
Age 18–24	21.1	35.2	45.2	43.0
Age 25–29	6.7	10.6	11.5	13.0

Sources: BC Statistics, labour force statistics, October 1998 (release 6 November, 1998, issue 98-10), figure 2: PSE participation rates by age, Canada and provinces, p. 3. BC Statistics, labour force statistics, August 2001 (release 7 September, 2001, issue 01–08), figure 2: PSE participation rate, selected age groups, Canada and provinces, 1990 and 2000, p. 4.

had smaller increases of approximately 2 percent. All three provincial PSE systems moved from being "elite" through a "mass" phase to finally hover around the magical threshold of 40 percent, which marks the movement to a "universal" PSE system (Trow 1973; Scott 1995). By the end of the 1990s, Ontario's participation rates had fallen below Quebec's and British Columbia's in both age categories. This pattern corresponds to a period of cuts to PSE funding to universities and colleges, tuition increases, and restructuring of student assistance programs in Ontario and a concerted effort in British Columbia to increase a previously low participation rate in PSE.

When we use ministry data in British Columbia, we can see the same pattern as described above, although the numbers are slightly different. Between 1985–86 and 2001–02, the participation rate for 18- to 24-year-olds, using full-time equivalent enrolment figures, rose from 26 per cent to 41 per cent (see figure 2.7). The increase cut across the Socred and the NDP eras. Since 2002–03 there has been a slight decrease, but by 2009–10 the participation rate had levelled out at approximately 42 percent. Similarly, between 1985–86 and 2001–02 the participation rate for the 18- to 29-year-old age group rose from 15 percent to 24 percent and then levelled out at approximately 25 percent for the rest of the decade.

In Ontario, we can get a sense of the same pattern through an examination of university participation rates for 18- to 24-year-olds and 18- to 29-year-olds (see table 3.7). This rate for the former group remained relatively constant in the mid to upper 20 percent range for the 1990s but then increased from 28.2 percent in 2001–02 to 32.7 percent in 2004–05 and to 35.5 percent in 2008–09. Similarly, for the 18- to 29-year-olds the rate hovered around 15 percent for the 1990s but then increased from 16.3 percent in 2001–02 to 19.4 percent in 2004–05. By 2008–09, this rate had increased slightly to 19.8 percent. The best ministry data from Quebec illustrates a high participation rate, although one has to be reminded that high school students are expected to continue on to college. The best equivalent indicator of participation for the 18- to 24-year-old age group in the other two provinces is the rate of participation in "bachelor's programs" (see table 4.4). This rate hovered around the mid-30 percent range during the 1990s and then increased from 35.7 percent in 1999–2000 to 41.3 percent in 2006–07.

Given the varying policy orientations in the three provinces with regard to the appropriate emphasis on academic and vocational programs, one would expect to find some key differences in the outcomes between provinces and within each province depending on the party in power. Yet in British Columbia the evidence suggests that all governments during the period from 1985–86 through to 2004–05 were strongly committed to increasing access across the system. While on the surface the PSE policies of the three parties were different, particularly with respect to vocationalism, the outcomes were very similar (see figures 2.9 and 2.10, and table 2.3).[5] The academic/graduate part of the offerings continued to account for about two-thirds of the total FTE allocation and as a share of the total participation rate for both the 18- to 24-year-old and 18- to 29-year-old age groups. If anything, the vocational commitment was slightly higher in 1985–86 than in any later year. Just as colleges wished to be more academic, so successive governments were committed to increasing access to PSE in the Interior to programs leading to degrees.

For Ontario, the best evidence we have with regard to programs comes from the data on the highest level of schooling and on degree and diploma production (see tables 3.7 and 3.8). As in British

Columbia, the trends suggest some success in the policies directed at expansion of degree-granting spaces as well as an overall increase in attendance across most PSE sectors. Between 1992–93 and 2008–09, the university participation rates for the 18- to 24-year-olds and the 18- to 29-year-olds rose from 28.23 to 35.5 percent and from 15.09 to 19.83 percent, respectively. In vocational/skills training, the absolute number of spaces increased, but, relatively speaking, the sector remained constant when set against the academic sector. The proportion of Ontario's population with a trade or college certificate/diploma or university degree or higher has increased steadily since 1986. Between 1986 and 2006, the proportion of the population with some PSE increased by 19 percent, suggesting that Ontarians have increasingly engaged in PSE in the last two decades. In particular, the proportion of the population with a university degree has increased the most (by 9 percent), followed by those with a college certificate or diploma (7 percent), suggesting the continuing value Ontario's population places on a university or college education. University enrolment numbers decreased in the 1990s but then increased dramatically after 2003 when the Liberals took power.

The pattern in Quebec has been somewhat different, given the role of the CÉGEPs (see table 4.4). Over the period 1990–91 to 2006–07, participation in college programs has remained relatively constant at around 60 percent, although the internal distribution rates for the career and pre-university programs have decreased, the gap has been filled in the decade between 1996–97 to 2006–07 with enrolment in the orientation and integration path. The degree-granting programs have all increased over the same period, with the bachelor's program overtaking the 40 percent threshold in 2003–04.

The percentage of Quebecers age fifteen and over who had a university degree in 2006 (14.9 percent) was lower than the percentage for this age group in Canada as a whole (16.2 percent) or for British Columbia or Ontario (17.3 and 18.0 percent, respectively). Similarly, the proportion of Quebecers who had at least a college certificate or diploma, or a university diploma counting for less than a bachelor's degree (20.9 percent), was slightly lower than for Canada as a whole as well as for the other two provinces (see table 5.8).

These indicators show that, contrary to expectations, a lower proportion of young Quebecers obtain a college certificate or diploma, or a university certificate or diploma below a bachelor's degree, than do young people in Ontario or British Columbia. Further, a smaller

Table 5.8.
Canadian population 15 years and over by highest degree, certificate, or diploma (2006)

	Quebec (%)	Ontario (%)	British Columbia (%)	Canada (%)
High school graduation certificate	22.3	26.8	27.9	25.5
Trades certificate or diploma	15.3	8.0	10.9	10.9
College certificate or diploma	16.0	18.4	16.7	17.3
University certificate or diploma below bachelor	4.9	4.1	5.4	4.4
Bachelor's degree	10.6	12.7	12.2	11.6
University certificate or diploma above bachelor	1.6	2.5	1.9	1.9
Medical degree	0.5	0.6	0.6	0.5
Master's degree	3.1	4.0	3.7	3.4
Earned doctorate	0.7	0.8	0.8	0.7
At least a college certificate or diploma or university certificate or diploma below bachelor	20.9	22.5	22.1	21.7
At least a university degree	14.9	18.0	17.3	16.2

Source: Statistics Canada, 2006 census of population, Statistics Canada catalogue no. 97–560–XCB2006018 (Canada, Code01).

proportion of them get a university degree (bachelor's, master's, or doctorate) than in the other two provinces. Although the system has caught up to a large extent in relation to how far behind it was at the time of the reforms in the 1960s, it has not completely caught up as far as access to PSE.

Finally, a national survey of literacy and numeracy conducted in 2003 by Statistics Canada (2005) concluded that 42 percent of Canadians over sixteen years of age cannot meet most everyday reading and numeracy requirements. Of the three provinces, only British Columbia scored "significantly higher" than the national average on literacy and numeracy. Ontario hovered around the Canadian averages, while Quebec scores were uneven (see table 5.9). They were around the Canadian average in numeracy and problem-solving but below average on the two literacy measures.

When discussing participation rates in PSE in Canada it is important to note that participation for Aboriginal and Inuit students lags far behind the rates for the general population. While an increasingly large number of Aboriginal students have been funded through

Table 5.9
Literacy and numeracy scores (2003)

	Literacy scores	Numeracy scores
British Columbia	281	272
Ontario	270	261
Quebec	266	259
Canadian average	272	263

Indian and Northern Affairs Canada, completion rates are poor. Further, many eligible students do not receive support. The question remains as to whether the federal government will recognize PSE as a treaty/Aboriginal right.

Marketization

Currie et al. (2002, 85) document a general trend in PSE reform policies within Australia, Canada, the United States, the United Kingdom, Western Europe, and Eastern Asia "towards a new 'ideal' that is austere, cost cutting, privately funded, market driven, with slower expansion and diversification programs." The authors point out that, under the so-called new public management regime, PSE institutions are encouraged to replicate a private-sector model according to which students and research users are treated as customers. As Young (2002) notes, the introduction of market mechanisms does not preclude increasing government control; instead, it may involve a change in government's approach to reform and alter the nature of its control over the system in order to induce universities to adopt government-identified priorities.

The three case studies clearly reveal how Canadian PSE has come to embrace market philosophy. As noted earlier, this is particularly true of Ontario, where the Harris government initiated a major retreat in public spending on PSE. It is also a distinct policy strategy of the BC Liberal government. Marketization has not been as noticeable in Quebec PSE. Our work documents the role of five policy developments in pushing these systems towards the market: (1) increase in the number and range of private institutions, (2) deregulation of fees, (3) growth in enrolment of international students, and (4) matching-fund schemes.

PRIVATE INSTITUTIONS

The PC government in Ontario and the Liberal government in British Columbia introduced legislation aimed at encouraging more competition in their PSE systems through the growth of private degree-granting institutions. In both provinces, the government claimed that private universities would expand choice for students, enhance competition between publicly funded universities, and improve accessibility. In Ontario, the Ministry of Training, Colleges and Universities brought forward new legislation for degree granting and operating a university in the province: the PSE Choice and Excellence Act, 2000. This act permits organizations to offer programs leading to a degree, or to operate a university, either with the consent of the minister of training, colleges and universities or by an act of the Legislative Assembly of Ontario. PEQAB evaluates programs offered by out-of-province institutions, new free-standing institutions and college applied degree programs. Under the old Degree Granting Act, 1983, consent was given only when the institution was offering a "niche" program in areas in which Ontario universities were unable or unwilling to meet student demand or societal needs. However, current requests are for mainstream programs offered by Ontario universities, and they have come from both out-of-province public, non-profit universities and private, for-profit universities.

Seventeen institutions have been granted restricted degree-granting authority by the Legislative Assembly of Ontario. All are bible colleges or small religious-affiliated institutions. The Ontario government has also been lobbied extensively to allow private, for-profit universities such as the University of Phoenix, Lansbridge University (formerly Unexus University), and the British IMC University to offer degree programs in Ontario. In November 1999, the private, non-profit University of Southern California was granted permission to offer diploma programs in Ontario. By 2009, nine private (in-province and out-of-province) institutions were legitimately offering degree programs.

The policies adopted by each administration from 1985 reflect not only different ideologies but also different economic climates. Consistent among the administrations is the increasing tendency to view PSE policy as an instrument of economic development, with each administration also placing varying emphases on social, equitable, and educational goals and principles (Lang et al. 1999). Ideology has also provided the justification for governments to focus on eliminating the deficit, balancing the budget, and increasing the role of the market.

Private career colleges are privately owned and are operated as commercial enterprises. They must be registered under the Private Career Colleges Act and administered by the Ministry of Education and Training. The non-degree private sector was the only part of the Ontario system that experienced significant expansion. The number of these colleges rose from over 200 in 1990 (Jones 1997b, 137–61) to 320 in 1994–95, to over 450 in 2004, and, finally, to 600 in 2010 (Ministry of Education and Training website). While the number of institutions has more than doubled, it does not appear that enrolment has kept pace. Further, this includes only those private career colleges required to register with the ministry under the Private Career Colleges Act – that is, those that offer vocational programs. Other unregistered institutions offer a myriad of non-vocational programs, but neither government nor anyone else is keeping track.

In British Columbia, Bill 15, the Degree Authorization Act, 2002, set out criteria under which new institutions, including private and public institutions from outside the province, would be authorized to offer degree programs and to grant degrees in British Columbia. In addition, the bill allows public colleges and institutes to offer "applied baccalaureate degrees" and university colleges to offer "applied master's degrees" (*Hansard*, 11 April 2002). The minister responsible for PSE has the authority to give consent to an applicant to grant a degree if the applicant satisfactorily passes a quality assessment process administered by the government-appointed Degree Quality Assessment Board. Thus far, two private, for-profit universities (University Canada West and Lansbridge University) have been approved under this legislation. Neither university is still in operation.

The BC Liberals have also authorized three British Columbia-based private, not-for-profit universities by private members legislation. In 2002, Quest University Canada (originally Sea to Sky University) was established with its own legislation. Quest is a non-profit, non-sectarian institution founded by former University of British Columbia president David Strangway and located in Squamish. Since the fall of 2007, Quest has offered a non-discipline-based bachelor of arts and sciences as its only degree. In 2005, the World Trade University (WTU) was established by private legislation to offer degree and non-degree programs in international trade, economics, business, and related subjects. In 2007, Pacific Coast University for Workplace Health Sciences (PCU-WHS) was established to focus on the implementation of workplace-based reintegration programs for injured and disabled workers. The Port Alberni campus opened in 2011. Both Quest and PCU-WHS are operating, but WTU closed in 2008.

The Degree Authorization Act also provides for the provision of individual degree programs by private institutions. By 2011, only two British Columbia-based private non-university institutions (Sprott Shaw Community College and the Art Institute of Vancouver) had received permission to offer a baccalaureate degree program. Five institutions had received approval to offer two-year associate degrees. In addition, a number of private US-based universities operate branch campuses in the Vancouver area. Farleigh Dickenson University, the Adler School of Professional Psychology, and Lawrence Technical University are just a few of the schools that the BC Ministry of Advanced Education allows to offer degree-level programs in the province.

In British Columbia, the number of private institutions registered with the PPSEC has mushroomed from 358 in 1993 to approximately 840. The number of private institutions operating in the province is approximately twelve hundred. Over the same period, the number of students has increased dramatically from 48,000 to 115,000. As part of this expansion, the number of private ESL schools has risen from five in the early 1980s to over 180 in 2005 (Culos 2005).

The situation in Quebec appears to be relatively stable. Quebec has no private universities and only a small private sector at the college level. The system contains forty-eight small private colleges that teach mainly technical subjects. In 2010–11, 217,264 students were enrolled in colleges. While the private colleges account for half of the total number of colleges, they only account for 9.7 percent of the total number of students. Within the private sector, twenty-five colleges have a licence to operate and to receive operating funds from the Quebec government. The other twenty-three private colleges merely have a permit to operate but do not receive any public funds. Operating funds are allocated and calculated on the basis of five criteria: (1) number of students, (2) student's field of study, (3) renting value of building, (4) part-time students, and (5) specific activities supported by the Ministry of Education.

As we have seen, changes in PSE policy in Ontario and British Columbia in recent years have attempted to move the system closer to the market. During the 1990s and the 2000s, governments in these two provinces created policy environments that were meant to facilitate marketization, yet the results were not that impressive at the degree-granting level. Change did occur in the vocational college sector, where the number of institutions increased substantially in both provinces. In Quebec, the private sector and privatization role of government remains fundamentally unchanged. The strength of the public sector unions combined with the opinion polls probably accounts as much as anything for the lack of change in Quebec.

DEREGULATION OF TUITION FEES

As noted earlier in this chapter (see figure 5.2), while Quebec has maintained very low fees, the change in government policy in the mid-1990s in Ontario and then in 2001 in British Columbia led to dramatic increases in the fees charged. Through deregulation of some graduate and professional programs, and steep increases in the still regulated fees for general arts and science programs, the Ontario government's tuition policy has been to balance funding for colleges and universities by bringing tuition fees back to 35 percent of the cost of providing university and college courses. In British Columbia, the Liberal government deregulated the fees in 2001.

The changes in tuition policy suggest that the governments in Ontario and British Columbia are moving away from supporting students and shifting that responsibility to students and their families, universities, and the private sector. In so doing, they are keeping government costs to a minimum while increasing costs for students. In downloading the costs of the PSE system to the "consumer" student, government is adopting a market paradigm.

INTERNATIONAL STUDENTS

For revenue generation reasons it has become increasingly important for Canadian postsecondary institutions to compete around the globe for international students. Foreign undergraduate students pay, on average, just under three times the price that Canadian students pay. Between 1999–2000 and 2006–07 the number of FTE international students enrolled in Canadian universities doubled from 35,205 to 71,232 (see table 3.8; CAUT Almanac 2009–10). By 2010, approximately ninety thousand full-time international students were studying in Canadian colleges and universities (AUCC 2010). Ontario and British Columbia have been particularly active in the international student market and managed to increase the number of international students dramatically over the last decade. The trend is driven less by explicit government policies than by institutions that are trying to make up some of the revenue lost due to decreases in government funding. The language situation has made it more difficult for Quebec institutions to compete for international students. However, it may also be the case that marketization forces generally have been less strong in this province as there is not the same push to compete in the international student market.

MATCHING-FUND SCHEMES

Matching-grants schemes, whereby funds from the private sector can contribute to the financing of different parts of the system, is another mechanism for fostering marketization. This strategy was prevalent under the PC government in Ontario, which introduced matching funds for student aid aimed at increasing student enrolment in engineering and computing. It also introduced a matching-fund program for research, whereby the government contributed one-third of the total funds required to support research initiatives that secured private-sector financing. The Ontario government placed a greater emphasis on matching private-sector funding and increasing university spending on student assistance and discipline-specific scholarships than it did on enhancing the Ontario Student Assistance Program.

Matching-fund schemes are less developed in British Columbia, but the Liberal government has shown increased interest in moving in this direction. An indication of this was the 2002 budget decision to make provision for a $45 million partnership with the private sector to establish twenty research chairs in the fields of medical, social, environment, and technical research in fulfilment of another New Era promise. The government also increased its reliance on targeted grants for the expansion of FTE student spaces over the 2004–05 to 2009–10 period; and, through a graduate internship program, it increased its collaboration with industry. Tendencies to increase marketization through private-sector influence on research is also evident in Quebec, where the provincial government introduced a university research tax credit program to encourage business to invest in applied research – a topic we return to in the section on R&D.

The three Canadian case studies show that, while the neoliberal influences on PSE in Canada may be less pronounced than they are in other Anglo-Saxon countries, the push towards marketization is well under way. This is particularly the case in Ontario and British Columbia, where the Harris and Campbell governments, respectively, adopted policy agendas aimed at fostering an ethos of competitiveness and entrepreneurship within the postsecondary sector.

Accountability

An underlying but consistent theme across all three provinces and across party political lines has been the commitment by governments to make the connections between educational spending and useful outcomes more transparent and understandable to the general public. This policy priority has taken on different forms in the three provinces. Both Quebec and Ontario have emphasized the institutional aspect of accountability, while British Columbia has emphasized the general public interest aspect.

Quebec has the longest history of regulating universities. In the 1970s, MEQ created the CREPUQ committee and charged it with evaluating the "quality" of degree programs. The work performed by this committee is symptomatic of how successive governments have eroded the autonomy of the universities. In the 1980s, Conseil les Univerités began sector-based studies on engineering, social science, and education. Across the PSE system institutions are directly accountable to MEQ in that they are required to submit "success plans" and "annual reports" at the college and university levels, respectively. Since the early 1990s, and as part of the government's desire to promote both accountability and efficiency, universities were required to conduct internal evaluations, which, in turn, are monitored by government. All programs are evaluated with regard to quality and relevance. In 2000, the Quebec government first clearly stated its accountability priority: universities were to keep their autonomy and their power to organize their activities as they saw fit, and they were answerable to society and public authorities for their management of public funds (MEQ 2000).

In Ontario, institutional accountability has been the major priority. Institutions are required to account for public funds and to demonstrate achievements on government-prescribed benchmarks or indicators. A system-wide accountability perspective has been more problematic in Ontario because of the lack of system-level planning. Moreover, the form of accountability has proven more controversial in the PSE system and has been the area most subject to change.

Accountability first became a priority in the early 1990s, when the NDP government began an auditing system for universities that rested with the institutional governing bodies. The PCs were far more aggressive in their approach. Accountability and quality were identified as major thrusts of their PSE platform. KPIs were introduced, and all colleges and universities were required to report on a set of them for each program. In the 2000 budget the government started to put money back into the system by way of operating grants.[6] The new funding was tied to performance indicators: enrolment growth[7] and university performance.[8] In addition, the government increased the use of targeted and matching private-sector funds. This combination of funding mechanisms substantially increases the level of accountability that universities experience.

In British Columbia, NDP commitments to accessibility and to vocationalism are good examples of how governments have attempted to make the PSE system more accountable to the public interest. Through a series of skill and training initiatives, the PPSEC, and the use of other intermediary bodies, the government used KPIs to make institutions in both the public and the private parts of the college sector more directly accountable with regard to their planning and student outcomes. At the university level, the NDP created the New Programs Committee to monitor and approve all new degree programs. The creation of new vocational niche universities and the emergence of applied degrees increased the vocational orientation of the PSE system and were aimed at making it more accountable to provincial economic interests.

While the NDP took this direct approach during the 1990s, the Liberals in Ontario adopted a different definition of accountability. Accountability has come to mean both quality assurance in the most general sense and a blurring of the boundary between the public and the private sectors. As they put in place the Quality Assurance Board (2003) and dismantled much of the infrastructure created by the NDP (its purpose being to guarantee accountability), they put their faith in the market as the best means of making institutions accountable. In other words, they believed that being accountable to the marketplace was the best way of making the system accountable to the public. In the university sector, the government provided targeted funding for particular occupations and simply decreed that more students would be educated without an increase in funding.

More than any other province, Quebec has been concerned with efficiency. In 2000, the government introduced a new management framework focusing on outcomes, respect for the principle of transparency, and increased accountability. Likewise, according to the Quebec Policy on Universities, accountability is one of the principles on which government and university initiatives are based: universities are supported financially by the state and they must run their institutions efficiently by making optimal use of the resources at their disposal. The policy's second priority is to improve the universities' performance in terms of education quality, research excellence, and the system's overall efficiency (MEQ 2000, 17). These themes were taken up in 2008, when the government passed two bills on the governance of CÉGEPs and universities. Modified in 2009, the intent of MELS was to make the system far more accountable. Finally, in 2011 the new University Funding Plan included a monitoring system that made use of performance indicators.

Labour Force Development

In some ways federal involvement in vocational and technical training issues had more impact on provincial systems of education than did any other intervention. During the 1960s and 1970s, the federal government adopted a "grand design," the essence of which was the development of "manpower." "Manpower policy" used labour market training and job creation programs as a means of increasing economic growth, decreasing unemployment, and promoting economic stability. The massive infusion of funds enabled many provinces to expand their adult training systems and was the foundation upon which provinces built their community college systems.

Through the 1960s, 1970s, and into the 1980s, the federal government purchased training courses or seats from provincial training institutes for its clients, mainly unemployed persons. During the same decade, the federal government shifted away from the funding training facilities and programs in provincial training institutes. The introduction of the Canadian Jobs Strategy (CJS) in 1985 served notice to provinces that the federal government planned to reduce institutional training purchases in coming years and to redirect these funds to private and voluntary sectors. This led to reduced funding through federal-provincial training agreements in the late 1980s and a phasing out of such agreements by the early 1990s. The "grand design" was replaced by the Labour Force Development Strategy and the Canadian Labour Force Development Board.

By the mid-1990s, much of the responsibility and funding for training had been devolved to the provinces and territories, through negotiated labour market development agreements with every jurisdiction except Ontario. A patchwork of agreements emerged, including a "strategic partnership"; "co-management"; and, for five provinces and two territories, "devolution." In the early 2000s, some interest was expressed in expanding the federal role with the introduction of the Innovation Strategy, which also included a new emphasis on apprenticeship training.

While the Government of Canada's role in training and the labour market is ever-evolving, because of major demographic and labour demand shifts provincial and territorial jurisdictions have become increasingly interested in human capital and human resource strategies. While provincial policies are similar there are differences in emphasis. A defining characteristic of the NDP administrations during the period between 1991 and 2001 in British Columbia was their commitment to vocationalism and skill training. The underlying theme was that academic education had received most of the attention in previous decades and that now it was time to rectify this unevenness and to better serve the interests of labour. Through a series of reports and legislation, successive governments increased both economic and institutional resources for non-academic and applied education. The roadmap in British Columbia for the NDP's skills agenda was set by a series of reports during the early 1990s. The grand aim was to dramatically reduce structural unemployment. What followed was a massive expansion in the number of vocational spaces as the new funding mechanisms took effect. The BC Liberal government took a different approach. The "New Model for Industry Training" removed the government from its direct involvement with apprentices, gave business a dominant role in the governance of the training system, and introduced a system of "flexible," modular training courses that could be adapted to suit the needs of specific employers and delivered by private trainers (Ministry of Advanced Education 2002). The mandates of the regulatory mechanisms that emerged from this policy – that is, the Private Career Training Institutes Agency and the Industry Training

Authority – had mandates that were more explicitly tied to fulfilling what business determined were the priorities for the province.

In Ontario's PSE system we can observe a distinct shift in emphasis away from a liberal education towards a vocational, technical education. The change in funding mechanisms, which have moved towards tied and matched private-sector funding, has shifted the system towards the market and has placed a greater emphasis on vocational training as a means of meeting labour market demands. The challenges facing the Ontario economy were and are very different from those facing British Columbia. The technologically dominated economy pushed governments to look for ways to increase the links between industry, colleges, and universities. The PCS (1995–2003) favoured market principles in their attempt to achieve these objectives. This government's postsecondary policy emphasized serving labour market needs. In other words, educational training was linked to the labour market in order to build industry infrastructure and to sustain industrial competitiveness. This was accomplished through vocationally oriented programs and through market-oriented research. For example, the first new university created in forty years in Ontario under the new degree-granting legislation is an amalgamation of Durham College and the new Ontario University Institute of Technology. This is a publicly funded university, but one explicit component of its mission is to serve the needs of the surrounding labour market (and the automotive and power industry) in the neighbouring region. At the same time, the OUIT attempts to be like all the other Ontario universities. Since 2000, the government has used targeted funding mechanisms and matching-funding programs to emphasize its vocationalism and skill development, thereby inducing the postsecondary institutions to embrace its priorities.[9]

In Quebec, the commitment to this policy theme, while unequivocal, has been much more sporadic than in the other two provinces. At the same time, those who promote this vision in Quebec believe that technicians, professionals, and management should all learn more about internationalization, to the extent that they learn to deal with people in other countries or even work abroad. Successive governments have reaffirmed the foundational role of CÉGEPs in career training. Further, while pushing educational institutions towards industry and the needs of the marketplace, governments have also been clear that institutions should not be diverted from their primary education missions and that they should protect their institutional autonomy. According to the policy on universities, quality training must also be relevant. In other words, it must enable students to acquire the competencies, skills, and tools they need to develop as individuals and to play their part in society. At the college level, this policy is actualized through a vocational and career education committee composed of representatives from MEQ and public agencies, employers, and union and association representatives. The continuing mandate has been to examine issues concerning the three education levels from the angle of education-employment relationships, to coordinate programs and place them in a continuum, and to avoid duplication.

At the university level, several committees and commissions have been charged with the task of evaluating programs from the point of view of their relevance. According to CRÉPUQ's program evaluation policy, every university must develop its own policy for the periodic evaluation of all its programs, in keeping with scientific, socio-economic, and systemic and institutional criteria.

A number of clearly targeted funding initiatives also embody this priority. At the college level, these initiatives fall into three categories: (1) those concerning institution and business promotion and support for co-op programs; (2) refundable tax credits for training, applicable to internships; and (3) support for entrepreneurship, designed to promote the development of an entrepreneurial culture. At the university level, specific funding with regard to student services provides that part of the funding that may be used to manage co-op programs. A budgetary allowance makes it possible to offer more internships as well as career guidance and placement services.

Research and Development

As briefly discussed in the section on political economy, funding research policy has primarily been a federal matter. Successive federal Liberal governments have made a concerted effort to dramatically increase the research funding going to universities, which, in turn, has had a profound impact on the structure of PSE in Canada. As one might expect, Ontario, Quebec, and British Columbia receive a very large proportion of the federal research funding through the granting councils (CAUT 2010–11, 44, table 5.1), accounting for 38.8, 28.1. and 11.9 percent, respectively, in 2007–08. We can observe a similar distribution when we examine the share of the total sponsored research funding.

At the provincial level, a wide variation exists between the three provinces in the extent to which they have created their own R&D infrastructure. British Columbia has introduced a few programs, most recently its Chairs of Excellence Program, but it has tended to rely on federal provision. All three provinces have faced similar increases in the allocation of funds for research due to the matching requirements imposed through the CFI and the CRC programs.

Ontario has, in some ways, led this policy initiative with, for example, a centres of excellence program that preceded the NCE program and was used as a model for federal policy. The OCE, the University Research Incentive Fund, the Premier's Council Technology Fund, and the Industry Research Program were all established in 1987. Ten years later, the Ministry of Energy, Science and Technology was created and the R&D Challenge Fund was established. The R&D Challenge Fund emphasized university–industry liaisons to support job creation and economic growth and to attract and keep skilled researchers in Ontario.

Supporting the Ontario R&D Challenge Fund, a 20 percent refundable R&D tax credit was established for corporate-sponsored R&D in universities and other postsecondary institutions. A cooperative education tax credit in information technology was expanded, and an intellectual property tax credit was established. Other provinces have also introduced a tax policy (e.g., Quebec in 2001) to provide particular incentives for R&D and technology. In 2002, the Ontario Research Performance Fund was announced. The fund provides an additional $30 million annually to colleges, universities, and research institutes to cover the overhead costs associated with Ontario-funded research. The R&D Challenge Fund was also increased to $100 million.

Over the last two decades, Quebec has developed a parallel system of R&D funding agencies that covers all disciplines and is by far the most extensive such structure to be found in any Canadian province. The decision to create a parallel structure begins in the mid-1970s with the Parent Commission, which emphasized basic research and the idea of a "republic of science" in charge of its own decisions. It also emphasized the fact that Quebec's researchers needed to catch up with researchers in the rest of Canada in order to be able to compete with them. Quebec is the only province that established structures for directly supporting university research, and this was due, in large part, to this "catching-up" ideology.[10] In this sense, the focus on R&D has always been about nation building. This priority is based on the principle that research must contribute more than before to the state's socio-economic goals.

During the 1990s, the concept of "progress," which was generally associated with the above goals, was replaced by that of "innovation." According to the Quebec Policy on Science and Innovation, it is by focusing on inter-sector networks and partnerships that research will be able to truly contribute to innovation. In a 1980 White Paper on scientific research, university research was positioned in relation to government research and industry research. Its aim was described as the advancement of knowledge. However, universities were asked to start concerning themselves more with research spin-offs and their effect on regional economic development. In the economic policy published in 1982 regarding the high-tech boom, or technological turning point (*Le virage technologique*), the need to develop close ties with business and to see that programs better addressed industrial training needs was emphasized. In 1983, the Act to Promote the Advancement of Science and technology in Quebec created the Conseil de la Science et de la Technologie, whose mandate was to advise the Ministère de la Recherche, de la Science et de la Technologie on all matters relating to scientific and technological development in Quebec.

While Quebec's original focus was upon the human sciences, over time, the Quebec policy agenda regarding research has taken on an increasingly utilitarian, economic-driven agenda. The 2001 Quebec Policy on Science and Innovation was based on a certain concept of what constitutes the requirements of the knowledge society. University research was assigned an instrumental function: it had to be geared towards innovation. According to this concept, there are three different types of innovation: (1) product innovation, which involves perfecting and marketing a product that is better than those already on the market; (2) process innovation, which entails perfecting and adopting new or improved production and distribution methods; and (3) social innovation, which refers to any new approach, practice, or intervention – or any completely new product – developed to improve a situation or solve a social problem in connection with institutions, organizations, or communities.

By referring to the concept of social innovation in this way, the Quebec government distanced itself from the strict technological innovation marketing promoted by the OECD and other governmental organizations (Milot 2005, 3). More specifically, this policy aimed: (1) to adapt the research support provided by Quebec's subsidizing agencies, (2) to support companies ensuring knowledge transfer by recognizing and promoting the value of university research, and (3) to harmonize universities' intellectual property policies so that they all recognized research accomplishments as institutional property. On the heels of this policy, the government proceeded to restructure its granting councils (Formation de chercheurs et d'aide a la recherche [FCAR], Conseil québécois de la recherche sociale [CQRS], Fonds de la recherche en santé du Québec [FRSQ]) into three distinct organizations along the lines of the federal granting agencies: One for the natural sciences (Fonds de recherche du Québec [FQRNT]), one for the humanities and social sciences (Fonds québécois de la recherche sur la société et la culture [FQRSC]), and one for the medical sciences (FRSQ). To facilitate the new policy the government tabled a plan of action on intellectual property management and continued to offer companies a generous tax credit for R&D expenditures. Since 2001, the amount of funding provided by the FQRSC as a proportion of the amount coming to Quebec researchers from SSHRC/CRSH has increased dramatically. As the figures below indicate, between 2001 and 2003, the proportion has risen from 23 percent to 83 percent.[11]

Alongside the decline in federal transfers for PSE we can observe a phenomenal increase in the resources allocated to R&D. Between 1983–84 and 1992–93, federal cash transfers for PSE as a percentage of GDP declined from 0.56 to 0.41 per cent. By 1998–99, this figure had dropped to 0.25 per cent and to 0.19 per cent in 2004–05 (CAUT 2006, 14, fig. 1.1). As noted earlier, at the same time as federal transfer payments have decreased, Canada has strengthened its commitment to funding R&D in PSE institutions.

Between 1988–89 and 2010–11, the increase in federal spending on the four councils (SSHRC, NSERC, Canada Council, and Medical Research Council/Canadian Institutes of Health Research [MRC/CIHR]) was substantial. In constant 1988 dollars, the amount increased from $721 million to $2.392 billion, or 232 percent. While we can observe a dip in funding during the restraint years of the mid-1990s, the funding began to increase in 1997–98. The most dramatic change occurred for the MRC at the point it was transformed into the CIHR. Between 1999–2000 and 2003–04, the yearly funding for MRC/CIHR in constant 1988 dollars increased from $233 million to $474 million, an increase of approximately 100 percent. During the same time period, the comparable increases to NSERC and SSHRC were much less, at 18.25 percent and 34.38 percent, respectively.

In the 2009–10 fiscal year, the Networks of Centres of Excellence Program funded thirty-eight networks for a total of $122 million (NCE 2010, 26). Included here were 17 NCE ongoing networks,[12] 17 Centres of Excellence for Commercialization and Research, and 4 business-led NCEs. The latter two initiatives began in 2007. Over the twenty-year period, 1989 to 2009, the NCE program has invested a total of $1.53 billion in research (NCE 2009, 2). By January 2010, the CFI had awarded a total of $4.34 billion for both research and infrastructure (CAUT 2010–11, 45, table 5.3). By December 2010, all of the projected 2000 CRC chairs had been awarded. In addition to the original fund of $900 million, the federal government, over the period of 2005–06 to 2009–10, spent a total of $1.3 billion (CRC 2010). Finally, the government in 2008–09 distributed $325 million in indirect cost payments to 140 PSE institutions, including all those that grant degrees (AUCC 2009).

Furthermore, these policy decisions are set within a science and technology policy that emerged from competing definitions of science, utility, and the "public good" (Fisher and Rubenson 2010). At the policy level, the interests of capital are privileged under the guise of serving the national interest. By promoting industry access to publicly funded research, the science and technology policy recognizes that scientific research is simultaneously fundamental and useful. But the policy also skews the balance in favour of private interests and commercial science.

The balancing impact of the R&D agenda becomes apparent when we examine the total yearly federal program spending on PSE research. Between 1988–89 and 2010–11, this amount in constant 1988 dollars increased from $2.727 billion to $3.721 billion, for a total of $984 million, or 37 percent. At the same time, we recognize the imbalance within the R&D budget between groups of disciplines. Of the new research funding by the federal government between 1998–99 and 2004–05 (approximately $11 billion), only $1.02 billion, or 11.2 percent, funded research in the humanities and social sciences.[13]

When compared to other OECD countries between 1998 and 2002, Canada ranks among the top five on higher education expenditures on research and development (HERD) as a percentage of GERD. Of the thirteen countries reporting in 2004, Canada was at the top with 34.8 percent and twice the OECD average, which stood at 17.3 percent (OECD 2007; CAUT 2007, 53, fig. 8.4). Similarly, in 2004 Canada's HERD, as a percent of GDP at 0.69, was second only to Sweden in the OECD ranking. R&D spending rose from $10.3 billion in 1990 to $26.3 billion in 2005. Canada recorded the fastest growth in R&D spending in the G7 between 1997 and 2003. The federal government's support of university R&D in 2005–06, at $2.5 billion, for the first time exceeded its own internal R&D expenditures (Council of Canadian Academies 2006, 39–40, figs. 4.2 and 4.3). In 2004, the federal government intramural spending on R&D was almost $2.3 billion, a figure that had remained fairly constant the previous six years (Council of Canadian Academies 2006, 109 [box 6.4] and 39–40 [fig. 4.3]).

Yet when we examine GERD as a percentage of GDP, Canada does not have a high ranking. As a response to the 1997 bottom ranking (fifteenth) on the OECD table, the Liberal government made a commitment in 1998 to invest in R&D and bring Canada into the top five rankings. The latest ranking (2004) places Canada thirteenth (OECD 2007). At 2.01 percent, Canada was below the OECD mean of 2.25 percent and attained only half the score of the leader, Sweden (Council of Canadian Academies 2006, 38, fig. 4.1). In "Global PSE Rankings," Canada does reasonably well on accessibility but less well on affordability (Usher and Cervenan 2005). When compared to fifteen other countries, Canada ranked fifth on accessibility but a lowly eleventh on affordability.[14]

As noted earlier, Ontario, Quebec, and British Columbia account for a very large proportion of the federal research funding through the granting councils. We can observe a similar distribution when we examine the share of the total sponsored research funding. In 2007–08, Ontario accounted for 40.0 percent of this total, while Quebec and British Columbia accounted for 24.7 and 11.4 percent, respectively (CAUT 2010–11, 47, table 5.7). The same differential can be observed by focusing on the CFI. Between 1998 and 2010, Ontario received 44.0 percent of CFI awards, while Quebec and British Columbia received 26.2 and 12.2 percent, respectively (CAUT 2010–11, 45, table 5.2). Quebec and British Columbia were "winners" when it came to the allocation of CRC chairs, taking into account each province's proportion of "All Faculty" and "All Students." Between 2000 and 2008, Quebec accounted for 27.2 percent of the total number of chairs, and British Columbia accounted for 13.4 percent. Alberta was declared the other "winner," with Ontario trailing just under the winning ratio even though the province accounted for 37.2 percent of the total. The other six provinces were declared "losers" by CAUT (2010–11, 46, table 5.4).

As noted in the case study chapters, how much the provinces made R&D a priority may be illustrated by two indicators: (1) GERD expenditures as a percentage of GDP, which is a conventional indicator of research efforts, and (2) total R&D spending as a percentage by source.[15] In 2004, the total GERD in current dollars stood at just over $26 billion. Governments and higher education funded 23 and 16 percent, respectively, while business enterprise accounted for 49 percent. Of the total GERD, two provinces, Ontario and Quebec, accounted for $11.7 and $7.2 billion, respectively, or approximately 73 percent (Statistics Canada 2007). These are also the two provinces that have been most committed to creating provincial research funding structures in parallel to the federal ones. During the period 1990 to 2004, GERD as a percentage of GDP has been consistently above the Canadian statistic while British Columbia has been consistently below (see figure 5.3). Quebec overtook the OECD mean in 1998 at 2.2 percent and then remained substantially above the mean at around 2.75 percent in the years 2001 through 2004. Ontario overtook the OECD mean in 2001, and for the three years from 2002 to 2004 remained at approximately the same level. Throughout the period the Canadian statistic has been below the OECD mean (see Fisher and Rubenson 2010, 85, table 3.7). It follows that British Columbia has been substantially below the OECD mean.

Yet, despite all the rhetoric around the importance of R&D in a competitive global economy, when we examine total R&D expenditure by source of funding it appears that business has been far more committed than government. Between 1990 and 2004, the proportion of GERD provided by business increased in all three provinces (see figures 2.12, 3.9 ,and 4.7). If we extend the period to 2008 (see table 5.10), the increases in British Columbia, Quebec, and Ontario were 8, 7, and 4 percent, respectively. The pattern for government expenditures as a proportion of GERD for British Columbia and Quebec inversely mirrors that for business. The decreases between

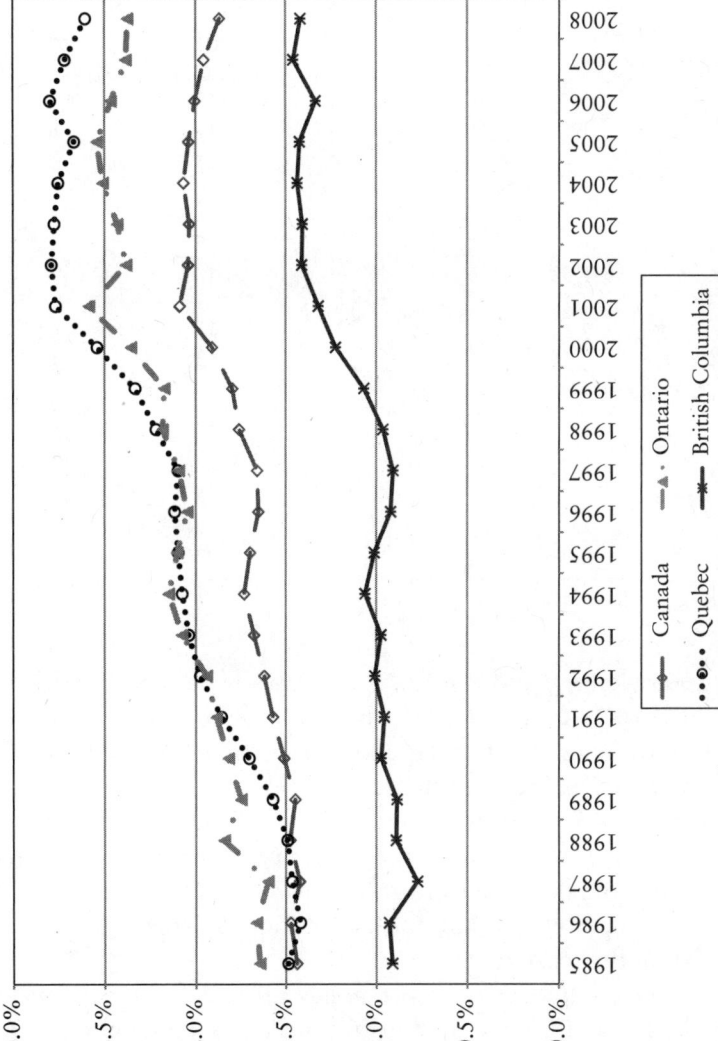

Figure 5.3
Gross domestic expenditures on research and development (GERD) as a proportion of GDP, 1985–2008.
Source: Statistics Canada.

Table 5.10
Proportion of GERD by source of funding and by province, 1990–2008

Province/source	1990 (%)	1998 (%)	2004 (%)	2008 (%)
BRITISH COLUMBIA				
Business	38	48	41	46
Government	38	23	21	24
Higher education	17	19	15	16
Foreign	4	8	17	11
Private non-profit	3	3	5	3
ONTARIO				
Business	45	48	56	49
Government	22	12	15	24
Higher education	14	11	15	16
Foreign	17	25	11	8
Private non-profit	2	2	2	3
QUEBEC				
Business	46	57	54	53
Government	28	17	22	22
Higher education	19	16	15	16
Foreign	5	8	7	7
Private non-profit	2	2	2	3

Source: CANSIM, table 385-001.

1990 and 2008 were 14 and 6 percent, respectively. While Ontario recorded a decrease through to 2004, by 2008 the proportion had increased slightly over the 1990 level. Foreign funding remained relatively stable in Quebec over the same period, while some contrary trends emerged in British Columbia and Ontario. Between 1990 and 2008, the foreign proportion rose from 4 to 11 percent in British Columbia and declined from 17 to 8 percent in Ontario. The proportion coming from private non-profit sources remained low and stable for all three provinces.

In overturning a fragmented science-policy history at the federal level, both the PC and Liberal administrations crafted a climate of commercialization by applying a multitude of mutually reinforcing policy instruments. Available data indicate that their efforts to drive science to the market have been successful. Business support of university research appears to be advancing more rapidly in Canada than elsewhere. However, the Canadian business sector remains a low performer, suggesting that Canada's industries continue to rely on publicly supported research rather than develop their own infrastructure. The federal government has promoted this tendency by providing the most favourable tax regime for investment in public R&D of any country among the G7.

In summary, at the provincial level it appears that, while governments across the political spectrum have clearly prioritized R&D in their policies, they have retreated from actual expenditures and have instead created the conditions that allow for investment from non-government funders, in particular business and, in the case of British Columbia, foreign sources.

Conclusion

DONALD FISHER AND KJELL RUBENSON

We began this book with a series of questions that revolved around the relation between PSE policy and its implementation across our three case study provinces from the early 1980s through to 2010. By documenting this relation in the PSE systems of British Columbia, Ontario, and Quebec, we laid the basis for a comparative analysis that would, in turn, allow us to clearly connect policy environments to outcomes. We set out to isolate those factors that enabled or constrained the attempts by state functionaries to achieve the envisaged policy outcomes. Our policy sociology orientation inevitably directed our gaze to the structural context and the play of social forces in both the creation of the policy environment and the restructuring of the state formation. Our assumption was that we could use an analysis of state PSE policy as a point of entry in order to locate these policies within what emerged as the key structural trends – namely, globalization, marketization, and academic capitalism. We could then attempt to provide a clearer understanding of the role of PSE in the transformation of the accumulation and legitimation functions of the state.

We accepted that, as in the rest of the Anglo-Saxon world, over the last two decades neoliberalism has come to comprise the raison d'être of Canadian politics. For Clement and Vosko (2003, viii), neoliberalism "has narrowed the discourse of political, economic, and social debate, transforming what it means to be liberal, social democratic, or even progressive conservative by asserting itself against social entitlements, rights, and citizenship." It followed that we were particularly interested in examining the connections between neoliberalism, PSE provincial policy, and the impact of that policy. In the 1990s, the battle against federal and provincial deficits and the adoption of neoliberal assumptions concerning the role of the state (Carroll and Shaw 2001) led governments to impose considerable budget cuts in education.

Our thesis regarding the broad political economy of PSE is that, over the last two decades, the adoption of this ideology has been a major cause of some dramatic changes in PSE policies and has brought about a fundamental transformation of PSE in Canada. The pressure for access has led to the emergence of new institutional types, raising new questions about differentiation, mandate, and identity and new lines of stratification. A trend towards vocationalism in the university sector has coincided with academic drift in the community college sector, leading to convergences in programming and institutional functions across systems as well as to competition for resources, students, and external partners. Unprecedented demand has made education a viable industry, sustaining both a proliferation of private providers and a range of new entrepreneurial activities within public institutions. Levels and objectives of public funding have swung dramatically over the period. Public investments in PSE, in the form of capital grants and tuition subsidies, have alternately expanded and contracted, being at some times applied across the board and at others targeted to specific social groups or economic sectors. Likewise, policy-makers have treated PSE at times as a mechanism for social inclusion and equality, at others as an instrument for labour force development, and at yet others as a market sector in its own right.

The rest of this chapter is divided into four segments. First is a comparison of the policy-making processes in the three provinces. The next two segments interpret our findings in relation to two of the three literature fields that inform our study. We begin with policy sociology and move on to the PSE literature. In these segments we focus on the interplay between the five policy themes that dominated our comparative analysis in chapter 5. These five themes are: (1 accessibility, (2) accountability, (3) marketization, (4) labour force development, and (5) research and development. The final segment focuses on the restructuring of the state.

POLICY-MAKING PROCESS

Three characteristics of the policy-making process stand out as we consider the similarities and differences between the three provinces. First is the degree to which the process has been consultative. Second, and closely related to the first, is the extent to which governments have used legislation as the means for setting policy. Both of these characteristics are part of the tension between pressure to centralize and pressure to decentralize – a tension that is a generic feature of all liberal democratic societies. Third is the role played by a systemic orientation to both planning and PSE.

Of the three provinces only Quebec can claim to have been consistent in adopting a consultative model. Governments across the political spectrum have created a wide range of venues for collaboration that has brought in all the stakeholders. Policy-makers use these collaborative endeavors to find points of convergence, which, in turn, lead to a consensus. The Quebec model of public management has at its heart inclusive consultative practices. In part, this is due to the presence of very powerful faculty and student unions that have not been afraid to exercise their power through strikes. Yet the approach is also housed in the rational, incremental approach to policy-making. The consistent assumption has been that, rather than making dramatic breaks, one should build incrementally on the policies in place.

At the same time, Quebec PSE, more than that of the other provinces, has a highly centralized decision-making process. The education ministries play a decisive steering role. The concentration of power in the state is used to steer systemic consultation and collaboration for the public good. Over the period of our study we have observed a certain decentralization of power in the college sector, while more power has been concentrated in the hands of the state at the university level. Changes in government policy in 2008 mark an increase in the control exercised by the state over both sectors.

In British Columbia and Ontario, the level of consultation has varied quite drastically. The changes are to some extent a result of different ideological orientations, individual leadership, and the ability of policy-making traditions to withstand forceful changes in the policy environment. The 1980s saw broad consultation taking place in both provinces. In British Columbia, the Social Credit Party's populist rural roots tied its extensive consultation exercises to its commitment to educational access. The government, and in particular Minister of Advanced Education Stanley Hagen, not only recognized the inherent and instrumental benefits of PSE but also regarded access as a democratic right. Similarly, the Liberals in Ontario maintained a broad consultation approach. The early 1990s saw a major divergence between the two provinces.

On the one hand, the NDP in British Columbia carried on the tradition of consultation through the 1990s, but it brought a stronger ideological commitment to these practices. It created a more inclusive tone to the policy discourse. The leadership believed that policy should be used to build foundations for a more social-democratic society. On the other hand, the NDP in Ontario drastically reduced the level of consultation as it responded to severe fiscal restraint. Government policy across the board, and including PSE, became a reactive, almost ad hoc, exercise rather than a measured rational process. Power was centralized and the policies took on a draconian quality. The trend was reinforced with the election of the neoliberal PC government. Public input was reduced at every turn. Power and decision making was increasingly centralized in the premier's office. PSE policy changed at a greater speed than at any other time in living memory as a massive legislative agenda aimed at rationalizing and reorganizing the system.

Since 2000, we have seen reversals of the above trends in both provinces. The election of the neoliberal government in British Columbia caused a radical rupture in the policy-making process. Consultation ceased to exist and a slew of legislation imposed the government's agenda. In contrast, the Liberals in Ontario went back to the historic traditions of transparent decision making and consultation through advisory bodies. The best symbol of their intregrative approach was the consultation exercise that resulted in the 2005 Rae Report.

While we can see many similarities in the structure of the three PSE systems, we also observe major differences in the extent to which governments adopted a systemic orientation to both planning and to PSE. In Quebec, the design of the system was decided in the 1960s and has not changed since. All governments have approached their planning and policy-making with a system orientation. This commitment, we argue, is connected to the Quebec model of public management and to the evidence-based rational incrementalism referred to earlier; but, more important, it is a central element in the nation-building identity that is taken for granted in Quebec. In contrast, neither British Columbia nor Ontario have had anything like a system orientation. While PSE in British Columbia is characterized by a degree of coordination, particularly around transfers between colleges and universities, policy-makers have never approached their task from a system perspective. The Liberal government was given the opportunity to change this state of affairs with the Campus 2020

Report in 2007 but chose not to implement its recommendations. Ontario records a complete absence of a system approach or system perspective. Even within the two sectors there is little evidence of policies designed with a system orientation in mind. This lack of system orientation has left a leadership vacuum that has often been exploited by individuals and institutions.

POLICY SOCIOLOGY

We conclude that the complexities uncovered in our comparative study are, at the very least, consistent with the policy sociology approach to PSE. We have documented how political, economic, and ideological factors have been the driving force behind the production and reproduction of PSE policy (Ball 1994; Taylor et al. 1997; Gale 1999, 2001; Rothstein 1999; Ozga 2000; Dale 2005; Robertson et al. 2007; and Rizvi and Lingard 2010). Following Bourdieu (1988), we have been able to document a number of "key moments" in PSE policy-making when governments changed direction. Four of these moments stand out and each is housed in the larger structural force of globalization and the force of political ideology. The first two occur in Ontario in 1995 and in British Columbia in 2001 with the election of governments with clear commitments to neoliberal ideology. The third moment occurred in the mid-1990s and had an impact on all three provincial governments as the federal government dramatically reduced its indirect, unconditional general funding of PSE and simultaneously began to dramatically increase its direct, conditional funding of R&D. Finally, the fourth moment occurred in the mid-2000s and had an impact on all three provincial governments as healthy economies and the global importance attached to PSE translated into rapid increases in provincial funding for PSE for the rest of the decade. As noted in chapter 5, this trend was encouraged in 2008, with increased federal allocations for PSE.

Over the last three decades provincial governments have linked Ontario's PSE policy to economic development and Ontario's competitiveness in the global economy. This has primarily been reflected in two ways: (1) through an emphasis on vocational and skills training and (2) through an emphasis on R&D (especially science and technology). There has been a distinct shift in emphasis in Ontario's PSE system away from liberal education and towards a vocational, technical education; and away from basic, curiosity-driven research and towards applied, market-driven research. The change in funding mechanisms towards tied and matched private-sector funding has moved the system towards the market and has placed a greater emphasis on vocational training, meeting labour market needs, and increasing market-oriented R&D.

PSE policy in Ontario is a reflection of the government employing fiscal strategies that include market mechanisms and market principles to assist in resource allocation and revenue generation, to address issues of accessibility and accountability, and to meet labour market needs. This policy approach does not involve outright privatization nor does it require the government to cede control of the PSE system to market forces; rather, it appears to represent a compromise whereby the universities maintain a degree of autonomy and the government maintains some degree of control over the postsecondary system. However, the introduction of market principles into Ontario's PSE policies comes within the historical context of a lack of system planning and the absence of a structural, co-coordinating component that oversees and integrates both/all sectors and develops coherent policy for the PSE system as a whole (as opposed to sectors within it). Market dynamics have crept into this void, providing direction and producing changes in the organizational arrangement of the system, even while the government promotes the structural status quo. This causes some concern, especially for those critical of allowing the market paradigm to operate in the public sphere. It also represents a significant divergence in recent years for PSE in Ontario, which, historically, has primarily been public and structurally stable. More than ever in its history, Ontario requires a clear vision of coordination and planning, along with a strong policy process, if it wishes to achieve a PSE system that is both public and structurally stable.

PSE in British Columbia has been and will continue to be a government priority. The public's perception that a good education is the passport to personal prosperity, coupled with the popular notion that an educated citizenry is necessary for a nation's prosperity, drives this policy priority. As long as the public continues to demand more PSE, any government, regardless of its political ideology, will accede. While funding has not always been generous for various reasons, including fiscal restraint, the budgets for education and PSE have often been spared when other areas have suffered deep cuts during economic downturns. In its attempt to cure the structural deficit and to balance the provincial budget by 2004–05, the Liberal government has protected the budgets of education and PSE while cutting the budgets of other ministries. Health is also exempted from cuts and has also experienced growth because, again, the voters have told government that it is the peoples' priority. As noted earlier, spending on health takes the largest proportion of the provincial budget in all three provinces. At the federal level, we noted in chapter 1 that, over the period from 1995–96 to 2010–11, transfers (tax points and cash) to the provinces for health increased dramatically while those for PSE and social assistance decreased slightly. Over the same period, the federal government turned its attention to funding R&D. Yet, here again, health was given a higher priority as the increases to CIHR far outstripped those for the other two granting councils.

The policy environment set by successive provincial governments has until recently been remarkably stable. Successive Social Credit and New Democratic administrations have been committed to "access" and vocationalism. The pressure for academic drift has come from within the system and from Interior communities who wanted more access to degree-granting programs outside the Vancouver and Victoria conurbations. Most recently, the operation of ideology can be recognized in the contrast between the NDP's freeze on student tuition fees versus the Liberal's program of re-regulation. While, since the mid-1980s no government as been able to ignore the importance of the market, the Liberal government elected in 2001 was the first to have enthusiastically supported the neoliberal approach to governing. Further, while the definition of what counts as a university has been changing, particularly with the advent of the university colleges and the "new" universities, British Columbia does seem to be on the verge of dramatic changes in the postsecondary system. Certainly, the link between political ideology and the implementation of marketization policies is clear in Ontario and British Columbia. The line of causation is clear and direct. In Quebec, the situation is more complex for the reasons given earlier. Still, we argue that the general move towards commodity production and academic capitalism described in the literature (Marginson 1997; Rooney and Hearn 2000; Slaughter and Rhoades 2004; Chan and Fisher 2008) is apparent and pervasive.

Yet it is important to highlight some of the tensions between political ideology, the theme of marketization, and practical politics when it comes to outcomes. First, while the NDP government in British Columbia in the 1990s did not follow the lead of the Ontario government and deregulate tuition fees, it did approve the creation of two public niche universities (Technical and RRU) as well as a private non-profit university (Sea to Sky, or Quest). Further, while the regulation of fees did fit well with this government's ideological stance it was also recognized as good electoral politics. Second, while the Liberal government in British Columbia was ideologically committed to deregulate tuition fees, it was also under tremendous pressure from university presidents to change this policy so they could fill the gap left by lower government transfers and increasing expenditures. Third, in Ontario the deregulation of fees was intertwined with the decline in federal funding, the ideological predisposition of the PCs to spend less on the public sector, and the funding gap that faced universities. Fourth, for all of the Liberal rhetoric in Quebec regarding raising tuition fess, the government simply faced too much opposition from all sides, but particularly from the students.

PSE policy at the federal and provincial levels has been driven by a changing political-economic imperative. The Canadian political establishment and the university community on the whole accept the position taken by the OECD (2003) that increased investment in R&D will enhance economic development. This acceptance, we argue, is due in part to what Gill (2003) labels "neoliberal constitutionalism" and supports the literature that documents how supranational organizations have helped proliferate neoliberal ideology (Schugurensky and Davidson-Harden 2003; Dale and Robertson 2003a, 2003b; Ginzburg et al. 2003). The OECD, through its reports, has consistently been an advocate of marketization. In working around the constitutional divisions of power, and as a means of increasing accountability, the Liberal federal governments of the 1990s followed the lead of the OECD by creating a raft of new policy instruments that were designed to dramatically increase R&D funding going to the academy. These investments would, it was argued, produce knowledge that, in turn, would lead to economic development and improved competitiveness in the international marketplace. At the same time, both PC and Liberal federal governments have used the political ideology of markets and quasi-markets to try to steer the academic community towards adopting commercial goals. The aim of science and technology policy since the late 1980s has been to soften the boundary separating the academy from industry (Fisher, Atkinson-Grosjean, and House 2001; Atkinson-Grosjean, House, and Fisher 2001; Fisher and Rubenson 2010).

At the provincial level, the "human resource" argument had, by the 1990s, replaced the language of "human capital" and was used, as in previous decades, to justify increased accessibility. Investing in human resources, it is argued, contributes to economic development at both individual and societal levels. While this language of justification cuts across political parties and all three provinces explored in this book, we can still see the force of different political ideologies. Quebec exceptionalism and nationalism had driven the relationship between the two levels of government to the extent that the province has benefited as much as have the others and, on many key occasions, has benefited more. The parallel R&D structures are designed to make the academic research enterprise in Quebec stronger than in any other province. The structure of the system and all of the provincial policies concerning students are designed to maximize accessibility. In contrast, British Columbia and Ontario, while very much in favour of increasing access, have also encouraged the creation of quasi-markets through the deregulation of fees. Again, the force of political ideology is clear as the NDP, PC, and Liberal regimes replace each other and, in turn, reverse or adopt new student tuition fee policies.

As we look across the five policy themes, we see that each of the three provinces intended to have an impact with regard to accessibility, accountability, labour force development, marketization, and R&D. Neoliberal ideology had the least impact in Quebec and, in that sense, it was in this province that the policy-making process was the most stable. Quebec's long-standing commitment to accountability translated into the strongest emphasis on efficiency in the PSE system. The emphasis on labour force development was sporadic but still important. Quebec was by far the leader in developing an R&D infrastructure and in providing for access and participation. This latter emphasis expressed itself though the mass-system structure, regulated low tuition fees, and strong financial assistance programs. In order, Ontario and British Columbia were the most affected by neoliberal ideology.

Ontario was at the forefront of creating quasi-markets by reducing funding and deregulating tuition fees. In conjunction with the pressure to move the system towards the market, we also observe a strong emphasis on accountability through performance indicators as well as a concomitant shift towards pushing the system to meet the demands of the labour market. While not as extensive as in Quebec, the Ontario government did more than any of the other eight provinces to support R&D. Whereas in British Columbia labour force development and general accessibility issues were dominant during the 1990s, we find that marketization and accountability become the dominant themes with the election of the Liberal government in 2001. R&D has been a minor theme in British Columbia.

Before leaving this section, it is important to emphasize the complex interplay between political, economic, and social forces. We have become increasingly aware of the difficulties that all policy researchers face when they attempt to explain the links between intent and outcome. In the body of this text, we document the numerous internal contradictions that emerged in each province. For example, the strong commitment to vocational education on the part of NDP governments in British Columbia through the 1990s did not translate into differential allocation of FTE between the vocational programs and the academic graduate programs. Similarly, during these years, in contrast to Ontario and Quebec, British Columbia maintained the total operating grant for PSE at a high level. Yet, when we look at the provincial funding per FTE enrolments, British Columbia recorded a substantial decrease while Ontario and Quebec remain stable. When we turn to accessibility and the overwhelming commitment by governments across the political spectrum to furthering this goal, it comes as a surprise to find that a lower proportion of people fifteen and over obtain PSE credentials, from a college diploma to a doctorate, in Quebec than in the other two provinces.

The policies adopted by the governments in all three provinces were housed in and contributed to the structural context. The examples given above speak to taking into consideration the importance of political ideology and political economy when trying to understand and to explain both the emergence of policy themes and their impact on PSE. Yet, as in the case with any social science endeavour, we become even more aware how difficult it is to move from narrative and description to a more general theory to explain changes in PSE systems.

HIGHER EDUCATION

Our examination of these three PSE systems confirms that the approach to coordination remains at the sector level. Yet, given the provision for movement between the colleges and universities in

British Columbia and Quebec, we can see a latent form of system-level coordination (Skolnik, Jones, and Soren 1998). Predictably, and in line with other OECD nations, each system experienced what Scott (1995) calls "massification" and, as in other industrialized, liberal democracies, continued along the road of the "Long Revolution" (Williams 1961). As part of this development we documented the increasing participation rate in PSE, which meant that all three provinces had moved beyond the "mass" threshold to hover around the 40 percent target that defines "universal" systems (Trow 1973). Again, this confirms the longer-term trend, which began in the mid-1960s, to move away from "elite" conceptions of PSE systems and, as noted earlier, was a direct result of the consistent emphasis on the accessibility theme. It should also be noted that, in comparison to other OECD countries, Canada is in the top rank with regard to participation rates.

As an outgrowth of the accessibility theme we show that academic drift continues to be an important trend. We document how successive governments in British Columbia expanded the number and type of institutions able to award degrees. This policy direction was driven by the desire to provide access to rural and Interior populations as well as by the pressure from institutional leaders (first in the colleges and then in the university colleges) for these changes. While not as extensive or as pronounced, the CAATs in Ontario were finally granted approval to offer applied degrees. Of our three cases, only Quebec has maintained the clear boundary between its colleges and its universities. This, we contend, is due to the breadth of the changes that took place in the 1970s. From the start, the creation of the Université du Québec, with its multiple campuses spread throughout the province, was designed to serve the whole population.

As a corollary to the developments described above, we have traced how these three PSE systems have changed, using the typology of system types developed by Clark (1987) and utilized by Scott (1995). By the beginning of our study, the BC and Ontario systems could best be characterized as "binary." By 2010, each system had moved into a mix of the four broad categories (binary, stratified, dual, and unified). Both British Columbia and Ontario lie somewhere between a binary and a stratified classification. We might simply call this type "differentiated." In such a system each sector is differentiated from the others; however, rather than having a single mission or function, the sectors have mixed functions. Quebec, on the other hand, has, throughout the period of our study, been stuck somewhere between the dual and unified categories. What we demonstrate is the need to rethink these categories by applying clear criteria across systems that become increasingly complex.

In any event, the changes in postsecondary system structure in British Columbia and Ontario are cases of "policy drift." These changes were for the most part reactive rather than predictive. Contrary to this, Quebec posited a systemic vision for PSE in the 1970s and has primarily stayed the course. Nation building is important here, but this resilience is also explained by the resistance to change due to the entrenched nature of PSE structural policies.

As noted earlier, the most important theme overall is accessibility. During the 1990s, British Columbia made the largest increase in funding. Quebec experienced a relatively steady state, while Ontario decreased funding. Between 1994 and 2008, tuition fees as a share of university operating revenue remained low in Quebec but increased dramatically in both Ontario and British Columbia following deregulation (see table 6.1). Participation rates go up in all three provinces. They go up the most in British Columbia, followed by Quebec and then Ontario.

Yet the dominance of accountability and marketization themes has not led to privatization; rather, as Slaughter and Rhoades (2004) point out, academic capitalism blurs the boundaries between public and private sectors, but it sustains a substantial level of public subsidy to PSE. Simultaneously, the public space in the academy is redefined as public monies shift to subsidize different activities, fields of work, and professionals. In many cases, capitalism academic style is not very successful in generating net revenues, and it leads to unanticipated, undesirable practices and outcomes. In the context of a conception of institutional purpose that is reduced to revenue enhancement, the academic knowledge/learning regime leads to an expanded range of educational services and to a reduced range of traditional-aged students. We also see an increasingly similar pattern in the effort of various types of universities and colleges to take advantage of global information and new economic opportunities in ways that reduce their distinctive involvement in local communities.

The redefinition of the public space as part of the academic capitalist knowledge/learning regime is particularly noticeable in Canada with regard to research policy (Metcalfe 2010). As previously noted, since 1997, the federal government has used a number of new policy

Table 6.1
Total government spending and tuition fees as a percentage of university operating revenue, 1994 to 2008

	Quebec		British Columbia		Ontario	
	Government Spending (%)	Tuition (%)	Government Spending (%)	Tuition (%)	Government Spending (%)	Tuition (%)
1994	80	14	73	18	73	23
2004	72	16	60	30	49	38
2008	70	21	58	40	49	42

Source: Adapted from CAUT Almanac, 2006, figure 1.4, p. 3. and CAUT Almanac, 2010–11, figure 1.2, p. 2.

instruments, as well as the three established funding councils, to dramatically increase the research funding going to universities. As a result, a key development in the academic research enterprise over the last fifteen years has been the emergence of a clearly distinguishable group of research-intensive universities. The increase in research funding has been concentrated in this relatively small group of universities. In 2008, fifteen[1] of the eighty-three universities listed by CAUBO accounted for approximately 80 percent of the total university research income.[2] Within all Canadian universities the natural, applied, and health sciences have been favoured, thereby exacerbating the level of internal stratification. All three provincial governments have been allies in this process through engaging in the matching-funds policy and, in the case of Quebec and Ontario, through their own R&D programs.

The redefinition is illustrated by the increases in federal funding going to support university R&D. In 2005–06, federal spending, at $2.5 billion, for the first time exceeded its own internal R&D expenditures (Council of Canadian Academies 2006, 39–40, figs. 4.2 and 4.3).[3] At the same time, and in spite of the very generous tax credits offered as an incentive to make these investments, Canada records a relatively low business expenditure on research (BERD) as compared to other OECD countries (41, fig. 4.4).

While successive federal governments fully intended to favour the natural, applied, and health sciences with increases in R&D, it is unclear whether or not they intended to create a new strata of "national" research-intensive universities. The "group of ten" (now thirteen) universities quickly took on the new identity as they enthusiastically competed for the R&D dollars. Alongside the increased differentiation across regions and between different types of universities, we have seen the academic model become more uniform across all universities. In this way, all Canadian universities have become part of a quasi-market.

RESTRUCTURING OF THE STATE

In general we find that PSE policy at the federal and provincial levels has been driven by a changing political-economic imperative. Political ideology is at times a critical factor and at other times is overwhelmed by larger structural forces such as globalization and marketization. We argue that, as PSE has become more central to the legitimation and accumulation functions served by the state, so PSE policy has become more closely tied to economic and social development. If R&D and labour force development primarily serve the accumulation function of the state, then accessibility and accountability serve its legitimation function both directly and indirectly by guaranteeing individual economic security (Spitzer 1987; Sears 2003).

The structural force of the discourse of the knowledge-based economy and globalization became clear in the mid-1990s as the federal government, in a whole "ensemble" of policies, decreased federal transfers to the provinces. As noted earlier, we regard this change in direction as a critical turning point in PSE policy and, further, in the restructuring of the state formation. The move away from unconditional transfers to the provinces for PSE and towards conditional R&D funding was grounded in the global neoliberal project. In this respect, we agree with Rizvi and Lingard (2010) as well as Dale (2005); Dale and Robertson (2003a); Schugurensky and Davidson-Harden (2003); Mundy and Iga (2003); Vidovich and Slee (2001); and Cohen and Kennedy (2007), who regard neoliberal ideology (marketization) as a key element in globalization. Further, we agree with Dale and Robertson (2003a) that, in general, social policy has been subjugated to economic policy. PSE policies at both levels of government have clearly favoured the creation of quasi-markets by encouraging postsecondary institutions, particularly research-intensive universities, to compete for research funding and graduate students. National well-being housed in free-market ideology became the watchword in PSE policy. Yet, at the same time, since the mid-1990s federal governments have become stronger and more dominant in the federal-provincial relationship in the PSE sector. Direct funding to individuals and institutions and the frequent requirement for the provinces to match this funding are the clear manifestation of the restructuring referred to above.

Globalization, by definition, is a force at the provincial level. The division of powers in any federal system means that the federal government must be concerned with national economic development. Yet, in the Canadian system, where the provinces are constitutionally responsible for education (including universities), we see heightened activity at the provincial level as these governments see themselves as competing nationally and at times globally. The concern with provincial economic development translates into massive investment in R&D in Ontario and Quebec. The anomaly here is British Columbia, which has responded much more slowly to this challenge. So for the most part we see a convergence around the ideas that, against the background of globalization and the knowledge-based economy, neoliberalism, competition, innovation, and economic development are linked together. In these ways, both levels of government are creating the conditions for capital accumulation and, at the same time, showing how they are accountable for the collective economic well-being.

Simultaneously, we have documented how all three provincial governments have consistently been concerned with accessibility. Provincial governments recognize their responsibility for the provision of access so that individuals can obtain postsecondary credentials and thereby attain some degree of economic security. Yet here, too, the force of globalization is clear as these governments utilize the general faith in markets to justify the increase in tuition fees. The anomaly here is Quebec, where successive administrations have either chosen or been pressed to maintain low tuition fees. In these ways, provincial administrations use PSE policies on accessibility to legitimate their governments while at the same time appearing to be accountable for individual economic security. Nowhere is this clearer than in the period from 2005 to 2010. Set within the influences of globalization and the knowledge economy, the policy environment drove Liberal governments in each province to increase their funding commitment to PSE in major ways. This happened in spite of the 2008–09 worldwide recession.

As we attempt to explicate the role of PSE policy in the restructuring process we use a model with three axes, each containing two cells. These axes are (1) provincial/federal, (2) legitimation/accumulation, and (3) accessibility/accountability. Our primary interest is in the series of relations that start at the provincial level, but we include the federal level because of the inter-relationships described above. Where variation between provinces exists we argue that, in the main, this is due to political ideology, in particular the force of globalization and neoliberal ideology. The four sets of provincial relations in our model are as follows: (1) accessibility/legitimation, (2) accessibility/accumulation, (3) accountability/legitimation, and (4) accountability/accumulation. In the first relational set, administrations across the political spectrum in all three provinces have consistently used PSE policies on accessibility to legitimate their governments. This has occurred in a number of ways, such as the increases in funding to move the participation rates into the "universal" category; the extension of degree-granting status to more institutions, thereby changing the structure of the PSE systems in both Ontario and British Columbia; and changes in tuition fee regulation associated with the election of neoliberal regimes. In the second relational set, again accessibility fulfills an accumulation function at the individual level as the opportunity to obtain credentials both academic and vocational is extended to a larger share of the population. We argue that PSE state policy on accessibility at the provincial level has primarily been aimed at achieving greater economic security for individuals. The connection between educational opportunity, the accumulation of what Bourdieu would call "cultural capital," and getting a job has become part of our taken-for-granted assumptions about modern society. It is in this way, we argue, that all three provincial governments have made PSE more central to the way they fulfill the legitimation and accumulation functions at the state level.

In the third relational set, we have documented the different ways that administrations have used PSE policy to make the systems more accountable to the state and, in turn, accountable to the population at large. Quebec, more than the other provinces, has practised a strict internal accountability regime, followed by Ontario. British Columbia has been the least inclined to adopt measures that apply to all institutions in the system. We argue that all three provinces have used PSE policy as a means towards attaining general accountability to the electorate and, thereby, have contributed to its legitimation function. The final relational set is most prominent in Ontario and Quebec, which have adopted clear science and technology policies that align with the federal initiatives around "innovation" and that have led to significant investments in R&D at the provincial level. Successive governments in both provinces have thereby made themselves accountable in a collective sense for linking the production of new knowledge to economic development. In so doing, these PSE policies have contributed to the accumulation function at the collective level both provincially and (by extension) nationally.

The long-term trend towards "universal" education is confirmed in our study as the "Long Revolution" has been extended to include PSE. We argue that this is not just a matter of political expediency but part of the accountability theme as governments want voters to see how responsive they are to all the issues associated with economic security at the individual level and with economic competitiveness at the collective level. As Bourdieu would put it, the connection between PSE and economic sustainability at both levels has become part of the Canadian "habitus" (see Harvey 2005). This connection has become a common orientation not only across the three provinces but also nationally as they account for approximately 75 percent of the total Canadian population. The mindset involved here becomes a taken-for-granted assumption about the way things work. In Gill's (2003) language, this is an example of "disciplinary neoliberalism" as governments and individuals internalize neoliberal ideology and, through self-governance and self-regulation, pursue a neoliberal agenda. Referring to Rizvi and Lingard (2010) and Harvey (2005), Phelps (2013, 39–40) concludes that neoliberalism, through the global social imaginary, fundamentally shapes "what is imagined to be possible and desirable by peoples (and especially policy-makers) all over the world" so that "we now imagine our world in market terms."

Our comparative approach also allows us to contribute to the debate among globalization theorists with regard to convergence and divergence (Wagner 2004; Mok 2003). As we have seen, there are many points of convergence, especially with regard to policies on accessibility and accountability. Yet, with regard to neoliberal ideology, which we regard as a defining characteristic of globalization, we found Quebec to be exceptional and therefore divergent. Even with the election and re-election of the Charest right-wing Liberal government (2003, 2007 [minority], and 2008), the province has not moved the PSE system in any significant way towards the market. The connection between nationalism and strong public-sector unions is the most likely explanation for this resistance. The refusal of the NDP government in British Columbia, during the 1990s, to pass the burden of reduced transfers from the federal government onto students by deregulating tuition fees is another example of divergence. Both of these examples provide strong evidence against the inevitability of globalization. Indeed, our study confirms the work of others (Brodie 1995; Hallak 2000; Green 2000; Amaral, Jones, Karseth 2002; Mundy and Iga 2003; Mok 2003; McBride 2001; King, Marginson, and Naidoo 2011), which shows that at some times governments help construct globalization by buying into neoliberalism while at other times they do not.

Changes in PSE policy at both levels of government illustrate the central part that universities are playing in the restructuring of the state (Amaral, Jones, and Karseth 2002; Morrow and Torres 2000). The willingness of the provinces, including Quebec, to allow the federal government to trespass across the constitutional divide with respect to R&D (NCE, CFI, CRC, indirect costs) is remarkable and, we argue, a significant indicator of structural change. Further, the acceptance of the matching-funding provisions as well as the adoption of science and technology innovation policies at the provincial level provides further insight into these changes. As we focus on the intersection between the state, PSE, and the market (Pusser 2008), we observe a redefinition of the public space and what is regarded as appropriate activity in that space. Here we have observed the creation of quasi-markets as universities compete with each other for research funds and for students. At the same time the state is alive and well. Rather than a retreat or a decline in state activity (Ohmae 1990; Giddens 2000a), we have documented, at the provincial level, differential outcomes in PSE that were a direct result of state policies.

In this volume, we argue that state PSE policy is a central component of state restructuring and mediation processes (Barrow 2005; Wood 2003). State PSE policy is a major way for the Canadian state to be globally competitive and, through increased accessibility, to provide for individual economic security. The marked differences we have documented in PSE policy across and between the provinces with respect to student fees and marketization is, we think, in part explained by the fact that Canada fits what Hall and Soskise (2001) refer to as the Anglo-Saxon model of welfare provision. These are countries they label as "liberal market" economies, and they contend that these countries have been more affected than "coordinated market" economies by the rhetoric, rather than the reality, of neoliberalism. We argue that this distinction provides some insight into Quebec exceptionalism.

In conclusion, we hope to have demonstrated how state PSE policy in Canada has, over the period of our study, taken on a more prominent role in guaranteeing and enhancing both capital accumulation and democratic legitimization (Offe 1984). Yet, in unravelling some of the complexity of the production and implementation of these policies, we find ourselves agreeing with the Third Way and "inclusive liberal" theorists (Saul 2005; Giddens 2003; Craig and Porter 2003, 2004; Roelvink and Craig 2004). Certainly, we have seen the force of neoliberal ideology at various critical turning points, but these changes in direction have to be set against the backdrop of governments that have avoided the extremes of privatization. The state has increasingly embedded PSE institutions in the market but, at the same time, has kept its long-term attachment to "welfare liberalism."

APPENDICES

Appendix 1
BC political parties, ministers responsible for post secondary education, ministries, and legislation

Party: Premier	Minister	Ministry	Policy/bill/reform/act
SOCIAL CREDIT			
William Vander Zalm 1986–91	Stan Hagen 1985–89	Advanced Education & Job Training	• 1989–Bill 72, Science Council Act • 1990–Bill 18, Science and Technology Fund Act
Rita Johnston 1991	Bruce Strachan 1990–91	Advanced Education, Training and Technology	• 1990–Bill 24, Private Post Secondary Education Act • 1990–Bill 40, UNBC Act
NEW DEMOCRATIC PARTY			
Mike Harcourt 1991–96	Thomas Perry 1991–93	Advanced Education, Training & Technology	• 1992–Bill 2, Repeal of BC Assoc. of Colleges Incorporation Act. Creation of Advanced Education Council of BC. • 1992–Bill 23, University Amendment Act: (1) repeal of section 80 prohibiting university faculty from forming faculty associations or trade unions; (2) authorization of public colleges and institutes to grant associate degrees.
	Dan Miller 1993–96	Skills, Training and Labour (Super-Ministry)	• 1993–Bill 15, allows for government to recover savings resulting from strikes or lockouts. • 1994–Bill 37, Skills Development and Fair Wage Act • 1994–Bill 22, College and Institute Amendment Act: (1) university colleges and institutes given the power to grant baccalaureate degrees; (2) allows colleges and institutes to elect faculty students and staff to governing boards. • 1994–Bill 23, Institute of Technology Amendment Act
	Elizabeth Cull 1993–96	Minister of Finance and Corporation Relations	• 1995–Bill 49, Royal Roads University Act • 1994–Bill 52, Public Education Labour Relations Act

Appendix 1
BC political parties, ministers responsible for post secondary education, ministries, and legislation (*Continued*)

Party: Premier	Minister	Ministry	Policy/bill/reform/act
NEW DEMOCRATIC PARTY			
Glen Clark 1996–99	Paul Ramsey 1996	Education, Skills and Training	• 1996–University Foundations Act • 1996–Accountants (Certified General) Act • 1996–Accountants (Chartered) Act
	Moe Sihota 1996		• 1996–Accountants (Management) Act • 1996–Applied Science Technologists and Technicians Act
	Joy MacPhail 1996–97	Education, Skills and Training/Labour	• 1996–Architects Act • 1996–Architects (Landscape) Act • 1996–Engineers and Geoscientists Act • 1996–Music Teachers (Registered) Act
	Paul Ramsey 1997–98	Education, Skills and Training	• 1997–Bill 30, Technical University of BC Act: established TechBC as degree granting
	Andrew Petter 1998–2000	Advanced Education, Training and Technology	• 1997–Bill 43, Industry Training and Apprenticeship Act: replaced previous apprenticeship Act • 1998–Bill 8, Tuition Freeze Act • 1999–Bill 59, Tuition Freeze Act • 2000–Bill 6, Tuition Freeze Act
Dan Miller 1999–2000	Graeme Bowbrick 2000	Advanced Education, Training and Technology	

Ujjal Dosanjh 2000–01		
	Cathy McGregor 2000–01	• 2001–Bill 9, Access to Education Act: reduced tuition fees, froze mandatory ancilliary fees, provided compensation for fee institutions for fee differentials
LIBERAL		
Gordon Campbell 2001–11		
	Shirley Bond 2001–04	Advanced Education	• 2001–Bill 28, Public Education Flexibility and Choice Act: removed issues of class size, length of academic year, and use of distance education methods from the bargaining table. • 2001–Bill 22, Skills Development & Fair Wage Repeal Act • 2002–Bill 15, Degree Authorization Act: (1) private and public institutions to offer degree programs; (2) public colleges and institutes to offer applied baccalaureate degrees; (3) university colleges to offer applied master's degrees. • 2002–Bill 50, Advanced Education Statutes Amendment Act: repealed TechBC and moved programs to SFU. • 2002–Private Members Bill, Sea to Sky University Act (Quest University) • 2003–Bill 35, Advanced Education Statutes Amendment Act • 2004–Bill 52, Private Career Training Institutions Act (replaced Private PSE Act)
	Graham Bruce 2001–05	Skills Development and Labour	• 2002–Bill 28, Public Education Flexibility and Choice Act
	Ida Chong 2004–05	Advanced Education	• 2005–Bill 2, Thompson Rivers University Act
	Murray Coell 2005–09	Advanced Education	• 2007–Bill 23, Knowledge Network Corporation Act • 2008–Bill 34, University Amendment Act

Appendix 1
BC political parties, ministers responsible for post secondary education, ministries, and legislation (*Continued*)

Party: Premier	Minister	Ministry	Policy/bill/reform/act
	Moira Stilwell 2009–10	Minister of Advanced Education and Labour Market Development	
Christy Clark 2011–present	Naomi Yamamoto 2011–present		• 2011–Bill 18, Advanced Education Statutes Amendment Act: (1) the Personal Education Number system, which tracks students in the BC educational system, to include private educational institutions; 2) board members of colleges and universities are to act in the best interests of the institution; 3) update of the Architects Act.

Appendix 2
Ontario's publicly-funded universities

Brock University	University of Toronto	Ryerson Polytechnic
Lakehead University	University of Western Ontario	Carleton University
Nipissing University	University of Ottawa	Laurentian University
Queen's University	University of Waterloo	Wilfrid Laurier University
Trent University	University of Guelph	McMaster University
University of Windsor	York University	University of Ontario Institute for Technology (OIT)
Ontario College of Art and Design	Royal Military College[1]	Algoma University

Note:
1 The Royal Military College was created by the Government of Canada in 1874 and is funded by the federal government. It has the authority to grant degrees under an Ontario provincial act passed in 1959.

Appendix 3
Privately funded degree-granting institutions in Ontario

1 Baptist Bible College Canada and Theological Seminary
2 Masters College and Seminary (formerly Eastern Pentecostal Bible College)
3 Canada Christian College and School of Graduate Theological Studies
4 Ner Israel Yeshiva College
5 Emmanuel Bible College
6 Redeemer University College
7 Faithway Baptist College
8 St Phillips Seminary
9 Great Lakes Bible College
10 Talpiot College
11 Heritage Baptist College and Heritage Theological Seminary (formerly Central Baptist Seminary and Bible College and London Baptist Bible College)
12 Theological College of Reformed Canadian Churches
13 Institute for Advanced Judaic Studies
14 Toronto Baptist Seminary and Bible College
15 Institute for Christian Studies (ICS)
16 Tyndale College and Theological Seminary (formerly Ontario Bible College)
17 Maimonides Schools for Jewish Studies

Appendix 4
Ontario, political parties, ministers, ministries and major initiatives

Party: Premier	Minister	Ministry	Selected major policy and legal initiatives
LIBERAL David Peterson 1985–90	Gregory Sorbara 1985–87 Lyn McLeod 1987–89 Sean Conway 1989–90	Ministry of Colleges and Universities	1986–90: The Corridor Funding Negotiations related to implementation of a new university funding system 1988:*The Report of the External Advisor to the Minister of Colleges and Universities on the Future Role and Function of the Ontario Council on University Affairs and its Academic Advisory Committee* (the Stubbs Report) 1986: Premier's Council Report –*Competing in the New Global Economy* 1986: Premier's Council on Technology (Fund) –*People and Skills in the New Global Economy* 1987: creation of Ontario Centres of Excellence (OCE) 1990: Premier's Council Report –*People and Skills in the New Global Economy* 1990: Freedom of Information and the Protection of Privacy Act, R.S.O. c. F.31
NEW DEMOCRAT PARTY Bob Rae 1990–95	Richard Allen 1990–93 Dave Cooke 1993–95	Ministry of Colleges and Universities and Ministry of Skills Development Ministry of Education and Training[1]	1990: *Vision 2000: Quality and Opportunity* 1990: Trades Qualification and Apprenticeship Act, R.S.O., c.17 as amended 1991:Commission of Inquiry on Canadian University Education (Stuart Smith Commission) AUCC 1992: *Transfer of Undergraduate Course Credit among Ontario Universities: Report and Recommendations* (Baker Report) –COU

PROGRESSIVE CONSERVATIVE			
Michael Harris 1995–2002	John Snobelon 1995–97		1992–93: *New Directions II: A Blueprint for Learning in Ontario*
	David Johnson 1997–99		1993: Task Force on Advanced Training-*No Dead Ends*. (Pitman Task Force)
	Janet Ecker 1999–2002		1993: *University Accountability: A Strengthened Framework Report of the Task Force on University Accountability* (Broadhurst Report)
	Elizabeth Witmer 2002–present	Ministry of Education[2]	1994: College University Consortium Council
			1996: *Excellence Accessibility Responsibility: Report of the Advisory Panel on Future Directions for Post secondary Education* (David Smith Commission)
			1998 Access to Opportunities Program (ATOP)
			1999: College-university degree completion accord
			1999: SuperBuild fund created
			1999: KPI's introduced for colleges and universities
			2000: Investing in Students Task Force – *Portals and Pathways*
	Dianne Cunningham 2002–present	Ministry of Training, Colleges and Universities[3]	2000: PSE Quality Assessment Board created
Ernie Eves 2002–03			2000: PSE Choice and Excellence Act
			2000: Tuition deregulation (partial)
			2001: Aim for the top Scholarship Fund created
			2001: UOIT created
			2002: University of Ontario Institute of Technology Act, S.O. c.8 Schedule. O as amended

Appendix 4
Ontario, political parties, ministers, ministries and major initiatives (*Continued*)

Party: Premier	Minister	Ministry	Selected major policy and legal initiatives
Dalton McGuinty 2003–07	Mary Anne Chamber 2003–05	Ministry of Training, Colleges and Universities	2002: Ontario Colleges of Applied Arts and Technology Act, S.O. c. 8 Schedule F as amended 2002: Ontario Colleges of Art and Design Act, S.O. c.8, Schedule. E as amended 2002: Ontario College of Trades and Apprenticeship Act, S.O. chapter 22 2003: Tuition freeze 2005: *Ontario: A Leader in Learning* (Rae Report) 2005: *Reaching Higher: The McGuinty Government Plan for PSE* 2005: Private Career College Act reviewed. S.O. c. 28. Sched. L 2005: The Ontario Trust for Student Support created
2007–12	Chris Bentley 2005–07		2005: Expanding the Ontario Youth Apprenticeship Program (OYAP) 2005: Quality Improvement Fund created 2005: Facilities Renewal Program created 2005: Higher Education Quality Council of Ontario Act created HEQCO 2005: Accessibility for Ontarians with Disabilities Act passed 2005: Apprenticeship Enhancement fund (AEF) created 2005: Ontario Youth Apprenticeship Program (OYAP) created 2005: Historic Labour Market Partnership Agreements/Labour Market Development Agreements (LMDA/LMPA) signed with federal govenrment

	2005: Ministry of Research and Innovation created that funds research across ministries-Ontario Research fund (ORF) created under this Ministry
	2006: Universities brought under the *Freedom of Information and Protection of Privacy Act*
	2006: Tuition freeze lifted and regulated tuition framework instituted until 2009-10
	2006: Fair Access to the Regulated Professions Act, S.O., c. 31
	2007: Announcement of plans to introduce legislation to establish an independent Algoma University
	2007 Office of the Fairness Commissioner created
	2007: Announcement of plans to introduce legislation to establish an independent Algoma University.
John Milloy 2007–2011	2008: Algoma University Act, S.O.2008, c.13. Algoma University College converted into Algoma University.
	2008: Colleges Collective Bargaining Act, 2008, S.O. 2008, c.15
	2009: Canada-Ontario Labour Market Agreement on Training and Skills Development to complement LMDA.
	2009: Ontario Labour Mobility Act S.O. c. 24 passed
	2009: Ontario College of Trades and Apprenticeship Act passed
	2010: Colleges Integrating Immigrants to Employment (CIITE) program
	2010: Open Ontario plan and Ontario Online Institute announced
	2011: Ontario Council on Articulation and Transfer (ONCAT) created.
	2011: Postsecondary Education and Training Policy Framework for Aboriginal Learners released

Notes:
1. Super ministry with elementary, secondary, and postsecondary education integrated into one ministry.
2. Ministry of Education and Training is split into two: Ministry of Education and Ministry of Training, Colleges and Universities. Ministry of Education is responsible for elementary and secondary education.

Notes: (*Continued*)

3. In the area of postsecondary education, the Ministry of Training, Colleges and Universities is responsible for:
   - developing policy directions for universities and colleges of applied arts and technology
   - planning and administering policies related to basic and applied research in this sector
   - authorizing universities to grant degrees
   - distributing funds allocated by the provincial legislature to colleges and universities
   - providing financial assistance program for postsecondary school students
   - defining courses of study at faculties of education
   - registering private career colleges

   In the area of training, the Ministry of Training, Colleges and Universities is responsible for:
   - developing policy directions for adult education and labour market training
   - managing provincial relations with the federal government concerning training programs
   - setting standards for occupational training, particularly for trades under the Trades Qualification and Apprenticeship Act
   - managing provincial programs to support workplace training and workplace preparation, including apprenticeship, career and employment preparation and adult literacy and basic skills
   - undertaking labour market research and planning

Appendix 5
Quebec's universities

	Number of students (autumn 2011)	Website
Bishop's University (1853)	2,762	www.ubishops.ca
Concordia University (1974)	35,207	www.concordia.ca
Université Laval (1852)	41,523	www.ulaval.ca
McGill University (1829)	35,847	www.mcgill.ca
Université de Montréal + HEC + École polytechnique	63,935	www.umontreal.ca
Université de Montréal (1920)	44,901	www.umontreal.ca
École Polytechnique (1873)	6,946	www.polymtl.ca
HEC-Montréal (1907)	12,088	www.hec.ca
Université de Sherbrooke (1954)	22,131	www.usherbrooke.ca
Université du Québec (1968) with the exception of TÉLUQ	83,803	www.uquebec.ca
Université du Québec à Chicoutimi (UQAC)	6,533	www.uqac.ca
Université du Québec à Montréal (UQAM)	40,791	www.uqam.ca
Université du Québec à Rimouski (UQAR)	6,430	www.uqar.ca
Université du Québec en Abitibi-Témiscamingue (UQAT)	2,832	www.uqat.ca
Université du Québec en Outaouais (UQO)	6,390	www.uqo.ca
Université du Québec à Trois-Rivières (UQTR)	12,161	www.uqtr.ca
École nationale d'administration publique (ENAP)	1,981	www.enap.ca
École de technologie supérieure (ETS)	6,164	www.etsmtl.ca
Institut national de la recherche scientifique (INRS)	521	www.inrs.uquebec.ca
TOTAL	268,167	

Source: CREPUQ http://www.crepuq.qc.ca/spip.php?article102&lang=fr

Appendix 6
Summary of targets and indicators and percentage of additional revenue allocated to them (percentage rate)

Targets	Indicators	Percentage of additional revenue
QUALITY OF TEACHING AND STUDENT SERVICES		
• Improve the equality of training and the graduation rate at all levels • Improve the supply of student support services • Improve the accessibility of university education for emerging clienteles	• Rate of student support and supervision by regular professors • Student retention rate • Graduation rate • Number of additional positions dedicated to supporting emerging clienteles	50 to 60%[1]
QUALITY OF RESEARCH		
• Step up research activities	• Resources allocated to research infrastructure and complementary training infrastructure (information technologies, libraries, etc.) • Number and amount of grants and research contracts obtained from the private sector and federal research funds	15 to 25%[1]
COMPETITIVE POSITIONING OF UNIVERSITIES IN CANADA AND ABROAD		
• Increase investment in clusters of excellence • Enhance the reputation of universities	• Number of world-class professors or researchers hired • Number of foreign students • Number and scope of projects carried out in clusters of excellence in cooperation with national and international partners	10 to 20%
ADMINISTRATION AND MANAGEMENT		
• Improve governance • Improve the financial situation of universities	• Members of the board of directors who sit on committees of strategic importance in the management of the university • Result targets associated with maintaining balanced budgets and eliminating annual deficits and the accumulated deficit • Growth rate of total remuneration compared with the government's pay policy • Annual targets for revenue from donations collected during fund-raising campaigns	5 to 15%

Source: Gouvernement du Québec (2011), 55.

1 The additional revenue derived from the tuition fee increase must be devoted exclusively to "quality of teaching and student services" and "quality of research."

Appendix 7
Québec political parties, ministers responsible for postsecondary education, ministries and measures in PSE, 1960–2011

Party: Premiers	Minister	Ministry	Policy/Bill/Reform/Act
PARTI LIBÉRAL			
Jean Lesage 1960–62 1962–66	Paul Gérin-Lajoie 1964–66	Ministère de l'Éducation	Building the system: Parent Report (1961–66) Universal program of student loans and grants Creation of the ministère de l'Éducation and the Conseil supérieur de l'Éducation (1964)
UNION NATIONALE			
Daniel Johnson 1966–68	Jean-Jacques Bertrand 1966–67	Ministère de l'Éducation	Creation of the cégeps (1967) Creation of the Université du Québec (1968)
Jean-Jacques Bertrand 1968–70	Jean-Guy Cardinal 1967–70		Creation of the Conseil des universités Creation of FCAC (1969)
PARTI LIBÉRAL			
Robert Bourassa 1970–73 1973–76	Guy Saint-Pierre 1970–72	Ministère de l'Éducation	First document of scientific policy (1971) Operation "General objectives of Higher Education" of the Conseil des universités (1973–76)
	François Cloutier 1972–75		
	Jérôme Choquette 1975–75		Creation of Concordia University (1974) Evaluating the collegial system: Nadeau Report (1975)
	Raymond Garneau 1975–76		
	Jean Bienvenue 1976–76		

Appendix 7
Québec political parties, ministers responsible for postsecondary education, ministries and measures in PSE, 1960–2011 (Continued)

Party: Premiers	Minister	Ministry	Policy/Bill/Reform/Act
PARTI QUÉBÉCOIS			
René Lévesque 1976–81	Jacques-Yvan Morin 1976–80	Ministère de l'Éducation	Commission of studies on the universities (1978)
1981–85	Camille Laurin 1980–84	Ministère de l'Enseignement supérieur et de la Science et de la technologie	Création du Conseil des collèges (1979)
	Yves Bérubé 1984–85		White et green books about scientific research (1979–80)
			Creation of the Conseil de la science et de la technologie (1983)
			First sectoral studies of the Conseil des universités on the engineering sector
Pierre-Marc Johnson 1985–85	Jean-Guy Rodrigue 1985–85		Creation of the ministère de l'Enseignement supérieur et de la science (1984)
PARTI LIBÉRAL			
Robert Bourassa 1985–89	Claude Ryan 1985–90	Ministère de l'Enseignement supérieur et de la Science (et de la technologie)	CRÉPUQ's policy of periodic evaluation of programs
1989–94	Lucienne Robillard 1990–94		New sectoral studies of the Conseil des universités
			Increase of university tuition fees (1993)
			Réforme de l'enseignement collégial
			Dissolution of the Conseil des collèges and the Conseil des universités (1993)
Daniel Johnson (fils) 1994–94	Jacques Chagnon 1994–94		Creation of the Commission d'évaluation de l'enseignement collégial

PARTI QUÉBÉCOIS			
Jacques Parizeau 1994–96 Lucien Bouchard 1996–2001 Bernard Landry 2001–03	Jean Garon 1994–96 Pauline Marois 1996–98 François Legault 1998–2002 Sylvain Simard 2002–03	Ministère de l'Éducation	Universities Commission on programs Bill 95: more accountability First universities' policy (2000) University funding policy (2000) Performance contracts between MEQ and the universities (2000–03) Science and innovation policy (2001)
PARTI LIBÉRAL			
Jean Charest 2003–2007 2007–2008 2008–	Pierre Reid 2003–2005 Jean-Marc Fournier 2005–07 Michelle Courchesne 2007–	Ministère de l'Éducation, du Loisir et du Sport	Parliamentary commission on the quality, accessibility and funding (2004) Forum on the future of collegial system (2004) Merger of TÉLUQ with UQAM (2005) Indirect cost of research policy (2005) New university funding formula (2005) Increase of university tuition fees (2007) Bills on the governance of cégeps and universities

Notes

CHAPTER ONE

1 Currently, Paul Axelrod and his collaborators on a SSHRC project (Making Policy in Post-Secondary Education) are using an analytic framework that bears a strong resemblance to policy sociology.
2 Dr Claude Trottier (Laval University) is the principal investigator for the Quebec case study. Dr Donald Fisher (UBC) and Dr Kjell Rubenson (UBC) are the principal investigators for the British Columbia case study and the coordinators for the whole study. Dr Theresa Shanahan (York University) is the principal Investigator for the Ontario case study.
3 These statistics are all taken from CAUT (2010–11).
4 The three teams in British Columbia, Ontario, and Quebec conducted nine, eleven, and eleven interviews, respectively.
5 These distinctions refer to thresholds of participation rates for the eighteen- to twenty-four-year-old population in higher education systems. The transition from "elite" to "mass" is at 15 percent, and from "mass" to "universal" is at 40 percent.
6 When comparing and categorizing systems using this typology, it is important to keep in mind that the definition of "higher" education varies somewhat by jurisdiction so that certain types of institutions may be included or excluded in "higher education" in different jurisdictions. This typology adopts the local definitions of what constitutes "higher" education without accounting for such discrepancies. Canada has tended to adopt a more inclusive definition of PSE. Additionally, this formulation takes no account of the division between public and private sectors in systems (which mark both the United States and Japan).

7 This whole section draws heavily on Fisher et al. (2006). We have updated the five appendices to 2010–11 and charts 3 through 10 accordingly. Detailed information on the years between 2003–04 and 2010–11 is available on request.
8 The federal spending power draws on the historic prerogative of the Crown to make gifts to its citizens (Cameron 2004, 7).
9 Through the 1970s and into the 1990s, federal responsibility for health and social welfare was housed in the federal Department of Health and Welfare. Upon its creation in 1994, Human Resources Development Canada (HRDC) took over the responsibility for social welfare. Finally, in 2003, when HRDC was split into two ministries – Social Development Canada and Human Resources and Skills Development Canada (HRSDC) – the former took over social welfare and the latter took over the educational skills development components.
10 For the first time after the 2004 election, the Liberal government appointed a parliamentary secretary responsible for PSE in HRSDC.
11 Section 93 of the Canadian Constitution Act, 1982, gives primacy to provincial authority over education.
12 These are outlined in Section 91 of the Canadian Constitution Act, 1982.
13 Registered Indian families living off reserve do not come under federal jurisdiction. Métis and non-status Aboriginal students come under provincial jurisdiction. Inuit peoples, by force of a 1939 Supreme Court decision, became "Indian" under the Constitution and, therefore, their affairs are also administered under the Indian Act (Miller 2004). Early implementation of the Indian Act saw the government enlist churches to operate schools within Indian communities. Their aim was to Christianize and assimilate Aboriginal people(s) into the lower strata of the dominant society, often brutally and without regard for local culture, language, traditions, and values. In the 1950s, the federal government began to operate its own schools. In the 1960s, attempts were made to integrate Indian children into provincial school systems. Since the 1970s, Aboriginals have struggled to assert jurisdiction over their own education within their claim of self-government. By 1973, the federal government accepted local control of education (Government of Canada 1996).
14 This program saw the federal government enter into bilateral agreements with the provinces to provide money for support of minority languages programs, including immersion programs, and also protected other minority language opportunities (Young and Levin 2002).
15 Until the late 1980s, there was an assistant deputy minister of postsecondary education in the Secretary of State Department.

16 It should be noted that various federal ministries, like Industry Canada, HRSDC, Social Development Canada, and Heritage Canada, do directly fund a small amount of academic research.
17 For details of the impact of these policy instruments, see Fisher and Rubenson (2010).

CHAPTER TWO

1 All of the population numbers are derived from Population Estimates contained in Table 510001, Cansim II (Statistics Canada 2012).
2 In 2002, the incoming Liberal government had dismantled OLA, established in 1988 by the Scored government, and replaced it as a distance education network of publicly funded postsecondary institutions in British Columbia.
3 The first private university in British Columbia was the now defunct Notre Dame University in Nelson. The institution was founded as a junior Roman Catholic college in 1950, operating under the name Notre Dame University College. In 1963, it received a charter from the Government of British Columbia and was renamed Notre Dame University. In 1977, at the request of its Board of Directors, ownership of the institution was transferred to the provincial government. It was renamed David Thompson University Centre and operated as a branch campus of UVic. In 1984, citing high costs of operation, the provincial government permanently closed the institution.
4 See appendix 1 for a list of the ministers responsible for PSE.
5 The successor to Notre Dame University.
6 The change in accounting practices refers to where the debt of Crown corporations was placed.
7 These recommendations included a more stable funding process that would allow for long-term institutional planning; more funds for literacy and adult basic education; assured provision of first- and second-year university courses through all regional colleges; and a range of services specially tailored to underrepresented groups such as remote communities, Aboriginals, students with disabilities, and the prison population.
8 Confidential interview by authors, October 2004. The implication here is that the initiative contained a high level of political capital as it appeared that university education had in one fell swoop been expanded to three interior population centres.
9 Cariboo College in Kamloops, Malaspina College in Nanaimo, and Okanagan College in Kelowna.

10 See "Opening Remarks by Premier Mike Harcourt," Premier's Summit: Skills Development and Training, summary of proceedings, 23–25 June 1993 (BC Government 1994a, 48; 1994b).
11 Confidential interview by authors, October 2003.
12 Another solution was the colleges' rapid entry into the international education market. Foreign student recruiting by Canadian institutions increased steadily since the 1980s and, in 2000, was estimated to be worth $203 million in annual direct investment to the BC economy alone and $2.5 billion nationally (British Columbia Centre for International Education [BCCIE], 2000). By the mid-1990s it was not uncommon, according to one researcher, "for the revenue from international education activities to represent between 10 percent and 20 percent of the entire college budget" (Knowles 1995).
13 These six were: Malaspina University College, Okanagan University College, University College of the Cariboo, University College of the Fraser Valley, Emily Carr College of Art and Design, and BCIT.
14 In 1996, Glen Clark took over the leadership of the party and became premier.
15 Confidential interview by authors, October 2004.
16 At the same time, schools offering only English as a second language (ESL) programs were removed from the oversight of this new body. This was in response to pressure from ESL school operators for relief from the burden of government regulation.
17 The legislation was motivated, in part, by complaints from administrators in the public colleges, university colleges, and institutes that they were prevented by collective agreements from implementing innovations to improve efficiency. As a consequence of the outrage from BC educators and CAUT's threat to censure any institution that used the powers granted under Bill 28, to date no institution has used this authority. Still, the threat of using these powers did result in some changes to collective agreements in the normal course of bargaining. The universities were not included in this legislation because, when approached by government, university presidents said they had all the flexibility they needed.
18 Formally known as *First Ministers and National Aboriginal Leaders: Strengthening the Relationship and Closing the Gap* (British Columbia First Nations, the Province of British Columbia and the Government of Canada 2005).
19 Confidential interview by authors, October 2003.
20 Ibid.
21 Ibid.

22 This shorter time period takes into account the demise of the university colleges.
23 Included here are the incomes from any wholly owned enterprise, such as a hall of residence, a cafeteria, or a car park.

CHAPTER THREE

1 All of the population numbers are derived from Population Estimates contained in Statistics Canada, 1 July 2010, table 510001, estimates of population, by age group and sex, for 1 July, Canada, provinces, and territories, annually (persons unless specified)), CANSIM database, Census Canada.
2 This number continues to change annually. See http://tcu.gov.on.ca/eng/general/postsec/opconsents.html for all degree programs offered under ministerial consent. See http://www.peqab.ca/completed.html for most recent completed applications.
3 This includes two new universities: (1) the Ontario College of Art and Design and (2) Algoma University. Also, the Royal Military College, which is funded by the Government of Canada, has degree-granting authority under provincial legislation. Further, Dominican University College, described as a bilingual Roman Catholic University that offers civil and pontifical degrees in theology and philosophy, receives funding from MTCU but is not part of the Council of Ontario Universities nor is it treated as part of the university sector. It received its Ontario University Charter in 1967. It is a publicly funded, degree-granting institution with limited degree-granting authority that is not considered a university or a CAAT. See appendix 2 for a listing of the universities.
4 This act provides that institutions seeking to offer degrees, or programs of postsecondary study leading to degrees, or seeking to be known as a university must either have the authorization of an act of the Legislative Assembly of Ontario or have the consent of the MTCU.
5 Humber College, Conestoga College, Sheridan College, Seneca College, and George Brown College all have ITAL designation and authority to offer up to 15 percent of their programming at the baccalaureate level; however, only Conestoga, Humber, and Sheridan have employed the ITAL designation. See Charles (2011).
6 See http://www.tcu.gov.on.ca/eng/generak/postsec/opconsents.html. See also http://www.peqab.ca/completed.html.
7 Many institutions offer non-vocational training that does not lead directly to employment (e.g., driving instruction for non-commercial vehicles, speed-reading, health and fitness, and tax preparation). These programs

are non-vocational in nature, and the colleges offering them are not required to register under the Private Career Colleges Act. Non-registered programs are not included as PCCs listed by the ministry and are not scrutinized by the Ministry of Training, Colleges and Universities.

8 The COU consists of the president of each Ontario university and an "academic colleague" elected by the university senate. It provides research and information shared among the universities and advocates for university interests vis-à-vis the government and its agencies (Royce 1998). It also serves its members by providing co-coordinating and planning and the central processing of university applications. (For more information on the COU, see http://www.cou.on/HOME/about_cou.htm.)

9 See Charles (2011) for a full discussion of the policy process leading to the Colleges of Applied Arts and Technology Act, 2002.

10 On 1 October 2010, this appointment process was amended under O. Regulation 301/10 under the Ontario Colleges of Applied Arts and Technology Act, 2002, S.O. 2002, c. 8, and appointment powers shifted to the lieutenant-governor in council. See Ministry of Training, Colleges and Universities Act, R.S.O. 1990, c.M.19 and Ontario Colleges of Applied Arts and Technology Act, 2002, S.O. 2002, c. 8 under Regulation 34/03.

11 Another important organization in this sector is "Colleges Ontario," formerly known as the Association of Colleges of Applied Arts and Technology of Ontario. Colleges Ontario provides a forum for the development of collaborative initiatives within the sector, and it advocates (to government) on behalf of CAATs.

12 One of Ontario's newest universities, the University of Ontario Institute of Technology (UOIT), received initial financial support from the provincial Ministry of Finance as well as from the MTCU. The Ministry of Energy and Infrastructure plays a role in supporting university and college capital infrastructure projects. The Ministry of Research and Innovation operates a number of postsecondary research funding mechanisms.

13 Trent University and the University of Nipissing have received Differentiation Grants to help them develop their unique mission and approach to education. For example, Trent University has a unique interdisciplinary mission, and its approach to pedagogy and instruction is student-centred, which, with small class sizes and tutorials, can be resource-intensive. These grants go into the operating budget of the institution and were continued in 2011. For a full discussion of differentiation within the system see Council of Ontario Universities (2011a); Weingarten and Deller (2010).

14 These currently include, but are not limited to: tuition freeze compensation fund, sustainability fund, Access to Opportunities Fund (ATOP), access to opportunity, transformation grants, quality assurance fund, various funds for nursing programs, and equipment and renewal funds (Colleges Ontario 2007).
15 In the 2009–10 transition period to the next sets of negotiated agreements, institutions were expected to maintain commitments as outlined in the original MYAA, and no additional targets were expected for 2009–10. However, institutions were expected to identify how improvements strategies would be extended in 2009–10. See HEQCO (2009a, 2009b).
16 The MTCU does not provide funding to institutions in advance to help them reach their targets and to speed their improvements; rather, institutions have to show the improvements first (i.e., accept the enrolment, implement the access/quality initiative, etc.). This means that there is a front-end expenditure for institutions: they must grow/improve in advance of receiving the funding for growth/improvement. There is an uncertainty to this arrangement that raises potential challenges for institutional planning should targets not be met and funds ultimately withheld.
17 Institutions are required to post their MYAAs on their websites. They must show their performance against identified targets. "Report back" reviews are also posted and easily accessible on the web. However, it is not clear if there is ever a summative evaluation of institutional performance (i.e., a final date for demonstrating achievement of specific targets at which time funding is granted or denied) or if what we have is a formative, continuous improvement – an evaluation process whereby institutions must continuously work towards and demonstrate to the MTCU their plans for improvement regarding their identified targets. Furthermore, the MYAAs are crafted in the language of improvement rather than in the language of meeting a specific number. For example, anecdotally, we were told by key informants that universities did not always meet specific, numerical, internal institutional enrolment targets for various programs (such as graduate enrolment targets). However, a general aggregate "increase in enrolments" towards the target would suffice for the purposes of MYAA reporting. And we were unable to identify instances in which the government held back quality funding after an institution's "report back" process.
18 Grants and contracts consisted of primarily of operating grants from the MTCU and other federal and provincial research grants and contracts. See Council of Ontario Universities (2011b, 2–3). See also http://www.cou.on.ca/statistics/cofu-uo/financial reports.

19 See Government of Ontario at http://www.gov.on.on/ont/. See also Statistics Canada (2007).
20 See appendix 4, which documents the political parties, ministers, and ministries responsible for PSE as well as major policy initiatives and legislation during each administration.
21 See Government of Ontario (1988a). The Premier's Council was established by the Liberals with a mandate to "steer Ontario into the forefront of economic leadership and technological innovation." The premier chaired the council, along with senior cabinet ministers from trade, treasury, skills, labour, education, and colleges/universities.
22 "The corridor funding provided stable shares of operating support as long as institutions did not go beyond plus or minus 3% of the formula enrolment calculations" (Jones 1997b, 149). For more information on the additional envelopes of funding, such as the accessibility envelope, see OCUA 1988.
23 For more information, see Government of Ontario (1988b).
24 According to Jones (1997b, 150): "Institutions that increased enrolment at a higher rate than their peers received a larger share of available support."
25 In 1987, the minister of Colleges and Universities commissioned another report by Jeffrey Gandz, a professor of business at the University of Western Ontario, to review and advise the ministry on the effectiveness of the collective bargaining process for CAATs. Gandz's report, entitled *The Report of the Colleges Collective Bargaining Commission,* also recommended structural changes in CAATs governance and a new collective bargaining framework (Government of Ontario 1988c). Some of these called-for changes were pursued by the Liberal government and were before the Legislature when the government changed in 1990. However, the proposed bill subsequently died in the house in 1992 (Cameron and Royce 1996).
26 Glen Jones observes that the OCEs are interesting for a number of reasons (including the fact that the Conservative Mulroney government used a similar model on a national basis). First, they were driven by a policy discussion that took place outside the normal Ontario higher education policy community. In fact, the Ministry of Colleges and Universities was largely excluded from the discussions. The initiative was driven by economic policy and notions of innovation for the new economy. Second, OCEs were essentially new entities that were distinct from existing universities – that is, they were new corporations that had complex contractual relationships with government and with affiliated universities (Jones 1994).

27 Funding for the OCEs was renewed by the NDP and PC governments that followed, but the PC government reduced the number of centres from seven to four.
28 In 2001, the PCs decided to close one of the French-language colleges, Collège des Grand Lacs, a distance-education college located in southwestern Ontario. The college ceased operations in 2002, and its programs were taken over by another French-language college, Collège Boréal.
29 Courchene and Telmer (1998) suggest that fiscal disaster would have befallen any government in power during this period, given the performance of the economic indicators over the 1990–95 period.
30 In response to the fiscal situation the NDP enacted austerity legislation to curtail the ballooning deficit. One of these measures was the Social Contract (Bill 48) introduced in the 1993 budget. "Via the Social Contract the Ontario government planned to shave $2 billion from planned expenditures on wage compensation from the broader public sector" by imposing wage freezes and giving civil servants unpaid days off per year (Courchene and Telmer 1998, 141). However, rather than just cut transfer payments to the various public institutions, the government chose to leave it to the individual employers and unions to deal with what was essentially a 5 percent rollback of the public sector – not a huge amount given that Alberta introduced a 20 percent rollback (albeit in much better financial times). The Social Contract legislation included a failsafe that permitted employers to negotiate new compensation to meet government savings targets; but, failing that, it gave them the power to unilaterally institute measures to reduce compensation. Under this arrangement the unions lost power once negotiations were abandoned. As a result, the NDP lost the support of much of the labour movement. When Bill 48 expired in 1996, employee wages returned to their precontract levels; however, by this point, the Harris Conservative government had been elected and it chose to implement a new round of budget cuts. See Courchene and Telmer 1998, 141–2) for a full discussion. See also Monahan (1995).
31 The employment equity legislation (Bill 79) was aimed at workplace discrimination against four designated groups: Aboriginals, people with disabilities, racial minorities, and women. It applied to every public-sector employer with more than ten employees and every private-sector employer with more than fifty employees, and it required Ontario employers to implement an employment equity plan that would eliminate barriers and establish timetables to recruit/promote members in the designated groups. See Courchene and Telmer (1998, 143–4) and Monahan (1995, 221–32).
32 See OCUA (1994b, 1994a, 1995).

33 OCUA (1994a, 1995).
34 For a discussion of this issue and the tensions between OCUA and the COU see Royce (1998, esp. 221); Cameron and Royce (1996); Monahan (2004); and Graham (1989).
35 The employment equity legislation began to change the face of faculty and staff in the postsecondary institutions. The social contract legislation shifted the locus of power and the roles of agencies in the university sector, especially the COU, which now acted on behalf of management in sector-wide discussions and negotiations to meet the target reductions required by the government. The Ontario Confederation of Faculty Associations (OCUFA) acted for faculty in discussions and negotiations. Although the government delegated negotiations to the institutions, the prescribed process left little room for autonomy or traditional collective bargaining (Jones 1997b).
36 For example, in September 1993 the University of Western Ontario, with government support, proposed closing the School of Journalism due to financial constraints. The university reversed itself after intense lobbying from the graduates of the journalism school. In the same year, the University of Toronto agreed to cap its enrolments in medicine. Royce (1998) notes that these agreements were made directly with the minister, who sought to reduce the number of doctors produced by the universities in exchange for the assurance that the institution would not suffer due to loss of tuition. Tuition in the dentistry programs at the University of Toronto and the University of Western Ontario were also deregulated at this time (1996) through a special agreement with the minister and the two universities. By 1996, a new bachelor of fine arts degree at the University of Ottawa resulted from consolidating the existing programs, and this led to the elimination of fifty courses in the Department of Fine Arts (Royce 1998, 345). Additionally, two engineering programs at McMaster University were products of rationalization and involved the closure of six existing programs. Royce (1998, 342) suggests that these changes reflect the ad hoc nature of the system planning and coordination that was occurring during this period, illustrating the "complete absence of any ongoing master planning activity on the part of the Ministry responsible for universities, the advisory body OCUA, or the university collectivity."
37 Nipissing had a special undergraduate teaching-oriented mission and was restricted to education, liberal arts, and sciences. See Government of Ontario (1992). The university's charter was later revised to provide expanded degree-granting authority.

38 The initial amendments limited Ryerson's university powers to granting degrees in areas of applied knowledge and research. See Government of Ontario (1993a).
39 Ontario Progressive Conservative Caucus (1992).
40 See Government of Ontario (1996a, 3ff.). See also the discussion paper, put out by the minister of education and training, that preceded the Smith Commission and outlined the issues it was to address (Government of Ontario 1996b).
41 The CUCC was established in 1996 by the COU and the Association of Colleges of Applied Arts and Technology of Ontario (ACAATO). Its mandate is to promote joint education and training ventures, establish electronic credit transfer guides, and undertake research on postsecondary student mobility.
42 See MTCU (2001). For more information about Ontario's KPI's, or to view the full set of statistics, see: www.edu.on.ca/eng/general/postsec/ps_overview.html.
43 The first envelope was tied to enrolment growth of first-entry undergraduate and second-entry professional and graduate programs. The second envelope was for performance-based funding and was distributed on the basis of an institution's graduation rates, employment rates, and student loan default rates.
44 In 2003, after the province eliminated the OAC (Grade 13 to the fifth year of secondary school), both the OAC and Grade 12 students graduated and entered the PSE system at the same time. These were the first students in the new four-year high school program who graduated at the same time as the last graduates of the old five-year program, thereby doubling the graduating cohort that was eligible to apply to the postsecondary stream.
45 For more information see: http://www.edu.gov.on.ca/eng/general/postsec/atop/.
46 In order to qualify, the private-sector contributions had to be pledged by 15 April 1999 and received by the university or college no later than 31 March 2001.
47 Concerns emerged that the funding under the Super Build Program was directed to projects in the applied technology, health, and general sciences, even though students in the liberal arts programs constitute the largest area of the university program demand. See OCUFA (2001, 12).
48 See MTCU (2002, 3). Available at http://www.edu.gov.on.ca/eng/general/postsec/postsec.html. In 1997–98, university income from tuition represented 37.6 percent of university revenue, while 57 percent came from

operating grants and 5.1 percent came from other sources. See OCUFA (2001, 13).
49 See OCUFA (2001, 8).
50 See Ministry of Training Colleges and Universities (2000).
51 The PC policy document states: "The restriction on private, degree granting universities should be lifted. However anyone wishing to start a private university should be subject to intense government scrutiny to ensure that the institution will be self-supporting and that its curriculum will not only meet provincial standards, but will focus on areas of emerging need" (Ontario Progressive Conservative Caucus 1992, 26).
52 See MTCU (2000).
53 Eight pilot projects per year for three years (starting September 2001) were established and evaluated by the Post-Secondary Quality Assessment Board. These programs could not duplicate programs normally offered at an Ontario university.
54 The board was chaired by Donald Baker at the time and consisted of ten part-time stakeholder representatives.
55 Initially, the degree-granting powers of the UOIT were held in abeyance, and it offered programs leading to degrees subject to ministerial consent, which meant its degree programs were assessed by PEQAB. The unlimited degree-granting powers of the UOIT Act (section 6) were proclaimed by the Government of Ontario in 2007. For procedures and standards associated with ministerial consent, see MTCU (2000).
56 See Ministry of Finance (2002). Prior to UOIT, the last entirely new publicly funded university created in Ontario was Brock University, which opened in St Catharines in 1964. Other new universities, such as Nippissing and Algoma, have involved the change in status of an existing institution.
57 University of Ontario Institute of Technology (2008).
58 See Government of Ontario (2006b).
59 For a full fiscal report, see Government of Ontario (2012).
60 See MTCU (2005).
61 MTCU (2002–03, 2003–04, 2004–05).
62 See Government of Ontario (2005a, 2005b).
63 Government of Ontario (2007). The additional funding included funds for facility renewal, existing building maintenance costs, capital projects, upgrade and new equipment, and technology.
64 Algoma College was established in 1965 in Sault Ste Marie as an affiliate campus of Laurentian University in Sudbury. The legislation would give the college its independence. See http://ogov.newswire.ca/ontario.

65 The Council of Ontario Universities attributes the enrolment surge to a number of factors, including: the double cohort that emanated from the decision to allow secondary school students to graduate from high school in four years instead of five, increasing population of 18- to 24-year-olds, increasing percentage of 18- to 25-year-olds attending university, increasing number of students completing four-year degrees rather than three-years degrees, and more students staying in university (COU 2007).
66 An additional $17 million over four years was provided in 2008 for the Mathematics of Information Technology and Complex Systems Inc. Accelerate program to create 1,750 new research internships for graduate students at leading companies and research institutes (MTCU 2010, 22).
67 Government of Ontario (2006a). The new framework came into place in the 2006–07 academic year and continued until 2009–10. Differential fees are allowed to be charged for certain programs, but the average increase cannot exceed 5 percent. Further, institutions are required to set aside some of the tuition funds for students in the form of financial aid. Currently, this set-aside level stands at 30 percent of any tuition increase (Colleges Ontario 2007, 2010).
68 Colleges were to receive $1.1 billion in total operating grants (including the funding for the Collaborative Nursing Program), and universities were to receive $2.6 billion in total operating grants. See MTCU (2005–06).
69 When QIF was first established in 2005 it provided $211 million to colleges and universities in 2005–06 so that they could improve quality by increasing faculty, purchasing resources, and improving student support services to accommodate higher enrolment and to augment access initiatives. Of the $211 million, $87.3 million was ear-marked for the colleges and $124.2 million was for the universities. See MTCU (2005–06).
70 The Higher Education Quality Council of Ontario was created by the Higher Education Quality Council Act, 2005, S.O. 2005, c. 28, sched. G.
71 The six areas are: (1) expansion and enhancement of apprenticeship, (2) labour market integration of recent immigrants, (3) literacy and essential skills, (4) workplace skills development, (5) Aboriginal peoples, and (6) assistance to others facing labour market barriers. See MTCU (2006–07).
72 MTCU (2004–05).
73 The Office of the Fairness Commissioner is housed in the Ministry of Citizenship and Immigration. It is the creature of the landmark Fair Access to Regulated Professions Act, 2006, which became law in March 2007.
74 Since the passage of the Postsecondary Choice and Excellence Act, 2002, growth of private postsecondary degree-granting institutions has been

modest. As of 2007, only six private in-province and out-of-province institutions had been given degree-granting approval by ministerial approval under the act (in addition to the seventeen private religious institutions already in existence and described earlier in the chapter.) Of these six institutions, two had denominational, not-for-profit status; two were US-based with not-for-profit status, one was Canadian with charitable status, and one was Canadian private and for-profit – namely, Radio College Canada (RCC) a private career college that obtained applied degree-granting powers. There were many more public institutions (institutes, colleges, and universities), in-province and out-of-province, that were given degree-granting powers. By 2010 (ten years after the PSCE Act had been passed), twenty-five private institutions (inside and outside the province) had made forty-seven applications for new, renewed, or amended consents to offer undergraduate and graduate programs in various disciplines (PEQAB 2010, 9).

75 Confidential interview no. 2 by authors, 20 April 2004; confidential interview no. 10B by authors, 29 April 2004; confidential interview no. 10J by authors, 29 April 2004.
76 Universities are required to set aside 30 percent of tuition increases for student aid.
77 Examples include the provincial Aim for the Top scholarships, the federal CMSF, the OGS, the OSOTF, and the Work Study Program.
78 It is important to note that HEQCO maintains that it is not a buffer body, nor does it operate in the way that previous intermediary bodies (such as OCUA) operated. The history here is instructive. OCUA was an advisory body to the minister, and it provided a checks and balance between universities and government. Unfortunately, and perhaps unfairly, OCUA came to be seen by the university sector as only acting on government issues. The COU saw OCUA as acting "increasingly as a buffer body protecting government from the demands of universities" and becoming increasingly involved in system management when it should only have been providing advice (Monahan 2004, 131). By comparison, HEQCO is constituted as "an arm's-length, incorporated agency of the Government of Ontario," governed by a board of directors that provides recommendations to the minister, based on research and evaluation, to improve the PSE sector. HEQCO reports to the Minister of Training, Colleges and Universities. It is chaired by a former Supreme Court of Canada judge who was also interim president of the University of Toronto. However, HEQCO members are appointed through the lieutenant-governor of Ontario by an Order in Council. At least one non-voting member of the

council is an employee of the Ministry of Training, Colleges and Universities. No HEQCO member may be a governing board member, executive, or administrative person at a PSE institution or a PSE association. The lieutenant-governor also makes regulations pertaining to the operation of HEQCO. These arrangements raise the question of whether, and to what extent, HEQCO is truly independent from the government. For details on Ontario's intermediary bodies, see: Higher Education Quality Council of Ontario Act, 2005 S.O. 2005, c. 28, sched. G.; Hardy (1996, 28); Monahan (2004), 131); Graham (1989).

79 By 2007, UOIT degree-granting powers had been proclaimed, and UOIT now resembles and behaves like other publicly funded universities in the province, offering a range of undergraduate and graduate programs.

80 The previous PC administration also funded research outside of the postsecondary ministry through the Ministry of Economic Development.

81 See Clark et al. (2009, 80ff), who ask: "How has postsecondary funding changed over time?" Their answer is nuanced. They observe: "It is indisputable that per-student revenue from these sources [government operating grants, tuition, and mandatory student fees], adjusted for CPI inflation, fell in the 1970s and early 1980s in both university and college sectors" (81). And again in the 1990s government reduced funding to universities in absolute terms on two occasions. However, the authors point out that, at the same time, the government permitted increases in tuition, which allowed *total university operating revenue* (made up of provincial operating grants plus tuition fees plus mandatory student fees plus other sources of soft variable money tied to programs [such as federal government research funds]) to remain relatively stable from mid-1980 to mid-2000. Their analysis, reflected in figure 4.3 (Clark et al. 2009, 83), shows that, over the last two decades, government operating grants have decreased per student while, to make up for this loss, student tuition and mandated fees have increased accordingly. Clark et al.'s analysis clearly shows the shift of university operating revenue away from government operating grants towards tuition and soft federal research money.

82 For example, the Ontario Student Opportunity Trust Fund (OSOTF I and II), established by the PC government in 1996 and re-established and expanded by the Liberals as the Ontario Trust for Student Support (OTSS), is a matching program whereby the Government of Ontario matches all funds raised in the private sector for student aid. See Government of Ontario (1996c, 2005c). The Access to Opportunity Program aimed at doubling computer and engineering graduate rates in these fields. In this program the government matches funds raised by the

private sector to fund the program. The Ontario Research and Development Challenge Fund was also a matching fund program, whereby the government contributed one-third of the total funds required to support research initiatives that had secured private-sector financing.

83 Confidential interview no. 10 by authors, 29 April 2004.
84 Confidential interview no. 9 by authors, 20 April 2004.
85 Confidential interview no 2 by authors, 20 April 2004.
86 Lang et al. (1999, 158) observe that the notable exception to this general approach in Ontario's higher education policy is in the area of tuition fees and student aid, where policy is "highly symmetrical."
87 Confidential interview no. 9 by authors, 20 April 2004.
88 Ibid.
89 Confidential interview no. 6 by authors, 29 April 2004; Royce 1998.
90 See Royce (1998); Confidential interview no. 6 by authors, 29 April 2004; Confidential interview no. 9 by authors, 20 April 2004; Confidential interview no. 10J by authors, 29 April 2004; Confidential interview no. 10B by authors, 29 April 2004.
91 The Ministry of Research and Innovation collaborates across ministries. The Learning to 18 strategy and several access initiatives, including Pathways to Success and the First Generation strategy, also work across ministries, including the MTCU, Health, and Children and Youth Services. Finally, the Fairness Commissioners Office works with the MTCU, citizenship and immigration, as well as with external professional and trade associations.
92 Relative to other comparator jurisdictions, such as the United Kingdom and Australia, the Canadian trends in certain PSE policy areas such as research are less dramatic.
93 Confidential interview no. 9 by authors, 20 April 2004.
94 Higher Education Quality Council of Ontario Act, 2005, S.O. 2005, c. 28 s. 6.
95 Clark and Trick (2006) suggest that environmental and process variables as well as political acuity contributed to the success of the Rae Report. Environmental variables include: the economy, the fiscal situation, and the political cycle. Process variables include reporting relationships, character of commissioner, and stakeholders' strategies.
96 Confidential interview no. 9 by authors, 20 April 2004.
97 See COU (2011b); Colleges Ontario (2007); MTCU (2009).
98 The Council of Ontario Universities attributes the enrolment surge to a number of factors, including: the double cohort that emanated from the decision to allow secondary school students to graduate from high school

in four years instead of five; the increasing population of 18- to 24-year-olds; the increasing percentage of 18- to 25-year-olds attending university; the increasing number of students competing for four-year degrees instead of three-year degrees; and more students staying in university (COU 2007).
99 In 2010–11 this figure jumped to 17.4 percent and then, in 2011–12, to 19 percent.
100 Under certain conditions full-time students change to part-time status and vice versa, which complicates the analysis of trends in enrolment.
101 Previous research on PSE participation rates reveal that many factors contribute to participation of groups in PSE (Barr-Telford et al. 2003; Shaienks and Ghuszynski 2007). Studies have broken down participation rates demographically using multivariate analysis to identify factors and characteristics of groups within the population that have an impact on PSE participation rates, such as: family background characteristics (Frenette 2007; Shaienks et al. 2006, 2007), high school experiences (Lambert et al. 2004), and the need for student loans (Shaienks et al., 2006, 2007). For the purposes of our study we are concerned with the impact of policy decisions on various system outcomes, one being participation. Moreover, our analysis does not show the breakdown of participation by groups, some of which have been traditionally under-represented in PSE in Ontario (e.g., Aboriginal students, students with disabilities, first generation students). This is another dimension of the participation story. To this extent, our data are selective and not intended to provide an exhaustive study of participation, defined broadly, in PSE.
102 The Ontario College of Art and Design (OCAD) was the first to be allowed degree-granting status in 2001 and to have been treated as part of the university sector.
103 Guelph University at Humber College offers parallel courses in the university and college, ultimately leading to a degree.
104 For a discussion of the cost drivers in PSE, especially faculty salaries and inflation as well as technology, debt servicing for capital construction, and the cost of complexity and competition, see Clark et al. (2009, 91–7).

CHAPTER FOUR

1 Statistics Canada, March 2011: http://www.statcan.ca/Daily/Francais/110324/dg11024b-fra.htm.
2 Statistics Canada, January 2008: http://www41.statcan.gc.ca/2009/10000/tbl/cybac10000_2009_000_t01–fra.htm.

3 Secrétariat des afffaires autochtones, November 2004: http://www.gouv. qc.ca/relations_autochtones/profils_nations_profil_en.htm.
4 Statistics Canada, CANSIM 11, Table 051–0001, Estimates of Population, by age group and sex: Canada, Provinces and Territories, annual, 1971–2012.
5 Percentages calculated from the data of the Direction de la recherche, des statistiques et de l'information en date du 26–02–2011, Ministère de l'Éducation, du Loisir et du Sport (MELS).
6 Percentages calculated from the data of the Direction de la recherche, des statistiques et de l'information en date du 26–02–2011, MELS.
7 This name replaced that of "Ministère de l'Éducation" when ministries were reshuffled in February 2005. In this chapter, we use both names, in keeping with the year and context to which we are referring.
8 Three federations of teachers' unions: Quebec Federation of College Students; Association québécoise de pédagogie collégiale (Quebec College Pedagogy Association); Quebec Intercollegiate Network of Sociocultural Activities.
9 Quebec Federation of University Professors and the Quebec Federation of University Students.
10 It should be noted that Quebec universities also belong to the Association of Universities and Colleges of Canada, which represents Canada's ninety-three not-for-profit public and private universities and university colleges. It offers a range of services, emphasizing three spheres of activity: (1) government policy and defending university interests, (2) communication and information exchange, and (3) partnerships and contract management.
11 Régime budgétaire et financier des CÉGEPS, 23 août 2011 (budgetary rules for CÉGEPS). See http://www.meq.gouv.qc.ca/sections/publications/index.asp?page=fiche&id=1554.
12 Régime budgétaire et financier des établissements privés d'ordre collégial, 14 septembre 2011 (budgetary rules for private colleges). See http://www.mels.gouv.qc.ca/ens-sup/ens-coll/reg-pri-vig.asphttp://meq.gouv.qc.ca/sections/publications/index.asp?page=fiche&id=1553.
13 Règles budgétaires et calcul des subventions de fonctionnement des universités québécoises pour l'année universitaire 2010–2011, 28 avril 2011. See http://www.Mels.gouv.qc.ca/sections/publications/index.asp?page=fiche&id=10448&type=2&. These MELS budgetary rules do not cover research grants coming from programs or agencies under MDEIE (in particular, the three research funds).
14 The federal cash transfers for PSE, however, had already begun to decrease by the mid-1980s as both federal and provincial governments

were looking to alter the relationship between the state and PSE (Fisher et al. 2006).

15 Its adoption coincided with the repealing of the Act Respecting the Reduction of Personnel in Public Bodies and the Accountability of Deputy Ministers and Chief Executive Officers of Public Bodies, voted for by the Liberal government in 1993.

16 Included here were (1) the challenge to municipal mergers and holding referendums on whether or not to rescind the law on amalgamations in the former municipalities; (2) the reorganization of the health care services; (3) the adoption of the Act to Amend the Labour Code, notably with regard to transferring the right to operate to subcontractors; and (4) social welfare reforms in the shape of benefit cuts for certain categories of beneficiaries.

17 Other projects stirred up opposition: (1) the project to build a powerhouse that would use natural gas for the production of electricity, which it renounced; (2) the construction of a highway that would be managed by a public-private partnership in northeastern Montreal (despite the opposition of the city of Montreal); and (3) the sale of part of a provincial park to a developer in the Eastern Townships. Moreover, in its negotiations with the employees of the public sector and the physicians, the government also imposed settlements by decrees instead of concluding collective agreements with the unions.

18 The objective of this fund created in 2006 is to reduce the public debt ($118 billion at that time) from 43 percent of GDP to 25 percent in 2025–26. It is supplied by sources of revenue constituted by royalties originating mainly from Hydro Québec, private producers of electricity, and from donations to the Ministry of Finance.

19 This type of demand was referred to by other higher education systems, in English Canada for instance, as "academic drift," or the propensity of institutions to demand university-style autonomy and organizational structure as well as the possibility of offering university-level programs. MEQ, without actually acknowledging that this was a direction that should be taken, in fact mentioned this possibility in the Forum consultation document.

20 Finally an agreement was concluded with the enterprise in November 2010 at the cost of $45.5 million.

21 See Toulouse (2007).

22 Projet de loi 107, *Loi modifiant la Loi sur les établissements d'enseignement de niveau universitaire et la Loi sur l'Université du Québec en matière de gouvernance*; et Projet de loi 110, *Loi modifiant la Loi sur les*

collèges d'enseignement général et professionnel en matière de gouvernance.

23 Loi instituant le poste de Commissaire aux plaintes concernant les mécanismes de reconnaissance des compétences professionnelles.

24 An Act to abolish the Ministère des Services gouvernementaux and to implement the Government's 2010–2014 Action Plan to Reduce and Control Expenditures by Abolishing or Restructuring Certain Bodies and Certain Funds.

25 The former designations were: the Fonds de la recherche en santé du Québec, the Fonds québécois de la recherche sur la nature et les technologies, and the Fonds québécois de la recherche sur la société et la culture.

26 In 2009–10, the tuition fees for a full-time student were among the lowest in Canada: $2,168 compared with $5,535 (mean tuition fees paid by students of the other provinces). As already indicated, they will increase by $325 per year up to $3,793 in 2016–17. Even then, they will represent 69 percent of the present mean tuition fees of the other provinces. And, if we take inflation into account, they will be at the level of the 1968 Quebec fees, and they will count for 16.9 percent of the student contribution to the global funding of universities (Gouvernement du Québec 2011a).

27 The Commission on the General Estates on Education had recommended that MEQ assumes this responsibility. But, as the universities were rather reluctant, the government entrusted the CREPUQ with this mandate.

28 The annual budget of CÉGEPS has to be approved by MELS. The data banks of the universities on student admissions and grade completion are audited. They also have to provide data on their funding, personnel, and research grants and contracts.

29 These sums are $500, $1,000 and $7,000, respectively, per BA, MA, and PhD.

30 In their opinion, however, the roots of this idea went back to the beginning of the 1980s, when the then minister of education talked about his vision for university development with a view to eventually formulating a policy (Laurin 1981).

31 The programs leading to an attestation of college studies (ACS) are short programs of studies elaborated locally by a CÉGEP. Unlike the DCS, the ACS is delivered by the institution, not MELS. They do not include general education components and only have specific training to allow adult students to acquire further skills in specialized fields.

32 These requirements are related, among others, to the education of highly qualified personnel, the increase in the interaction between the universities and various stakeholders, and the adoption of strategies to help graduates enter the workforce.

33 The Professional Code is the framework law that regulates the fifty-one professions in Quebec. It is implemented by an autonomous government agency, the Office des professions, which has the power to monitor the functioning of each professional order.
34 The Quebec government closely monitors the success rates of Quebec's researchers vis-à-vis federal programs. For instance, with 23.2 percent of Canada's population, according to Statistics Canada, 27.0 percent of SSHRC's spending was in Quebec (2008–09), which was good, whereas only 23.2 percent of NSERC's spending (2007–08) was in Quebec, which was only average.
35 Actually these objectives were not reached. In 2010, these percentages were, respectively, 2.49 and 59 percent. See the Tableau synoptique du Tableau de bord du système d'innovation québécois, du Ministère du développement économique, de l'innovation et de l'exportation (Gouvernement du Québec 2013).
36 See Gouvernement du Québec (2006a).
37 In 2009–10, the funds allocated to universities (operating funds, Quebec research funds, and investment funds) corresponded to 1.97 percent of the GDP compared to 1.82 percent for Canada without Quebec (Gouvernement du Québec 2013).
38 As has already been pointed out, this summit brought together representatives of the business community, the unions, the community groups, and other interest groups, including the students associations, and it contributed to building a consensus in Quebec society to write off the annual $4 billion deficit over three years.
39 The global provincial expenses refer to the expenses related to operating grants, fixed assets, and research.
40 The share of the two other sources of own revenue – investment income and other own sources of revenue – has also augmented by 0.7 percent in the case of the former and by 2.5 percent in the case of the latter.
41 CAUT Almanac 2011–12, table 3.2, p. 40.
42 This augmentation seems paradoxical as the Parti Québécois government decided to freeze the tuition fees on its arrival in power. As already indicated, this increase depends on its decision to raise fees for out-of-province students. Both in- and out-of-province students are included in the weighted average calculation of Statistics Canada.
43 As indicated previously, this new path was created in 1995 following the college education reform.
44 The interviews enabled us to circumscribe government's role more clearly.

CHAPTER FIVE

1 The best estimate we have of the decline in the amount of the federal transfer being spent on PSE comes from a briefing note to the minister of human resources and skills development obtained under the access to information legislation. This note was first reported in the *Ottawa Citizen*, 5 April 2005, and then in the CAUT April 2005 bulletin. We would like to thank Sarah Schmidt of the *National Post* Ottawa Bureau for sharing a copy of the original document. We have updated this chart using the same assumptions.
2 The data for this table are drawn from tables 2.1, 3.2, and 4.1 presented in the case study chapters. The data reported for Quebec in the last column are from 2006–07 (explanation in table 5.2).
3 The data for this table are drawn from figures 2.4, 3.3, and 4.3 presented in the case study chapters.
4 The statistics used in this table are not available in all three provinces after 2000.
5 In figure 2.9 and table 2.3 the data was not available beyond 2004–05.
6 They have also created the SuperBuild Fund, which allows for capital expansion (upgrades, renovations of existing building, and new residences) but does not contribute to operating costs.
7 Enrolment growth is determined by growth of first-entry undergraduate programs and second-entry professional and graduate programs.
8 Performance is determined by institutions' graduation and employment rates, and by student loan default rates.
9 As previously mentioned, examples of targeted funding initiatives include the Access to Opportunity Program (ATOP), which was intended to increase the number of new spaces in computer science and high demand engineering programs by almost 40 percent between 1998–99 and 2000–01 (see above).
10 The Quebec government closely monitors the success rates of Quebec's researchers vis-à-vis federal programs. For instance, with 23.7 percent of Canada's population, 27.89 percent of SSHRC's spending in 2002–03 was in Quebec, which was good, whereas only 23.08 percent of NSERC's spending in 2001–02 was in Quebec, which was only average.
11 Conseil de recherches en sciences humaines et sociales du Canada (CRSH)
2001 $28,491,862
2002 $32,115,710
2003 $36,685,486
Total $97,293,058

Fonds Québécois de la Recherche sur la Société et la Culture
2001 $6,658,113
2002 $24,720,132
2003 $30,488,310
Total $61,866,555

12 Between 1988 and 2009, the NCE created a total of thirty-nine NCE networks. Some of the ongoing established networks began in the mid-1990s.
13 The foregoing section on the federal role with regard to PSE is drawn from Fisher et al. (2006).
14 This conclusion is somewhat misleading because Usher and Cervanan used the OECD/United Nations Educational, Scientific and Cultural Organization (UNESCO) definitions of tertiary education, which means that, in Canada, they excluded the most accessible and affordable part of the PSE – namely, the non-university sector (e.g., college transfer program, community colleges, Collèges d'enseignement général et professionnel [CEGEPs] and Colleges of Applies Arts and Technology (CAATS).
15 The following section draws heavily on Fisher and Rubenson (2010).

CONCLUSION

1 The fifteen universities in order of the amount of research funds received are: University of Toronto, University of Alberta, University of British Columbia, McGill University, Université de Montréal, McMaster University, Université Laval, University of Ottawa, University of Calgary, University of Western Ontario, University of Saskatchewan, Queen's University, University of Manitoba, Guelph University, and Waterloo University.
2 Calculated from CAUT Almanac 2010–11, table 5.5, p. 46.
3 In 2004, the federal government intramural spending on R&D was almost $2.3 billion, a figure that has remained fairly constant for the previous six years (Council of Canadian Academies 2006, 109, box 6.4 and 39–40, fig. 4.3).

References

ACTS

Freedom of Information and the Protection of Privacy Act, R.S.O. 1990, c. F.31.
An Act to amend The Ryerson Polytechnical Institute Act, 1977, Royal Assent, 1 June 1993.
Bill Pr.70, (Chapter Pr. 52 Statues of Ontario, 1992) an Act Respecting Nipissing University, Royal Assent December 10, 1992.
Apprenticeship and Certification Act, 1998, S.O. 1998, c. 22, as amended.
Colleges Collective Bargaining Act, R.S.O. 1990. c. 15, as amended.
Higher Education Quality Council Act, 2005, S.O. 2005, c. 28, Sched G.
Accessibility for Ontarians with Disabilities Act, 2005, S.O. 2005, c. 11.
Ministry of Training, Colleges and Universities Act, R.S.O. 1990, c. M.19, as amended.
Ontario Colleges of Applied Arts and Technology Act, 2002, S.O. 2002, c. 8, Sched. F, as amended.
Ontario College of Art & Design Act, 2002, S.O. 2002, c. 8, Sched. E, as amended.
PSE Choice and Excellence Act, 2000, S.O. 2000, c. 36, as amended.
Private Career Colleges Act, 2005, S.O. 2005, c. 28, Sched. L.
Trades Qualification and Apprenticeship Act, R.S.O. 1990, c. T.17, as amended.
University Expropriation Powers Act, R.S.O. 1990, c. U.3, as amended.
University Foundations Act, 1992, S.O. 1992, c. 22, as amended.
University of Ontario Institute of Technology Act, 2002, S.O. 2002, c. 8, Sched. O, as amended.
Fair Access to the Regulated Professions Act, 2006, S.O. 2006, c. 31.

SOURCES

Alberta. 2005. *A Learning Alberta: Advanced Education – Across-Jurisdictional Overview of Accessibility, Affordability and Quality.* Edmonton: Government of Alberta.

Altbach, P.G. 1998. *Comparative Higher Education: Knowledge, the University, and Development.* Greenwich, CT: Ablex Pub. Corp.

– 2007. *Tradition and Transition: the International Imperative in Higher Education.* Rotterdam: Sense Publishers.

Altbach, P.G., R.F. Arnove, and G.P. Kelly, eds. 1982. *Comparative Education.* New York: Macmillan.

Altbach, P.G., R.O. Berdhal, and P.J. Gumport, eds. 1999. *American Higher Education in the Twenty-First Century: Social, Political, and Economic Challenges.* Baltimore: Johns Hopkins University Press.

Amaral, A., G.A. Jones, and B. Karseth. 2002. "Governing Higher Education: Comparing National Perspectives." In *Governing Higher Education: National Perspectives on Institutional Governance*, ed. A. Amaral, G.A. Jones, and B. Karseth, 279–307. London: Kluwer Academic Publishers.

Andres, L., and J. Dawson. 1998. *Investigating Transfer Project. Phase 3: A History of Transfer Policy and Practice in British Columbia.* Research report prepared for the BC Council on Admissions and Transfer. Vancouver: British Columbia Council on Admissions and Transfer.

Anisef, P., N.R. Okihiro, and C. James. 1982. *Losers and Winners: The Pursuit of Equality and Social Justice in Higher Education.* Toronto: Butterworths.

Arnove. R.F., and C.A. Torres, eds. 2003. *Comparative Education: The Dialectic of the Global and the Local.* Lanham: Rowman and Littlefield.

Association of Universities and Colleges of Canada (AUCC). 1991. *Report of the Commission of Inquiry on Canadian University Education* (Smith Report). Ottawa: AUCC.

– 2009. *Funding the Institutional Costs of Research: An International Perspective.* Ottawa: AUCC.

– 2010. *The Value of a Degree in a Global Marketplace.* Ottawa: AUCC.

Axelrod, P. 1982. *Scholars and Dollars: Politics, Economics, and the Universities of Ontario, 1945–1980.* Toronto: University of Toronto Press.

– 2002. *Values in Conflict: The University, the Marketplace, and the Trials of Liberal Education.* Montreal and Kingston: McGill-Queen's University Press.

Bakvis, H. 2002. A Checkerboard Federalism? Labour Market Development Policy in Canada. In *Canadian Federalism: Performance, Effectiveness, and Legitimacy*, ed. H. Bakvis and G. Skogstad, 197–219. Don Mills, ON: Oxford.
Ball, S.J. 1990. *Politics and Policy Making in Education: Explorations in Policy Sociology*. London: Routledge.
– 1993. "What Is Policy? Texts, Trajectories and Toolboxes." *Discourse* 13(2): 10–17.
– 1994. *Education Reform: A Critical and Post-Structural Approach*. Buckingham: Open University Press.
– 1997. "Policy Sociology and Critical Social Research: A Personal Review of Recent Education Policy and Policy Research. *British Education Research Journal* 23 (3): 257–74.
– 1999. "Labour, Learning and the Economy: A 'Policy Sociology' Perspective." *Cambridge Journal of Education* 29 (2): 195–206.
Barrow, C.W. 2005. "The Return of the State: Globalization, State Theory, and the New Imperialism." *New Political Science* 27 (2): 123–45.
Barr-Telford, L., F. Cartwright, S. Prasil, and K. Shimmons. 2003. *Access, Persistence and Financing: First Results from the PSE participation survey (PEPS)*. Ottawa: Statistics Canada 81–595–MIE-No.007.
Bastow, S., and J. Martin. 2003. *Third Way Discourse: European Ideologies in the Twentieth Century*. Edinburgh: Edinburgh University Press.
Beatty, J. 2002. "Online Learning Strategy to Open Up Higher Education: Optimism Follows Tech BC Meeting," *Vancouver Sun*, 30 October.
Bédard, D. 2003. *Les études secondaires et postsecondaires: Propositions de réorganisation pour améliorer la performance du système d'éducation au Québec*. Québec: Fédération des commissions scolaires.
Bélanger, P.W., V. Harvey, G. Rocher, et C. Trottier. 1975. "Le Rapport Nadeau: Les besoins des étudiants." *Prospectives* 11 (4): 215–21.
Bélanger, P.W., G. Rocher, et C. Trottier. 1975. "Les besoins des étudiants." *Prospectives* 11 (4) : 215–22.
Berland, D., and A. Lecours. 2006. "Sub-State Nationalism and the Welfare State: Quebec and Canadian Federalism." *Nations and Nationalism* 12 (1): 77–96.
Bok, D. 2003. *Universities in The Marketplace: The Commercialization of Higher Education*. Princeton, NJ: Princeton University Press.
Bourdieu, P. 1988. *Homo Academicus*. Trans. P. Collier. Stanford, CA: Stanford University Press.
Bourdieu, P. 1999. *The Tyranny of the Market*. London: Routledge.
Bowe, R., S. Ball, and A. Gold. 1992. *Reforming Education and Changing Schools: Case Studies in Policy Sociology*. London: Routledge.

Brennan, J., M. Kogan, and U. Teichler, eds. 1996. *Higher Education and Work: A Conceptual Framework.* Bristol, PA: J. Kingsley.
British Columbia. 1993. *Report of the Commission of Inquiry into the Public Service and Public Sector.* Victoria: Queen's Printer.
– 1994a. *Premier's Summit on Skills Development and Training. Summary of Proceedings. June 23–25, 1993.* Victoria: Queen's Printer.
– 1994b. "Real Skills for the Real World." Training plan unveiled by Premier Harcourt. News release. 3 May.
– 2002. *Electoral History of British Columbia: Supplement, 1987–2001.* Victoria: Legislative Library.
British Columbia Centre for International Education (BCCIE). 2000. *10 Years of Excellence.* Available at http://www.bccie.bc.ca/aboutBCCIE/resource.asp
British Columbia Chamber of Commerce. 2002. *2002–2003 Policy and Positions Manual.* Vancouver: British Columbia Chamber of Commerce.
British Columbia Council of Admission and Transfer. 2003. *2002–2003 Annual Report to the Ministry of Advanced Education.* Vancouver: British Columbia Council of Admission and Transfer.
British Columbia First Nations, the Province of British Columbia, and the Government of Canada. 2005. *Transformative Change Accord.* Available at http://www.gov.bc.ca/arr/social/down/transformative_change_accord.pdf.
British Columbia Labour Force Development Board (BCLFDB). 1995. *Training for What? Report of the British Columbia Labour Force Development Board.* N.p.
British Columbia Labour Force Development Board. 1996. *Training for Whom: Research Background Paper.* Victoria: British Columbia Labour Force Development Board.
British Columbia Ministry of Finance. 2001. *Economic and Fiscal Update.* Available at http://www.fin.gov.bc.ca/archive/efu/pdf/update.pdf.
British Columbia Progress Board. 2002. *Learning to Win: "Ready Set Go": Report of the Panel on Education, Skills, Training and Technology Transfer.* Vancouver: BC Progress Board.
Brodie, J. 1995. *Politics on the Margins: Restructuring and the Canadian Women's Movement.* Halifax: Fernwood.
– 2002. "Citizenship and Solidarity: Reflections on the Canadian Way." *Citizenship Studies* 6: 377–94.
Burawoy, M. 2005. "For Public Sociology." *American Sociological Review* 70 (1): 4–28.

Callinicos, A. 2001. *Against the Third Way: An Anti-Capitalist Critique.* Cambridge, UK: Polity Press.

Calvert, J. 2000. "The BC College, University College, Institutes and Agencies Accord." Paper presented at the Labour Education and Training Research Network conference entitled "The Provision of Training in Canada: Regional Comparisons, National Perspectives," 2–22 October, Vancouver.

Cameron, D.M. 1991. *More Than an Academic Question: Universities, Government and Public Policy in Canada.* Halifax: Institute for Research on Public Policy.

– 2004. *Collaborative Federalism and PSE: Be Careful What You Wish For.* Available at http://jdi.econ.queensu.ca/Files/Conferences/pseconferencepapers/Cameronconferencepaper.pdf.

Cameron, D., and D. Royce. 1996. "Prologue to Change: An Abbreviated History of Public Policy and PSE in Ontario." Background paper to the Advisory Panel on Future Directions for PSE. Toronto: Government of Ontario.

Canadian Association of University Teachers. 2005. *Almanac of Post-Secondary Education in Canada.* Ottawa: CAUT Publicaitons.

– 2006. *Almanac of Post-Secondary Education PSE in Canada.* Ottawa: CAUT Publications.

– 2007. *Almanac of Post-Secondary Education <PSE?> in Canada.* Ottawa: CAUT Publications.

– 2010–11. *Almanac of Post-Secondary Education PSE in Canada.* Ottawa: CAUT Publications.

– 2011–12. *Almanac of Post-Secondary Education PSE in Canada.* Ottawa: CAUT Publications.

Canadian Research Chair Program (CRC). 2010. *Program Statistics.* December. Available at www.chairs.gc.ca.

Carnoy, M. 2000. "Globalisation and Educational Reform." In *Globalization and Education*, ed. N. Stromquist and K. Monkman, 43–62. Lanham, MD: Rowman and Littlefield.

Carrier, G. 2001. *A Review of Performance Indicators, Funding and Benchmarking in the United States and Canada.* Québec: Direction générale de l'enseignement et de la recherche, Ministère de l'Éducation.

Carroll, W.K. 2010.. *Corporate Power in a Globalizing World: A Study in Elite Social Organization.* Rev. ed. Toronto: Oxford University Press.

Carroll, W., and J. Beaton. 2000. "Globalization, Neo-liberalism, and the Changing Face of Corporate Hegemony in Higher Education." *Studies in Political Economy* 62: 71–98.

Carroll, W.K., and R. Ratner, eds. 2005. *Challenges and Perils: Social Democracy in Neoliberal Times*. Halifax: Fernwood.

Carroll, W.K., and M. Shaw. 2001. " Consolidating a Neoliberal Policy Bloc in Canada, 1976–1996." *Canadian Public Policy* 27: 195–217.

Castells, M. 2000. *The Rise of the Network Society*, vol. 1, 2nd ed. Malden, MA: Blackwell Publishing

Chan, A.S., and D. Fisher, eds. 2008. *The Exchange University: Corporatization of Academic Culture*. Vancouver: UBC Press.

Charles, A.C. 2011. "Policy Windows and Changing Arrangements: An Analysis of the Policy Process Leading to the Colleges of Applied Arts and Technology Act, 2002." PhD diss., University of Toronto.

Clark, B.R. 1978. *Academic Differentiation in National Systems of Higher Education*. New Haven, CT: Higher Education Research Group, Institution for Social and Policy Studies, Yale University.

– 1983. *The Higher Education System: Academic Organization in Cross-National Perspective*. Berkeley, CA: University of California Press.

–, ed. 1987a. *The Academic Profession: National, Disciplinary, and Institutional Settings*. Berkeley, CA: University of California Press.

– 1987b. *The Academic life: Small Worlds, Different Worlds*. Princeton: Carnegie Foundation for the Advancement of Teaching.

– 1998. *Creating Entrepreneurial Universities: Organizational Pathways of Transformation*. Oxford: Pergamon.

Clark, I., and D. Trick. 2006. "Advising for Impact: Issues from the Rae Review on the Use of Special Purpose Advisory Commissions. *Canadian Public Administration* 49 (2): 180–95.

Clark, I., G. Moran, M. Skolnik, and D. Trick. 2009. *Academic Transformations: The Forces Reshaping, Higher Education in Ontario*. Montreal and Kingston: McGill-Queens University Press.

Clement, W., and L. Vosko, eds.. 2003. *Changing Canada: Political Economy and Transformation*. Montreal and Kingston: McGill-Queen's University Press.

Coalition of BC Businesses. 2001. *The Industry Training and Apprenticeship Commission: What Is Its Future?* Vancouver: Coalition of BC Businesses.

Cohen, R., and P. Kennedy. 2007. *Global Sociology*, 2nd ed. New York: New York University Press.

Colleges Ontario. 2006. *Annual Report*. Toronto: Colleges Ontario.

– 2007. *Environmental Scan*. Toronto: Colleges Ontario.

– 2010. *Colleges Resources: Environmental Scan 2010: An Analysis of Trends and Issues Affecting Ontario*. Toronto: Colleges Ontario.

Comité consultatif sur l'accessibilité financière aux études. 2003. *Vers une accessibilité financière à la réussite de son projet d'études*. Document de consultation. Québec: Gouvernement du Québec.

Commission for the Estates General on Education. 1996. *Estates General on Education. Rénover notre système d'éducation : Dix chantiers prioritaires*. Québec: Gouvernement du Québec.

Commission des universités sur les programmes (CUP). 2000. *Pour une vision intégrée de la formation universitaire: Diversité et complémentarité*. Rapport final présenté au ministre d'État à l'Éducation et à la Jeunesse. Montréal: Conférence des recteurs et des principaux des universités du Québec.

Conférence des recteurs et principaux des universités du Québec. 2009. *Mémoire présenté par la Conférence recteurs et principaux des universités du Québec dans le cadre de la consultation générale sur le projet de loi no 38, Loi modifiant la Loi sur les établissements d'enseignement universitaire et la Loi sur l,Université du Québec en matière de gouvernance*. Montréal: Conférence des recteurs et des principaux des universités du Québec.

Conseil des collèges. 1992. *L'enseignement collégial: Des priorités pour un renouveau de la formation*. Québec: Conseil des collèges.

Conseil des universités. 1973. *Les universités québécoises: Situation, orientations, réalisations. Rapport du Comité des objectifs de l'enseignement supérieur au Conseil des universités*. Québec: Conseil des universités.

Conseil des universités. 1984. *Le secteur du génie et de la technologie en génie: Bilan factuel*. Québec: Conseil des universités.

– 1987. *Le secteur le l'éducation dans les universités du Québec: Une analyse de la situation d'ensemble*. Québec: Conseil des universités.

– 1990. *Le secteur des sciences sociales:Voies de développement et cibles d'action*. Québec: Conseil des universités.

Conseil du trésor. 1999. *Pour de meilleurs services aux citoyens: Un nouveau cadre de gestion pour la fonction publique – Énoncé de politique sur la gestion gouvernementale : sommaire*. Québec: Conseil du trésor.

Conseil supérieur de l'éducation (CSE). 1975. *Le collège: Rapport sur l'état des besoins de l'enseignement collégial* (Nadeau Report). Québec: Gouvernement du Québec.

– 1988. *Le rapport Parent, 25 ans après. Rapport annuel 1987–1988 sur l'état des besoins de l'éducation*. Québec : Gouvernement du Québec.

– 1999. *L'évaluation institutionnelle en éducation: Une dynamique propice au développement*. Sainte-Foy, Québec: Gouvernement du Québec.

– 2002. *Les universités à l'heure du partenariat: Avis du Conseil supérieur de l'éducation au ministre de l'Éducation*. Québec: Gouvernement du Québec.

- 2009. *Rappel des positions du Conseil supérieur de l'éducation sur la gouvernance de l'éducation. Document préparé à la suite des projets de loi sur la gouvernance des cégeps et des universités.* Québec: Gouvernement du Québec.
Cormier, M., et M. Nadeau. 2006. "Et que la formation continue." Dans *Les CÉGEPS: Une grande aventure collective québécoise*, dir. L. Héon, D. Savard et T. Hamel, 235–49. Québec: Presses de l'Université Laval.
Coyne, A. 2000. "Haven't We Been This Way Before?" *National Post*, 2 June. Available at http://andrewcoyne.com/columns/NationalPost/2000/20000602.html.
Council of Canadian Academies, Committee on the State of Science and Technology in Canada. 2006. *The State of Science and Technology in Canada*. Ottawa: Council of Canadian Academies.
Council of Ministers of Education Canada (CMEC). 1995. *Pan-Canadian Protocol on the Transferability of University Credits*. Toronto: CMEC.
Council of Ontario Universities (COU). 1992. *Transfer of Undergraduate Course Credits among Ontario Universities: Report and Recommendations* (Baker Report). Toronto: COU.
- 2007. Ontario Universities-2007: Resource Document. Toronto: COU
- 2011a. *Advancing University Education for the Benefit of Ontarians.* COU No. 843, ISBN No. 0-88799459-8.
- 2011b. *Financial Report of Ontario Universities, 2009–2010, Highlights*. Toronto: COU.
Courchene, T., and C. Telmer. 1998. *From Heartland to North American Region State: The Social, Fiscal and Federal Evolution of Ontario.* Toronto: Monograph Series on Public Policy, Centre for Public Management, Faculty of Management, University of Toronto.
Craig, D., and D. Porter. 2003. "Poverty Reduction Strategy Papers: A New Convergence." *World Development* 31: 53–69.
- 2004. "The Third Way and the Third World: Poverty Reduction and Social Inclusion Strategies in the Rise of 'Inclusive' Liberalism." *Review of International Political Economy* 11 (2): 387–423.
Culos, G. 2005. "Electric with Education: Private PSE Policy in British Columbia." MA Thesis, University of British Columbia.
Currie, J. 1998. "Globalization Practices and the Professoriate in Anglo-Pacific and North American Universities." *Comparative Education Review* 42 (1): 15–29.
- 2004. "The Neoliberal Paradigm and Higher Education: A Critique." In *Globalization and Education*, ed. P. Manicas, and J. Odin, 42–63. Honolulu: University of Hawai'i Press.

Currie, J., and J. Newson, eds. 1998. *Universities and Globalization: Critical Perspectives.* Thousand Oaks, CA: Sage.

Currie, J., B. Thiele, and P. Harris. 2002. *Gendered Universities in Globalized Economies : Power, Careers and Sacrifices.* Lanham, MD: Lexington Books.

Dale, R. 1997. "The State and Governance of Education: An Analysis of the Restructuring of the State-Education Relationship." In *Education, Culture, Economy, Society,* ed. A. Halsey, H. Lauder, P. Brown, and A.S. Wells, 273–82. Oxford: Oxford University Press.

– 1999. "Specifying Globalisation Effects on National Policy: Focus on the Mechanisms." *Journal of Educational Policy* 14: 1–17.

– 2005. "Globalisation, Knowledge Economy and Comparative Education." *Comparative Education* 41 (2): 117–51.

Dale, R., and S. Robertson. 2003a. "Changing Geographies of Power in Education: The Politics of Resealing and Its Contradictions." Paper presented at the joint BERA/BAICE conference on globalization, culture and education, 12 June, 1–26.

– 2003b. "This Is What the fuss Is About! The Implications of GATS for Education Systems in the North and the South." published by the EU-funded GENIE (the Globalization and Europeanization Network in Education)

Dandurand, L. 2005. "Réflexion autour du concept d'innovation sociale: Approche historique et comparative." *Revue française d'administration publique* 115 : 332–77.

Deem, R. 2001. "Globalisation, New Managerialism, Academic Capitalism, and Entrepreneurialism in Universities: Is the Local Dimension Still Important?" *Comparative Education* 37 (1): 7–20.

Dennison, J.D. 1987. "Universities under Financial Crisis: The Case of British Columbia." *Higher Education* 16: 135–43.

– 1995a. Organization and Function in PSE. In Dennison (1995d), 121–40.

– 1995b. "Introduction." In Dennison (1995d), 3–12. .

– 1995c. "Community College Development in Canada since 1985." In Dennison (1995d), 13–104.

–, ed. 1995d. *Challenge and Opportunity: Canada's Community Colleges at the Crossroads.* Vancouver: UBC Press.

Dennison, J., and P. Gallagher. 1986. *Canada's Community Colleges.* Vancouver: UBC Press.

Department of Finance, Canada. 2000. *The Budget Speech 2000.* Available at fin.gc.ca/budgetoo/pdf/speech.pdf.

Dill, D.D. 1997a. "Markets and Higher Education: An Introduction." *Higher Education Policy* 10: 163–66.

- 1997b. "Higher Education Markets and Public Policy." *Higher Education Policy* 10: 167–85.
Dill, D.D., and F.A. Van Vught, eds. 2010. *National Innovation and the Academic Research Enterprise.* Baltimore: Johns Hopkins University Press.
Doern, G.B., and M. Sharaput, 2000. *Canadian Intellectual Property: The Politics of Innovating Institutions and Interests.* Toronto: University of Toronto Press.
Domhoff, G.W. 1998. *Who Rules America: Power and Politics in the Year 2000*, 3rd ed. Mountain View, CA: Mayfield.
Donald, J.G. 1997. "Higher Education in Québec: 1945–1995." In *Higher Education in Canada: Different Systems, Different Perspectives*, ed. G.A Jones, 161–88. New York: Garland.
Doray, P., E. Comoe, C. Trottier, F. Picard, J. Murdoch, B. Laplante, S. Moulin, M. Marcoux-Moisan, and A. Groleau. 2009. *Transitions: Parcours scolaires et modes de transition dans l'enseignement postsecondaire canadien / Transitions: Educational Pathways and Transition Modes in Canadian Post-Secondary Education.* Montréal: Fondation canadienne des bourses du millénaire.
Drucker, P. F. 2002. *Managing the Next society.* New York: St Martin's Press.
Enders, J. 2005. "Border Crossings: Research Training, Knowledge Dissemination and the Transformation of Academic Work." *Higher Education* 49: 119–33.
Esping-Andersen, G. 1985. *Politics against Markets: The Social Democratic Road to Power.* Princeton, NJ: Princeton University Press.
Etzkowitz, H., A. Webster, and P. Healey. 1998. *Capitalizing Knowledge: New Interactions of Industry and Academe.* Albany: SUNY Press.
Everett, S. 2003. "The Policy Cycle: Democratic Process or Rational Paradigm Revisited. *Australian Journal of Public Administration* 62 (5): 65–70.
Fairclough, N. 1989. *Language and Power.* London: Longman.
- 1995. *Critical Discourse Analysis.* Boston: Addison Wesley.
Feagin, J., A. Orum, and G. Joberg, eds. 1991. *A Case for the Case Study.* Chapel Hill: University of North Carolina.
Fédération des CÉGEPS. 2004. *Les CÉGEPS, une réussite québécoise: Mémoire présenté au Forum sur l'avenir de l'enseignement collégial.* Montréal: Fédération des CÉGEPS.
Ferretti. 2000. "La révolution tranquille. " *Action nationale*, janvier.
Fisher, D., and J. Atkinson-Grosjean. 2002. "Brokers on the Boundary: Academy-Industry Liaison in Canadian Universities." *Higher Education* 44: 449–67.

Fisher, D., J. Atkinson-Grosjean, and D. House. 2001. Changes in Academy/Industry/State Relations in Canada: The Creation and Development of the Networks of Centres of Excellence. *Minerva: A Review of Science and Policy* 39: 299–325.
Fisher, D., and B. Gilgoff. 1987. "The Crisis in BC Public Education: The State and the Public Interest." In *A Sociology of Education: Readings in the Political Economy of Canadian Schooling*, ed. T. Wotherspoon, 68–93). Toronto: Methuen.
Fisher, D., and K. Rubenson. 1998. "The Changing Political Economy: The Private and Public Lives of Canadian Universities." In *Universities and Globalization: Critical Perspectives*, ed. J. Currie and J. Newson, 77–99. Sage.
– 2010. "Canada." In *National Innovation and the Academic Research Enterprise: Public Policy in Global Perspective*, ed. D.D. Dill and F.A. Van Vught, 62–116. Baltimore: Johns Hopkins University Press.
Fisher, D., K. Rubenson, T. Shanahan, C. Trottier, J. Bernatchez, R. Clift, G. Jones, J. Lee, M. MacIvor, and J. Meredith. 2006. *Canadian Federal Policy and PSE*. Vancouver: Centre for Policy Studies in Higher Education and Training.
Frauley, J. 2012. "Post-Social Politics, Employability, and the Security Effects of Higher Education." *Journal of Pedagogy* 3 (2): 219–41.
Frenette, Marc. 2007. *Why Are Youth from Lower-Income Families Less Likely to attend University? Evidence from Academic Abilities, Parental Influences, and Financial Constraints*. Ottawa: Statistics Canada.
Friedman, M. 1991.. *Monetarist Economics*. Cambridge, MA: Blackwell.
Gale, T. 1999. "Policy Trajectories: Treading the Discursive Path of Policy Analysis." *Discourse* 20 (3): 393–407.
– 2001. "Critical Policy Sociology: Historiography, Archaeology and Genealogy of Policy Analysis." *Journal of Education Policy* 16 (5): 379–93.
Gerring, J. 2007. *Case Study Research: Principles and Practices*. Cambridge: Cambridge University Press.
Giddens, A. 1999. *The Third Way: The Renewal of Social Democracy*. Malden, MA: Polity Press.
– 2000a. *The Third Way and Its Critics*. Malden, MA: Polity Press.
– 2000b. *Runaway World: How Globalization Is Reshaping Our Lives*. New York: Routledge.
– 2003. *The Progressive Manifesto: New Ideas for the Centre-Left*. Cambridge: Polity Press.
Gill, S, 2003. *Power and Resistance in the New World Order*. New York: Palgrave Macmillan.

Gingras, Y., B. Godin, et Y. Trépanier. 1999. "La place des universités dans les politiques scientifiques et technologiques canadiennes et québécoises." Dans *L'État québécois et les universités: Acteurs et enjeux*, dir. P. Beaulieu et D. Bertrand, 69–99. Ste-Foy: Presses de l'Université du Québec.

Ginzburg, M., O. Espinoza, S. Popa, and T. Mayumi. 2003. "Privatization, Domestic Marketization, and International Commercialization of Higher Education: Vulnerabilities and Opportunities for Chile and Romania within the Framework of WTO/GATS. *Globalisation, Societies and Education* 1 (3) : 413–45.

Godin, B., M. Trépanier, et M. Albert. 2000. "Des organisations sous tension: Les conseils subventionnaires et la politique scientifique." *Sociologie et sociétés* 32 (1): 17–42.

Goldberg, M.P. 2005. "Ideology, Policy and the (Re)production of Labour Market Inequality: A Critical Discourse Analysis of Access to Professions and Trades." PhD diss., University of Toronto.

Gould, E. 2003. *The University in a Corporate Culture*, Yale: Yale University Press.

Gouvernement du Québec. 1963–66. *Report of the Royal Commission of Inquiry on Education in the Province of Québec*. Québec: Gouvernement du Québec.

– 1979. *Commission d'études sur les universités*. Québec: Gouvernement du Québec.

– 1980. *Pour une politique québécoise de la recherche scientifique*. Québec: Éditeur officiel.

– 2000. *Québec Policy on University Funding*. Québec: Ministère de l'Éducation.

– 2001. *Politique québécoise de la science et de l'innovation: Savoir changer le monde*. Québec: Gouvernement du Québec.

– 2006a. *Indicateurs de l'activité scientifique et technologique au Québec: Compendium édition 2006*. Québec: Gouvernement du Québec. Available at http://ps.public.pncmedia.com/cgi/affiche_doc.cgi?dossier=9057&table=0.

– 2006b. *Moderniser la gouvernance des sociétés d'État: Enoncé de politique*. Québec. Gouvernement du Québec.

– 2007. *Tableau de bord du système d'innovation du Québec: Édition 2007*. Québec: Ministère du Dévelopement économique, de l'Innovation et de l'Exportation.

– 2007/2011. *Tableau de bord du système d'innovation du Québec: Éditions 2007 et 2011*. Québec : Ministère du Développement économique, de l'Innovation et de l'Exportation.

- 2008. *Statistiques de l'éducation: Enseignement primaire, secondaire, collégial et universitaire*. Québec. Ministère de l'Éducation du Loisir et du Sport.
- 2010. *Stratégie québécoise de la recherche et de l'innovation 2010-2013: Mobiliser, innover, prospérer*. Québec: Ministère du développement économique, de l'innovation et de l'exportation.
- 2011a. *Un plan de financement des universités équitable et équilibré pour donner au Québec les moyens de ses ambitions*. Québec: Finances Québec.
- 2011b. Indicateurs de l'éducation, Édition 2011. Québec: Gouvernement du Québec.
- 2013. Indicateurs de l'éducation, Édition 2012. Québec: Gouvernement du Québec. Available at statistiques/innovation/tableauxsynoptiques/tableausynoptiquetableaudebord innovation.pdf.

Government of British Columbia. 1993. *Premier's Summit, Skills Development and Training, June 23-25, 1993: Summary of Proceedings*. Victoria: Government of British Columbia.
- 1996. *Report of the Royal Commission on Aboriginal Peoples*, 3 vols. Ottawa: Canada Communications Group.

Government of Ontario. 1985. *The Report of the Advisor to the Minister of Colleges and Universities on the Governance of the Colleges of Applied Arts and Technology*. (Pittman Report). Toronto : Government of Ontario.
- 1988a. *The Accessibility Envelop, Ontario Council on University Affairs, Advisory Memorandum 87– III, The On-going Accessibility Envelope for 1987-1988, Fourteenth Annual Report, 1987-1988*. Toronto: Ministry of Colleges and Universities.
- 1988b. *Competing in the New Global Economy: Report of the Premier's Council*. Vol. 1. Toronto: Government of Ontario.
- 1988c.*The Report of the Colleges Collective Bargaining Commission* (Jeffrey Gandz Report). Toronto: Gov
- 1990. People and Skills in the New Global Economy. Report of the Premier's Council. Toronto: Government of Ontario.
- 1992. Bill Pr. 70 (Chapter Pr. 52, Statues of Ontario, 1992) an Act Respecting Nipissing University, Royal Assent 10 December.
- 1993a. An Act to Amend The Ryerson Polytechnical Institute Act, 1977, Royal Assent, 1 June.
- 1993b. *University Accountability: A Strengthened Framework* (Broadhurst Report). Toronto: Taskforce on University Accountability.
- 1996a. *Excellence, Accessibility and Responsibility: Report of the Advisory Panel on Future Directions for Postsecondary Education* (Smith Report). Toronto: Government of Ontario, MTCU.

- 1996b. *Future Goals for Ontario Colleges and Universities.* Toronto: Government of Ontario.
- 2005a. *Backgrounder-Reaching Higher: The McGuinty Government Plan for PSE, Ontario.* Toronto: Government of Ontario.
- 2005b.Investing in People: Strengthening Our Economy. Toronto: Government of Ontario.
- 2005c. MTCU news release. 9 November.
- 2006a. Building Opportunity. Toronto: Government of Ontario, Ministry of Finance.
- 2006b. *Economic Outlook and Fiscal Review.* Toronto: Government of Ontario, Ministry of Finance.
- 2007. *Budget-Backgrounder: Expanding Opportunities for Students.* Toronto: Government of Ontario, Ministry of Finance.
- 2012. *Ontario's Economic Outlook and Fiscal Plan, 2012.* Toronto: Government of Ontario, Ministry of Finance.

Graham, C. 1989. "The Ontario Council on University Affairs: A Buffer Agency." *Philanthropist* 8 (4): 17–23.

Green, A. 2000. "Education and Globalization in Europe and East Asia: Convergent and Divergent Trends. *Journal of Education Policy* 14 (1): 55–71.

Habermas, J. 1989. *The Structural Transformation of the Public Sphere: An Inquiry into a Category of Bourgeois Society.* Trans. Thomas Burger with the assistance of Frederick Lawrence. Cambridge, MA: MIT Press

Hall, P.A., and D. Soskice. 2001. *Varieties of Capitalism: The Institutional Foundations of Comparative Advantage.* Oxford: Oxford University Press

Hallak, J. 2000. "Globalization and Its Impact on Education." In *Globalization, Educational Transformation and Societies in Transition,* ed. T. Mebrahtu, M. Cranly, and D. Johnson, 21–40. London: Symposium Books.

Hamel, P. et B. Jouve. 2006. *Un modèle québécois? Gouvernance et participation dans la gestion publique.* Montréal: Presses de l'Université de Montréal.

Hardy, Cynthia. 1996.*The Politics of Collegiality: Retrenchment Strategies in Canadian Universities.* Montreal and Kingston: McGill-Queen's University Press.

Harvey, D. 2005. *A Brief History of Neoliberalism.* Oxford: Oxford University Press.

HEQCO. 2009a. Letter of advice from HEQCO Chair Frank Iacobucci to the Honourable John Milloy, Minister of Training Colleges and Universities, Toronto.

- 2009b. *Towards an Accountability Framework for Ontario PSE*. Toronto: HEQCO.
Hirst, P., and G. Thompson. 1996. *Globalization in Question*. Cambridge, UK: Polity Press.
Hommen, L. 1997. "The British Columbia Labour Force Development Board: Delivering Consensus." In *Social Partnerships for Training*, ed. A. Sharpe and Rodney Haddow, 217–50. Kingston: School of Policy Studies, Queen's University.
Jessop, B. 1990. *State Theory: Putting the Capitalist State in Its Place*. Cambridge, UK: Polity Press.
- 2002. "Globalization and the National State." In *Paradigm Lost: State Theory Reconsidered*, ed. S. Aronowitz and P. Bratsis, 185–220. Minneapolis: University of Minnesota Press.
K. Jothen, D.S. Avison, G. Cormode, J. Merkel, J.R. Rae, and R. Young. 2011. *Final Report: Evaluation of the BC Aboriginal Post-Secondary Education Strategy*. Victoria: Ministry of Advanced Education. Available at http://www.aved.gov.bc.ca/aboriginal/docs/APSES_evaluation_report.pdf
Jones, G. 1994. "Higher Education Policy in Ontario." In *Higher Education Policy: An International Comparative Perspective*, ed. L. Goedegebuure, F. Kaiser, P. Maassen, L. Meek, F. van Vught, and E. de Weert, 214–38. Oxford: Pergamon.
- 1996. "Governments, Governance, and Canadian Universities." In *Higher Education: Handbook of Theory and Research*, vol. 11, ed. J.C. Smart, 337–71. New York: Agathon Press.
–, ed. 1997a. *Higher Education in Canada: Different Systems, Different Perspectives*. New York: Garland.
- 1997b. "Higher Education in Ontario." In *Higher Education in Canada: Different Systems, Different Perspectives*, ed. G. Jones, 137–61. New York: Garland.
- 1997c. "The Structure of University Governance in Canada." In *Governing Higher Education: National Perspectives on Institutional Governance*, ed. A. Amaral, G.A. Jones, and B. Karseth, 213–33. London: Kluwer Academic Publishers.
- 2004. "Ontario Higher Education Reform, 1995–2003: From Modest Modifications to Policy Reform." *Canadian Journal of Higher Education* 34 (3): 39–54.
- 2006. "Canada." In *International Handbook of Higher Education*, ed. J.K. Forest and P.G. Altbach, 627–45. Dordrecht, The Netherlands: Kluwer Academic Publishers.

Jones, G.A., M.L. Skolnik, and B. Soren. 1998. "Arrangements for Coordination between University and College Sectors in Canadian Provinces, 1990–1996." *Higher Education Policy* 11 (1): 15–27.

Jones, G.A., and S. Young. 2004. "'Madly Off in All Directions": Higher Education, Marketization, and Canadian Federalism." In *Markets and Higher Education: Rhetoric or Reality?*, ed. P. Teixeira, B.B. Jongbloed, D.D. Dill, and A. Amaral, 185–205. Dordrecht, The Netherlands: Kluwer Academic Publishers.

Kelsey, J. 2002. "The Third Way: A Road to Nowhere." In *At the Crossroads: Three Essays*, ed. J. Kelsey, 47–88. Wellington, NZ: Bridget Williams Books.

Keynes, J.M. 2007. *The General Theory of Employment, Interest and Money*. New York: Palgrave Macmillan.

King, R., S. Marginson, and R. Naidoo, eds. 2011. *Handbook on Globalization and Higher Education*. Williston, VT: Edward Elgar.

Knowles, J. 1995. "A Matter of Surivival: Emerging Entrepreneurship in Community Colleges in Canada." In *Challenge and Opportunity: Canada's Community Colleges at the Crossroads*, ed. J.D. Dennison, 184–207. Vancouver: UBC Press.

Kogan, M. 1975. *Educational Policy-Making: A Study of Interest Groups and Parliament*. London: Allen and Unwin.

Kunz, J.L. 2001. "Social Inclusion and Diversity: Fries or Stir-fry?" Paper presented at the conference entitled "A New Way of Thinking? Towards a Vision of Social Inclusion," 10–12 November, Ottawa, Ontario.

Lambert, M., K. Zeman, M. Allen, and P. Bussière. 2004. *Who Pursues PSE? Who leaves and Why? Results from the Youth in Transitions Survey*. Ottawa: Statistics Canada and Human Resources and Social Development Canada.

Lang, D., D. House, S. Young, and G. Jones. 1999. *University Finance in Ontario*. Toronto: OISE/UT.

Laurin, C. 1981. "L'avenir des universités québécoises: Vers une politique des universités." Discours prononcé par le ministre de l'Éducation devant des représentants de la communauté universitaire québécoise, à l'Université de Montréal, le 3 février.

Lee, J.S.H. 2005. "Access to PSE: A Comparative Study of British Columbia and Ontario." Ed.D. diss., University of British Columbia.

Lesemann, F. 2003. "La société des savoirs et la gouvernance: La transformation des conditions de production de la recherche universitaire." *Lien social et politiques – RIAC* 50: 17–37.

Lindblom, C. 1980. *The Policy-Making Process*. Englewood Cliffs, NJ: Prentice-Hall.

Lingard, R. 1993. "The Changing State of Policy Production in Education: Some Australian Reflections on the State of Policy Sociology." *International Studies in Sociology of Education* 3 (1): 25–47.

Lingard, R., S. Rawolle, and S. Taylor. 2005. "Globalising Policy Sociology in Education: Working with Bourdieu." *Journal of Educational Policy* 20 (6): 759–77.

Macdonald, J.B. 1962. *Higher Education in British Columbia and a Plan for the Future*. Vancouver: UBC Press.

MacIvor, M.K. 2012. *Aboriginal Post-Secondary Education Development Policy in British Columbia, 1986–2011*. PhD diss., Univsersity of British Columbia.

Magnusson, W., W.K, Carroll, C. Doyle, M. Langer, and R.B.K. Walker, eds. 1984. *The New Reality: The Politics of Restraint in British Columbia*. Vancouver: New Star Books.

Marchak, M.P. 1983. *Green Gold*. Vancouver: UBC Press.

Marginson, S. 1997. *Markets in Education*. St Leonards, AU: Allen and Unwin.

– 1997. *Educating Australia. Government, Economy and Citizen since 1960*. Cambridge: Cambridge University Press.

Marginson, S., and M. Considine. 2000. *The Enterprise University: Power, Governance, and Reinvention in Australia*. Cambridge: Cambridge University Press.

McBride, S. 2001. *Paradigm Shift: Globalisation and the Canadian State*. Halifax: Fernwood.

McKee, C. 2009. *Treaty Talks in British Columbia: Building a New Relationship*, 3rd ed. Vancouver: UBC Press.

Merriam, S. 1998. *Qualitative Research and Case Study Applications in Education*. San Francisco: Jossey-Bass.

Metcalfe, A.S. 2009. "The Geography of Access Aad Excellence: Spatial Diversity in Higher Education System Design." *Higher Education* 58 (2): 205–20.

– 2010. "Revisiting Academic Capitalism in Canada: No Longer the Exception." *Journal of Higher Education* 81 (4): 489–514.

Miller, J.R. 2004. *Lethal Legacy: Current Native Controversies in Canada*. Toronto: McClelland and Steward.

Miliband, R., L. and Panitch, eds. 1994. *Socialist Register 1994: Between Globalism and Nationalism*. London: Merlin Press.

Milot, P. 2005. *Note de recherche: La commercialisation des résultats de la recherche universitaire: une revue de la littérature*, Rapport soumis au Conseil de la science et de la technologie, Montréal, Centre interuniversitaire de recherche sur la science et la technologie.

Ministère de la Recherche de la Science et de la Technologie. 2001. *Politique québécoise de la science et de la technologie: Savoir changer le monde*. Québec: Gouvernement du Québec.

– 2002. *Gestion de la propriété intellectuelle dans les universités et les établissements du réseau de la santé et des services sociaux où se déroulent des activités de recherche: Plan d'action*. Québec : Gouvernement du Québec.

Ministère de l'Éducation (MEQ).1977. *L'enseignement primaire et secondaire au Québec: Livre vert*. Québec. Gouvernement du Québec.

– 1979. *L'école québécoise: Énoncé de politique et plan d'action*. Québec: Gouvernement du Québec.

– 1982. *L'école: Une école communautaire et responsable*. Québec: Gouvernement du Québec.

– 1997a. *L'école, tout un programme: Énoncé de politique éducative*. Québec: Gouvernement du Québec.

– 1997b. *Prendre le virage du succès: Plan d'action ministériel pour la réforme de l'éducation*. Québec: Gouvernement du Québec.

– 2000. *Québec Policy on Universities: Priorities for Our Future*. Québec: Gouvernement du Québec.

Ministère de l'éducation du loisir et du sport. 2006. *Régime budgétaire et financier des établissements privés d'ordre collégial*. Québec: Ministère de l'éducation.

Ministère de l'éducation du loisir et du sport. 2011. *Règles budgétaires et calcul des subventions de fonctionnement aux universités du Québec pour l'année 2010–2011*. Québec: Ministère de l'éducation.

Ministère de l'Enseignement Supérieur et de la Science (MESS). 1993. *L'enseignement collégial québécois: orientations d'avenir et mesures de renouveau: Des collèges pour le Québec du XXIe siècle*. Québec: MESS.

Ministère du Développement Économique, de l'Innovation et de l'Exportation (MDEIE). 2006. *Un Québec innovant et prospère: Stratégie québécoise de la recherche et de l'innovation*. Québec: MDEIE.

– 2009. *Tableau synoptique du Tableau de bord du système d'innovation québécois, édition 2009*. Québec: MDEIE.

Ministère d'état au développement économique. 1982. *Le virage technologique, Bâtir le Québec. Phase 2: Programme d'action économique 1982–1986*. Québec: Gouvernement du Québec.

Ministry of Advanced Education. 1988. *Access to advanced education and job training in British Columbia*. Report of the Provincial Access Committee. Victoria: Ministry of Advanced Education.
- 2002. *A New Model for Industry Training in British Columbia*. Victoria: Ministry of Advanced Education.
- 2003. Aboriginal PSE and Training Policy Framework Draft for Discussion, 14 November. Private possession of Dr. Madeleine MacIvor.
- 2004. *Aboriginal Post-Secondary Education and Training Policy Framework*. Final draft. October. Private possession of Dr. Madeleine MacIvor.
- 2006. *Annual Service Plan Report 2006/07*. Available at http://www.bcbudget.gov.bc.ca/Annual_Reports/2006_2007/ae/ae.pdf .

Ministry of Advanced Education, Training and Technology. 1992. *Forces of Change Influencing Education and Training*. Victoria: British Columbia Ministry of Advanced Education, Training and Technology.

Ministry of Education, Skills and Training. 1996a. *Aboriginal Post-Secondary Education and Training Policy Framework*. Victoria: British Columbia Ministry of Education, Skills and Training.
- 1996b. *Charting a New Course: A Strategic Plan for the Future of British Columbia's College, Institute and Agency System*. Victoria: Province of British Columbia. Available at http://www.aett.gov.bc.ca/strategic/newcourse/.

Ministry of Skills, Training and Labour. 1995. *Skills Now: Year One Report*. Victoria: Province of British Columbia.

Ministry of Finance. 2002. "Canada's Newest University to Meet the Demand for Market-Driven Degree Programs: Province to Invest $60 Million in Ontario Institute of Technology." News release, 4 October. http://www.gov.on.ca/FIN/english/nre-oit.htm
- 2009. *Public Account of Ontario, 2009–2010: Annual Report and Consolidated Financial Statement*. Toronto: Government of Ontario.

Ministry of Training, Colleges and Universities (MTCU). 2000. *Investing in Students Task Force*. Government of Ontario. http://www.edu.gov.on.ca/eng/general/postsec/taskhme.html
- 2001. *Update: Reporting on Performance at Ontario's Colleges and Universities*. Toronto: Government of Ontario.
- 2002. *Update: Ontario's Plan for Students in the Double Cohort*. Toronto: Government of Ontario.
- 2005. *Ontario: A Leader in Learning*. Toronto: Government of Ontario.
- 2002–03. *Annual Report*. Toronto: Government of Ontario.

- 2003–04. *Annual Report.* Toronto: Government of Ontario.
- 2004–05. *Annual Report.* Toronto: Government of Ontario.
- 2005–06. *Results-Based Plan, Annual Report.* Toronto: Government of Ontario.
- 2006–07. *Results-Based Plan, Annual Report.* Toronto: Government of Ontario.
- 2009. *Published Result-Based Plan, 2009–2010.* Toronto: Government of Ontario.
- 2010. *Results-Based Plan Briefing book, 2010–2011.* Toronto: Government of Ontario.

Mok, J..H.K. 2002. From Nationalization to Marketisation: Changing Governance in Taiwan's Higher-Education System. *Governance: An International Journal of Policy, Administration and Institutions* 15 (2): 137–59.

- 2003. "Similar Trends, Diverse Agendas: Higher Education Reform in East Asia." *Globalisation, societies and education* 1 (2): 201–21.

Monahan, E. 2004. *Collective Autonomy: A History of the Council of Ontario Universities, 1962–2000.* Waterloo: Wilfrid Laurier University.

Monahan, P. 1995. *Storming the Pink Palace: The NDP in Power – A Cautionary Tale.* Toronto: Lester Publishing.

Moran, L. 1991. "Legitimation of Distance Education: A Social History of the Open Learning Institute of British Columbia, 1978–1988." Ph.D diss., University of British Columbia.

Morrow, R.A., and C.A. Torres. 2000. The State, Globalization, and Educational Policy. In *Globalization and education: Critical Perspectives*, ed. N.C. Burbules and C.A. Torres, 27–56. London: Routledge.

Mundy. K, and M. Iga. 2003. "Hegemonic Exceptionalism and Legitimating Bet-Hedging: Paradoxes and Lessons from the US and Japanese Approaches to Education Services under GATS." *Globalization, Societies and Education* 1 (3): 281–319.

Neave, G., and F.A. van Vught, eds. 1991. *Prometheus Bound.* Oxford: Pergamon.

Networks of Centres of Excellence Program (NCE). 2009. *Annual Report.* Ottawa: Ministry of Supply and Services.

- 2010. *Annual Report.* Ottawa: Ministry of Supply and Services.

Newman, O., and R. De Zoysa. 2001. *The Promise of the Third Way: Globalization and Social Justice.* Houndmills, Basingstoke, Hampshire: Palgrave Macmillan.

Noble, D.F. 1976. *America by Design: Science, Technology, and the Rise of Corporate Capitalism.* New York: Knopf.
– 2001. *Digital Diploma Mills: The Automation of Higher Education.* New York: Monthly Review Press.
Noël, A. 2002. Without Quebec: Collaborative Federalism with a Footnote? In *Building the Social Union: Perspectives, Directions and Challenges*, ed. T. McIntosh, 17–18. Regina: Saskatchewan Institute of Public Policy.
Offe, C. 1984. *Contradictions of the Welfare State.* Cambridge, MA: MIT Press.
– 1996. *Modernity and the State: East, West.* Cambridge, UK: Polity Press.
Office québécois de la langue française. 2008. *Rapport sur l'évolution de la situation linguistique au Québec 2002–2007.* Montréal: Gouvernement du Québec.
Ohmae, K. 1990. *Borderless World.* London: Collins.
Olssen, M., J. Codd, and A.M. O'Neil. 2004. *Education Policy: Globalisation, Citizenship, Democracy.* London: Sage.
Ontario Council on University Affairs (OCUA). 1988. *Fourteenth Annual Report, 1987–1988, the Accessibility Envelope, Advisory Memorandum 87–III, the On-going Accessibility Envelope for 1987–1988.* Toronto: Ministry of Colleges and Universities.
– 1994a. *Sustaining Quality in Changing Times: Funding Ontario Universities – A Discussion Paper.* Toronto: Ministry of Colleges and Universities.
– 1994b. *Twentieth Annual Report, 1993–94:An Advisory Memorandum 93–VI, Academic Quality Reviews.* Toronto: Ministry of Colleges and Universities.
– 1995. *Advisory Memorandum 95–III: Resource Allocation for Ontario Universities.* Toronto: Ministry of Colleges and Universities.
Ontario Council of University Faculty Associations (OCUFA). 2001. *Ontario Government Directions Concerning Higher Education.* Toronto: OCUFA. www.ocufa.on.ca/lobby/ogd.asp.
– 2006a. *The Measured Academic: Quality Controls in Ontario Universities.* Toronto: OCUFA
– 2006b. *Performance Indicator Use in Canada, the US, and Abroad.* Toronto: OCUFA
– 2007a. *Quality in the Balance.* Toronto: OCUFA.
– 2007b. *University Degree Program Academic Quality Assessment in Ontario.* Toronto: OCUFA

Ontario Ministry of Colleges and Universities. 1990. *Vision 2000: Quality and Opportunity*. Toronto: Ontario Ministry of Colleges and Universities.

Ontario Ministry of Training, Colleges and Universities. 2000. *Directives and Guidelines for Applying for Ministerial Consent Under the PSE Choice and Excellence Act, 2000*. Toronto: MTCU.

Ontario Progressive Conservative Caucus. 1992 *New Directions*: Vol. 2: *A Blueprint for Learning in Ontario*.Toronto: Ontario Progressive Conservative Caucus.

Organization for Economic Co-operation and Development (OECD). 1989. *Education and the economy in a changing society*. Paris: OECD.

- 2003. *The Sources of Economic Growth in OECD Countries*. Paris: OECD.
- 2006. *Main Science and Technology Indicators, 2006–1*. Paris: OECD.
- 2007. *Main Science and Technology Indicators, 2007–1*. Paris: OECD.

Orum, J. 1992. *Review of BC Student Assistance and Barriers to Postsecondary Participation*. Final Report. N.p.

Ozga, J. 1987. "Studying Education Policy through the Lives of Policy Makers: An Attempt to Close the Macro-Micro Gap. In *Changing Policies, Changing Teachers, New Directions for Schooling*, ed. L. Barton and S. Walker, 138–50. Milton Keynes, Open University Press.

- 2000. *Policy Research in Educational Settings: Contested Terrain*. Philadelphia, PA: Open University Press.

Panitch, L. 1994. "Globalization and the State." In *Socialist Register 1994: Between Globalism and Nationalism*, ed. R. Miliband and L. Panitch, 60–93. London: Merlin Press.

Paquet, G. 2002. *Robert Bourassa et la méso-économie: l'homme de Buridan et ses demi-mesures*. Communication au colloque Robert Bourassa, Université du Québec à Montréal, 21–23 mars.

Patterson, L.L. 2006. *Aboriginal Roundtable to Kelowna Accord: Aboriginal Policy Negotiations, 2004–2005*. Ottawa: Library of Parliament.

Phelps, J.M. 2013. "Otherwise, Elsewhere: International Doctoral Students in Globalized Transnational Spaces." PhD diss., University of British Columbia.

Plant, G. 2007. *Campus 2020: Access and Excellence: The Campus 2020 Plan for British Columbia's post-secondary Education System*. Available at http://www.aved.gov.bc.ca/campus2020/campus2020-thinkingahead-report.pdf.

Poggi, G. 1990. *The State: Its Nature, Development, and Prospects*. Stanford, CA: Stanford University Press.
Postsecondary Education Quality Assessment Board (PEQAB). 2010. *Ontario: A Global Leader in Quality Assurance, Annual Report 2009/2010*. Toronto: PEQAB.
Poulantzas, N. 1978. *Classes in Contemporary Capitalism*. London: Verso.
Proulx, J.-P. avec la collaboration de J.-P. Charland. 2009. *Le système éducatif du Québec: De la maternelle à l'Université*. Montréal: Chenelière Education.
Provincial Advisory Committee on Post-Secondary Education for Native Learners. 1990. *Report of the Provincial Advisory Committee on Post-Secondary Education for Native Learners*. Victoria: Provincial Advisory Committee on Post-Secondary Education for Native Learners.
President of the Treasure Board. 2002. *Canada's Performance 2002*. Available at http://www.tbs-sct.gc.ca/rma/communic/communie.asp.
Prince, M.J. 1996. "At the Edge of the Canadian Welfare State: Social Policy Making in British Columbia". In *Politics and Government in British Columbia*, ed. R.K. Carty, 236–72. Vancouver: UBC Press.
Pusser, B. 2008. "The State, the Market and the Institutional Estate: Revisiting Contemporary Authority Relations in Higher Education." In *Higher Education: Handbook of Theory and Research*. Vol. 23, ed. J.C. Smart, 105–39. Dordrecht, The Netherlands: Association for Institutional Research and the Association for the Study of Higher Education, Springer.
Ragin, C. 1987. *The Comparative Method: Moving beyond Qualitative and Quantitative Strategies*. Berkeley: University of California Press.
Rayner, W. 2000. *British Columbia's Premiers in Profile*. Surrey, BC: Heritage House.
Reich, R. 1992. *The Work of Nations: Preparing Ourselves for 21st-Century Capitalism*. New York: Vintage.
Richardson, R. 2004. *A Conceptual Framework for Comparative Studies of Higher Education Policy: Working Paper*. New York: AIHEPS.
Richardson, R.C., K. Reeves Bracco, K.P. Callan, and J.E. Finney. 1999. *Designing State Higher Education Systems for a New Century*. Phoenix, AR: American Council on Education and the Onyx Press.
Rizvi, F., and F. Lingard. 2010. *Globalizing Education Policy*. New York: Routledge.
Robertson, S., M. Novelli, R. Dale, L. Tickly, H. Dachi, and A. Ndibelema. 2007. *Globalisation, Education and Development: Ideas, Actors and*

Dynamics. London: Department for International Development, Educational Paper No. 68.

Robinson, E.I., and R. Simon. 1999. "The Dynamics of Canadian Federalism." In *Canadian Politics*, 3rd ed., ed. Alain-G. Gagnon and James P. Bickerton, 366–88. Peterborough: Broadview Press.

Rocher, G. 2004. *À la défense du réseau collégial*. Montréal: Les Presses de l'Université de Montréal.

Roelvink, G., and D. Craig. 2004. "The Man in the Partnering State: Regendering the Social through Partnership." Paper presented at conference entitled "Strengthening Communities through Local Partnerships," 5–8 April, University of Auckland, New Zealand, Local Partnerships and Governance Group. Available at http://www.arts.auckland.ac.nz/lpg/Researchpaper13.pdf.

Rooney, D., and G. Hearn. 2000. "Of Minds, Markets, and Machines: How Universities Might Transcend the Ideology of Commodification." In *The University in Transformation: Global Perspectives on the Future of the University*, ed. S. Inayatullah and J. Gidley, 91–104. Westport, CT: Bergin and Garvey.

Rose, N. 1999. *The Powers of Freedom: Reframing Political Thought*. Cambridge, UK: Cambridge University Press.

Rothstein, B. 1999. *Just Institutions Matter*. Cambridge: Cambridge University Press.

Royce, D. 1997. "University System Co-ordination and Planning in Ontario, 1945–1996." Phd diss., University of Toronto.

Rubenson, K. 2003. "Adult Education and Cohesion." *Lifelong Learning in Europe* 8 (1): 22–31.

Saul, J.R. 2005. *The End of Globalism*. Toronto: Viking Canada.

Scheurich, J.J. 1997. *Research Method in the Postmodern*. London: Falmer Press.

Schugurensky, D. 2003. "Higher Education Restructuring in the Era of Globalization: Toward a Heteronomous Model?" In *Comparative Education: The Dialectic of the Global and the Local*, 2nd ed., ed. R. Arnove and C. Torres, 257–76. Lanham: Rowman and Littlefield.

Schugurensky, D. and A, Davidson-Harden. 2003. "From Cordoba to Washington: WTO/GATS and Latin American Education." *Globalisation, Societies and Education* 3 (3): 321–57

Schworm, W., and G. Rosenbluth. 1984. "British Columbia Provincial Budget." *Western Economic Review* 3: 50–63.

Scott, P. 1995. *The Meanings of Mass Higher Education*. Buckingham, UK: SRHE and Open University Press.

Scott, P., ed. 2000. *Higher Education Re-Formed*. London: Falmer.
Sears. A. 2003. *Retooling the Mind Factory: Education in a Lean State*. Aurora, ON: Garamond.
Shaienks, D., J. Eisl-Culkin, and P. Bussière. 2006. *Follow-up on Education and Labour Market Pathways of Young Canadian Aged 18–20: Results from YITS Cycle 3*. Ottawa: Statistics Canada and human Resources and Social Development Canada.
Shaienks, D., and T. Gluszynski. 2007. *Participation in pse: Graduates, Continuers and Drop Outs, Results from YITS Cycle 4*. Ottawa: Statistics Canada and Human Resources and Social Development Canada.
Shanahan, T. 2002. "Legal Scholarship: An Analysis of Law Professors' Research Activities in Ontario's English-Speaking Common Law Schools." PhD diss., University of Toronto.
– 2008. "Hoisted by our own Petard: Accountability Agreements, Key Performance Indicators and Funding Mechanisms in Ontario's PSE." Paper presented at the plenary panel, Annual Conference of the Canadian Society for the Studies in Higher Education, 2 June.
Shanahan, T., and G. Jones. 2007. "Shifting roles and approaches: Government co-ordination of PSE in Canada, 1995–2006." *Higher Education Research and Development* 26 (1): 31–43.
Skocpol, T. 1980. "Political Responses to Capitalist Crises: Neo-Marxist Theories of the State and the Case of the New Deal." *Politics and Society* 10: 155–99.
Skolnik, M. 1987. "State Control of Degree Granting: The Establishment of a Public Monopoly in Canada." In *Governments and Higher Education: The Legitimacy of Intervention*, ed. C. Watson, 56–83. Toronto: Higher Education Group, OISE.
– 1992. "Higher Education Systems." In *Higher Education in Canada*, ed. A.D. Gregor and G. Jasmin, 15–26. Ottawa: Secretary of State of Canada in cooperation with the Association for Canadian Studies.
– 1994. "Toward the Creation of a CAAT-University Partnership for an Integrated Baccalaureate Program in Nursing." *College Quarterly* 1 (3): 15–20.
– 1997. "Putting It All Together: Viewing Canadian Higher Education from a Collection of Jurisdiction Based Perspectives." In *Higher Education in Canada: Different Systems, Different Perspectives*, ed. G.A. Jones, 325–42). New York: Garland.
Skolnik, M., G. Jones, and B. Soren. 1998. "Arrangements for Coordination between University and College Sectors in Canadian Provinces: 1990–1996." *Higher Education Policy* 2 (1): 15–27.

Skolnik, M.L., and G.A, Jones. 1993. "Arrangements for Coordination between University and College Sectors in Canadian Provinces." *Canadian Journal of Higher Education* 23 (2): 56–73.

Slaughter, S., and L. Leslie. 1997. *Academic Capitalism: Politics, Policies and the Entrepreneurial University*. Baltimore: Johns Hopkins University Press.

Slaughter, S., and G. Rhoades. 1996. "The Emergence of a Competitiveness Research and Development Policy Coalition and the Commercialization of Academic Science and Technology." *Science, Technology, and Human Values* 21 (3): 303–39.

– 2004. *Academic Capitalism and the New Economy: Markets, State, and Higher Education*. Baltimore: Johns Hopkins University Press.

– 2008. "The Academic Capitalist Knowledge/Learning Regime." In *The Exchange University: Corporatization of Academic Culture*, ed. A. Chan and D. Fisher, 19–48. Vancouver: UBC Press.

Smith, D. 2011. "Manitoba's Post-Secondary System since 1967: Stability, Change and Consistency." *Canadian Journal of Higher Education* 41 (1): 48–60.

Spitzer, S. 1987. "Security and Control in Capitalist Societies: The Fetishism of Security and the Secret Thereof. In *Transcarceration: Essays in the Sociology of Social Control*, ed. J. Lowman, R. Menzies and T. Palys. 43–58. Brookfield, VT: Gower.

Stake, R.E. 1995. *The Art of Case Study Research*. Thousand Oaks, CA: Sage.

Statistics Canada. 2005. *International Adult Literacy and Skills Survey(IALSS)*. Ottawa: Statistics Canada.

– 2007. *Eastern Ontario Health Unit Ontario (Code 3558) 2006 Community Profiles 2006 Census, Statistics Canada*. Catalogue no. 92-591-XWE. Ottawa. Released 13 March.

– 2012. Table 510001, Cansim II, Statistics Canada. Available at http://www5.statcan.gc.ca/cansim/a05?lang=eng&id=0510001.

Task Force on Advanced Training. 1993. *No Dead Ends: Report of the Task Force on Advanced Training to the Minister of Education and Training*. Toronto: Ontario Ministry of Education and Training.

Taylor, S. 1997. "Critical Policy Analysis: Exploring Contexts, Texts, and Consequences." *Discourse: Studies in the Cultural Politics of Education* 18 (19): 23–35.

– 2004. "Researching Educational Policy and Change in 'New Times': Using Critical Discourse Analysis." *Journal of Educational Policy* 19 (4): 433–51.

Taylor, S., F. Rizvi, B. Lingard, and M. Henry. 1997. *Educational Policy and the Politics of Change*. London: Routledge.
Teichler, U., and J. Sadlack, eds. 1998. *Higher Education Research: Its Relationship to Policy and Practice*. New York: Pergamon.
Thompson, P. 2005. "Bringing Bourdieu to Policy Sociology: Codification, Misrecognition and Exchange Value in the UK Context." *Educational Policy* 20 (6): 741–58.
Thurow, L.C. 1977. "Education and Economic Equality." In *Power and Ideology in Education*, ed. J.A.H. Karabel, 325–35. New York: Oxford University Press.
Toulouse, Jean-Marie. 2007. *Rapport de recherche sur la gouvernance des institutions universitaires remis au Groupe de travail sur la gouverance des universités*. Montréal: Institut sur la gouvernance d'organisations privées et publiques.
Trow, M. 1973. *Problems in the Transition from Elite to Mass Education*. Berkeley, CA: Carnegie Commission on Higher Education.
University of Ontario Institute of Technology. 2008. *Strategic Plan, 2008–2011*. Oshawa: UOIT.
Usher, A., and A. Cervenan. 2005. *Global Higher Education Rankings: Accessibility and Affordability in Comparative Perspective*. Toronto: Educational Policy Institute.
Van Damme, D. 2002. "Higher Education in the Age of Globalization." In *Globalization and the Market in Higher Education: Quality, Accreditation and Qualifications*, ed. S. Uvalic-Trumbic, 21–33. Paris: UNESCO/IAU/Economica.
Vidovich, L., and R. Slee. 2001. "Bringing Universities to Account? Exploring Some Global and Local Policy Tensions." *Journal Education Policy* 16 (5): 431–53.
Volgy, T., and A. Bailin. 2003. *International Politics and State Strength*. Boulder, CO: Lynne Rienner.
Von Hayek, F.A. 1976. *The Road to Serfdom*. Chicago, IL: University of Chicago Press.
Wagner, P. 2004. "Higher Education in an Era of Globalization: What Is at Stake?" In *Higher Education and Globalization*, ed. J.K. Odin and P.T. Manicas, 7–23. Honolulu: University of Hawaii Press.
Watkins, M. 2003. "Politics in the Time and Space of Globalization." In *Changing Canada: Political Economy and Transformation*, ed. W. Clement and L. Vosko, 3–24). Montreal and Kingston: McGill-Queen's University Press.

Weingarten, Harvey, and Fiona Deller. 2010. *The Benefits of Greater Differentiation in Ontario's University Sector*. Toronto: Higher Education Quality Council of Ontario.

Williams, R. 1961. *Long Revolution*. London: Chatto and Windus.

Wolf, A. 2002. *Does Education Matter? Myths about Education and Economic Growth*. London: Penguin.

Wood, E. 2003. *Empire and Capital*. London: Verso.

Yin, R. 2003. *Case Study Research Design and Methods*, 3rd ed. Thousand Oaks, CA: Sage.

York University. 2006a. Multi-Year Accountability Agreement 2006–07 to 2008–09. Available at http://www.yorku.ca/president/mya.

– 2006b. Multi-Year Action Plan, submitted to MTCU in September. Available at http://www.yorku.ca/president/mya.

Young, J., and B. Levin. 2002. *Understanding Canadian Schools: An Introduction to Educational Administration*, 3rd ed. Toronto: Thompson Nelson.

Young, S. 2002. "The Use of Market Mechanisms in Higher Education Finance and State Control: Ontario Considered." *Canadian Journal of Higher Education* 32 (2): 79–102.

Index

Page numbers followed by *f* or *t* indicate figures or tables.

Aboriginal peoples: New Relationship, 77; policies, 14–15, 57, 66–7, 83; population, 134, 201
Aboriginal Post-Secondary Education and Training Policy Framework, 67, 77
Aboriginal programs: funding, 16; goals, 78; outreach, 153; participation rates, 312–13; support, 131, 250
academic capitalism, 4, 23, 24, 25, 268, 334, 345
academic drift, 35, 82, 108, 115, 117, 286, 298, 299, 335, 343, 344
academic programs, enrolment rates, 108
Access for All, 88, 94
accessibility: as accumulation function, 349; BC policy, 82; comparison, 298–313, 343–4; definition of, 8, 161; and globalization, 348; infrastructure funding, 157; integration with accountability, 165; meeting objectives, 288–9; northern regions, 146, 153, 154;

OECD comparison, 329; ON policy, 162–4; QC policy, 248–51, 274–5; tuition fees, 101, 103, 105, 181
accessibility/accumulation, 349
Accessibility for Ontarians with Disabilities Act (AODA), 157, 164
accessibility fund, 136
accessibility/legitimation, 347, 348, 349
Access to Opportunities Fund (ATOP), 146
accountability: attempts at, 115–16; audits for, 144; BC, 85–7; comparison, 319–21; constraints of, 80; definition of, 8; funding by priorities, 228–9; and governance, 239–40; by governing bodies, 145; indicators, 241; management frameworks, 227; of managers and directors, 223; ON, 164–5; QC, 251–5; research councils, 156–7; shift of responsibilities, 25; universities, 140–2
accountability/accumulation, 349, 350

accountability/legitimation, 347, 348, 349–50
accumulation function, 4, 32–3, 34, 334, 347, 349–50, 352
l'Action démocratique du Québec (ADQ), 235, 236
Act Respecting Educational Institutions at the University Level, 205, 222, 224, 227, 254
Act Respecting Private Education, 203, 210
Act Respecting the Conseil supérieur de l'Éducation, 248
Act Respecting the Reduction of Personnel in Public Bodies, 223, 254
Act to Promote the Advancement of Science and Technology, 220, 260, 326
Act to Promote the Maintenance and Renewal of Public Infrastructure, 237
Act to Promote Workforce Skills Development and Recognition, 205
adult basic education (ABE), 105, 108, 109f, 110f, 111t
Advanced Education Council of British Columbia (AECBC), 90
advanced training, 138
advisory bodies, 170
Advisory Committee on the Financial Accessibility of Education, 248
Advisory Panel on Future Directions for PSE, 145, 149, 170–1
affordability, 329
AIHEPS model, 6f
Aim for the Top Scholarships, 148
Albert, M., 262
Alberta, Government of, 130, 133, 156
Alberta, tuition fees, 11

Alexander College, 45
Algoma University, 153
Allen, Richard, 140
Alliance for International Higher Education Policy Studies (AIHEPS), 3
Alpha College, 58
Altbach, P.G., 23
Amaral, A., 23, 28, 351
Andres, L., 48
Anisef, P., 23
Applied General Education Path, 202
Apprenticeship Enhancement Fund Program (AEF), 158
apprenticeship programs: access, 157–8; consultation process, 90; efficiency, 81; enrolment rates, 105; expansion of, 84, 85; vs vocational training, 69–70
Arnove, R.F., 23
Art Institute of Vancouver, 45, 316
Association des collèges privés du Québec, 208
Association of Universities and Colleges of Canada, 143, 318, 328
Association pour la solidarité syndicale étudiante, 245
Athabasca University, 45
Atkinson-Grosjean, J., 342
attestation of college studies (ACS), 204
automotive and power industries, 150
autonomy, 145, 286
Avison, Don, 69
Avison, D.S., 78
Axelrod, P., 23

Bailin, A., 29
Baker, Donald, 143
Baker Report, 143, 162
Bakvis, H., 14

Ball, S., 11, 21, 22, 338
Barrow, C.W., 32, 351
Bastow, S., 31
Bayh-Dole Act, 229
BC Campus, 75, 80–1
BC Knowledge Development Fund (BCKDF), 69
BC Progress Board, 90
BC Task Force on Employment and Training, 59–60
Beaton, J., 33
Bédard, D., 232
Bélanger, P.W., 215
Bennett, Bill, 52, 53
Berdhal, R.O., 23
Berland, D., 301
Bernatchez, J., 18, 265, 292
bible colleges, 126, 314
bilingual programs, 131, 162
binary systems, 12, 163, 171, 194, 196, 299
Blaney, Jack, 79
block operating grants, 50–1
boards, 239–40
Bok, D., 24
Bouchard, Lucien, 224
bounded rationality model, 198
Bourassa, Robert, 217, 221, 265
Bourdieu, P., 22, 23, 24, 338, 349, 350
Bovey, Edmund, 168
Bowbrick, Graeme, 68
Bowe, R., 21, 22
Brennan, J., 23
British Columbia: accessibility, 82–4; accessibility comparison, 298–313, 343–4; accountability, 85–7; accountability comparison, 319–21; conclusions, 114–21; credit transfer system, 48–9; current design and funding, 36–51; expenditures, 97t, 297t; funding, 50–1, 91–101; funding comparison, 292–8, 294f; globalization, 351; grants per funded FTE, 95f; intermediary bodies, 47–50; labour force development comparison, 321–4; marketization, 9, 87; marketization comparison, 313–19; ministers and policies, 355–8; outcomes, 101–14; policy making process, 87–90; policy making process comparison, 335–8; policy sociology, 338–43; political context, 51–82; political ideology trends, 11–12; population, 36–7; private sector design, 42–7; public sector design, 37–42; R&D comparison, 324–33; representation by, 10–11; revenue sources, 99f, 100t; trends, 35; vocationalism, 84–5
British Columbia, government of, 64, 84
British Columbia Association of Institutes and Universities (BCAIU), 48
British Columbia Chamber of Commerce, 90
British Columbia Council on Admissions and Transfer (BCCAT), 48, 299
British Columbia *Hansard*, 65, 68, 76, 81, 87, 90, 315
British Columbia Institute of Technology (BCIT), 41, 54, 57
British Columbia Labour Force Development Board (BCLFDB), 61–2, 67
British North America Act, 14
Broadhurst, William, 140
Brodie, J., 29, 31, 351
Burrawoy, Michael, 20
business. *See* private sector

Caisse de dépôt et placement du Québec, 238
Callan, K.P., 286

Callinicos, A., 31
Calvert, J., 64
Cameron, D., 14, 54, 127, 136, 137, 138, 140, 168
Campbell, Gordon, 11, 52, 72, 77, 80, 90
The Campus 2020 Plan for British Columbia's PSE System (Plant), 40, 337–8
Canada: enrolment, 185t, 187t; GERD, 331f; and globalization, 29–30; higher education attainment, 312t; literacy and numeracy scores, 312, 313t; participation rates, 184t; per student funding, 296t; student awareness of, 15; study provinces representation, 10–11; values, 31
Canada Assistance Plan, 136, 139
Canada Council, 327–8
Canada Foundation for Innovation (CFI), 10, 16, 18, 69, 230, 325, 329–30
Canada Health and Social Transfer (CHST), 16–17, 18, 19–20, 91, 172, 238, 265, 292, 340, 347
Canada Millennium Scholarship Foundation (CMSF), 16, 79, 148, 154–5, 233, 308
Canada Research Chairs (CRCs), 10, 18, 69, 325
Canada Social Transfer and Equalization Program, 201
Canada Student Loans Program (CSLP), 16, 148, 233
Canada Studies Program, 15
Canadian Association of University Business Officers (CAUBO), 295, 347
Canadian Association of University Teachers (CAUT), 16, 87, 295, 324, 329, 330

Canadian Constitution Act, 15
Canadian Graduate and Professional Student Survey (CGPSS), 133, 156
Canadian Institutes of Health Research (CIHR), 18, 327–8, 340
Canadian Jobs Strategy, 321
Canadian Labour Force Development Board (CLFDB), 62, 322
Canadian Way, 30–1
Capilano University, 38
capital: in PSE, 24; and state, 26
capital accumulation, 32–3
capitalist state, 32–3
career certificate programs, 204
career colleges, 153
career training, 203
Carnoy, M., 29
Carrier, G., 229
Carroll, W., 31, 33, 54, 335
case study method, 9–10
Castells, M., 25
CAUT Almanac, 87, 317
CCPA/BC, 68
CÉGEP International, 208
central marketing agency, 64
Centre for Curriculum, Transfer and Technology (C_2T_2), 49, 63, 75
Centre for Education Information Standards and Services (CEISS), 49, 63–4, 75
Centres of Excellence for Commercialization and Research, 328
Centro de Investigacion y Estudios Avanzados, 3
Cervenan, A., 329
Chairs of Excellence Program, 325
Chan, A.S., 9, 24, 33, 340
Charest, Jean, 12, 230, 237
Charles, A.C., 130

Charlottetown Accord, 222
Charter of the French Language, 218–9
Charting a New Course: A Strategic Plan for the Future of British Columbia's College, Institute and Agency System, 62–3, 64, 75, 85, 88–9
Chowdhury, Sujit, 44–5
Chrétien, Jean, 30, 31
civil society, consultation, 284
Clark, B.R., 12, 23, 24, 25, 194, 344
Clark, Christy, 52
Clark, Glen, 52, 67, 84
Clark, I., 170
Clement, W., 334
Clift, R., 18, 265, 292
Coalition of BC Businesses, 76, 90
Codd, J., 21
Cohen, R., 347
collective agreements, 76, 244
College and Institute Act, 37, 41–2, 53, 67
College and Institute Amendment Act, 65
college boards, 169
College Centres for Transfer of Technology, 235
college funding model, 131
Collège militaire royal de Saint-Jean, 222
colleges: coordinating bodies, 207–8; QC network, 202–5. *See also* colleges and institutes (BC); Collèges d'enseignement général et professionnel (CÉGEPS); Colleges of Applied Arts and Technology (CAATS)
colleges and institutes (BC): budget submissions, 51; degree programs, 76; funding, 91, 92f, 93f, 94, 96; governance, 41–2; grants per funded FTE, 95f; intermediary bodies, 48–9; marketization, 64; operating grants, 118f; participation rates, 107f; reform goals, 62–3, 86; revenue sources, 98, 100–1
Colleges Collective Bargaining Act, 129
Colleges Compensation and Appointments Council (CCAC), 129–30
Collèges d'enseignement général et professionnel (CÉGEPS): career training, 255–6, 257–8; collaboration, 204; decentralization, 232–3; failing tax, 253; funding, 209–10, 238, 252, 266; geographical accessibility, 299; governance, 239–40; grants per funded FTE, 269f; operating grants, 267f; organization of, 203, 217–18; participation rates, 278, 279t; policy influences, 244; research and development, 262, 264; revenue sources, 271; revitalization, 223, 249; tuition fees, 274
Colleges Integrating Immigrants to Employment Program, 158–9
Colleges of Applied Arts And Technology (CAATS): accountability, 146; alternative funding sources, 178; binary systems, 145; collaboration, 162, 168, 170–1; competition among, 136; creation, 127; degree completion arrangements, 149; design, 125–6; funding, 155; governance, 129–30, 169; grants per funded FTE, 176f; intermediary bodies, 128; operating grants, 173f, 197f; participation rates, 184; revenue sources, 172, 174; review of, 137–8

Colleges Ontario, 129, 133, 172, 174
College Standards and Accreditation Council (CSAC), 138
College University Consortium Council (CUCC), 138, 145
Collins, Gary, 73
Columbia College, 45
Comité consultatif sur l'accessibilité financière aux études (CCAFE), 207, 232
commercialization, 24
Commission consultative de l'enseignement privé, 203
Commission de la culture et de l'éducation, 240
Commission de l'enseignement collégial (CEC), 207, 223, 256
Commission de l'enseignement et de la recherche universitaires (CERU), 207, 223
Commission des universités sur les programmes (CUP), 228, 252–3, 259
Commission d'évaluation de l'enseignement collégial (CEEC), 207–8, 223, 244, 251, 252
Commission for the Estates General on Education, 225, 228, 248
Commission of Inquiry on Universities, 219
Commission on the Future Development of the Universities of Ontario, 168
Commission on Universities, 222
Commission sur l'éthique en science et en technologie, 241
Committee of University Program, 244
Committee on the Future Role of Universities in Ontario, 168
Committee on University Affairs, 127, 168

commodification: of knowledge, 4; in universities, 23–4
Common Sense Revolution, 172, 301
Commonwealth Co-operative Federation (CCF), 52
community colleges. *See* colleges and institutes (BC); Collèges d'enseignement général et professionnel (QC); colleges of applied arts and technology (ON)
Comoe, E., 203
Competing in the New Global Economy, 165
completion rates, 289
computer science, 146, 147
Confederation of University Faculty Associations of BC, 77
Conference of Rectors and Principals of the Universities of Québec (CRÉPUQ): accountability, 225, 252–3; career training, 258; decision-making process, 244, 254; evaluation policy, 224; funding, 211, 234, 238; overview, 208; professional skills, 240–1; programs, 228, 232
Conseil de la Fédération, 231
Conseil de la Science et de la Technologie (CST), 256, 260, 326
Conseil des collèges, 207, 223, 255
Conseil des universités, 207, 216, 218, 220, 221–2, 244, 252, 256, 319
Conseil du Trésor, 227, 244, 245
Conseil interprofessionnel du Québec, 241
Conseil québécois de la recherche sociale, 327
Conseil supérieur de l'éducation (CSE), 207, 216, 218, 223–4, 251, 255
Conservative government (federal), 231
Considine, M., 9, 24

Constitution Act, 15, 219
consultation, 169, 246, 284, 287, 335–8
continuing education, 249
Contract Training Marketing Society (CTMS), 64, 85
convergence, 26–7, 350–1
Cooke, Dave, 141, 142
coordinated market system economies, 30
Coquitlam College, 45
Cormier, M., 204
Cormode, G., 78
Corpus Christi College, 45
corridor funding, 131, 136, 162
cost of living, 308
Council of Canadian Academies, 329, 346
Council of Ministers of Education Canada (CMEC), 16, 143
Council of Ontario Universities (COU), 127, 133, 141, 143, 146, 149, 154, 174, 175
Council of Regents, 136–7
Council of Technology, 166
Council of Universities, 169
Courchene, T., 134, 135, 139, 144, 161
Coyne, A., 30, 31
Craig, D., 30, 32, 352
Credentials Validation Service (CVS), 129
credit transfer systems: BC, 48–9, 56; ON, 138, 143, 149, 155–6, 162
CREPUQ committee, 319
critical moments, 23
critical sociology, 20
Culos, G., 58, 316
Culture and Education Commission, 252
current design and funding: BC, 36–51; ON, 123–4; QC, 214–17
Currie, J., 23, 24, 25, 313

Dachi, H., 22, 338
Dale, R., 22, 23, 25, 26, 27, 28, 338, 341, 347
Dandurand, L., 261
David Smith Commission, 145
Davidson-Harden, A., 27, 28, 341, 347
Dawson, J., 48
DCS-BA programs, 204
debt, 50, 308
decentralization, 115
decision-making process: BC, 87–90; comparison, 335–8; ON, 167–71; QC, 206–9, 242–8, 286–7
Deem, R., 25
Degree Authorization Act, 42–6, 76, 77, 81, 87, 315, 316
Degree Granting Act, 125, 126, 128, 314
degree-granting authority: and accessibility, 162; BC, 42–3; control by, 128; ON, 124, 171; QC, 222
Degree Program Review Committee, 71, 86
degree programs: BC transfer system, 45; completion rates, 289; expansion of, 149–50; monitoring, 86; private institutions, 126; rural access, 55–6; university colleges, 65; US-based institutions, 45–6
Degree Quality Assessment Board, 47, 315
demand, 335
Dennison, J., 53, 54, 56
dentistry, tuition fees, 102f, 103, 182f, 276f, 304t
Department of Finance, Canada, 31
Department of Foreign Affairs and International Trade (DFAIT), 15
De Zoysa, R., 31
Differentiation Grants, 131

Dill, D.D., 23, 25
diploma of college studies (DCS), 202–4
diploma of vocational studies (DVS), 202
diploma programs, completion rates, 289
direct funding, 17
disciplinary neoliberalism, 26
distance learning, 75, 249, 299, 300
divergence, 26–7, 350–1
diversification, 144
Doern, G.B., 18
Domhoff, G.W., 26
Donald, J.G., 246
Doray, P, 203
Dosanjh, Ujjal, 52, 69
Doubling the Opportunity initiative, 79–80
Doyle, C., 54
Drucker, P.F., 13
dual systems, 12, 282–3
Durham College, 150–1, 166, 323

economic activity: importance of PSE, 28, 58–9; renewal, 55
economic development: and PSE policy, 4, 160, 165–7; and R&D, 15–6, 235, 347; state intervention, 215
economic policy, 137, 347
economic priorities of study, 7
economic security, 4
education: highest level attained, 190t, 312t; jurisdiction of, 14
Education Quality and Accountability Office (EQAO), 141
efficiency: and accountability, 251–4; definition of, 8
Emily Carr Institute of Art and Design, 57
Emily Carr University of Art and Design, 38

Eminata Group, 44
employee associations, 244
employees. *See* labour force development
employment equity, 142
employment income, 308
Enders, J., 28
engineering, 146, 147
English schools, 238
enrolment: accessibility measures, 163–4; initiatives to increase, 156, 160; ON, 186f, 187t, 188t; participation measurement, 181, 184–5, 187–8, 190; QC, 203, 205–6; targeted funding support, 153–4. *See also* per student funding
entrepreneurship, 24
equalization payment, 151
equity, 140
ESL schools, 316
Esping-Andersen, G., 30
Espinoza, O., 28, 341
established programs financing (EPF), 16
Estates General on Education, 230, 251, 289
Etzkowitz, H., 24
Everett, S., 22
Eves, Ernie, 134, 144–5
Excellence, Accessibility and Responsibility, 145
exceptionalism, 17, 242, 252
expansion funding, 147
expenditures: comparison, 297t; percentages, 97t, 270t

Facilities Renewal Program, 155, 157
Fair Access to the Regulated Professions Act, 158
Fairclough, N., 21
Fairleigh Dickinson University, 45
fairness commissioner, 158
Feagin, J., 9

federal government: effect of policies, 6f, 161; labour force development, 321–2; labour market training, 158; relationship with provinces, 13–20, 201, 284, 292; research and development, 327–8, 346–7; research regulation, 230, 243, 261–2; responsibilities, 348; stabilization payments, 136, 139; transfer payments, 16–17, 18, 19–20, 91, 172, 238, 265, 340, 347
Fédération des CÉGEPs, 208, 232, 240, 243, 283, 287
Fédération étudiante collégiale du Québec, 245
Fédération étudiante universitaire du Québec, 245
Ferretti, L., 215
finance. *See* funding
financial aid. *See* student financial assistance programs
Finland, R&D expenditures, 279
Finney, J.E., 286
first-generation students, 153
fiscal policy. *See* funding; student financial assistance programs; tax credits
fiscal restraint, and policy-making process, 168–9
Fisher, D., 9, 18, 24, 33, 54, 265, 292, 330, 340, 342
Fisher, Harry, 168
Fonds de recherche du Québec – Nature et technologies, 208, 241, 327
Fonds de recherche du Québec – Santé, 208–9, 241, 327
Fonds de recherche du Québec – Société et culture, 208, 241, 327
Fonds des générations, 231
Forces of Change, 60
Ford Foundation, 3
foreign research funding, 113f, 193f, 281f

forest industry, 89
Formation de chercheurs et d'aide a la recherche (FCAR), 327
Formation des chercheurs et action concertée (FCAC), 217
Forum des générations, 231
France, critical moment, 23
francophone students (ON), 153, 162, 300
Fraser International College, 45
Frauley, J., 27
Freedom of Information and Protection of Privacy Act, 157, 164
French-language programs, 138
Friedman, M., 30
Front de libération du Québec (FLQ), 217
FTE funding. *See* per student funding
funding: and accountability, 141–2, 146, 165, 253; BC, 50–1, 91–101; budget cuts, 53–4; for career training, 258–9; comparison, 292–8, 346t; core service, 72–4; effect of constraints, 142; federal government priorities, 13–14; federal-provincial relationships, 16–17; grants per funded FTE, 95f, 176f; new formula, 234–5; ON, 130–3, 171–80; and policy goals, 167; by priorities, 228–9; QC, 265–73; sources, 87; strategies promoting access, 249–50; structure for R&D, 17–18; targeted, 74–5, 153–4; tuition freeze, 68–9. *See also* revenues (all sources)
funding envelopes, 146

Gale, T., 21, 22, 291, 338
Gallagher, P., 53
General and Vocational Colleges Act, 203, 223, 227
General Education Path, 202

general funding expenditures, 211–12
General Purpose Operating Grants (GPOG), 130
geographical accessibility, 249, 250, 299–300
Gerring, J., 9, 10
Giddens, A., 27, 30, 31, 351, 352
Gilgoff, B., 54
Gill, S., 26, 341, 350
Gingras, Y., 217, 218
Ginzburg, M., 28, 341
globalization, 23, 25, 26–30, 165–7, 334, 347, 348, 350–1
global neoliberalism, 26–7
Godin, B., 217, 218, 262
Gold, A., 21, 22
Goldberg, M.P., 22
Gould, E., 28
governments: approach to globalization, 28–9; division of power, 10; ideology of, 6–7; view of PSE, 3–4
government training contracts, 64–5, 85
graduate programs: capital support, 155; degrees granted, 191t; enrolment, 154, 184–5, 187t; FTE by programs, 111t; participation rates, 109f, 110f; quality review process, 140; tuition fees, 102f, 103, 147, 182f, 276f, 304t
Graham, Colin, 142
granting councils, 18, 20, 324, 329–30
Green, A., 28, 351
Green Report, 57
Groleau, A., 203
gross domestic expenditures on research and development (GERD), 19, 329–30, 332, 332t
gross domestic product: and operating grants, 120f; and R&D expenditures, 112f, 192f, 193f, 280f, 330, 331f
Gumport, P.J., 23

Habermas, J., 26
Hagen, Stanley, 55–6, 88, 336
Hall, P.A., 30, 352
Hallak, J., 29, 351
Hamel, P., 215
Harcourt, Mike, 52, 58, 61
Harper, Stephen, 231
Harris, Mike, 11, 134, 143–4
Harris, P., 313
Harvey, D., 350
Healey, P., 24
health professions, 79, 152
health sector funding, 19, 96, 175, 268, 340
Hearn, G., 24, 340
Henry, M., 22, 291, 338
higher education expenditures on research and development (HERD), 329
Higher Education Presidents' Council (HEPC), 49
Higher Education Quality Council of Ontario (HEQCO), 127, 132, 133, 156–7, 165, 170, 198
Hirst, P., 28
Holland, 12
Hommen, L., 61
Homo Academicus (Bourdieu), 23
Hood, Christopher, 29
House, D., 137, 140, 167, 168, 314, 342
Human Resources and Development Canada (HRDC), 15, 16
Human Resources and Skills Development Canada (HRSDC), 15, 16
hybrid systems, 163

Iacobucci, Frank, 132
Iga, M., 27, 28, 29, 347, 351

inclusive liberalism, 30–2
Indian and Northern Affairs Canada (INAC), 14, 15
Indirect Costs Program, 263
indirect research cost policy, 211, 233–4, 263
indirect transfers, 17
industry. *See* private sector
Industry Research Program, 325
Industry Training and Apprenticeship Commission (ITAC), 71, 76, 81, 85
Industry Training Authority (ITA), 76, 85, 119, 322–3
information access and privacy, 157
infrastructure: for accessibility, 157; funding, 147, 155
innovation, 326
Innovation Strategy, 322
Institute for Christian Studies, 126
Institute of Indigenous Government, 37, 38, 67
Institute of Technology and Advanced Learning (ITALS), 126
institutes. *See* colleges and institutes (BC)
institutionalization of neoliberalism, 26
Institut national de la recherche scientifique (INRS), 205, 217
intermediary bodies, 165, 168
Inter-Ministry Committee on Equity in Apprenticeship, 70
internationalization, 155, 259, 323
internationalization of neoliberalism, 26
internationally trained individuals, 158–9, 240–1
international research centres, 156
international students, 154, 206, 317–18
international studies, 154
inter-provincial certification, 159
Inuit students, 14, 16, 201, 312

Investing in Students Task Force, 148–9
investment funds, 209
investments, 237

James, C., 23
Jessop, B., 32
Jewish schools, 231
Joberg, G., 9
Johnson, Daniel, Jr., 221
Johnson, Rita, 52
joint degree programs, 149
Jones, G., 12, 14, 18, 23, 28, 37, 47–50, 127, 128, 131, 136, 137, 138, 140, 157, 161, 163, 167, 168, 190, 265, 287, 292, 314, 315, 344, 351
Jothen, K., 78
Jouve, B., 215

K-12 education: funding, 98, 175; in QC, 201–2; years to complete, 308
Karseth, B., 23, 28, 351
Kelly, G.P., 23
Kelowna Accord, 77–8
Kelsey, J., 31
Kennedy, P., 347
key moments, 338
Keynes, J.M., 30
key performance indicators (KPIS), 131–3, 146, 153, 156, 164, 320
King, R., 351
Kingston College, 44, 47
knowledge: commodification of, 4; and the state, 25
knowledge-based economy, 23, 347
Knowledge Network, 75
knowledge society, emergence of, 13
knowledge transfer, 167
Kogan, M., 11, 23
Kwantlen College, 65
Kwantlen Polytechnic University, 38

labour force development: in accumulation function, 347; comparison, 321–4; definition of, 8; links to PSE, 255–60; recommendations, 60–2; targeting, 166; training, 157–8; university ties, 223–4. *See also* apprenticeship programs; vocational and technical training
Labour Force Development Strategy, 322
Labour Market Development Agreement (LMDA), 158
Labour Market Partnership Agreements (LMPA), 158
labour mobility, 240–1
Lakehead University, 152
Landry, Bernard, 225
Lang, D., 137, 140, 167, 168, 314
Langer, M., 54
languages, 15, 201
Lansbridge University, 44
Laplante, B., 203
Laurentian University, 152
Laurin, C., 219
law, tuition fees, 102f, 103, 182f, 276f, 304t
Leading Edge Endowment Fund, 74
Learning and Work: The Way Ahead for British Columbians (Strand Report), 59–61
Leblanc, 14
Lecours, A., 301
Lee, J., 18, 23, 31, 265, 292
legislation, 335–8
legitimation function, 4, 25, 27, 32, 34, 334, 347, 349–50, 352
Lesage, Jean, 215
Lesemann, F., 263
Leslie, L., 24, 25
Lévesque, René, 218
Levin, B., 14
liberal-democratic state, 4

Liberal government (BC): accessibility, 83–4, 302; accountability, 86; funding, 91, 94, 96, 98, 100–1, 118f; ideology, 52; labour force development, 321–2; marketization, 87, 313; matching-fund schemes, 318; ministers and policies, 357–8; new public structures, 37, 38; overview, 72–82; policy-making process, 89–90, 337; political ideology trends, 11–12; priorities, 117, 119, 121; private institutions, 46, 47, 314; structure implementation, 49; tuition fees, 67, 103, 306; vocational policy, 85
Liberal government (federal): marketization, 161, 341–2; research and development, 324, 332
Liberal government (ON): accessibility, 162, 163, 302; accountability, 164–5, 320–1; funding, 171–2, 175, 197f; globalization, 165–7; ministers and policies, 360; overview, 134–8, 151–60; participation rates, 187; policy-making process, 336, 337, 341; tuition fees, 306
Liberal government (QC): accessibility, 301, 302; effect of governance style, 285; evolution of system, 214–15, 217–18, 221–4, 230–42; funding, 265, 266, 271; ministers and policies, 367, 368, 369; policy-making process, 341; R&D expenditures, 279; research support, 261; tuition fees, 274–5
liberalism, 30–2
liberal market economies, 30
Liberal-NDP Accord, 135
Lindblom, C., 246
Lingard, R., 21, 22, 291, 338, 347
literacy, 312, 313t
Lo, Michael, 44

Loans and Bursaries Program, 213, 230–1, 233
Loi sur les investissements universitaires, 211
Long Revolution, 344, 350

MacIvor, M., 18, 57, 67, 265, 292
Magnusson, W., 54
manpower policy, 321
Marcoux-Moisan, M., 203
Marginson, S., 9, 24, 302, 340, 351
marketization: BC, 81, 86–7; comparison, 313–9; definition of, 9; effect, 347; focus on, 4, 8, 334; OECD, 341; ON, 160–1, 166, 171, 196; QC, 286; state restructure, 25; in universities, 23–4
Martin, J., 31
Martin, Paul, 30–1
matching-fund schemes, 318–19
Mayumi, T., 28, 341
McBride, S., 28, 29, 30, 351
McGuinty, Dalton, 134, 151, 159, 170
McKee, C., 78
Medical Research Council, 327–8
Medical School initiative, 79–80
medicine: capital support, 155; enrolment, 154; tuition fees, 102f, 103, 182f, 276f, 304t
Meech Lake Accord, 221, 222
Meredith, J., 18, 265, 292
Merkel, J., 78
Merriam, S., 9
Metcalfe, A.S., 38, 345
Métis, 15
Miliband, R., 26
Miller, Daniel, 52, 65
Miller, Frank, 134
Milot, P., 261, 327
Ministère de la Recherche, de la Science et de la Technologie, 229, 326
Ministère de l'Éducation (MEQ), 216, 219, 221, 226, 227, 228, 233, 248, 249, 252, 254, 257, 263, 286, 319, 321
Ministère de l'Éducation du Loisir et du Sport (MELS): centralization, 243–4; control, 239; decision-making process, 242, 244–5; diplomas, 202, 204; funding, 210, 236, 238; indirect research cost policy, 233–4; investments, 211, 237; regulations, 287; responsibilities, 206, 209, 212; role, 240, 286
Ministère de l'Enseignement supérieur, de la Science et de la Technologie, 221
Ministère de l'enseignement supérieur et de la science, 223, 255, 256
Ministère d'état au développement économique, 220
Ministère du Commerce extérieur, 221
Ministère du Développement Économique, de l'Innovation et de l'Exportation (MDEIE), 206, 233, 235, 242, 243, 245, 261, 262, 279
Ministère du Développement économique et régional et de la Recherche (MDERR), 233
ministers, 19
Minister's Committee on Entry-Level Trades Training and Apprenticeship, 70
Ministry of Advanced Education (BC), 50–1, 55–6, 74, 77, 78, 81, 85, 90, 322
Ministry of Advanced Education Training and Technology (BC), 60
Ministry of Colleges and Universities Act, 126, 128

Ministry of Education, Skills and Training (BC), 62, 67, 88
Ministry of Education and Training (ON), 142
Ministry of Energy, Science and Technology (ON), 325
Ministry of Finance (ON), 159
Ministry of Research and Innovation (ON), 159
Ministry of Skills, Training and Labour (BC), 61
Ministry of Training, Colleges and Universities (ON), 125, 126, 153, 154, 156, 157, 159, 160, 314
Mok, J.H.K., 25, 28, 29, 350, 351
Monahan, P., 139
Moran, L., 54
Morrow, R.A., 351
Moulin, S., 203
Mulroney, Brian, 55
multi-year accountability agreements (MYAAS), 132–3, 157, 187
Mundy, K., 27, 28, 29, 347, 351
Murdoch, J., 203

Nadeau, M., 204
Nadeau Report, 218, 223, 251
Naidoo, R., 351
National Assembly, 210, 254
National Assembly Culture and Education Commission, 207, 223, 227, 249
National Centre for Public Policy and Higher Education, 274, 302–3
National Institute of Disability Management and Research (NIDMAR), 43
nationalism, 31, 242, 246
national organizations, 16
National Sciences and Engineering Council of Canada, 327–8
National Survey on Student Engagement (NSSE), 133, 156

nation-states: approach to globalization, 28–9; transition of, 32
Natural Sciences and Engineering Research Council (NSERC), 18
Ndibelema, A., 22, 338
NDP government (BC): accessibility, 83, 301; accountability, 86, 320; funding, 91, 94, 96, 98, 100–1, 118f; ideology, 52; labour force development, 322; ministers and policies, 355–7; new public structures, 37, 38; overview, 58–72; policy-making process, 88–9, 337, 341; priorities, 117, 119; private institution financial assistance, 46; tuition fees, 103, 306; vocational policy, 84–5
NDP government (ON): accessibility, 162; accountability, 164, 320; funding, 172, 197f; globalization initiatives, 166; ministers and policies, 360; overview, 138–43; policy-making process, 168–9, 337
Neave, G., 23
neoconservatism, 54–5
neoliberalism: in BC, 81; effect, 27–8, 30, 224, 334–5, 341, 342–3, 347, 352; funding, 87; institutionalization, 26; in QC, 221, 222, 230, 286; in restructuring, 349–50; themes in, 25; trends, 11–2
Networks of Centres of Excellence Program, 18, 166, 325, 328
New Directions II: A Blueprint for Learning in Ontario, 144
Newfoundland and Labrador, tuition fees, 10
Newman, O., 31
New Model for Industry Training, 322

Index   437

New Programs Committee, 320
New Programs Evaluation
    Commission, 244, 252, 258
New Public Management
    approach, 239
Newson, J., 23
New York University, 3
Nicola Valley Institute of
    Technology (NVIT), 37, 38, 67
Nipissing College, 142
Noble, D.F., 24
*No Dead Ends: Report of the Task
    Force on Advanced Training to
    the Minister of Education and
    Training*, 138
Noël, A., 14
non-degree programs, 46
Nortel, 146
northern grants, 146
Northern Ontario School of
    Medicine, 152
Northern School of Medicine, 154
Novelli, M., 22, 338
numeracy, 312, 313t

O'Brian, David, 26
October Crisis, 217
Offe, C., 32, 352
Office Québécois de la langue française, 201
Official Languages in Education
    Program, 15
Ohmae, K., 27, 351
Okanagan University College, 38
Okihiro, N.R., 23
Olssen, M., 21
O'Neil, A.M., 21
One Stop Training and
    Employment System, 157
on-line learning, 75
Ontario: accessibility, 161–4; accessibility comparison, 298–313, 343–4; accountability, 164–5;

accountability comparison, 319–21; conclusions, 194–9; coordination, 127–33; current design and funding, 123–4; degrees granted, 191t; enrolment, 187t; expenditures, 177t, 297t; funding, 171–80; funding comparison, 292–8, 294f; grants per funded FTE, 176f; higher education attainment, 190t; labour force development comparison, 321–4; marketization, 9, 160–1; marketization comparison, 313–9; ministers and policies, 360–3; operating grants, 173f; outcomes, 180–94; policy-making process, 167–71; policy-making process comparison, 335–8; policy sociology, 338–43; political context, 133–60; political ideology trends, 11–2; population with PSE, 188; private institutions, 126–7; public institutions, 124–6; R & D, 165–7; R & D comparison, 324–33; representation by, 10–1; revenue sources, 179f, 180t; universities, 359; vocationalism, 165
Ontario, government of, 137, 165
Ontario: A Leader in Learning, 152, 153
Ontario Bridging Partnership
    Assistance Program, 158
Ontario Centres of Excellence, 137, 165–6, 325
Ontario College of Art and Design, 150
Ontario Colleges of Applied Arts
    and Technology Act, 128–9, 152
Ontario Colleges Quality Assurance
    Service (OCQAS), 129
Ontario Council of Regents for
    Colleges of Applied Arts and
    Technology, 128, 168

Ontario Council of University Faculty Associations (OCUFA), 133, 156
Ontario Council on Graduate Studies, 140
Ontario Council on University Affairs (OCUA), 127, 131, 136, 140–2, 143, 168, 169
Ontario Graduate Fellowships, 154–5
Ontario Graduate Scholarships, 148
Ontario Green Jobs Strategy, 159
Ontario Institute for Studies in Education (OISE), 142
Ontario Labour Mobility Act, 159
Ontario Online Institute, 160
Ontario Progressive Conservative Caucus, 144
Ontario Public Service Employees Union (OPSEU), 129
Ontario Research Fund (ORF), 159
Ontario Research Performance Fund, 325
Ontario Second Career Program, 159
Ontario Student Assistance Program (OSAP), 147, 154, 160, 318
Ontario Student Opportunity Grant program, 154
Ontario Student Opportunity Trust, 148
Ontario Trust for Student Support (OTSS), 155
Ontario University Institute of Technology, 323
Ontario Youth Apprenticeship Program, 158
Open Learning Agency (OLA), 38, 54, 56, 63, 75
Open Ontario Plan, 159–60
operating expenditures, 211–12
operating grants: BC, 50, 91, 92f, 93f, 94, 197f; comparison, 292–3; and GDP, 120f; ON, 130–2, 155, 156, 167, 172, 173f; per funded FTE, 172, 174, 176f; QC, 209–13, 265, 267f
Organization for Economic Co-operation and Development (OECD), 29–30, 59, 329, 341
Orum, A., 9
Orum, J., 54
outcomes: BC, 101–14; management frameworks, 227; ON, 180–94; QC, 273–82
Ozga, J., 21, 22, 338

Pacific Coast University for Workplace Health Sciences (PCU-WHS), 43, 315–16
Pacific Vocational Institute, 54
Pan-Canadian Protocol on the Transferability of University Credits, 143, 162
Panitch, L., 26, 32
Paquet, G., 221
Parent Commission, 260, 325–6
Parent Report, 215–17
Parizeau, Jacques, 224
participation, 105, 108
participation rates: BC, 106f, 107f, 109f, 110f, 111t; comparison, 184t, 308–13, 309t; ON, 188t, 189f; QC, 278, 279t, 289
Parti de l'Action démocratique, 237
Parti Québécois: accessibility, 301; effect of governance style, 285; election results, 235–6, 237; evolution of system, 218–21, 224–7; funding, 265–6, 271; ministers and policies, 368, 369; R&D, 261, 279; tuition fees, 275
Parti Québec Solidaire, 238
Pascal, Charles, 142
Patterson, L.L., 77
Pay Equity Act, 231

People and Skills in the New Global Economy, 137, 162
performance indicators, 131–3
Perry, Tom, 65
per student funding: BC, 68, 74, 94, 95f; comparison, 295–6, 296t; ON, 130–1, 136, 171, 174, 176f; QC, 266, 268, 269f
Peterson, David, 134, 135
Petter, Andrew, 67–8
Phelps, J.M., 350
Picard, F., 203
Piper, Martha, 79
Pittman, Walter, 136, 138
Placements Universités, 213–14
Plant, G., 37, 40, 49
Poggi, G., 25
policies: analysis of, 11; focus on, 4–5; formation of, 29; and neoliberalism, 334–5; and operating grants, 118f, 197f; and restructuring, 351; study of PSE performance links, 5–9, 6f
policy drift, 345
policy-making process: BC, 87–90; comparison, 335–8; key moments, 338; ON, 167–71; QC, 206–9, 242–8, 286–7
Policy on Universities, 252, 253
policy priorities, 291
policy sociology, 4, 20–3, 291, 338–43
policy themes: BC, 82–7; emphasis of, 33; ON, 160–7; QC, 248–65; in study, 8–9
political context: BC, 51–82; ON, 133–60
political economy: funding comparison, 292–8; and trends, 335
political ideology: effect of, 117, 119, 349; and practical application, 340–1, 347; trends, 11–12
political priorities, of study, 6–7

Polonsky, Gary, 150
Popa, S., 28, 341
population: BC, 36–7; ON, 123–4, 133–4; QC, 200–1
Porter, D., 30, 32, 352
Postsecondary Assistance Program, 16
Postsecondary Choice and Excellence Act, 171
Postsecondary Education Quality Assessment Board (PEQAB), 128, 129t, 150, 300, 314
Postsecondary Student Assistance Program, 16
Poulantzas, N., 32
Premier's Council on Technology, 135, 137
Premier's Council Technology Fund, 137, 325
pre-university programs, 203–4
Prince, M.J., 53, 54, 59
private career colleges, 126–7, 315
Private Career Colleges Act, 126–7, 152–3, 315
Private Career Training Institutes Act, 46
Private Career Training Institutions Agency (PCTIA), 46–7, 75, 119, 322
private institutions: comparison, 314–17; creation of, 149–50; degree programs, 77, 81, 124; design, 42–7; funding, 210, 231, 238, 252; governance, 58, 86, 203; ON, 359; operating grants, 267f
privately financed, not-for-profit universities, 149
Private PSE Commission (PPSEC), 46–7, 58, 75, 81, 86, 320
private sector: contribution to research, 218; in decision-making process, 245; matching-fund schemes, 318–19;

partnerships, 19, 165–7, 255–7, 262, 341–2; research access, 18; research funding, 113f, 193f, 242–3, 279, 281f, 282; student financial assistance, 148
privatization, 25, 351
process innovation, 326
product innovation, 326
production, 32
professional programs, 147
professional skills, recognition of, 240–1
professional sociology, 20
Program Evaluation Review Commission, 244, 252, 258
Program Quality Assurance Process Audit (PQAPA), 129
program relevance, 228
Progressive Conservative government (federal), 161, 332, 341–2
Progressive Conservative government (ON): accessibility, 163, 300, 301–2; accountability, 164, 320; funding, 172, 197f; globalization initiatives, 166; intermediary bodies, 127; labour force development, 323; marketization, 161, 313; matching-fund schemes, 318; ministers and policies, 361–3; overview, 143–51; policy-making process, 169; political ideology trends, 11–12; private institutions, 314; tuition fees, 306
Proulx, J.-P., 223
Provincial Access Committee (PAC), 56
Provincial Advisory Committee on PSE for Native Learners, 57
Provincial Apprenticeship Board, 60
provincial government: relationship with federal government, 13–20, 201, 284, 292; responsibilities, 348
PSE: federal government view of, 14; vs other sector funding, 175, 178; sociology of, 20, 23–5; system definition, 12–13; system design, 337–8
PSE Choice and Excellence Act (PSCE Act), 124, 125–6, 128, 149–50, 184, 314
Public Administration Act, 225, 227, 230, 237, 252
public choice, 25
public consultation, 89–90, 284
Public Education Flexibility and Choice Act, 76
public institution design: BC, 37–42; ON, 124–5
public-private partnerships, 31–2
Public Sector Accountability Act, 146
public-sector employees, 231
public servant training, 64–5, 85
Public Service Restraint Act, 53
public sociology, 20
public space, 24, 345–6
public sphere, 26
Pusser, B., 351

quality assurance, 129, 153, 155–7, 320. *See also* accountability
Quality Assurance Board, 320
Quality Improvement Fund (QIF), 132, 156, 157
quality review process, 140–1
quasi-markets, 19, 24, 87, 302, 341, 347, 351
Quebec: accessibility, 248–51; accessibility comparison, 298–313, 343–4; accountability, 251–5; accountability comparison, 319–21; conclusions, 282–90; current system, 214–17;

decision-making process, 242–8; decisions and orientations, 227–42; evolution of system, 217–27; expenditures, 270t, 297t; funding, 265–73; funding comparison, 292–8, 294f; globalization, 350–1; labour force development comparison, 321–4; labour market links, 255–60; marketization comparison, 313–19; ministers and policies, 366; outcomes, 273–82; policy-making process, 206–9; policy-making process comparison, 335–8; policy sociology, 338–43; political ideology trends, 12; protection of power, 17; R&D, 260–5; R&D comparison, 324–33; recent events in, 5; relationship with federal government, 13; representation by, 10–11; revenue sources, 272f, 273t; system design, 200–6; targets and indicators, 366; universities, 365
Québec, Gouvernement du, 203, 206, 210, 212, 216, 219, 220, 239, 241, 243, 260, 275, 289
Quebec Charter of Human Rights and Freedoms, 217
Quebec Federation of School Boards (FCSQ), 232
Quebec model, 287
Quebec Policy on Science and Innovation, 229, 243, 260, 261, 326
Quebec Policy on Universities, 210, 212, 248–9, 256, 321
Quebec Policy on University Funding, 228
Quebec Professional Code, 259
Quebec University Funding Plan, 214, 242, 245
Quebec Youth Summit, 225, 226

Quest University Canada, 43, 44, 315
Quiet Revolution, 215, 217, 283–4

R&D Challenge Fund, 325
Rae, Bob, 134, 135, 138, 152, 172
Rae, J.R., 78
Rae Report, 152, 153, 155, 156, 170
Ragin, C., 9
Ratner, R., 31
Rawolle, S., 22
Reaching Higher Plan, 153, 156, 159, 171, 174, 185
Recherche Québec, 241
Redeemer University College, 126
Reeves Bracco, K., 286
referendum, 219, 225
Régime budgétaire et financier des établissements privés d'ordre collegial, 210
regional learning councils (RLCs), 49
Reich, R., 28
religious-affiliated institutions, 126
Report of the Advisor to the Minister of Colleges and Universities on the Governance of the Colleges of Applied Arts and Technology, 136–7
Report of the Commission of Inquiry on Canadian University Education (Smith Report), 143, 162, 169
Report of the Provincial Advisory Committee on Post-Secondary Education for Native Learners (Green Report), 57
research and development: in accumulation function, 347; advocacy, 69; and commodification of knowledge, 4; comparison, 324–33; definition of, 9; and economic development, 165–7;

expenditures, 112f, 113f, 192f, 193f, 280f, 281f, 332t; federal policies, 15–16; federal regulation, 230; funding, 17–19, 111, 114, 159, 191, 194, 345–6; funding agencies, 208–9; in high-tech fields, 74; indirect costs, 211, 233–4; innovation, 326; objectives, 235; policy and restructure, 351; policy-implementing organization, 229; private sector funding, 144, 161, 242–3; QC, 260–5, 278–9, 282; reorganization of funding, 241–2; structure, 263; support, 217; ties to business, 220, 224; university role, 218
research councils: funding, 15–16, 18, 327; ON, 156–7
research-intensive universities, 346–7
research on PSE, 170
Research Universities' Council of British Columbia (RUCBC), 47–8, 51
Réseau Trans-tech, 208
restructuring, 25–6, 145, 347–52
revenues (all sources): BC, 98, 99f, 100–1, 100t; comparison, 297–8, 298t, 332t; ON, 172, 174–5, 179f, 180t; QC, 271, 272f, 273t
Rhoades, G., 24, 268, 340, 345
Richardson, R., 199, 286
Rizvi, F., 22, 291, 338, 347, 350
Robertson, S., 22, 26, 27, 28, 338, 341, 347
Robinson, E.I., 14
Rocher, G., 215, 232
Roelvink, G., 30, 352
Roman Catholic Church, 215
Rooney, D., 24, 340
Rose, N., 27
Rosenbluth, G., 53
Rothstein, B., 22, 23, 338

Royal Commission of Inquiry on Education in the Province of Quebec (Parent Report), 215–17
Royal Roads University, 37, 40–1, 65–6, 87
Royce, D., 127, 131, 136, 137, 138, 140, 141, 142, 143, 145, 167, 168
Rubenson, K., 18, 24, 116, 265, 292, 330, 342
Ryerson Polytechnic Institute, 142

Sadlack, J., 23
Saul, J. R., 30, 352
Scheurich, J. J., 21
scholarships, 148
school completion objectives, 248
Schugurensky, D., 22, 27, 28, 341, 347
Schworm, W., 53
science and technology policy, 18, 328, 341–2
Scott, P., 12, 23, 194, 282–3, 309, 344
Sears, A., 27, 347
Sea to Sky University, 43, 77, 87
secondary education, 308
sector funding, 19, 96, 175, 178, 268
Shanahan, T., 9, 18, 127, 156, 157, 265, 292
Shapiro, Bernard, 142
Sharaput, M., 18
Shaw, M., 335
Sihota, Moe, 70
Simon, R., 14
Skill Development and Fair Wage Act, 70, 76, 85
skills and literacy training, 159
Skills Now, 61, 70, 84, 89, 94, 96
skills training. *See* vocational and technical training
Skocpol, T., 26

Skolnik, M., 12, 37, 127, 128, 140, 344
Slaughter, S., 24, 25, 268, 340, 345
Slee, R., 27, 347
Smith, D., 37
Smith, Stuart L., 143
Smith Report, 143, 162, 169
Snobelon, John, 145
social assistance, 19, 340
social change, 215
social contract, 142
Social Credit government (BC): accessibility, 82–3, 301; accountability, 86; funding, 91, 96, 98, 100–1, 118f; ideology, 52; ministers and policies, 355; new public structures, 37; overview, 53–8; policy-making process, 88, 336; priorities, 119; tuition fees, 103
social inclusion, 88
social innovation, 261, 326–7
social mobility, 140
social policy, 135, 347
Social Sciences and Humanities Research Council (SSHRC), 18, 123, 327–8
social services sector funding, 268
sociology of education, 20
sociology of PSE, 20, 23–5
Soren, B., 12, 127, 344
Soskice, D., 30, 352
special missions component, 211–12
special purpose, teaching universities: budget submissions, 51; creation, 38; mandate, 39–40
Special Purpose Operating Grants (SPOG), 130
specific funding expenditures, 211, 212
Spitzer, S., 27, 347
Sprott Shaw Community College, 45, 77, 316
Stake, R.E., 9

Standing Senate Committee on National Finance, 14
state: and capital, 26; restructuring, 25–6, 347–52
state policy: divergence of, 28–9; evolution of, 352; and performance, 6f
state theory, 20, 25–33
Statistics Canada, 271, 295, 312, 330
STEP down initiative, 139
Strachan, Bruce, 55, 57–8
Strand, Kenneth, 60
Strand Report, 59–61
Strange, Susan, 29
Strangway, David, 43, 315
Stratégie de la recherche et de l'innovation, 261
stratified systems, 13
Strong, David, 43
student associations, 236
student experience, 155–6
student financial assistance programs: for accessibility, 147–8, 154–5, 163, 275; bursary reduction, 233; comparison, 302–8, 307t; federal policies, 16; market concepts, 79; PCCs, 127; private institutions, 152–3; in QC, 213, 216, 278t
students: FTE expansion, 50; international, 154, 206, 317–18. See also enrolment; participation rates
students' associations, 226, 243, 245, 247, 250–1
students in need, 148, 153
students with disabilities, 131, 153
Student Training Completion Fund, 46–7
study: background, 3; design and purpose, 5–9; key concepts, 4; policy sociology, 22–3; research design, 9–13

subsidiarity, 221
success: initiatives to increase, 226, 227; link to access, 248, 250
Summit on the Economy and Employment, 226, 265
Super Build Fund, 147, 150
Sweden: HERD, 329; R&D expenditures, 279
system-level accountability, 164
system orientation, 337–8
system structure, 344–5

targeted funding envelopes, 136, 162, 167
Task Force on Advanced Training (ON), 138
Task Force on University Accountability, 140
Tax and Consumer Rate Freeze Act, 67
tax credits: apprenticeship, 158; R&D, 262, 318, 325, 327, 346; training, 258, 324; tuition fees, 213
Taylor, S., 21, 22, 291, 338
teachers' unions and associations, 66, 243, 245
Technical University of British Columbia (Tech BC), 37, 66, 85, 86
technological innovation, 135, 166, 261, 286, 327. *See also* research and development
technology fields, 61–2, 66, 135–6, 146
technology transfer and liaison centres (TTLCs), 263
technology transfer centres (TTCs), 262, 264
Teichler, U., 23
Télé-université (TÉLUQ), 205, 234, 249, 299
Telmer, C., 134, 135, 139, 144, 161

Thiele, B., 313
Third Way, 30–2, 352
Thompson, G., 28
Thompson, P., 22
Thompson Rivers University (TRU), 38, 75
Thurow, L.C., 23
Tickly, L., 22, 338
Torres, C.A., 23, 351
trades training. *See* apprenticeship programs; vocational and technical training
Training Accord, 81, 85
Training Completion Assurance Fund (TCAF), 153
Training for What?, 62
Transfer of Undergraduate Course Credits among Ontario Universities: Report and Recommendations (Baker Report), 143, 162
transfer payments, 16–17, 18, 19–20, 91, 172, 238, 265, 292, 340, 347
Transformative Change Accord, 78
Treasury Board, 50–1
Trépanier, M., 262
Trépanier, Y., 217, 218
Trick, D., 170
Trinity Western University, 43
Tri-University Presidents' Council (TUPC), 47–8, 69, 79–80, 90
Trottier, C., 18, 203, 215, 265, 292
Trow, M., 12, 309, 344
trust funds, 148
tuition fees: accessibility measures, 101, 103, 105, 163, 181, 274–5; comparison, 303, 304t, 305f, 306, 346t; deregulation, 147, 148, 155, 302, 317, 341, 345; framework, 153; freeze, 67–9, 83, 152; increases, 10–11, 73–4, 78–9, 213, 222, 236; opposition

Index 445

to increases, 247; percent of revenue, 101, 133, 174, 271; percent of total funding, 297–8; policy, 212; by program, 102f, 182f, 276f; proportion of after-tax income, 104f, 183f, 277f
Tuition Freeze Act, 67

undergraduate programs: degrees granted, 191t; enrolment, 184–5, 185t, 186f; FTE by programs, 111t; participation rates, 109f, 110f; quality review process, 140–1; tuition fees, 102f, 103, 104f, 147, 182f, 183f, 276f, 277f, 304t, 305f
unemployment, 59–60
Unexus University, 44
unified systems, 12–13
Union Nationale government, 214, 215–16, 367
unions, 217, 244
United States: and globalization, 29; R&D expenditures, 279
universal education, 350
Université du Québec, 205, 216, 235, 249, 250, 299, 343
Université du Québec à Montréal (UQAM), 234, 236–7, 239
universities: and academic capitalism, 24; binary systems, 145; budget submissions, 51; career training, 256–7, 258–9; collaboration, 79–80, 137–8, 162, 168, 170–1, 203; coordinating bodies, 208–9; creation of, 150; degree completion arrangements, 149; designation of, 222; effect of globalization, 28; evaluation of, 225; funding, 91, 94, 133, 174–5, 238, 241, 266; funding formula, 234–5; governance, 38–40, 239–40; grants per funded FTE, 95f, 176f, 269f; intermediary bodies, 47–8, 127; management accountability, 227–8; national credit transfer, 143; ON, 124–5, 359; operating grants, 92f, 93f, 118f, 173f, 197f, 210–11, 267f; participation rates, 107f, 184–5, 187, 278, 279t; policy orientations, 228; pre-university programs, 203–4; program development, 244; QC, 205–6, 232, 365; quality review process, 140–1; reinvestment, 226; research-intensive, 346–7; revenue sources, 98, 100–1, 172, 174–5, 178, 213–14, 271; student endowments, 155; system planning, 218; vision for, 220
University Accountability: A Strengthened Framework, 140
University Act, 38–40, 47
University Amendment Act, 66
University and College Entrance Preparation Program, 16
University Canada West, 43–4, 77, 81
University College of the Cariboo, 38, 75
university colleges: degree programs, 56–7, 65, 71, 76, 86; development of, 37–8; funding, 91, 92f, 93f, 94; operating grants, 118f
university-community liaison offices, 263
university-dominated systems, 12
university-entrepreneurship centres (UECs), 263
University Funding Plan, 212–13, 253, 266, 274, 286
University Investment Act, 237
university networks, 205–6

University of British Columbia
 (UBC), 38, 79–80
University of Northern British
 Columbia (UNBC), 56, 57, 58,
 65, 79–80
University of Ontario Institute of
 Technology (UOIT), 150–1, 166,
 300
University of Southern California,
 314
University of the Fraser Valley, 38
University of Toronto, 142
University of Victoria (UVic), 79–80
University Presidents' Council of
 British Columbia, 47
University Research Incentive Fund
 (URIF), 137, 166, 325
University Restructuring Steering
 Committee, 142, 166
Usher, A., 329

Valorisation-Recherche Québec,
 229, 235
Vancouver Island University, 38
Vancouver University, 45–6
Van Damme, D., 27
Vander Zalm, William, 52, 55
van Vught, F.A., 23
Vidovich, L., 27, 347
Vision 2000, 43
vocational and career education
 committee, 257
vocational and technical training:
 accessibility, 298; vs apprenticeship, 69–70; BC, 61, 70–1, 76,
 84–5; and economic development, 165–6; emphasis on, 117;
 enrolment rates, 105, 108; federal government involvement,
 15; FTE by programs, 111t;
 interprovincial certification, 159;
 ON, 157–8, 188, 190; participation rates, 109f, 110f, 310–1;
 QC, 255–60; recommendations,
 60; in universities, 335
Vocational Training Path, 202
Volgy, T., 29
von Hayek, F.A., 30
Vosko, L., 334

Wagner, P., 27, 350
Walker, R.B.K., 54
Wallerstein, Immanuel, 29
Watkins, M., 26
Watson, John, 47
Watson Report, 47
Weber, 4
Webster, A., 24
welfare liberalism, 30, 352
welfare provision model, 352
Williams, R., 344
Wolf, A., 116
Wood, E., 32, 351
Work-Oriented Training Path, 202
Work Study Program, 148
World Trade University (WTU),
 44–5, 315–16

Yin, R., 9, 10
York University, 133, 137, 156, 157
Young, J., 14
Young, R., 78
Young, S., 137, 140, 161, 163, 167,
 168, 313, 314
Yukon College, 45

Zimmerman, Wolfgang, 43